A Book of
Lands and Peoples

A Book of Lands and Peoples

assembled by
ERIC NEWBY

assisted by
SONIA ASHMORE

HarperCollins*Publishers*

HarperCollins*Publishers*
77–85 Fulham Palace Road,
Hammersmith, London w6 8jb

www.harpercollins.co.uk

Published by HarperCollins*Publishers* 2003
1 3 5 7 9 8 6 4 2

A catalogue record for this book
is available from the British Library

ISBN 0 00 714939 5

Maps by Leslie Robinson

Set in PostScript Linotype Minion with Photina display by
Rowland Phototypesetting Ltd,
Bury St Edmunds, Suffolk

Printed and bound in Great Britain by
Clays Ltd, St Ives plc

To Wanda,
my constant companion in my travels

CONTENTS

ACKNOWLEDGEMENTS

I would like to thank my daughter, Sonia Ashmore, for her great help in compiling this book, Michael Fishwick at HarperCollins, and my editor, Lucinda McNeile, for her pursuit of perfection.

INTRODUCTION

I have called the second volume of my anthology of writing by travellers *A Book of Lands and Peoples*, because this was the title of a glossy magazine to which my parents gave me a subscription back in the 1920s. What excitement was generated in our house when it came in through the letter box. It suddenly opened up new worlds to me, all of which appeared to be brought to my doorstep exclusively for my pleasure. *The Children's Colour Book of Lands and Peoples*, edited by Arthur Mee, a distinguished journalist, turned me into an embryonic traveller.

Although at the time the photographs in these publications were more appealing to me than the text, I was later to discover the remarkable accounts left by travellers throughout history which have continued to inspire and impress me. The examples that have been chosen for this anthology have been written by a great variety of people: Greek historians, Arab scholars, medieval monks, Elizabethan adventurers, amateur and professional explorers and naturalists, poets, intrepid Victorian women, and those who just felt the urge to wander. Whether they were merely 'gadding about' or because travel 'Stirreth up Wisdome', in the words of Thomas Coryate, the literary legacy of these miscellaneous travellers is an extraordinary compendium of advice, fortitude, strange experiences and sheer wonder at the world they encountered.

Then I felt like some watcher of the skies
When a new planet swims into his ken;
Or like stout Cortez when with eagle eyes
He star'd at the Pacific – and all his men
Look'd at each other with a wild surmise –
Silent, upon a peak in Darien.

(John Keats, Sonnet XI, 'On First Looking into Chapman's Homer'

I only hope that this anthology will give you as much pleasure as Arthur Mee's publication gave me all those years ago. As it has been impossible to provide detailed maps for the journeys of so many travellers, I recommend a good atlas, and bags of determination.

Notes on Travel

Pliny the Elder

(AD 23–79)

A Roman soldier, scientist and scholar from Como, North Italy, Gaius Plinius Secundus was a friend of Emperor Vespasian. The *Historia Naturalis* is taken from 160 volumes of Pliny's observations of the world as it was then known. Although not reliable, the book gives us the most complete picture of knowledge of the world at the time. Pliny became a Commander of the Roman fleet in AD 79, but in the same year died of asphyxiation while enthusiastically trying to observe the great eruption of Vesuvius. Besides the *Natural History* he wrote a treatise on javelin-throwing from horseback, the life of a Roman general, two history books and a work on grammatical problems.

Description of the world in thirty-seven bookes

The first Booke containeth the Dedicatorie Epistle or Preface of the whole worke, addressed to *Titus Vespasian* the Emperour. Also the names of the Authors out of which hee gathered the Historie, which he prosecuteth in 36 Bookes: together with the Summarie of everie Chapter:

The second, treateth of the World, Elementts, and Starres:

The third, describeth the first and second gulfe, which the Mediterranean sea maketh in Europe:

The fourth, compriseth the third gulfe of Europe,

The fifth, containeth the description of Affricke,

The sixt, handleth the Cosmographie of Asia,

The seventh treateth of man, and his inventions, the eighth sheweth unto us, land creatures and their kindes,

The ninth, laieth before us all fishes, and creatures of the water,

The tenth speakes of flying foules and birds,

The eleventh telleth us of Insects,

The twelfth treateth of drugs and odoriferous plants,

The thirteenth describeth strange and forreine trees:

The fourteenth sheweth of vine-plants &c.,

The fifteenth comprehendeth all fruitfull trees,

The sixteenth describeth unto us all wild trees,

The seventeenth containeth tame trees within hortyards,

The eighteenth booke treateth of the nature of corne, and all sorts
thereof, together with the profession of husbandmen, and agriculture,

The nineteenth discourseth of Flax, Spart, and Gardenage,

The twentieth sheweth of garden herbs, good to serve both the kitchin
for meat, and the Apothecaries shop for medicine,

The one and twentieth treateth of flours and garlands,

The two and twenty containeth the chaplets and medicines made of
hearbes,

The three and twentie sheweth the medicinable vertues of wine, and
tame trees growing in hortyards,

The foure and twentie declareth the properties of wild trees serving in
Physick,

The five and twentie treateth of the herbes in the field coming up of
their own accord,

The six and twentie sheweth of many new and strange maladies, the
medicinable vertues also of certaine herbes, according to sundry
diseases,

The seven and twenty goeth forward to certaine other hearbes and their
medicines,

The eight and twentie setteth downe certaine receits of remedies in
Physicke, drawne from out of man and other bigger creatures,

The nine and twentie treateth of the first authours and inventors of
Physicke, also of medicines taken from other creatures,

The thirtieth booke speaketh of Magicke, and certaine medicines appro-
priat to the parts and members of mans bodie,

The one and thirtie containeth the medicinable vertues of fishes and
water creatures,

The two and thirtie sheweth other properties of fishes, &c.,

4

The three and thirtie treateth of gold and silver mines,
The foure and thirtie speaketh of copper and brasse mines, also of lead,
 also of excellent brasse-founders and workemen in copper,
The five and thirtie discourseth of painting, colour, and painters,
The six and thirtie treateth of marble and stone for building,
The seven and thirtie concludeth with pretious stones.

Sir John Maundeville

(fl. 1322–56)

> Maundeville or Mandeville claimed to be a knight, born
> at St Albans. 'Ravished with a mightie desire to see the
> greater parts of the world ... he departed from his
> Countrey, in the Yeere of Christe 1322; and, as another
> Ulysses, returned home, after the space of 34 Yeeres',
> according to the editor of the 1725 edition. His book of
> travels was published in French in 1366 and widely trans-
> lated. Although the author claimed that even the Pope
> said the book was true, it is actually a compilation from
> the works of other writers including Odoric of Pordenone
> (q.v.); but it is a very good read.

The way to Paradys

And bezonde the Lond and the Yles and the Desertes of Prestre Johnes
Lordschipe, in goynge streyght toward the Est, men fynde nothing but
Mountaynes and Roches fulle grete: and there is the derke Regyoun,
where no man may see, nouther be day ne be nyght, as thei of the
Contree seyn. And that Desert, and that place of Derknesse, duren fro
this Cost unto Paradys terrestre; where that Adam oure foremest Fader,
and Eve weren putt, that dwelleden there but lytylle while; and that is
towards the Est, at the begynnynge of the Erthe. But that is not that
Est, that wee clep oure Est, on this half, where the Sonne risethe to us:
for whenne the Sonne is Est in tho partyes, toward Paradys terrestre, it

5

is thanne mydnyght in oure parties o this half, for the rowndenesse of the Erthe, of the whiche I have towched to zou before. For oure Lord God made the Erthe alle round, in the mydde place of the Firmament. And there as Mountaynes and Hilles ben, and Valeyes, that is not but only of Noes Flode, that wasted the softe ground and the tendre, and felle doun into Valeyes: and the harde Erthe, and the Roche abyden Mountaynes, whan the soft Erthe and tendre wax nessche, throghe the Water, and felle and becamen Valeyes.

Of Paradys ne can not I speken propurly: for I was not there. It is fer bezonde; and that forthinkethe me: and also I was not worthi. But as I have herd seye of wyse men bezonde, I schalle telle zou with gode Wille. Paradys terrestre, as wise men seyn, is the highest place of Erthe, that is in alle the World: and it is so highe, that it touchethe nyghe to the cercle of the Mone, there as the Mone makethe hire torn. For sche is so highe, that the Flode of Noe ne myght not come to hire, that wolde have covered alle the Erthe of the World alle aboute, and aboven and benethen, saf Paradys only allone. And this Paradys is enclosed alle aboute with a Walle; and men wyte not whereof it is. For the Walles ben covered alle over with Mosse; as it semethe. And it semethe not that the Walle is Ston of Nature. And that Walle streccethe fro the Southe to the Northe; and it hathe not but on entrée, that is closed with Fyre brennynge; so that no man, that is mortalle, ne dar not entren.

Sir Walter Raleigh

(c. 1552–1618)

English soldier, navigator, writer and courtier. A favourite of Queen Elizabeth I who endowed him with land, favours and a knighthood. Raleigh organised the expeditions to colonise Virginia, and planted his Irish estate with tobacco and potatoes they brought back. He sailed with Davis in search of the North-West Passage and in 1593 to Trinidad and Guiana (now Venezuela). He travelled three hundred miles up the Orinoco river, in his search for the city of

El Dorado. The victim of court intrigue at the end of Elizabeth's reign, he was condemned to death, but spared at the scaffold and put in the Tower, where he passed the time studying and writing a *History of the World*. He then returned to the Orinoco in search of gold, but the journey was beset by disaster. On his return, Raleigh was executed; before his death, he wrote an *Apology for the Voyage to Guiana*.

Inventory of things found with Raleigh's body, 15 August 1618

The phantom to which he sacrificed his reputation, his fortune, and his life, namely the gold-mines of Guiana, haunted him to his last moments. His Apology expresses a continued assurance in the existence of gold-mines near the banks of the Orinoco; and in 'the inventory of such things as were found on the body of Sir Walter Rawleigh, Knight, the 15th day of August, 1618', which document was sent to Sir Thomas Wilson by Sir Robert Naunton, Secretary of State, occur the following objects:

A Guiana idol of Gold.
A Spleenstone, (left with him for his own use).
One wedge of fine gold at 22 carratts.
An other stob of coarser gold.
Item one plott of Guiana and Nova (R –) and another of the
   river of Orenoque.
The description of the river Orenoque.
A plott of Panama.
A tryal of Guiana ore with a description thereof.
A Sprig jewel.
Five assays of the Silver myne.

These articles were probably taken from him after his recommittal to the Tower, when in the act of making his escape.

Thomas Coryate

(c. 1577–1617)

English eccentric and traveller, born at Odstock Rectory
in Somerset. Coryate became an unofficial jester at the
court of James I. In 1608 he set off on a 1975-mile walk
across Europe, described in his book, *Coryat's Crudities.
Hastily gobled up in Five Moneths Travelles in France . . .
Newly digested in the hungry aire of Odcombe in the County
of Somerset and now dispersed to the nourishment of the
travelling members of this Kingdome.* On his return to
Odstock, he hung up the shoes in which he had walked
back from Venice in the village church. In 1612 he set off
again in an easterly direction via Greece and Constantinople. He died at Surat on the west coast of India five
years later, presumably worn out himself.

What travell meaneth

Therefore that my Oration may derive her beginning even from this, I
will ask this first question: how many travellers there are that when
they undertake any voyage do rightly understand what travell meaneth.
Since many doe fondly imagine that it is nothing else then a certayne
gadding about, a vaine beholding of sundry places, a transmigration
from one country to another, whose feete doe only move from place
to place, and whose eyes are conveighed from one field to another. Of
whom thou mayest very rightly use that knowen speech of the Poet.

> The climate, not their minds they change,
> That sayling over every Sea doe range.

But we will say that he is the man that visiteth forraine Kingdomes and
doth truly travell, and that according to the censure of all learned men,
the consent of Historians, and the opinion of politicians, he I say, who
whither soever he directeth his journey, travelleth for the greater benefit

of his wit, for the commodity of his studies, and the dexterity of his life, who moveth more in minde then body, who attayneth to the same by the course of his travel, that others doe at home very painfully and with great study by turning of bookes. Will you have me (my worthy Auditors) speake more plainly to you? It is travell that stirreth up wisdome, purchaseth fortitude, confirmes it being purchased, gives light unto us for the instruction of our manners, makes us from barbarous to be gentle and milde natured: it rooteth out a fond selfe love, it availeth to suffer labours, to undergoe dangers, and with a valiant and manly minde to endure them, and sheweth us the nearest way to the solid learning of all things. What need many words? Let travell be the plentifull institution of all our life. For histories doe teach us that men of old time did travell to that end.

William Bligh

(c. 1753–1817)

Bligh was born at Plymouth; went to sea at fifteen and sailed with Captain Cook on his second voyage round the world (1772–4). As Commander of HMS *Bounty* he set off for Tahiti to collect plants of the breadfruit tree for planting in West Indies in 1787. After six months at Tahiti, the crew mutinied against Bligh's alleged cruelty. Bligh was cast adrift in a 23-foot open boat with eighteen volunteers; the boat was intended for ten. After a six-week journey of incredible hardship, they landed at Timor, Java, 3618 miles across the Pacific, thanks to Bligh's skilled seamanship and good care of the men.

Washing clothes in salt-water

(June 1789)

With respect to the preservation of our health, during a course of sixteen days of heavy and almost continual rain, I would recommend to every one in a similar situation the method we practised, which is to dip their clothes in the salt-water and wring them out as often as they became filled with rain. It was the only resource we had, and I believe was of the greatest service to us, for it felt more like a change of dry clothes than could well be imagined. We had occasion to do this so often that at length all our clothes were wrung to pieces, for except the few days we passed on the coast of New Holland we were continually wet either with rain or sea.

Charles Kingsley

(1819–75)

English author, academic and cleric, and an exponent of muscular Christianity. Kingsley was the author of *Westward Ho!* and *The Water Babies*. The son of a clergyman, he started writing sermons at the age of four; was fond of plants and geology; and learned boxing under a black prizefighter at Oxford. In 1869 he visited the West Indies at the invitation of his friend, the Governor of Trinidad. Kingsley had a bad stammer; and, according to Leslie Stephen in the *Dictionary of National Biography*, 'The excessive fervour of his emotions caused early exhaustion.'

A dream of travel

At last we, too, were crossing the Atlantic. At last the dream of forty years, please God, would be fulfilled, and I should see (and happily, not alone) the West Indies and the Spanish Main. From childhood I had studied their Natural History, their charts, their Romances, and alas! their Tragedies; and now, at last, I was about to compare books with facts, and judge for myself of the reported wonders of the Earthly Paradise. We could scarce believe the evidence of our own senses when they told us that we were surely on board a West Indian steamer, and could by no possibility get off it again, save into the ocean, or on the farther side of the ocean; and it was not till the morning of the second day, the 3d of December, that we began to be thoroughly aware that we were on the old route of Westward-Ho, and far out in the high seas, while the Old World lay behind us like a dream.

Sir Francis Galton

(1822–1911)

English scientist and traveller. Like his cousin Charles Darwin, Galton was a man of enormous scientific curiosity. He studied meteorology, coining the word 'anticyclone'; he invented modern fingerprinting, devised the correlation coefficient, did research in experimental psychology and colour blindness, and through his investigations into heredity, became the founder of eugenics. His travels in North Africa, Syria, Egypt and remote parts of South West Africa produced two books including his inimitable and indispensable *Art of Travel*.

Blistered feet

To prevent the feet from blistering, it is a good plan to soap the inside of the stocking before setting out, making a thick lather all over it. A raw egg broken into a boot, before putting it on, greatly softens the leather: of course the boots should be well greased when hard walking is anticipated. After some hours on the road, when the feet are beginning to be chafed, take off the shoes, and change the stockings; putting what was the right stocking on the left foot, and the left stocking on the right foot. Or, if one foot only hurts, take off the boot and turn the stocking inside out. These were the plans adopted by Captain Barclay. When a blister is formed, 'rub the feet, on going to bed, with spirits mixed with tallow dropped from a candle into the palm of the hand; on the following morning no blister will exist. The spirits seem to possess the healing power, the tallow serving only to keep the skin soft and pliant. This is Captain Cochrane's advice, and the remedy was used by him in his pedestrian tour.'

What to do with a drowned man

A half-drowned man must be put to bed in dry, heated clothes, hot stones, &c., placed against his feet, and his head must be raised moderately. Human warmth is excellent, such as that of two big men made to lie close up against him, one on each side. All rough treatment is not only ridiculous but full of harm; such as the fashion – which still exists in some places – of hanging up the body by the feet, that the swallowed water may drain out of the mouth.

Bivouacking

Bivouacking is miserable work in a wet or unhealthy climate; but in a dry and healthy one, there is no question of its superiority over tenting. Men who sleep habitually in the open, breathe fresher air and are far more imbued with the spirit of wild life, than those who pass the night within the stuffy enclosure of a tent. It is an endless pleasure to lie half awake watching the stars above, and the picturesque groupings of the encampment round about, and to hear on all sides the stirrings of animal life. And later in the night, when the fire is low, and servants and cattle are asleep, there is no sound but of the wind and an occasional plaintive cry of wild animals, the traveller finds himself in that close communion with nature which is the true charm of wild travel. Now all this pleasure is lost by sleeping in a tent. Tent life is semi-civilization, and perpetuates its habits. This may be illustrated by a simple trait; a man who has lived much in bivouacs, if there be a night alarm, runs naturally into the dark for safety, just as a wild animal would; but a man who travels with tents becomes frightened when away from its lights, or from the fancied security of its walls.

In a dangerous country there can be no comparison between the hazard of a tent and that of a bivouac. In the former a man's sleep is heavy; he cannot hear nearly so well; he can see nothing; his cattle may all decamp; while marauders know exactly where he is lying, and may make their plans accordingly. They may creep up unobserved and spear him through the canvas. The first Napoleon had a great opinion of the advantages of bivouacking over those of tenting. He said it was the healthier of the two for soldiers.

William Kitchiner

(fl. 1827)

English doctor, author of *The Cook's Oracle*, *The Art of Invigorating Life* etc., his book of advice to travellers includes songs set to music by himself. Volume II is *The Horse and Carriage Keeper's Oracle*, written by 'An Old Coachman'.

How to avoid a damp bed

The Receipt, therefore, to sleep comfortably at Inns, is to *take your own Sheets*, to have plenty of flannel gowns, and to promise, and take the care to pay, a handsome consideration for the liberty of choosing your Beds.

Damp Beds are oftenest found in Inns that are least visited; they ought to be carefully avoided, for they not only produce dreadful *Disorders*, but have often proved the *Death* of the person who has had the misfortune to sleep in them.

Especially in Winter, not only examine the Beds, to see whether they are quite Dry, but have the Bed-clothes in your presence put before the fire.

Just before you go to Bed, order a pan of hot Coals to be run through it, then place a clean tumbler inverted between the Sheets, and let it remain there for a few minutes – if on withdrawing it the slightest cloud is observable on the inner surface, be certain that either the Sheets or the Bed are damp: sleeping in the Blankets is a disagreeable, but the safest way of escaping such danger: there are many persons in the habit of travelling who make it a constant practice.

A Wash Leather Sheet, about 8 feet by 5, is not an unpleasant substitute for Linen.

If a friend offers you a Bed, have it warmed with the necessary precautions, because there are in certain houses, certain state beds, kept for certain Visitors, which are very likely to be damp ...

S. Leigh Hunt and Alexander S. Kenny

(c. 1833)

Hunt was a major in the Madras Army, Kenny a Demonstrator of Anatomy at King's College, London. Their book was aimed at preparing women for the ordeals of life in tropical countries. Their advice ranges from diet suggesting, curiously that cocoa is a suitable drink for hot countries, how to care for orchids, remedies for Burmese ringworm and bunions, wet nurses, and a reminder to take a tuning fork for pianos.

Ship's etiquette

EARLY RISING: EN DÉSHABILLE – In the very early morning in the tropics, people are glad to escape from the close confinement of their cabins; the ladies generally congregate in the saloon and ladies' cabin, while the gentlemen proceed on deck. All are more or less *en déshabille*, and a sort of tacit understanding exists, that before a certain hour – say 7 or 7.30 a.m. – no lady shall make her appearance on deck, nor shall any gentlemen encumber the saloon with his presence for a longer time than may be necessary for him to hurry through from cabin to deck. Morning greetings are not exchanged between the sexes under these circumstances, and Mrs A. is discreetly unconscious of the identity of Mr B. as he hurries past in dressing-gown and slippers.

Henry Major Tomlinson

(1873–1958)

Tomlinson worked in a shipping office from age of 13, and then became a journalist. In 1909, tired of his London life, he caught a tramp steamer at Swansea that sailed to Brazil and then 2000 miles along the Amazon and Madeira rivers, returning via Jamaica and Florida. He was a war correpondent in the 1914–18 war. Here he evokes an experience of leaving home that will strike a familiar chord with many travellers.

The Sea and the Jungle

It had never occurred to me (any more than it did to you when you got this book to learn about the tropic sea and the jungle) that the Open Road, where the chains fall from us, would include Swansea High Street four hours before sunrise in a steady winter downpour. But there I discovered that trade wind seas by moonlight, flying fish, Indians, and forests and palms, cannot be compelled. They come in their turn. They are mixed with litter and dead stuff, like prizes in a bran tub. Going down the drear and aqueous street it was clear that if there are exalted moments in travel, as on the instant when we discover we really may prepare to go, yet exaltation implies the undistinguished flats from which, for a while, we are translated. This is a travel book for honest men. I am still on the flat. It will be to-morrow presently. My chief fear was that my waterproof, rattling in the wind, would alarm silent and sleeping Swansea. I found a policeman standing at a street corner, holding out his cape to help away the rain. He could give me no hope. He knew where the dock was, but the way thither was difficult and tortuous. I had better follow the tram lines, and ask again, if I saw anybody. Therefore the tram lines I followed till my portable estate, by compound interest, had increased to untold tons; but the empty tram way went on for ever down the rows of frozen and desolate lamps, so that I surrendered all my chances of the seas of the tropics and the jungle of the Brazils, and turned aside from the course which the policeman said led to ships and the deep, entered the dark portico of a shop, where it was only half wet, and lit my pipe, there to wait for the shy goods to turn my luck.

Harvard Travellers Club

Their *Handbook of Travel* (1917) included logarithmic tables for making astronomical observations, advice on how to travel with sled dogs and on portable darkrooms. The advice on how to prevent plague: 'leave promptly if you can. Otherwise avoid the vicinity of filth and protect your legs with high boots.'

On camel travel

SELECTION OF CAMELS

The traveller will first consider whether, in view of the nature of his journey, it is better for him to buy his camels or to hire them. For long or dangerous journeys the purchase of camels is to be recommended, as the traveller can then take risks which under other circumstances the camel-eers might reasonably refuse. Prices fluctuate according to the season, the state of the camel-market, the number of beasts bought or hired, etc. In hiring, the price ought to include pack saddles and the services of the drivers. One man is usually allowed to every five camels. Riding saddles must be especially arranged for, and unless obtained from a trustworthy source (e.g., some Government department) should be given a stiff trial. There is something wrong with a saddle that creaks when in use.

It is always advisable, and usually possible, to find some reputable European familiar with camel travel whose advice can be obtained in making arrangements. The advice of professional guides and dragomans should only be taken with the greatest caution, since this class almost always involve the traveller in difficulties, and have only their own extravagant pretensions to recommend them. When the camels are secured, the traveller should note their brands and general appearance, in order to be quite sure afterward that he sets out with the same beasts he has bought or hired. Rheumy-eyed camels, or those which slavver over-much, camels which on rising are seen to tremble slightly in the hind legs, are to be looked on with suspicion; those with bad gall-spots or other obvious ills are to be rejected. A camel which has often been branded about the joints and withers has probably been cauterized for a bad sprain, an infirmity very apt to reappear on a hard march. Most good riding camels have very thick coats of comparatively straight hair, faintly lustrous. The best indication of a camel's general condition is its hump. The hump may be baggy and flaccid, owing to bad or scanty feeding, or else distended with fat as a result of too much green food and too frequent watering. A camel thoroughly fit for desert work will have a hump firm and well filled, but not bloated in appearance.

HIRE OF CAMELEERS
It is usual when hiring men for a journey of more than three weeks to make part payment (but not more than 25 per cent) of wages in advance. Once the bargain has been struck, it is well to promise the men a *bakhshish*, or present. Such promises ought, however, to be left vague, and it should be plainly stated that if the work is not satisfactory there will be no rewards. It is also well to hint, in cases where a number of men are employed, that the best man of the lot will receive, in addition to his own *bakhshish*, that of the worst man of the crew as well. It often happens that at the end of a journey a traveller, in the pleasurable satisfaction of his safe arrival, good-naturedly gives rewards irrespective of the services his men have rendered him. By so doing he stultifies himself in the eyes of his cameleers and raises difficulties for the next European who employs them.

BAGGAGE AND RIDING CAMELS
The many local varieties of camels all fall into two great classes: riding camels (*hagîn*) and baggage camels.

CARE OF THE CAMELS
The pace of a caravan in good condition travelling over easy country

in winter may approach 2½ miles an hour. An ill-packed, ill-nourished caravan, or one travelling in hot weather or over damp or rocky ground, will make much slower progress. The Bactrian camel travels best in the cold months, even over snow and frozen ground. In summer the animals used in Mongolia and Manchuria are packed for short trips only, or else entirely laid off. In winter the Bactrian is protected by exceedingly long hair over an undercoat of wool. When warm weather approaches, both these coverings are shed, leaving the animals unprotected against the sudden climatic changes of extraordinary seasons or hill travel. Camels are extremely susceptible to cold, and when they have prematurely lost their winter coats, the drivers often tie blankets about the necks, chests, and bellies of the animals. As a rule it is hopeless for the white traveller to attempt the cure or alleviation of any of the many ills which may befall his beasts, but it is well to provide a strong antiseptic dressing for sore backs and wounds, and to inquire before setting out if the camel-leader is provided with tar in case a smear is necessary when the camels shed their hair.

Frank Tatchell

(fl. 1920)

English clergyman, the Vicar of Midhurst, Sussex. His charming book *The Happy Traveller: A Book for Poor Men*, published in 1923, suggests that he must have been something of an absentee vicar. His book was one of the inspirations of my own youth and must have lured innumerable Britons from their hearths in search of new horizons.

How to deal with brigands

The traveller soon finds out that a peasant with every mark of being a brigand may be a very peaceable person. His wild appearance is probably due to your seeing him at the wrong end of the week, because, on the Continent, poor men only get shaved on Saturday. If you *do* meet a real 'suspicious character' in a lonely place, do not hesitate, but keep on with an added jauntiness; and do not go round him, which would argue you afraid, but rather steer more directly for him. If you like, you can finger an imaginary revolver in your hip-pocket, but a cheery and confident good-day is enough. Do not look back.

Tipping

Tips will be expected wherever you go, and are called *backsheesh* or *comshaw* in the East. They need not always be given in money; a present of a cigar or a stick of trade tobacco will not only save your pocket but will be accepted without loss of self-respect. To stint yourself is the mark of a fool and to be niggardly in these little gifts is a mistake. I counteract my own tendency to meanness in these matters by unfailing liberality to children and *old* beggars. In the South Seas you have to carry trade 'truck', because in the more virgin islands money has no value. Beads have lost their glamour and are besides heavy to carry, but aluminium thimbles and hanks of red cotton are well received and pack into a small parcel. In Europe I take spare trout flies to give away to local anglers, and flower seeds for garden-lovers in other parts of the world.

Advice on camping

The cosiest place for camping is under a rock overhanging a dry spot near a stream; the draughtiest is under a tree, but if I chance on a walnut tree I sleep beneath it as it is clear of midges and mosquitoes. These pests can also be kept at bay in the open by covering yourself with ferns. Your fire should be built in the shape of a half-moon with the points towards the wind. Build it quite small at first, using bark peelings of birch as tinder. Sleep on the lee side of it with your feet to the fire (the smoke will drive over your head), and have some spare wood by you to throw on during the night. If it is warm, use the beachcomber's pillow, your boots rolled in your coat. If it is chilly, your coat thrown over the head and shoulders is more protection than when kept on. To sleep snugly you must take off every perspired garment and wrap up well the coldest part of the body, from the waist to the knees. Scrape a good big hole for your hipbone and use an old newspaper as a ground-sheet. Do not dread an occasional night in the open when you are benighted and have no camp. There are few beds more comfortable than a dry ditch in England in June.

What to do when lost

If you are lost, you are exposed to three dangers – fear, cold and hunger – of which the first is the deadliest. Sit down until the first panic is over. Then resist the temptation to go uphill to get into freer spaces. Instead, *go downhill*; you will find water, and most settlements are in valleys. You are not likely to be travelling for pleasure in a really cold country, and at night you can cover yourself with heather or bracken. As to hunger, a man can live on his own fat for a week and it is a poor country where there are no lichens. These boiled for an hour will keep you going, and it is useful to know that no toadstool growing on a tree is poisonous. If you have any food left when you first realize that you have lost your way, save it until nightfall and eat half of it when you camp. In the morning only have a drink and eat your last food at midday. After that, drink only a sip at a time and chew pieces of your boots. Water above house-level is sure to be pure and good to drink.

An emergency compass can be contrived by laying your watch face upwards on the palm with the hour hand pointing to the sun. Half-way between the hour hand and XII will be due south in the northern hemisphere. To try to find a lost track at night is labour thrown away; but you ought at least to be able to recognize the Pole Star and the Southern Cross and know that Orion is upright when south and slanting east or west.

How to avoid a watery grave

Should you have the bad luck, when at sea, to fall overboard, get your boots off and turn the coat pockets inside out; but do not take off your clothes, because they keep you warm. Make no attempt to swim anywhere, but just keep yourself afloat until you are picked up. If there are sharks about, keep splashing the water.

Travellers' ailments

Carry some simple medicines in tabloids or pills, and a clinical thermometer. A man's normal temperature is 98.4°F.; his pulse should beat seventy to eighty-four times a minute and he should breathe fifteen to eighteen times. If he breathes over twenty-two times a minute something is wrong.

Care of the feet. Cut the toe nails straight across, not round; and soap your socks. Wash the feet night and morning with soap and *cold* water, and powder your evening socks with a little Fuller's earth.

Cold feet. Kneel on a chair or tree trunk for a few minutes ... Two pairs of thin socks are warmer and more comfortable than one thick pair. Mittens can impart a glow to the whole frame, but how few will condescend to wear them!

Constipation. Sip hot water before meals. Sea water is better still, if you can drink it hot without being sick. In the tropics take two grains of Cascara three times daily until relieved, or, if the water is above suspicion, sip a glass of it cold before breakfast.

Diarrhoea. Take first a dose of Cascara and then a Chlorodyne tabloid.

Dysentery. Symptom – blood in the excrement. Take Chlorodyne. Salol tabloids in a little whisky lessen the chances of your having the disease. If you catch it in the wilds and have no drugs, chew wood charcoal or scrape a powder from a charred stick and swallow it with water.

Eczema. Live for a week or two on nothing but milk and oranges, with an occasional dose of Epsom salts.

Grit in the eye. Rub the *other* eye, when both eyes will water. Carry a small camel's hair brush for getting grit out, and, after you have done so, put a drop of castor oil in the eye. Sulphate of zinc is a good soothing lotion and you can rest your eyes by fixing them on the horizon. Snuff is good for the eyes. The Zulus, who are inveterate snuff-takers, have the finest eyesight in the world. Never touch the eyes just after scratching an insect bite. Indeed, the Spaniards have a proverb: 'Never rub your eyes except with your elbow.'

Indigestion. Before meals take in a glass of water enough baking powder (bicarbonate of soda) to cover a shilling. Drink nothing with your food.

Malaria. At first you feel hot and yet shiver. Then there are three stages – cold, hot and sweating. Take Magnesium Sulphate at once, dissolved in water. Then 15 grains of quinine twice a day. You can buy it at any post office in India, and, if the country is malarial, you should take five grains daily. But to take quinine daily in the tropics, whether there is fever there or not, is wrong. The system gets used to the drug and will not respond when there is need of a dose; besides, to take it constantly makes you deaf. Wear a cholera belt east of Suez, but only wear it at night. There is no malaria east of 170°E., that is to say, none in Fiji or in any part of Polynesia.

Neuralgia. Take ten grains of aspirin, or drink a cup of tea with three or four cloves in it; but do not start a journey without having your teeth seen to.

Prickly heat. Smear the skin with Izal cream; or with a paste of Fuller's earth and lime juice. A simpler but longer remedy is to lie up for a day or two, constantly bathing the itching places with a handkerchief dipped in cold water.

Rheumatism. Eat nothing for a time except oranges and lemons and only drink milk.

Simple fever. Go to bed and take ten grains of aspirin. This cures the headache and lowers the temperature. Repeat the dose after four hours. If the tongue is dirty take castor oil.

Sore throat. Put a little table salt on the tongue and keep it there until it has dissolved. To avoid colds wash your nostrils with your fingers when they are soapy.

Sea sickness. Try stopping both ears tightly with cotton wool. For it is now thought to be caused by a loss of the sense of equilibrium, which resides, not in the stomach, but in the ears.

Snake bite. Cut round the wound, make it bleed and rub in crystals of Permanganate of Potash. A special lancet for this can be got for ninepence from Messrs Arnold & Co. Giltspur St, EC1. Take no alcohol.

Sunstroke. Keep in a darkened room, and after sunset, *not before*, dissolve a teaspoonful of ordinary salt in a wineglassful of cold water. Trickle a little into both ears a drop at a time. This takes away the pain, and you will sink into a delightful sleep and be nearly all right next day. This is a Greek remedy and has cured me several times when I have had a touch of the sun.

Vermin on the body. Smear the underclothes with paraffin or with mercurial ointment. If you should become infested with fleas, sleep out in a bed of bracken one night and in the morning you will be free of the pests.

You can quite easily pack your medical kit in a tin box 3½″ × 2¼″ × ⅝″, weighing no more than 2½ ozs. For cuts, take a roll of surgical bandage, 2′ × 3″, already treated with iodiform, a piece of surgical tape, 16″ by 12″, and a small tube of carbolated vaseline. Put up ten of each of the tabloids that you think you may want in little paper packets, and fill up the tin with a sewing needle and thread, a heavy needle and shoe thread, and a paper of burnt rag which is good tinder in an emergency. But try my plan of having all responsible buttons sewn on in duplicate before you start. An air cushion, 18″ × 36″, will keep the necessary parts of your body off the ground when sleeping out. If you wear shoes in the tropics and not boots, wrap some thin notepaper round your ankles underneath your socks and so foil the mosquitoes. If you *do* get bitten hold a lighted cigarette as close as you can to the bite without scorching the skin.

Army and Navy Stores

The Army and Navy Stores was started as a Co-operative Society in 1871 by a group of officers, intending to reduce costs and share profits. It expanded to military and naval centres in Britain and overseas. In the 1930s it had branches in Bombay, Calcutta and New Delhi (telegraphic address 'Armistice') as well as Plymouth, Portsmouth, Aldershot and Chatham. The company could supply almost everything required for life at home or abroad.

Camp equipment, etc.

The 'Lorimer' Canteen

A practical device – after many years' personal experience – to meet the daily needs of Officials who require to be away from their headquarters on tour for many days at a time. One wearies of the tin mug and other picnic adjuncts for such long periods.

The canteen provides ordinary Glasses, China Cups and Saucers, brown China Teapot, a container for Knives, Forks and Spoons (which can be removed bodily for cleaning), and ordinary cruet (always ready for use), Corkscrew, Tin-Opener, Pots for tea, Sugar, Jam (screwed lids).

Tumblers, China Cups, etc., are secured in baize lined nests and have been found to travel quite safely both by Head Carriage and by Animal Transport.

Beneath the tray are the heavier items, Sparklet Syphon, Thermos, Cooked-food Container, Tea-tray, Dishes and Plates.

Price, Complete   £7   12   6

Marquees and tents. Double-roof ridge tent

The Best tent for Africa is the Double-Roof Ridge Tent made from Green Rotproof Canvas as supplied to

Sir H.M. Stanley   Sir H. Johnston

Col. von Wissman   Bishop Hannington

H. M. Government

The Congo State

Uganda, Gold Coast, and Lagos Railways

Tropical School of Medicine, etc.

Price £12   15   0 – £28   10   0

. . . can be supplied with ground sheets, verandah, bathrooms, mosquito nets, etc.

Naturalist section

Skins, Heads, Horns, Spears Etc., Suitable for Hall Decoration. Skins, Fur Rugs Etc. The Society employs none but the best Skin Dressers, and the greatest care is always taken in the dressing of the skins entrusted to it. Notwithstanding this it occasionally occurs that some skins do not turn out quite satisfactorily in the process of dressing. This is due to various causes such as their being tainted, improperly preserved by Natives, or some other imperfection . . .

The prices given below for Mounting DRESSED Skins are APPROXI-MATE only . . .

Lining Tiger skins with canvas and bordering felt	90/-
Half raising heads of the above skins and inserting eyes, extra from	25/-
Filling-in Leopard skin with black goat skin as hearth rugs, lined black canvas	150/-

Travel tickets, and baggage arrangements. HM Transports

The Society's Representatives are in attendance before sailing and upon arrival of steamers at Bombay, and will make arrangements for the shipment and clearance of luggage . . .

Officers at Indian Up-Country Stations can forward their baggage to the Society's Depot, Bombay, so as to arrive five days clear prior to the date of the Transport Sailing.

Foreign expeditions

The Society's large experience in fitting out, in every detail, exploring, shooting, and other expeditions, enables it to bring special knowledge to bear when executing orders for such. Cases of assorted provisions and other necessaries for use on journeys to and in the interior, are packed to come within the weight for head, mule or camel loads.

Funerals and cremations

FUNERALS can be conducted to and from places ABROAD, ship-ments, Consular matters, and Permits being dealt with by thoroughly experienced Managers . . . Instructions by TELEPHONE can be received and will be immediately dealt with, at any time day or night: 'VICTORIA 8500'.

John Hatt

(1948–)

English traveller, publisher and writer who has travelled to innumerable countries, reprinted many great books of travel writing, and written the modern *vade mecum*, *The Tropical Traveller*.

How to pack

Packing used to make me anxious as I was always sure I would leave out some vital piece of equipment. So I now keep a permanent 'abroad packing-list' and thereby eliminate most of my anxiety. First I pack without looking at the list; then, when I have finished packing, I check down the list to see if I have left anything out. You can use the same slightly updated list year after year.

If you are unlucky enough to have your luggage stolen, this list will facilitate the preparation of an insurance claim.

How to deal with sharks

Basking shark and the Whale shark feed only on plankton and small fish.

Unless you are a California surfer, your most likely problem with sharks arises if you are a spear-fisherman. Don't keep fish attached to your belt; instead put them into some type of floating container towed behind you. Spear-fishermen frequently notice that they can swim for long periods unmolested, but the moment they spear a fish, a shark appears, apparently from nowhere. For a long time it was believed that the shark was attracted by blood; though the best evidence now seems to show that they are attracted by vibration from the *wriggling* fish.

When you know there are any lethal sharks in the area, keep away from fish: Most of the attacks have been on divers with fish in the vicinity, on their belts, spear, or float, or being towed or speared nearby, or when the fish are being cleaned. In one instance a shark even jumped out of the water and took off the arm of a man walking along a reef with a fish he was carrying.

How to deal with dogs

On approaching some villages by foot, you are beset by ferocious dogs. This is terrifying. The cardinal rule is not to run away; if you turn your back you may well be bitten. Face the dog, look as ferocious as you can, and bend down as if to pick up a stone. This is what the locals do and, surprisingly, the dog nearly always shies away, even before you have picked up the stone – probably because it has unpleasant memories of rocks being bounced off its head. Should the dog still be gnashing its teeth, forget the British attitude to dogs and lob a few stones at it. If this doesn't work, arm yourself with a stout stick, hold your ground and wait until someone calls it off.

While on the subject of facing an animal – rather than running away – here is the true story of an acquaintance. He was walking with two guides in a Nepali game reserve, when they were charged by a tiger (who was almost certainly with cubs). One of the guides fled; the other, yelling at full pitch, advanced towards the tiger. The tiger retreated.

Africa

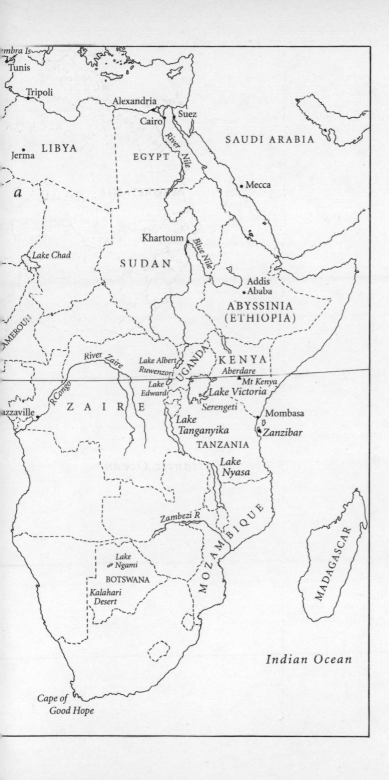

Lambra Is
Tunis
Tripoli
Alexandria
Cairo   Suez
Jerma   LIBYA
EGYPT
SAUDI ARABIA
a
River Nile
Mecca
Khartoum
Blue Nile
SUDAN
Lake Chad
Addis
Ababa
ABYSSINIA
(ETHIOPIA)
CAMEROUN
River Zaire
Lake Albert
Ruwenzori   UGANDA   KENYA
R Congo   Lake   Aberdare
Edward   Mt Kenya
ZAIRE   Lake Victoria
Serengeti   Mombasa
azzaville   Lake   Zanzibar
Tanganyika
TANZANIA
Lake
Nyasa
Zambezi R
MOZAMBIQUE
Lake
Ngami   MADAGASCAR
BOTSWANA
Kalahari
Desert
Indian Ocean
Cape of
Good Hope

Ibn Battuta

(c. 1304–77)

An Arab, born at Tangier, Ibn Battuta was perhaps the greatest traveller in world history. His travels started in 1325 with a pilgrimage to Mecca and Medina, via the North African coast, Egypt, the Nile and the Levant. He did not stop there but continued through the Near East, returning to Mecca to spend three years studying law, before sailing as a trader from Yemen to Somalia and on to Mombasa. He eventually reached Hangchow and the China Sea via Constantinople, Afghanistan, India, and the Maldive Islands, where he took an official position and four wives, eventually moving on to Ceylon with one of them. Battuta covered some 75,000 miles in thirty years of travel in Asia and Africa, not including detours. He settled in Fez to dictate the account of his journeys; this took thirty years. Afterwards he travelled across the Atlas Mountains and the Sahara to Timbuktu.

The lighthouse at Alexandria

I went to see the lighthouse on this journey and found one of its faces in ruins. One would describe it as a square building soaring into the air. Its door is high above the level of the ground, and opposite its door and of the same height is another building; wooden planks are laid from one to the other, and on these one crosses to the doorway. When they are removed there is no means of approach to it. Inside the door there is a place for the guardian of the lighthouse to sit in, and within the lighthouse itself there are many chambers. The breadth of the passage

33

in its interior is nine spans, and the breadth of the wall ten spans; the breadth of the lighthouse on each of its four faces is 140 spans. It is situated on a high mound and lies at a distance of one *farsakh* [three miles] from the city on a long tongue of land, encompassed on three sides by the sea up to the point where the sea is immediately adjacent to the city wall, so that the lighthouse cannot be reached by land except from the city. On this peninsula connected with the lighthouse is the cemetery of Alexandria. I visited the lighthouse [again] on my return to the Maghrib in the year 750 [1349], and found that it had fallen into so ruinous a condition that it was impossible to enter it or to climb up to the doorway.

Alvise da Cadamosto

(c. 1432–1483)

Venetian navigator and trader, sent by Prince Henry the Navigator to the coast of West Africa by way of Madeira and the Canaries. Cadamosto's wonderful account describes the interior of Mauretania, the desert camel routes and the Sahara gold for salt trade. He continued to Senegal and Gambia where he sailed up the vast Gambia River to be met with hails of arrows, since the natives believed the white men to be cannibals. Here Cadamosto noted that the 'Pole Star sank so low that it seemed to touch the sea,' and was the first to describe the Southern Cross at 13°23 N: 'Six large and wonderfully bright stars. We measured them with the compass,' having no astronomical instruments. On a subsequent voyage he discovered the Cape Verde Islands.

Great serpents which can swallow a goat

There are divers sorts of animals, and large numbers of snakes, great and small: some are poisonous, others not. Of the bigger, some are two paces and more in length, but without wings or feet which serpents [are said to] possess. They are so large that snakes are found which swallow a goat whole, without tearing it to pieces. It is said that these great ones are found in swarms in some parts of the country, where there are also enormous quantities of white ants, which by instinct make houses for these snakes with earth which they carry in their mouths. When these are made they resemble ovens. Of these houses they make a hundred or a hundred and fifty in one spot, like fine towns.

These negroes are very great charmers of all things, and especially of these serpents. I have heard it said by a Genoese, a man worthy of credence, that having found himself the year previous to me in the country of this Budomel, and being asleep one night in the house of his nephew, Bisboror, where I lodged, he heard in the middle of the night much hissing outside the house. On rousing himself, he saw that the said Bisboror had arisen, and having summoned two of his negroes was preparing to mount a camel and to depart. The Genoese demanded of him whither he wished to go at such an hour. He replied it was on one of his duties – and suddenly made off. After an interval he returned to the house. The Genoese again questioning him, he replied: "Did you not hear hissing a while ago – hisses outside the house?" The Genoese replying in the affirmative, this is what Bisboror told him: "They were serpents, which, if I had not gone to perform a certain incantation which we of these parts employ, and by which I have turned them away, would have slain many of my animals this night."

The women who dance by night

The women of this country are very pleasant and light-hearted, ready to sing and to dance, especially the young girls. They dance, however, only at night by the light of the moon. Their dances are very different from ours.

These negroes marvelled greatly at many of our possessions, particularly at our cross-bows, and, above all, our mortars. Some came to the ship, and I had them shown the firing of a mortar, the noise of which frightened them exceedingly. I then told them that a mortar would slay more than a hundred men at one shot, at which they were astonished, saying that it was an invention of the devil's. The sound of one of our country pipes, which I had played by one of my sailors, also caused wonderment. Seeing that it was decked out with trappings and ribbons at the head, they concluded that it was a living animal that sang thus in different voices, and were much pleased with it. Perceiving that they were misled, I told them that it was an instrument, and placed it, deflated, in their hands. Whereupon, recognising that it was made by hand, they said that it was a divine instrument, made by God with his own hands, for it sounded so sweetly with so many different voices. They said they had never heard anything sweeter.

They were also struck with admiration by the construction of our ship, and by her equipment – mast, sails, rigging, and anchors. They were of opinion that the portholes in the bows of ships were really eyes by which the ships saw whither they were going over the sea. They said we must be great wizards, almost the equal of the devil, for men that journey by land have difficulty in knowing the way from place to place, while we journeyed by sea, and, as they were given to understand, remained out of sight of land for many days, yet knew which direction to take, a thing only possible through the power of the devil. This appeared so to them because they do not understand the art of navigation [the compass, or the chart].

They also marvelled much on seeing a candle burning in a candlestick, for here they do not know how to make any other light than that of a fire. To them the sight of the candle, never seen before, was beautiful and miraculous. As, in this country, honey is found, they suck the honey from the comb, and throw away the wax. Having bought a little honeycomb, I showed them how to extract the honey from the wax, and then asked whether they knew what it was that remained. They replied that it was good for nothing. In their presence, therefore, I had some candles made, and lighted. On seeing this, they showed much wonderment, exclaiming that we Christians had knowledge of everything.

Father Francisco Alvarez

(fl. 1480s)

Portugese priest sent on a mission to Abyssinia in 1487. He tempered the selfish and quarrelsome behaviour of the Portugese Ambassador, and gave marvellous descriptions of the country and his encounters with the Abyssinian ruler, Prester John who asked him numerous questions on religious points. Alvarez's book may have inspired Dr Johnson's *Rasselas*.

In Abyssinia

In this dry river bed there were many trees of different species, amongst which were jujube trees, and other trees without fruit. Whilst we were thus resting at the river bed there came to us a gentleman named Frey Mazqual, which in our tongue means servant of the cross. He in his blackness was a gentleman, and said he was a brother-in-law of the Barnagais, a brother of his wife. Before he reached us he dismounted, because such is their custom, and they esteem it a courtesy. The ambassador Mattheus, hearing of his arrival, said he was a robber, and that he came to rob us and told us to take up arms: and he Mattheus took his sword, and put a helmet on his head. Frey Mazqual, seeing this tumult, sent to ask leave to come up to us. Mattheus was still doubtful, but withal he came up to us like a well born man, well educated, and courteous. This gentleman had a very good led horse and a mule on which he came, and four men on foot.

Leo Africanus

(1494–1552)

Arab notary born Al-Hassan Ibn-Mohammed Al-Wezad Al-Fasi to a wealthy family in Spain, who travelled extensively in North and Central Africa, the Mediterranean and Near East. Captured by corsairs on his second voyage to Constantinople, he was taken to Rome as a gift to Pope Leo X, Giovanni de' Medici, who converted him to Christianity. He spent twenty years in Rome and wrote his great book, *The History and Description of Africa*, which was the authoritative work about the continent for some three hundred years, and gave the earliest account of Timbuktu.

Manners and customs of the Arabians of Africa

These Arabians when they travell any iourney (as they oftentimes doe) they set their women upon certaine saddles made handsomely of wicker for the same purpose, and fastened to their camels backes, neither be they anything too wide, but fit onely for a woman to sit in. When they goe to the warres each man carries his wife with him, to the end that she may cheere up her good man, and give him encouragement.

... The women of Barbarie use not [this] fond kind of painting, but contenting themselves only with their naturall hiew, they regarde not such fained ornaments: howbeit sometimes they will temper a certaine colour with hens-dung and safron, wherewithall they paint a little round spot on the bals of their cheeks, about the bredth of a French crowne. Like wise betweene their eie-browes they make a triangle and paint upon their chinnes a patch like unto an olive leafe. Some of them also doe paint their eie-browes: and this custome is very highly esteemed of by the poets and by the gentlemen of that countrie. Howbeit they will not use these fantasticall ornaments above three daies together: all which time they will not be seene to any of their friends, except it be to their husbands and children: for these paintings seeme to bee great allurements unto lust, whereby the said women thinke themselves more trim and beautifull.

Whale ribs and amber

Yea, some there are which sticke not to affirme, that the Prophet Jonas was cast forth by the Whale upon the shoare of Messa, when he was sent to preach unto the Ninivites. The rafters and beames of the said Temple are of Whales bone. And it is a usuall thing amongst them, to see Whales of an huge and monstrous bignesse cast up dead upon their shoare, which by reason of their hugenesse and strange deformitie, may terrifie and astonish the beholders. The common people imagine, that, by reason of a certaine secret power and vertue infused from heaven by God upon the said temple, each Whale which would swim past it, can by no meanes escape death. Which a mighty Whale cast up, unlesse a certaine Jew had told me, that it was no such strange matter: for (quoth he) there lie certaine rockes two miles into the Sea on either side, and as the Sea moves, so the Whales move also; and if they chance to light upon a rocke, they are easily wounded to death, and so are cast upon the next shoare. This reason more prevailed with me, then the opinion of the people. Myselfe (I remember being in this Region at the same time when my Lord the Seriffo bare rule over it) was invited by a certaine Gentleman, and was by him conducted into a Garden, where he shewed me a Whales rib of so great a size, that lying upon the ground with the convexe or bowing side upward, in manner of an arch, it resembled a gate, the hollow or inward part whereof aloft we could not touch with our heads, as we rode upon our Camels backs: this rib (he said) had laine there above an hundred yeares, and was kept as a miracle. Here may you find upon the sea-shore great store of Amber, which the Portugal and Fessan Merchants fetch from thence for a verie meane price: for they scarcely pay a Duckat for a whole ounce of most choice and excellent Amber. Amber (as some thinke) is made of Whales dung, and (as others suppose) of their Sperma or Seede, which being consolidate and hardned by the Sea, is cast upon the next shoare.

Pietro della Valle

(1586–1652)

An Italian who left Venice in 1614, spent a year in Constantinople and more than a decade travelling in Egypt, the Holy Land, Arabia, Persia and India. Four hundred years later, his observations still have great liveliness and charm.

Graffiti on pyramid

I had no less pleasure seeing the pyramid from the outside, because I climbed with no little exertion right up to the top, where there is a fine view to be enjoyed, revealing the sea and Egypt and many countries around. There above, at the highest point, on the part which looks towards Italy, I took pleasure in leaving my name carved, with that of someone else I do not feel badly about. I also took pleasure in having my *kapici* and other Turks who were there with us shoot from the summit, with the greatest possible force, a number of arrows. These, however forcefully they were launched, always fell back on to the steps of the pyramid, nor did anyone prove capable by a long way of projecting one beyond the steps or to where they ended.

The brothels of Cairo in 1616

Since the last letter I wrote from here, which if I remember aright was on 25 January, I have seen in Cairo some other curious little things that should not be omitted. And first of all (though these are matters offensive to every chaste ear, such as yours) so that you may nonetheless realise what barbarities hold sway where our faith does not, I shall not fail to tell you that in this Cairo, outside of the city, in several quarters there are certain places designated, let us say, as public brothels: in short they are inhabited by women who, with no fear of any chastisement, wish to practise openly the trade of the harlot.

Women such as these petition the Pasha, and he grants them his favour, provided that they pay I do not know what sum of money daily to the chief constable, who in turn stations policemen there to exact the money every day and guard the women from being harmed. And they do not spend the night in that place, since it is in the country, but just the livelong day, waiting for the arrival of customers, whom, as they come along one by one, they satisfy most courteously and for very little payment, say for a *maidino*, which is worth little more than a few pieces of small change in Naples. And when satisfaction is being given in this way to some lecher or other, because (as I said) there are no houses there, nor anywhere to stay under cover, they retire behind some little mounds of stones, which they build for this purpose, where on the bare ground they are scarcely concealed from the eyes of any passers-by. But what is still more abominable about this place is that these whores are brazen enough sometimes to ply their trade so publicly that quite often – not behind the retreat of stones but outside on the open road, in the sight of everyone – they freely expose themselves, clothed or stripped, to whoever wishes it, especially when there is some prurient lout who, giving them two or three of those *maidini*, wants, as often happens, to derive pleasure from seeing their debaucheries.

And what is more, for very little money, all the women there flock together and strip naked, and play a thousand and one outlandish games among themselves, skipping and dancing and doing other things, the craziest in the world, about which it is as well to keep quiet; and indubitably it is just as well that the doctor has not seen them, as I fear it would have robbed him of all forbearance. These women are nearly all of them ugly, being so dirt cheap as you have heard, yet not so ugly that they do not offer temptation to some lusting man.

Andrew Battel

(*fl.* 1589–1614)

An Englishman prone to a life of extreme adventure, Battel was captured by Indians in South America, handed over to the Portugese, and then taken to Zaire, on the Congo.

He made two unsuccessful attempts to escape, was banished to an even more remote place for six years on the first occasion and injured his leg badly on the second. He was later left as a hostage with a cannibal tribe, the Gagas, but impressed by his display of marksmanship, they decided not to eat him. After eighteen years of this sort of ordeal, he managed to return to England and write down his adventures.

Escape from prison at Loango

When I was sent to Longo [Loango], which is fifteen leagues to the northward of the River Zaire, and carried all commodities fit for that country, as long as glass beads, and round blue beads, and seed beads, and looking-glasses, blue and red coarse cloth, and Irish rugs, which were very rich commodities. Here we sold our cloth at a great rate, for we had for one yard of cloth three elephants' teeth, that weighed 120 pounds; and we bought great store of palm-cloth and elephants' tails. So, in little time we laded our pinnace. For this voyage I was very welcome to the governor, who promised me my liberty if I would serve him. So I went in his pinnace two years and a half upon the coast.

An attempted escape

Then there came a ship of Holland to the city, the merchant of which ship promised to carry me away. And, when they were ready to depart I went secretly on board, but I was betrayed by Portugals which sailed in the ship, and was fetched on shore by sergeants of the city and put in prison, and lay with great bolts of iron two months, thinking that the governor would have me put to death. But at last I was banished for ever to the Fort of Massangano, to serve in the conquest of those parts. Here I lived a most miserable life for the space of six years without any hope to see the sea again.

A second attempt at escape

In this fort there were Egyptians and Moriscoes that were banished as myself. To one of these Egyptians I brake my mind, and told him that it were better for us to venture our lives for our liberty than to live in that miserable place. This Egyptian was as willing as myself, and told me he would procure ten of his consorts to go with us. So we got three Egyptians and seven Portugals. That night we got the best canoe that we could find, and went down the river Cuanza, and being as far down as Mani Cabech, which is a little lord in the province of Elamba [Lamba], we went on shore with our twelve muskets, powder and shot. Here we sunk our canoe, because they should not know where we went on shore. We made a little fire in the wood, and scorched Guinea wheat, which we [had] brought from Massangano, to relieve us, for we had none other food.

As soon as it was night, we took our journey all that night and the next day, without any water at all. The second night we were not able to go, and were fain to dig and scrape up roots of trees, and suck them to maintain life. The third day we met with an old negro which was travelling to Mani Cabech. We bound his hands behind him, and made him lead us the way to the Lake of Casansa. And, travelling all that day in this extreme hot country we came to the Bansa [mbanza], or town, or Mani Casansa, which lyeth within the land twelve leagues from the city of San Paulo. Here we were forced to ask for water, but they would give us none. Then we determined to make them flee their houses with our shot; but seeing that we were desperately bent they called their Lord, Mani Casansa, who gave us water and fair speeches, desiring us to stay all night, only to betray us; but we departed presently, and rested that night in (sic) the lake of Casansa.

The fourth day, at night, we came to the river which towards the north, and passed it with great danger. For there are such abundance of crocodiles in this river that no man dare come near the riverside when it is deep.

Ingredients for a cannibal feast

And presently they were all in arms, and marched to the river side, where he had provided *Gingados*. And being ready with our boat and

Gingados, the general was fain to beat them back because of the credit who should be first. We carried over eighty men at once, and with our muskets we beat the enemy off, and landed, but many of them were slain. By twelve of the clock all the Gagas were over.

Then the general commanded all his drums, *tavales, petes, pongos*, and all his instruments of warlike music to strike up, and gave the onset, which was a bloody day for the Benguelas. These Benguelas presently broke, and turned their backs, and very great number of them were slain, and were taken captives, man, woman and child. The prince, Hombiangymbe, was slain, which was ruler of this country, and more than one hundred of his chief lords, and their heads presented and thrown at the feet of the great Gaga. The men, women and children that were brought in captive alive, and the dead corpses that were brought to be eaten, were strange to behold. For these Gagas are the greatest cannibals and man-eaters that be in the world, for they feed chiefly upon man's flesh [notwithstanding of their] having all the cattle of that country.

James Bruce

(1730–94)

Scottish explorer, nicknamed 'The Abyssinian'. Bruce was in the Portugese wine trade and became Consul-General at Algiers where he learned Arabic. He also studied antiquities in Italy and the Near East. In 1768 he travelled to Abyssinia, and spent four adventurous years looking for the source of the Nile, with the support of Ras Michael, the ruler. What he actually found was the Blue Nile, although two Portugese Jesuits preceded him, a hundred and fifty years earlier. He made his way back to Cairo, having travelled 3730 miles by his own reckoning. When his *Travels* were published, his stories were so extraordinary that many people, including Dr Johnson, did not believe him.

Abba Salama, guardian of the fire

Abba Salama, of whom we shall often speak, at that time filled the post of Acab Saat, or guardian of the fire. It is the third dignity of the church, and he is the first religious officer in the palace. He had a very large revenue, and still a greater influence. He was a man exceedingly rich, and of the worst life possible; though he had taken the vows of poverty and chastity, it was said he had at that time above seventy mistresses in Gondar. His way of seducing women was as extraordinary as the number seduced. It was not by gifts, attendance, or flattery, the usual means employed on such occasions; when he had fixed his desires upon a woman, he forced her to comply, under pain of excommunication. He was exceedingly eloquent and bold, a great favourite of the Iteghe's, till taken in to be a counsellor with Lubo and Brulhe. He had been very instrumental in the murder of Kasmati Eshte, of which he vaunted, even in the palace of the queen his sister. He was a man of pleasing countenance, short, and of a very fair complexion; indifferent, or rather averse to wine, but a monstrous glutton, nice in what he had to eat, to a degree scarcely before known in Abyssinia; a mortal enemy to all white people, whom he classed under the name of Franks, for which the Greeks, uniting their interests at favourable times, had often very nearly overset him.

Mungo Park

(1771–1806)

Scottish traveller. Park studied medicine and his first journey was as assistant surgeon on an East Indiaman bound for Sumatra. He was then sent by the African Association to explore the Niger basin and visit Timbuktu. He learned the Mandingo language in Gambia before setting off to meet the dangers of the interior with a local servant, an interpreter, two asses and one horse and wearing a top hat. Park narrowly avoided execution, and death from illness, was robbed of all his possessions, but saved by a trader at Kamilia. On his second attempt to map the Niger, he was ambushed by tribesmen, seven hundred miles from Timbuktu, and drowned as a result. He had explored over one thousand miles of the Niger, much of the time more or less on his own.

Some outlandish creatures

We rode nearly in a direct line through the woods, but in general went forwards with great circumspection. I observed that my guide frequently stopped and looked under the bushes. On inquiring the reason of this caution, he told me that lions were very numerous in that part of the country, and frequently attacked people travelling through the woods. While he was speaking my horse started, and looking round, I observed a large animal of the cameleopard kind standing at a little distance. The neck and fore-legs were very long; the head was furnished with two short black horns, turning backwards; the tail, which reached down to the ham joint, had a tuft of hair at the end. The animal was of a mouse colour, and it trotted away from us in a very sluggish manner – moving its head from side to side, to see if we were pursuing it. Shortly after this, as we were crossing a large open plain, where there were a few scattered bushes, my guide, who was a little way before me, wheeled his horse round in a moment, calling out something in the Foulah language which I did not understand. I inquired in Mandingo what he meant; '*Wara billi billi!*' ('A very large lion!') said he, and made signs for me to ride away. But my horse was too much fatigued; so we rode slowly past the bush from which the animal had given us the alarm. Not seeing anything myself, however, I thought my guide had been mistaken, when the Foulah suddenly put his hand to his mouth, exclaiming, '*Soubah an allahi!*' ('God preserve us!') and, to my great surprise, I then perceived a large red lion, at a short distance from the bush, with his head couched between his fore-paws. I expected he would instantly spring upon me, and instinctively pulled my feet from my stirrups to throw myself on the ground, that my horse might become the victim rather than myself. But it is probable the lion was not hungry; for he quietly suffered us to pass, though we were fairly within his reach. My eyes were so riveted upon this sovereign of the beasts, that I found it impossible to remove them until we were at a considerable distance.

Eugène Delacroix

(1798–1863)

French painter, the son of a politician, Delacroix was also
rumoured to be the son of Talleyrand. His early works
shocked traditionalists for their use of colour and loose
style of painting. He visited England in 1825, and was
impressed by the work of English artists. In 1832 he accompanied a diplomatic mission to Spain and Morocco. This
visit inspired a series of oriental paintings. Delacroix kept
a detailed daily journal for nearly sixty years.

Meknes

We have been in the Moroccan capital (one of three) for about a
fortnight and we are surrounded with honours and closely watched.
The custom is that envoys to the emperor remain shut up in the house
assigned to them until they are granted an audience. After that date
they are free to go about, but you shall see what sort of freedom this
is. You are allotted a certain number of soldiers, whom of course you
have to pay yourself, with whom you may walk about the town if the
fancy takes you. There you are surrounded by an execrable crowd, who
execrate the dress and appearance of Christians and who fling in your
face all sorts of insults which, luckily, you don't understand. It takes all
the curiosity I've got to run the gauntlet of this mob. The picturesque
is here in abundance. At every step one sees ready-made pictures, which
would bring fame and fortune to twenty generations of painters. You'd
think yourself in Rome or in Athens, minus the Attic atmosphere; the
cloaks and togas and a thousand details are quite typical of antiquity.
A rascal who'll mend the vamp of your shoe for a few coppers has the
dress and bearing of Brutus or Cato of Utica. I could go on forever
telling you about our reception, our audience with the emperor, his
parasol and his state coach, taken out of the stables especially for our
benefit; it's a kind of two-wheeled sedan, drawn by a mule. We were

granted an honour that nobody before us had enjoyed, that of visiting the palace, the garden and the private apartments of His Majesty. The day we entered Meknes there was pandemonium, and more rifle shots than they fire in their battles; we were almost smothered under all this bustling zeal, since the emperor had ordered all the inhabitants, on pain of the severest punishment, to shut up their shops and make merry for our benefit; as from this morning, the deal seems to have been concluded, and not without trouble.

René Caillié

(1799–1838)

A humbly-born Frenchman inspired by reading *Robinson Crusoe* to become an explorer. By the age of twenty he had been to Africa twice and to Guadeloupe. Illness forced his return to France where he lay on a couch outside his house answering questions about his travels. He then spent three years in Senegal preparing himself for his great journey to Timbuktu, then the richest city in Africa and forbidden to outsiders. He set off in 1827, in the guise of an Egyptian and penniless. A year later he reached Djenné on the Niger, traded his umbrella for a canoe, and sailed on to become the first European to enter Timbuktu. He was disappointed by the 'dreary aspect' of the city and returned to Fez and Tangier across the Sahara with a caravan of 1400 camels pulling hundreds of Negro slaves in chains.

Salt carriers of the Sahara

We met several *Foulahs* laden with salt, wax, honey or rice, and I was surprised to notice these unfortunate black men carrying loads of two hundred pounds on their heads, walking extremely fast, and crossing the mountains of Irnanké with astonishing agility. They carry a stick to help with their load, which is carried in a long basket three feet long and one foot wide, made of thin, flexible twigs. With the goods loaded in the basket, the lid is replaced and tied tightly with ropes made from tree bark. When the porters need a rest, they place one end of the basket between the branches of a tree and support the other end with a stick. Bearing these loads, they travel as far as Kankan to sell their salt.

Descent of the Niger by pirogue

The pirogues which travel from Djenné to Tombouctou are so numerous as to form veritable flottilas. Thirty to thirty five metres long, and with a capacity of sixty to eighty tons, they are made from planks lashed together with ropes, and roughly caulked. Two men are constantly employed in baling out water from the boats with calabashes, but there is always six inches of water in the bottom. The crew consists of sixteen to eighteen sailors, two men to steer and the *patron*. As there is no sail, the sailors punt with a pole, or pull on a rope from the bank. When the shore is too wooded or the river too deep, they paddle fast from the bow, for which a space is left clear. The *patron* keeps to the stern and steers with a long pole, ignoring the rudder. As steering is difficult, it often takes two or three men to do it. All the sailors and even some of the *patrons* are slaves; free men would consider the job degrading. These boats can only travel in calm weather; even the faintest wind (frequent on account of the low river banks) can create waves which can destroy or submerge the boat.

Edward Lane

(1801–76)

Lane started life as an engraver in Europe, but spent twelve years in Egypt, initially on account of his health. He became the leading Arabic scholar of his day, and dressed as an Egyptian man of letters. He made the first complete translation of the *Thousand and One Nights* and parts of the Koran and wrote the five-volume *Arab Lexicon*, completed by his great-nephew Stanley Lane-Poole (1854–1931).

Domestic life of the modern Egyptians

Before I describe the ordinary habits of the master of a family, I must mention the various classes of persons of whom the family may consist. The hareem, or the females of the house, have distinct apartments allotted to them; and into these apartments (which, as well as the person to whom they are appropriated, are called 'the hareem') no males are allowed to enter, except the master of the family, and certain other near relations, and children. The hareem may consist, first, of a wife, or wives (to the number of four); secondly, of female slaves, some of whom, namely, white and (as they are commonly called) Abyssinian (but more properly Galla) slaves, are generally concubines, and others (the black slaves) kept merely for servile offices, as cooking, waiting upon the ladies, &c.; thirdly, of female free servants, who are, in no case, concubines, or not legitimately so. The male dependants may consist of white and of black slaves, and free servants; but are mostly of the last-mentioned class. Very few of the Egyptians avail themselves of the license, which their religion allows them, of having four wives; and still smaller is the number of those who have two or more wives, and concubines besides. Even most of those men who have but one wife are content, for the sake of domestic peace, if for no other reason, to remain without a concubine-slave: but some prefer the possession of an Abyssinian slave to the more expensive maintenance of a wife; and keep a black slave-girl, or an Egyptian female servant, to wait upon her, to clean and keep in order the apartments of the hareem, and to cook. It is seldom that two or more wives are kept in the same house: if they are, they generally have distinct apartments. Of male servants, the master of a family keeps, if he can afford to do so, one or more to wait upon him and his male guests; another, who is called a *sakkà* or water-carrier, but who is particularly a servant of the hareem, and attends the ladies only when they go out; a *bowwáb*, or door-keeper, who constantly sits at the door of the house; and a *sáïs*, or groom, for the horse, mule, or ass. Few of the Egyptians have *memlooks* or male white slaves; most of these being in the possession of rich 'Osmánlees (or Turks); and scarcely any but

Turks of high rank keep eunuchs: but a wealthy Egyptian merchant is proud of having a black slave to ride or walk behind him, and to carry his pipe.

The Egyptian is a very early riser, as he retires to sleep at an early hour: it is his duty to be up and dressed before daybreak, when he should say the morning-prayers. In general, while the master of a family is performing the religious ablution, and saying his prayers, his wife or slave is preparing for him a cup of coffee, and filling his pipe, to present to him as soon as he has acquitted himself of his religious duties.

Many of the Egyptians take nothing before noon but the cup of coffee and the pipe: others take a light meal at an early hour. The meal of breakfast (*el-fatoor*) generally consists of bread, with eggs, butter, cheese, clouted cream, or curdled milk, &c.; or of a *fateereh*, which is a kind of pastry, saturated with butter, made very thin, and folded over like a napkin: it is eaten alone, or with a little honey poured over it, or sugar. A very common dish for breakfast is *fool mudemmes* or beans, similar to our horse-beans, slowly boiled, during a whole night, in an earthen vessel, buried, all but the neck, in the hot ashes of an oven or a bath, and having the mouth closely stopped: they are eaten with linseed-oil, or butter, and generally with a little lime-juice: thus prepared, they are sold in the morning in the sooks (or markets) or Cairo and other towns. A meal is often made (by those who cannot afford luxuries) of bread and a mixture called *dukkah*, which is commonly composed of salt and pepper, with *zaatar* (or wild marjoram) or mint or cumin-seed, and with one, or more, or all, of the following ingredients: namely, coriander-seed, cinnamon, sesame, and *hommus* (or chick-peas): each mouthful of bread is dipped in this mixture. The bread is always made in the form of a round flat cake, generally about a span in width, and a finger's breadth, or less, in thickness.

Harriet Martineau

(1802–76)

An English writer of Huguenot origin, Martineau was driven to writing through financial necessity. She wrote economic and social works, travel books and novels. Martineau was very hard of hearing from the age of eighteen and five years of her life were spent as an invalid; she claimed to have been cured by Mesmerism. Despite this she travelled widely, notably in America, Egypt and Palestine.

First sights of Africa

My first sight of Africa was on a somewhat lurid November evening, when the descending sun marked out by its red light a group of purple rocks to the westward, which had not been visible till then, and which presently became again invisible when the sun had gone down behind them, and the glow of the sky had melted away. What we saw was the island of Zembra, and the neighbouring coast of Tunis. Nothing in Africa struck me more than this its first phantom appearance amidst the chill and gathering dusk of evening, and with a vast expanse of sea heaving red between us and it.

My next sight of Africa was when I came on deck early on the morning of 20 November. A Libyan headland was looming to the south-east. Bit by bit, more land appeared, low and grey: then the fragments united, and we had before us a continuous line of coast, level, sandy, and white, with an Arab tower on a single eminence. Twice more during the day we saw such a tower, on just such an eminence. The sea was now of a milky blue, and lustrous, as if it were one flowing and heaving opal. Presently it became of the lightest shade of green. When a tower and a ruined building were seen together, everyone called out 'Alexandria!' and we expected to arrive by noon: but we passed the tower and ruins, and saw only a further stretch of low and sandy coast. It was three o'clock before we were in harbour. When we came on deck after dinner, we found that we were waiting for a pilot; and that we ought to be growing impatient, as there was only an hour of daylight left, and the harbour could not be entered after dark. There was no response from a pilot-boat which we hailed; and one of our boats was sent off to require the attendance of the pilot, who evidently thought he could finish another piece of business before he attended to ours. He was compelled to come; and it was but just in time. The stars were out, and the last brilliant lights had faded from the waters, before we anchored. As we entered the harbour, there was, to the south-west, the crowd of windmills which are so strange an object in an African port: before us was the town, with Pompey's Pillar rising behind the roofs: further north, the Pasha's palace and hareem, with their gardens and rows of palms coming down to the margin of the sea: further round, the light-house; and to the east, at the point of the land, a battery.

We saw this morning a *sakia* for the first time, little thinking how familiar and interesting an object the *sakia* would become to us in the course of three months, nor how its name would for ever after call up associations of the flowing Nile, and broad green fields, and thickets of sugar-canes, and the melancholy music of the waterwheel, and the picturesque figures of peasant children, driving the oxen in the shady circuit of the weed-grown shed. This, the first we saw, was a most primitive affair, placed among sand hillocks, foul with dirt, and its wooden cogwheels in a ruinous state. We presently saw a better one in the garden of the German Consul. It was on a platform, under a trellice of vines. The wheel, which was turned by a blind-folded ox, had rude earthen jars bound on its vanes, its revolutions emptying these jars into a trough, from which the water was conducted to irrigate the garden.

Richard Lemon Lander

(1804–34)

English traveller from Cornwall. Lander travelled as assistant to Hugh Clapperton on his second journey to Africa in 1825. From Ouidah, in Dahomey, they followed the Lagos and other rivers to Kano and Sokoto in central Sudan. Worn out by his ordeals, Clapperton died nearby. Lander wrote an account of the expedition and returned to explore the lower Niger with his brother John, who died of exhaustion after returning to England. Richard Lander was fatally wounded at the island of Fernando Po (now Bioko, off Equatorial Guinea).

King Adólee at Badagry

After crossing the river Formosa, which is about a mile in width, we arrived at Badagry at five o'clock in the afternoon, and were comfortably accommodated in the dwelling of Mr Houtson who had previously resided at that place. The house, like every other in the town, except the king's, is constructed of bamboo cane, and has but one story. On Friday, the 2d of December, the King, Adólee, sent us a present of a bullock, a fine pig, and some fowls; and on the following day honoured us with a visit, in all the pomp and barbarous magnificence of African royalty. He was mounted on a diminutive black horse, and followed by about one hundred and fifty of his subjects, who danced and capered before and behind him; whilst a number of musicians, performing on native instruments of the rudest description, promoted considerably the animation and vivacity of their motions and gestures. He was gorgeously arrayed in a scarlet cloack, literally covered with gold lace, and white kerseymere trowsers similarly embroidered. His hat was turned up in front with rich bands of gold lace, and decorated with a splendid plume of white ostrich feathers, which, waving gracefully over his head, added not a little to the imposing dignity of his appearance! Close to the horse's head marched two boys, each carrying a musket in his right hand; they wore plain scarlet coats, with white collars and large cocked hats, tastefully trimmed with gold lace, which costly material all classes excessively admire. Two fighting chiefs accompanied their sovereign on foot, and familiarly chatted with him as he advanced. On approaching within a short distance of us, the monarch dismounted, and squatting himself on the ground outside our house, an umbrella was unfurled and held over his head, whilst a dozen of his wives stood round their lord and master

> With diverse-colour'd fans, whose wind did seem
> To glow the *delicate* cheeks which they did cool!

for the atmosphere was sultry and the heat oppressive. After paying our respects to our august visitor, to do him honour, I was desired to hoist an English union-jack over him. This was the climax of his glory and his pride; he was sensibly delighted, and looked as childishly vain as a girl when she first puts on a new dress. All hands now began to drink rum, and the spectacle became highly and singularly grotesque. Laying aside all pretensions to superiority of rank, his Badagrian majesty forgot his illustrious birth, and was as cheerful and merry as the meanest and most jovial of his subjects. Seated on the ground, his splendid dress glittering in the rays of the sun, surrounded by his generals, pages, and wives, with a British flag held by a white floating over his princely head, his soul softened by the most inspiring and delicious music! and his animal spirits exhilarated by large and repeated draughts of his favourite cordial, he was in a transport of joy, and looked and spoke as if he had been the happiest man in the universe; while the shouts and bustle of the people, the cracking of fingers and clapping of hands, the singing, and dancing, and capering, all was so novel, and so African, that it made an impression on my memory which will never be erased from it. This debauch continued for a couple of hours; when all the rum being consumed, and Adólee becoming rather tipsy, his majesty begged me to favour him, before his departure, with a tune on my bugle horn, of which he had formed the most extravagant notions. To this modest request I cheerfully acceded, and played several English and Scotch airs, until I became so completely exhausted that my breath was entirely spent, the king not permitting me to drop the instrument till then.

Owing either to the effects of the liquor Adólee had partaken of so freely, or to the sound of the music, &c. he was quite in an extasy, and shook hands and thanked me at the close of every tune. The king then remounted, and the procession returned in the same order, and performed the same anticks as when it came. Captain Clapperton and his associates accompanied the monarch to his palace, whilst I and my companions repaired to our peaceful habitation.

Gérard de Nerval

(1808–55)

French writer, born Gérard Labrunie. Nerval travelled in North Africa and the Near East to recover from a broken heart. Eventually a victim of his own melancholy, he took his own life in Paris, on a night when the temperature was eighteen degrees below zero. His *Journey to the Orient* is far from cold and gloomy however; the first part is a very lively account of his stay in Cairo; the second part an orientalist fantasy of Caliphs and the Queen of Sheba.

The caravan from Mecca

As many as thirty thousand people were about to swell the population of Cairo. The streets of the Muslim district were already thronged with crowds, but I managed to make my way to Bab-el-Fotouh, the Gate of Victory; the whole of the main street which leads there was crammed with bystanders who were kept in orderly lines by government troops. The sound of trumpets, cymbals and drums directed the advancing procession; the various nations and sects were distinguished by their trophies and flags. The long files of harnessed dromedaries, which were mounted by Bedouins armed with long rifles, followed one another, however, at a fairly monotonous pace, and it was only when I reached the countryside that I was able to appreciate the full impact of a spectacle which is unique in the whole world.

A whole nation on the march was merging into the huge population which adorned the knolls of Mount Mokatam on the right, and, on the left, the thousands of usually deserted edifices of the City of the Dead; streaked with red and yellow bands, the turreted copings of the walls and towers of Saladin were also swarming with onlookers. I had the impression that I was present at a scene during the crusades, and this illusion of living in another age was perfected by the sight of the flashing breastplates and knightly helmets worn by the viceroy's guards, interspersed in groups among the crowd. Farther ahead, in the plain where the Calish meanders, stood thousands of chequered tents where the pilgrims halted to refresh themselves; there was no lack of dancers and singers; all the musicians of Cairo, in fact, competed with the horn-blowers and kettledrummers of the procession, an enormous orchestra whose members were perched on top of camels.

Most awesome of all was the vast multitude of Maghrebians which consisted of people from Tunis, Tripoli, Morocco, and also of our 'compatriots' from Algiers; I was sure that I would never again have the opportunity to admire such a bearded, shaggy and ferocious assortment. The majority of the Santon and Dervish brotherhoods were among them, too, ecstatically howling their canticles of love which were punctuated by the name of Allah. Flags of a thousand different colours, hampers overloaded with personal property and weapons, and, here and there, in their magnificent apparel, the emirs and sheikhs mounted upon caparisoned horses streaming with gold and precious stones ... all enhanced the overwhelming splendour of this somewhat disorderly advance. The numerous palanquins for the women were also a picturesque sight, to say the least; this singular apparatus, consisting of a bed surmounted by a tent, was fixed across the back of a camel. Entire families, with lots of children and furniture, appeared to be comfortably settled within these pavilions which, for the most part, were embellished by gorgeous tapestries.

Thomas Cree

(1814–1901)

Cree was a Royal Navy surgeon who spent most of his naval career abroad, much of it on the China Station during the Opium Wars. In the course of duty, he had to carry out amputations on the open deck of his ship, by candlelight. Despite such grim duties, Cree also describes a social life of great gaiety in the journals, which he kept throughout his travels, and illustrated them with lively watercolour sketches.

Alexandria

We had received an invitation to a ball at the Swedish Consul's in honour of the Swedish squadron here. We landed at 8.30 p.m. and found a crowd with torches outside the house and a guard of Swedish Marines from their ships. The squadron consists of a Swedish frigate and a corvette and a Norwegian corvette.

We ascended a handsome flight of steps to some fine large rooms brilliantly lighted and decorated, presenting a splendid appearance and crowded with company. Ladies of all sorts, sizes and complexion in all sorts of costumes, and the gentlemen in uniforms of various countries. The Swedish naval officers were all in full dress, so were we, and their uniform is much like ours. Most of them speak English and some of them have been in our service, and Smith found an old messmate amongst them. The rooms were elegantly furnished from Trieste and the ballroom had fine statues in the corners. About 700 people were present – Swedes, Norwegians, French, Russians, Dutch, Spanish, Italians, Greeks and Turks, in their various costumes. Not many English, as it was Sunday. There were lots of pretty girls, especially the daughter of the Spanish Consul, with whom I had the pleasure of waltzing, although we could not understand each other's speech. There was also a lovely Greek girl in the costume of her country. Many Turkish and

Egyptian officers in gaudy uniforms of scarlet and gold. The Admiral of the Fleet [Stopford] was there, but he sat looking on stroking his long white beard.

There were plenty of partners, though none of them that I met could speak English. I was introduced to a pretty Italian girl, whose name I forget, but we were so well pleased with each other that we danced together for the remainder of the evening. Sweetmeats were plentiful: 300 pounds, I hear, were ordered from one confectioner alone in Alexandria; and there was plenty of negus and lemonade, and claret and water. The supper was at a buffet in another room and there was plenty of cold chicken and cold meat, with jellies, creams and ices, which was done justice to, especially by the ladies who crowded up to the buffet and, after eating as much as they could, pocketed many of the good things. One stout middle-aged Frenchwoman was engaged in filling her pockets which were stuffed out with cold chicken and sweetcakes as she stood before me. I was eating a custard – the opportunity was tempting – so I emptied my glass into her open pocket, and a nice mixture she must have found when she got home.

We did not break up till 8 in the morning, but notwithstanding the broad daylight, I found my Italian partner stood the trying ordeal. We found our jolly-boat waiting at the jetty and we were glad to get on board to breakfast. My ankles were stiff enough with dancing so much on the stone floor.

David Livingstone

(1813–73)

Scottish missionary and explorer. He started work in a cotton mill at the age of ten and joined the London Missionary Society after studying Greek, divinity and medicine. His missionary vocation led him to become one of the most famous explorers of Africa, regarded as a hero in England in his day. Livingstone discovered Lake Ngami, the astonishing Victoria Falls of the Zambezi and later

Lakes Shirwa and Nyasa. He disappeared for three years and was thought to be dying near Lake Tanganyika. In 1871 he was found by Stanley, alive enough to embark on his penultimate expedition – to the Lualaba basin (now in Zaire), but died on the way. His last journey was made by his body, embalmed in salt and brandy, which was sent back to London via Zanzibar.

The Victoria Falls

After twenty minutes' sail from Kalai, we came in sight, for the first time, of the columns of vapour, appropriately called 'smoke', rising at a distance of five or six miles, exactly as when large tracts of grass are burned in Africa. Five columns now arose, and bending in the direction of the wind, they seemed placed against a low ride covered with trees; the tops of the columns at this distance appeared to mingle with the clouds. They were white below, and higher up became dark, so as to simulate smoke very closely. The whole scene was extremely beautiful; the banks and islands dotted over the river are adorned with sylvan vegetation of great variety of colour and form. At the period of our visit several trees were spangled over with blossoms. Trees have each their own physiognomy. There, towering over all, stands the great burly baobab, each of whose enormous arms would form the trunk of a large tree, beside groups of graceful palms, which, with their feathery-shaped leaves depicted on the sky, lend their beauty to the scene. As a hieroglyphic they always mean 'far from home', for one can never get over their foreign air in a picture or landscape. The silvery mohonono, which in the tropics is in form like the cedar of Lebanon, stands in pleasing contrast with the dark colour of the motsouri, whose cypress-form is dotted over at present with its pleasant scarlet fruit. Some trees resemble the great spreading oak, others assume the character of our own elms and chestnuts; but no one can imagine the beauty of the view from anything witnessed in England. It had never been seen before by European eyes; but scenes so lovely must have been gazed upon by angels in their flight. The only want felt, is that of mountains in the background. The falls are bounded on three sides by ridges 300 or 400 feet in height, which are covered with forest, with the red soil appearing among the trees. When about half a mile from the falls, I left the canoe by which we had come down thus far, and embarked in a lighter one, with men well acquainted with the rapids, who, by passing down the centre of the stream in the eddies and still places caused by many jutting rocks, brought me to an island situated in the middle of the river, and on the edge of the lip over which the water rolls. In coming hither, there was danger of being swept down by the streams which rushed along on each side of the island; but the river was now low, and we sailed where it is totally impossible to go when the water is high. But though we had reached the island, and were within a few yards of the spot, a view from which would solve the whole problem, I believe that no one could perceive where the vast body of water went; it seemed to lose itself in the earth, the opposite lip of the fissure into which it disappeared, being only 80 feet distant. At least I did not comprehend it until, creeping with awe to the verge, I peered down into a large rent which had been made from bank to bank of the broad Zambesi, and saw that a stream of a thousand yards broad, leaped down a hundred feet, and then became suddenly compressed into a space of fifteen or twenty yards. The entire falls are simply a crack made in a hard basaltic rock from the right to the left bank of the Zambesi, and then prolonged from the left bank away through thirty or forty miles of hills ... From [this cloud] rushed up a great jet of vapour exactly like steam, and it mounted 200 or 300 feet high; there condensing, it changed its hue to that of dark smoke, and came back in a constant shower, which soon wetted us to the skin. This shower falls chiefly on the opposite side of the fissure, and a few yards back from the lip, there stands a straight hedge of evergreen trees, whose leaves are always wet. From their roots a number of little rills run back into the gulf; but as they flow down the steep wall there, the column of vapour, in its ascent, licks them up clean off the rock, and away they mount again. They are constantly running down, but never reach the bottom.

Heinrich Barth

(1821–65)

German lawyer and archaeologist; the consummate scientific explorer of sub-Saharan Africa. Barth was engaged by the British Government to explore Lake Chad and to suppress slavery. The expedition started from Tripoli, crossed the Sahara and eventually reached the lake. The leader, Richardson, left the party at Agades; the other member, Overweg, was victim of the climate, and Barth continued alone through the Niger region for two years. He spent two years living secretly in Timbuktu, under the protection of a local sheikh, and wrote a history of the Songhai. He eventually returned to England, having travelled some twelve thousand miles under conditions of extreme difficulty.

The last day of 1850

A cold day, and a mountainous country. After we had crossed the sand-hills, there was nothing before us but one flat expanse of sand, mostly bare, and clothed with trees only in favoured spots. The most remarkable phenomenon was the appearance of the feathery bristle, the *Pennisetum distichum*, which on the road to A'gades begins much further northwards. Indeed, when we encamped, we had some difficulty in finding a spot free from this nuisance, though of course the strong wind carried the seeds to a great distance. All our enjoyment of the last evening of the old year centred in an extra dish of two ostrich eggs.

The shops of Kano

Here a row of shops filled with articles of native and foreign produce, with buyers and sellers in every variety of figure, complexion, and dress, yet all intent upon their little gain, endeavouring to cheat each other;

there a large shed, like a hurdle, full of half-naked, half-starved slaves torn from their native homes, from their wives or husbands, from their children or parents, arranged in rows like cattle, and staring desperately upon the buyers, anxiously watching into whose hands it should be their destiny to fall. In another part were to be seen all the necessaries of life; the wealthy buying the most palatable things for his table; the poor stopping and looking greedily upon a handful of grain: here a rich governor dressed in silk and gaudy clothes, mounted upon a spirited and richly caparisoned horse, and followed by a host of idle, insolent slaves; there a poor blind man groping his way through the multitude, and fearing at every step to be trodden down; here a yard neatly fenced with mats of reed, and provided with all the comforts which the country affords – a clean, snug-looking cottage, the clay walls nicely polished, a shutter of reeds placed against the low, well-rounded door, and forbidding intrusion on the privacy of life, a cool shed for the daily household work, a fine spreading *alléluba*-tree, affording a pleasant shade during the hottest hours of the day, or a beautiful *gónda* or papaya unfolding its large feather-like leaves above a slender, smooth, and undivided stem, or the tall date-tree, waving over the whole scene; the matron in a clean black cotton gown wound round her waist, her hair neatly dressed in *chókoli* or *bejáji*, busy preparing the meal for her absent husband, or spinning cotton, and at the same time urging the female slaves to pound the corn; the children naked and merry, playing about in the sand at the 'urgi-n-dáwaki' or the 'da-n-chácha' or chasing a stubborn goat; earthenware pots and wooden bowls, all cleanly washed, standing in order. Further on a dashing Cyprian, homeless, comfortless, and childless, but affecting merriment or forcing a wanton laugh, gaudily ornamented with numerous strings of beads round her neck, her hair fancifully dressed and bound with a diadem, her gown of various colours loosely fastened under her luxuriant breast, and trailing behind in the sand; near her a diseased wretch covered with ulcers, or with elephantiasis.

Kissed to suffocation

On arrival at the broad dry bed of a stream about two days' march from Gondokoro, we halted beneath the shade of a large tree for breakfast. The women and children now approached, and hesitatingly declared that this was their country, and their villages were near. They evidently doubted my sincerity in restoring them, which hurt me exceedingly.

'Go, my good women,' I exclaimed, 'and when you arrive at your homes, explain to your people that you were captured entirely against my will, and that I am only happy to have restored you.'

For a few moments they looked around them, as hardly believing the good news. In another instant, as the truth flashed across their delighted minds, they rushed upon me in a body, and before I had time for self-defence, I found myself in the arms of a naked beauty who kissed me almost to suffocation, and with a most unpleasant embrace licked both my eyes with her tongue. The sentries came to my assistance, together with the servants, who withstood the grateful crowd; otherwise both my wife and myself would have been subjected to this painful thanksgiving from the liberated Bari women.

Their freedom having been explained, we gave each a present of beads as a reward for the trouble they had undergone, and they went away rejoicing upon the road to their own homes.

Lady Lucie Duff Gordon

(1821–69)

English author, translator and traveller. A childhood friend of John Stuart Mill, she continued to keep brilliant company and conversation, and translated the works of German writers. She married Sir Alexander Duff Gordon, but in the 1850s was sent abroad for her health, to South Africa and then to Egypt where she spent seven years, the longest time a European had spent there. The publication of her spirited *Letters* home encouraged many others to follow her. She died in Cairo.

A Coptic Church

On Sunday we halted at Bibeh, where I caught sight of a large Coptic church, and sallied forth to see whether they would let me in. The road lay past the house of the head man of the village, and there 'in the gate' sat a patriarch surrounded by her servants and his cattle. Over the gateway were crosses, and queer constellations of dots more like Mithraic symbols than anything Christian; but Girgis was a Copt (Kubtee), though chosen head of the Muslim village. He rose as I came up, stepped out and salámed, then took my hand and said I must go into his house and enter the hareem before I saw the church. His old mother, who looked a hundred, and his pretty wife, were very friendly; but as I had to leave Omar at the door, our talk soon came to an end, and Girgis took me into the divan, without the sacred precincts of the hareem. Of course we had pipes and coffee, and he pressed me to stay some days, and to eat with him every day and to accept all his house contained. I took the milk he offered and asked him to visit me in the boat, saying I must return before sunset, when it gets cold, as I was ill. The house was a curious specimen of a wealthy man's house. I could not describe it if I tried; but I felt as if I were acting a passage in the Old Testament.

We went to the church, which looked like nine beehives in a box. Inside, the nine domes, resting on square pillars, were very handsome; Girgis was putting it into thorough repair at his own expense, and it will cost a good deal, I think, to repair and renew the fine old wood panelling of such minute and intricate workmanship. The church is divided by three screens; one in front of the eastern three domes is impervious, and conceals the Holy of Holies.

The hareem sit behind a third screen, the furthest removal from the holy screen, where also was the font, locked up ... The Copts have but one wife, but they shut her up even closer than the Arabs do. The children were sweetly pretty, so unlike the Arab brats, and the men very good-looking. They did not seem to acknowledge me at all as a *coréligionnaire*, and asked whether we of the English religion did not marry our brothers and sisters.

Samuel White Baker

(1821–93)

British explorer who regarded the pursuit of dangerous game as the best training for explorers and soldiers. Baker began travelling seriously after his wife died of typhoid fever, having previously lived in Mauritius and Ceylon, where he established an agricultural settlement with his brothers. While manager of the construction of a railway linking the Danube and the Black Sea, he met and married a beautiful Hungarian, Florence Von Saas, who was to travel with him through Africa. Baker learned Arabic, and how to use astronomical instruments in preparation for a journey to explore the Abyssinian tributaries of the Nile. At Gondokoro, they met the explorers Speke and Grant who had just discovered Lake Victoria. The Bakers went on to discover Lake Albert-Nyanza, catching their breathtaking first sight of it from a high cliff. On the way they had fallen in with ivory and slave traders. A local ruler had tried to obtain Florence by extortion; she became ill and had to be carried on a litter. They returned to Khartoum after two and a half years, having cleared up the question of the sources of the Nile. Afterwards, Baker accompanied the Prince of Wales to Egypt, became Governor-General of the Equatorial Nile basin with a mission from the pasha of Egypt to suppress the slave trade. He continued to travel after this.

Slaves purchased for needles

In Unyoro there was an established value for a healthy young girl. Such a person was equal to a single elephant's tusk of the first class, or to a new shirt. Thus a girl could be purchased for a shirt, and she might be subsequently exchanged for a large elephant's tusk.

In the country of Uganda, where the natives are exceedingly clever as tailors and furriers, needles are in great demand. A handsome girl may be purchased for thirteen English needles! Thus for slave-traders there existed an excellent opening for a profitable business. A girl might be bought for thirteen needles in Uganda, to be exchanged in Unyoro for an elephant's tusk that would be worth twenty or thirty pounds in England.

'I'll sell him to you for a molote!'

The sheik and I got on famously, and I found a good listener, to whom I preached a touching sermon upon the horrors of the slave trade, which I was resolved to suppress.

The good man was evidently touched at the allusion to the forcible separation of children from their parents.

"Have you a son?" he asked.

"My sons are, unfortunately, dead," I replied.

"Indeed!" he exclaimed. "I have a son – an only son. He is a nice boy – a very good boy; about so high [showing his length upon the handle of his spear]. I should like you to see my boy – he is very thin now; but if he should remain with you he would soon get fat. He's a really nice boy, and *always hungry*.

You'll be so fond of him; he'll eat from morning till night; and still he'll be hungry. You'll like him amazingly; he'll give you no trouble if you only give him plenty to eat. He'll lie down and go to sleep, and he'll wake up hungry again. He's a good boy, indeed; and he's my only son. *I'll sell him to you for a molote* [native iron spade]!"

The result of my sermon on the slave trade, addressed to this affectionate father, was quite appalling. I was offered his only son in exchange for a spade! and this young nigger knave of spades was warranted to remain *always hungry*.

Western novelties in the heart of Africa

On arrival in the divan he was much astonished and delighted. The room, twenty-eight feet by fourteen, was arranged with double rows of metal boxes on all sides, so closely packed that they formed either low tables or seats, as might be required. These were all covered with blue blankets, which gave a neat appearance, upon which, at the east end of the room, were exhibited samples of the various goods that I had brought for the establishment of a regular trade in Unyoro. There were tin plates as bright as mirrors, crockery of various kinds, glasses, knives of many varieties, beautiful Manchester manufactures, such as Indian scarfs, handkerchiefs, piece-goods, light blue serge, chintzes, scarlet and blue blankets, blue and crimson cotton cloth, small mirrors, scissors, razors, watches, clocks, tin whistles, triangles, tambourines, toys, including small tin steamers, boats, carriages, Japanese spinning tops, horn snakes, pop-guns, spherical quicksilvered globes, together with assortments of beads of many varieties.

"Are they all for me?" asked Kabba Réga.

"Certainly," I replied, "if you wish to exchange ivory. All these things belong to the Khedive of Egypt, and any amount remains in the maga-zines of Gondokoro. These are simply a few curiosities that I have brought as an experiment to prove the possibility of establishing a trade."

Among other things, the wheel of life attracted his attention. This had frequently been exhibited, but neither Kabba Réga nor his chiefs ever tired of the performance.

The magnetic battery was now called for, and Kabba Réga insisted upon each of his chiefs submitting to a shock, although he was afraid to experiment upon himself. He begged Lieutenant Baker, who managed the instrument, to give as powerful a shock as he could, and he went into roars of laughter when he saw a favourite minister rolling on his back in contortions, without the possibility of letting the cylinders fall from his grasp.

Every individual of his headmen had to suffer, and when all had been operated upon, the ministers sought outside the divan among the crowd for any particular friends that might wish to try "the magic".

At length one of the wires of the instrument gave way, as a patient kicked and rolled frantically upon the ground; this was a good excuse for closing the entertainment.

Anon.

The author of *Travels in Africa* (1824) admits to his nar-
rator being a composite figure, Tom Jackson, who leaves
his rural Irish hearth to travel the world. Shipwrecked off
the coast of Africa, he and his companions rowed ashore
in open boats to be met at first with kindness from
the natives. They later fell into the hands of 'savages' and
'Moors' and eventually travelled all over Africa, across the
desert to Egypt, to South Africa, up the Gambia and Niger
rivers, and eventually back to County Wicklow.

The people of Tombuctoo

The people of Tombuctoo are both stout and healthy, for they will
lie out in the sun in midday, when even I, after a long stay with
them, could not bear it; and also sleep without shelter at night, though
a heavy fog, which comes from the river, falls like dew upon the
ground. They also grease their bodies with butter, which makes the skin
smooth and shining, but if they neglect it, it will grow rough and very
ugly.

The men all have the marks of a deep cut from the forehead down
to the nose, from which others branch out at each side, over the eyebrows, into which, while the wound is fresh, they put a blue die, which
never afterwards washes out; but they are very dirty in their habits, for
sometimes they will not wash themselves in fourteen days together. The
king and queen changed their dress once a week.

Amelia Edwards

(1831–92)

English novelist. She went to Egypt by chance, with a
female companion. They 'had just taken refuge in Egypt
as one might turn aside into the Burlington Arcade or the
Passage des Panoramas – to get out of the rain . . . Without
definite plans, outfit, or any kind of Oriental experience,
behold us arrived in Cairo on the 29th November 1873,
literally, and most prosaically, in search of fine weather.'
They travelled up the Nile in a flat-bottomed boat 'not
very unlike the Noah's Ark of our childhood'. Their party
discovered an unknown tomb at Abu Simbel, which
they 'excavated'. Edwards subsequently became a serious
Egyptologist; she founded the Egyptian Exploration Fund
and endowed the first Chair of Egyptology in England.

A tomb is opened

The Boulak authorities keep a small gang of trained excavators always
at work in the Necropolis of Thebes. These men are superintended by
the Governor, and every mummy-case discovered is forwarded to Boulak
unopened. Thanks to the courtesy of the Governor, we had the good
fortune to be present one morning at the opening of a tomb. He sent
to summon us, just as we were going to breakfast. With what alacrity
we manned the felucca, and how we ate our bread and butter half in
the boat and half on donkey-back, may easily be imagined. How well I
remember that early morning ride across the western plain of Thebes
– the young barley rippling for miles in the sun; the little water-channel
running beside the path; the white butterflies circling in couples; the
wayside grave with its tiny dome and prayer-mat, its well and broken
kulleh, inviting the passer-by to drink and pray; the wild vine that trailed
along the wall; the vivid violet of the vetches that blossomed unbidden
in the barley. We had the mounds and pylons of Medinet Habu to the

left – the ruins of the Ramesseum to the right – the Colossi of the Plain and the rosy western mountains before us all the way. How the great statues glistened in the morning light! How they towered up against the soft blue sky! Battered and featureless, they sat in the old patient attitude, looking as if they mourned the vanished springs.

We found the new tomb a few hundred yards in the rear of the Ramesseum. The diggers were in the pit; the Governor and a few Arabs were looking on. The vault was lined with brickwork above, and cut square in the living rock below. We were just in time; for already, through the sand and rubble with which the grave had been filled in, there appeared an outline of something buried. The men, throwing spades and picks aside, now began scraping up the dust with their hands, and a mummy-case came gradually to light. It was shaped to represent a body lying at length with the hands crossed upon the breast. Both hands and face were carved in high relief. The ground-colour of the sarcophagus was white; the surface covered with hieroglyphed legends and somewhat coarsely painted figures of the four lesser Gods of the Dead. The face, like the hands, was coloured a brownish yellow and highly varnished. But for a little dimness of the gaudy hues, and a little flaking off of the surface here and there, the thing was as perfect as when it was placed in the ground. A small wooden box roughly put together lay at the feet of the mummy. This was taken out first, and handed to the Governor, who put it aside without opening it. The mummy-case was then raised upright, hoisted to the brink of the pit, and laid upon the ground.

It gave one a kind of shock to see it first of all lying just as it had been left by the mourners; then hauled out by rude hands, to be searched, unrolled, perhaps broken up as unworthy to occupy a corner in the Boulak collection. Once they are lodged and catalogued in a museum, one comes to look upon these things as "specimens", and forgets that they once were living beings like ourselves. But this poor mummy looked startlingly human and pathetic lying at the bottom of its grave in the morning sunlight.

Viscount James Bryce

(1838–1922)

Scottish historian, lawyer, statesman and mountaineer. In 1876 Bryce visited Russia, the Caucasus and Armenia; and wrote a charming book about his travels around Mount Ararat. He also visited South Africa.

On the Cape of Good Hope

An hour in the railway brings one to Simon's Bay, the station of the British naval squadron, a small but fairly well sheltered inlet under high hills. From this one drives for four hours over a very rough track through a lonely and silent country, sometimes sandy, sometimes thick with brushwood, but everywhere decked with brilliant flowers, to the Cape, a magnificent headland rising almost vertically from the ocean to a height of 800 feet. Long, heavy surges are always foaming on the rocks below, and nowhere, even on this troubled coast, where the hot Mozambique current meets a stream of cold Antarctic water, do gales more often howl and shriek than round these rocky pinnacles. One can well understand the terror with which the Portuguese sailors five centuries ago used to see the grim headland loom up through the clouds driven by the strong southeasters, that kept them struggling for days or weeks to round the cape that marked their way to India. But Sir Francis Drake, who passed it coming home westward from his ever-famous voyage round the world, had a more auspicious experience: "We ran hard aboard the Cape, finding the report of the Portuguese to be most false, who affirm that it is the most dangerous cape of the world, never without intolerable storms and present danger to travellers who come near the same. This cape is a most stately thing, and the finest cape we saw in the whole circumference of the earth."

Sir Henry Morton Stanley

(1841–1904)

Journalist and explorer. Born in Wales as John Rowlands and abandoned to the workhouse; he went to New Orleans as a cabin boy and was adopted by a merchant named Stanley whose name he took. He fought on both sides in the American Civil War and subsequently went to Abyssinia with Lord Napier's expedition in 1868 as a correspondent for the *New York Herald*. Three years later the paper sent him to find Livingstone, feared dead in Central Africa. Stanley found him, still alive, at Ujiji on the eastern shore of Lake Tanganyika. An immortal exchange ensued. The two men explored the lake, but Stanley failed to persuade the doctor to return to England with him. Stanley later returned to Lake Victoria, discovered a new source of the Nile, reached Lake Albert, and continued along the Congo, reaching the coast 999 days after leaving Zanzibar. He made two further expeditions to Central Africa, on the last of which he rescued Emin Pasha, ruler of the Sudan, from rebels, discovering Lake Edward and Mount Ruwenzori en route.

Mirambo

April 22nd:
Halt.

This day will be memorable for the visit of the famous Mirambo to me accompanied by his Chiefs. He was so different from all I ever conceived of such a redoubtable chieftain and a bandit of such terrible reputation. A man 5 feet 11 inches in height, about 35 years old, well-made but with not an ounce of superfluous flesh about him; handsome, regular featured, mild, soft spoken, with what you would call a meek demeanour, generous, open-handed with nothing of the small cent ideas of narrow mean-minded men. Indeed I did not let myself readily believe that this

73

could possibly be the ferocious Chief of the terrible Ruga-Ruga. I could not believe it until all the Arabs testified to it, for I had expected to see something of the Mtesa type – a man whose exterior would proclaim the man's life and rank – but this unpresuming quiet-eyed man of inoffensive meek exterior, whose language was so mild without a single gesture, indicated nothing of the Napoleonic genius which he has for five years displayed in the heart of Africa to the injury of Arabs and commerce and the nearly trebling the price of ivory. Nothing, I said, but I will except the eyes, which were composed and a steady calm gaze. And unlike all other Africans I have met, they met your own and steadily and calmly confronted them. Thus I had seen Mirambo.

A Madras Officer

Anonymous East India Company officer, describing his return journey to England by sea and over land in vivid detail.

The outskirts of Suez

The outskirts of Suez are in keeping with the interior of the town. Heaps of accumulated rubbish on all sides: filth of every description, and ruinous houses, lined the road for some distance. Dead dogs and donkeys, skeletons of camels presented themselves here and there; causing a stench sufficient to make one sick. Squalid huts inhabited by still more squalid wretches, with starvation and disease depicted on their miserable faces; in fact, every thing and object which we saw, gave us an idea of abject poverty – the acme of human woe. I was glad when we passed these pitiful scenes, and breathed more freely when we came upon the open plain.

A camp in the desert

We arrived at No. 4 at about twelve o'clock at night; the progress we made from the last station, was very slow certainly, but we had safety on our side, and that is better than going fast with the chance of a broken neck. Here we caught up those who had started before us. They were all bustling out of bed, to make room for the fresh arrivals. But I must mention to the reader that No. 4 is the principle halting ground in the desert. Here is a regular hotel. A large house with a range of apartments for families as well as single persons. There is a hall for meals, and a suite of six or eight bed-rooms. A flight of stone steps leads you up; underneath are the stables and other offices, kitchen, &c. &c. It was dreadfully cold when we arrived. Mr D. told me to seize a bed-room at once; which I forthwith did; securing one, which had but just been vacated by a married couple; so I bundled my wife into bed without delay, and ran down into kitchen to procure her a hot cup of coffee. There was such a noise and hubbub at this place, such hollooing and shouting; horses neighing, kicking, and fighting; Arab coachmen and ostlers wrangling; passengers on the start running up and down the steps, and shaking hands, and talking with those come; ladies calling frantically for their children; and children crying for the cold; maid-servants and nurses flying about with their dresses not fastened behind, some with caps and bonnets, others with stockings and garters in their hands; people rushing up against each other and begging pardon; one man running here and another there as if mad; in fact I never saw such a sight – 'twas confusion worse confounded most truly! I stood at the door of the kitchen, witnessing the amusing spectacle, and could not help laughing! Indeed it was a most ludicrous sight. The cook in the kitchen had been hard at work ever since six o'clock the previous morning; and was still at it, making coffee and swearing in fine style.

Joseph Thomson

(1858–95)

Scottish naturalist and explorer. He became leader of a pioneering journey to Lakes Nyasa and Tanganyika at the age of twenty, when the leader, Keith Johnston, died. His third expedition to Africa in 1883, from Mombasa through the Great Rift Valley to Uganda, took him through Masai country. These fearsome warriors tormented Thomson by making him take off his boots and wiggle his toes, pinched him, and made him take down his trousers; he retaliated by dissolving Epsom salts in water, White magic which made an impression. Things became trickier, but fortunately for Thomson, the Masai faced more serious enemies, and he was able to continue across the 13,000-foot Aberdare Range, past Mount Kenya to Lake Victoria. On the return journey, Thomson was badly gored by a buffalo, but eventually got back to the coast, after a journey of three thousand miles. In 1885 he travelled up the Niger to the Western Sudan, and later explored the Atlas Mountains, climbing some of its highest peaks.

Meeting a slave caravan

Camped at Mtowa, we found a huge caravan of ivory and slaves from Manyema, awaiting, like ourselves, means of transport across the lake. There were about 1000 slaves, all in the most miserable condition, living on roots and grasses, or whatever refuse or garbage they could pick up. The sight of these poor creatures was of the most painful character. They were moving about like skeletons covered with parchment, through which every bone in the body might be traced. It would be difficult to say what appearance they might have had if properly fed, but as we saw them they looked most ugly and degraded savages, not one whit more prepossessing than those we had met among such tribes as the Wakhutu, the Wapangwa, or Wanena. Livingstone describes the fine appearance of the Manyema in glowing terms. But assuredly the specimens we saw at Mtowa little deserved to be highly spoken of. Probably, however, the slaves were the riff-raff and criminals of the tribes, sold to the Arabs for some misdemeanour.

We learned that they had had a frightful march during which two-thirds fell victims to famine, murder, and disease; so that out of about 3000 slaves who started from Manyema, only 1000 reached Mtowa. Of those remaining, 600 belonged to the renowned Tippu Tib, mentioned by Cameron and Stanley. The poor wretches were carrying ivory to Ujiji and Unyanyembe, to be there disposed of, along with themselves, for stores to be taken back to Nyangwe.

It was reported that Tippu Tib, with his enormous accumulations of ivory and slaves, was about to commence his return to the coast as soon as the necessary stores reached him. He proposed to march by force, sweeping everything before him, and taking whatever he could lay his hands on. He would pass through Urua by the eastern side of the Lualaba, through Kabuirè, round the south end of the lake, and then cross Usango and Uhehè to the coast. It is highly improbable that ever this bold scheme will be carried into effect. Ruin and destruction would be the fate of such an expedition, if attempted. It is more than likely that Tippu Tib will never leave Manyema.

I was very much pleased with the Arabs at the head of this caravan. They certainly were not the brutal monsters we would be inclined to imagine on learning that they left their slaves to die of starvation, or to live on roots and grasses. At the risk of being misunderstood, I cannot but describe them as most courteous gentlemen, with as humane and kindly feelings on the whole as are found in the average European, but who have been accustomed from boyhood to a most abominable traffic, in which their traditions and customs said there was no harm. They looked upon such of their slaves as they bought and sold, simply as a European would look upon pigs or horses.

Mary Kingsley

(1862–1900)

Daughter of George Henry Kingsley, a travel writer and physician whose only prescription was foreign travel, accompanied by himself, and niece of the writer Charles Kingsley (q.v.). Mary Kingsley was self-taught, studying mechanics, chemistry, anthropology, ethnography. After spending four years nursing her parents, Mary set off for West Africa in a cargo ship. She went on to explore the Congo. She subsidised her extremely intrepid journeys, through swamps and canoeing deadly rapids, by making collections for the University of Cambridge and the British Museum. She also traded in oil and rubber. Her writing is marked by a great empathy with Africa and Africans, and by common sense. Finding herself trapped in a game pit lined with spikes, she praised 'the blessings of a good thick skirt'. Kingsley died while nursing prisoners of the Boer war.

Mangrove swamps

Soon the salt waters are shut right out, the mangrove dies, and that bit of Africa is made. It is very interesting to get into these regions; you see along the river-bank a rich, thick, lovely wall of soft-wooded plants, and behind this you find great stretches of death; miles and miles sometimes of gaunt white mangrove skeletons standing on grey stuff that is not yet earth and is no longer slime, and through the crust of which you can sink into rotting putrefaction. Yet, long after you are dead, buried, and forgotten, this will become a forest of soft-wooded plants and palms; and finally of hard-wooded trees. Districts of this description you will find in great sweeps of Kama country for example, and in the rich low regions up to the base of the Sierra del Cristal and the Rumby range.

You often hear the utter lifelessness of mangrove-swamps commented on; why I do not know, for they are fairly heavily stocked with fauna, though the species are comparatively few. There are the crocodiles, more of them than any one wants; there are quantities of flies, particularly the big silent mangrove-fly which lays an egg in you under the skin; the egg becomes a maggot and stays there until it feels fit to enter into external life. Then there are "slimy things that crawl with legs upon a slimy sea," and any quantity of hopping mud-fish, and crabs, and a certain mollusc, and in the water various kinds of cat-fish. Birdless they are save for the flocks of grey parrots that pass over them at evening, hoarsely squarking; and save for this squarking of the parrots the swamps are silent all the day, at least during the dry season; in the wet season there is no silence night or day in West Africa, but that roar of the descending deluge of rain that is more monotonous and more gloomy than any silence can be. In the morning you do not hear the long, low, mellow whistle of the plantain-eaters calling up the dawn, nor in the evening the clock-bird nor the Handel-Festival-sized choruses of frogs, or the crickets, that carry on their vesper controversy of "she did" – "she didn't" so fiercely on hard land.

But the mangrove-swamp follows the general rule for West Africa, and night in it is noisier than the day. After dark it is full of noises; grunts from I know not what, splashes from jumping fish, the peculiar whirr of rushing crabs, and quaint creaking and groaning sounds from the trees; and – above all in eeriness – the strange whine and sighing cough of crocodiles. I shall never forget one moonlight night I spent in a mangrove-swamp. I was not lost, but we had gone away into the swamp from the main river, so that the natives of a village with an evil reputation should not come across us when they were out fishing. We got well in, on to a long pool or lagoon; and dozed off and woke, and saw the same scene around us twenty times in the night, which thereby grew into an aeon, until I dreamily felt that I had somehow got into a world that was all like this, and always had been, and was always going to be so.

Gorillas at home

... I saw before me some thirty yards off, busily employed in pulling down plantains, and other depredations, five gorillas: one old male, one young male, and three females. One of these had clinging to her a young fellow, with beautiful wavy black hair with just a kink in it. The big male was crouching on his haunches, with his long arms hanging down on either side, with the backs of his hands on the ground, the palms upwards. The elder lady was tearing to pieces and eating a pineapple, while the others were at the plantains destroying more than they ate.

They kept up a sort of a whinnying, chattering noise, quite different from the sound I have heard gorillas give when enraged, or from the one you can hear them giving when they are what the natives call "dancing" at night. I noticed that their reach of arm was immense, and that when they went from one tree to another, they squattered across the open ground in a most inelegant style dragging their long arm with the knuckles downwards. I should think the big male and female were

79

over six feet each. The others would be from four to five. I put out my hand and laid it on Wiki's gun to prevent him from firing, and he, thinking I was going to fire, gripped my wrist.

Murray's Handbooks

With the German firm of Baedeker, John Murray's publishing house dominated the production of nineteenth and early twentieth-century travel books. Murray's, founded by the first John Murray in 1768, has been a publisher in the wider sense of the word; its authors have included Jane Austen, Byron, Darwin and Disraeli, to name but a few. The *Handbooks* appeared on the scene in 1836, kicked off by John Murray the third (1808–92). His guide to Holland was followed swiftly by *Handbooks* for France, Germany and Switzerland, remarkable feats considering that he compiled them all himself, as well as being the publisher. While Baedeker's guides were factual *tours de force*, Murray's *Handbooks*, while informative, were more literate and enjoyable to read.

An ascent of the Great Pyramid

Having now given the history, and described the exterior, of the Great Pyramid, the next thing is to accomplish the task, which most travellers think it necessary to set themselves, of getting to the top of it. The Ascent is usually made from the NE corner. Some pronounce the getting to the top to be a very fatiguing business, while others declare that it is the easiest thing possible. Some speak of the giddiness they experienced, and others affirm that the weakest head has nothing to fear. The truth may be said to lie between these two extremes, at least for those who are neither very old nor very young, very strong-headed nor very subject to vertigo: the not altogether inactive may find it a little fatiguing; and heads that are unaccustomed to going aloft, either on rigging or Alps, may feel a little dizzy.

Evelyn Waugh

(1903–66)

English writer. Although it is difficult to imagine Evelyn Waugh in his later years as a traveller, he visited the world extensively between 1928 and 1937, in Europe, the Near East, Africa and South America, writing a number of travel books. In 1930 he found himself in Addis Ababa for the Coronation of Ras Tafari as Emperor Haile Selassie of Ethiopia. The explorer Wilfred Thesiger (**q.v.**) witnessed the same event.

A coronation in Addis Ababa, 1930

This is what I saw at the coronation:

The Emperor and Empress were due to appear from their vigil at seven in the morning. We were warned to arrive at the tent about an hour before that time. Accordingly, having dressed by candlelight, Irene and I proceeded there at about six. For many hours before dawn the roads into the town had been filled with tribesmen coming in from the surrounding camps. We could see them passing the hotel (the street lamps were working that night) in dense white crowds, some riding mules, some walking, some moving at a slow trot beside their masters. All, as always, were armed. Our car moved slowly to Gorgis, hooting continuously. There were many other cars; some carrying Europeans; others, Abyssinian officials. Eventually we reached the church and were admitted after a narrow scrutiny of our tickets and ourselves. The square inside the gates was comparatively clear; from the top of the steps the machine-guns compromised with ecclesiastical calm. From inside the cathedral came the voices of the priests singing the last phase of the service that had lasted all night. Eluding the numerous soldiers, policemen, and officials who directed us towards the tent, we slipped into the outer ambulatory of the church, where the choir of bearded and vested deacons were dancing to the music of hand drums and little silver rattles. The drummers squatted round them; but they carried the rattles themselves and in their other hand waved praying-sticks. Some carried nothing, but merely clapped their empty palms. They shuffled in and out, singing and swaying; the dance was performed with body and arms rather than with the feet. Their faces expressed the keenest enjoyment – almost, in some cases, ecstasy. The brilliant morning sun streamed in on them from the windows, on their silver crosses, silver-headed rods, and on the large, illuminated manuscript from which one of them, undeterred by the music, was reciting the Gospels; the clouds of incense mounted and bellied in the shafts of light.

Elizabeth Marshall Thomas

(1931–)

The daughter of anthropologists, Thomas lived with four of the Kalahari bushmen language groups during the 1950s.

Looking for bi

We were going particularly to look for *bi*, a fibrous, watery root that is the mainstay of the Bushmen's diet during the hot season when the melons are gone. From the end of August, when the spring begins, the heat increases in intensity until December and January, when the rains come, relieving the drought. During this hot, dry season the sand reflects the sun until the air all over the veld shudders and dances, until human beings and animals alike gasp for air and water. This is the hardest season of all for the Bushmen, yet most of them remain alive by going into the veld early in the morning in the cooler light of dawn to gather *bi*. The *bi* they find is brought back to the werf before the sun is hot; it is scraped, and the scrapings are squeezed dry. The people drink the juice they squeeze. Then they dig shallow pits like graves for themselves in the shade. They urinate on the *bi* scrapings and line the pits with the now moist pulp, then lie in the pits and spend the day letting the moisture evaporating from the urine preserve the moisture in their bodies. They lie still all day and at dusk go into the veld again to gather food, perhaps a few roots or cucumbers, returning to their werf before it is utterly dark, for in the hot season the big snakes, too, move only at night, the mambas and the cobras out of their holes.

By the end of the season the Gikwe are emaciated from hunger and thirst, and it is because of this season that the Gikwe hear the jackals on the plains cry, "Water, water."

When we reached the little hill Twikwe had mentioned we found no *bi* root, but we found other kinds of veld food: a bush with red berries, several kinds of roots, and a spiny cucumber not three inches long, round and bristling with its spines like a sea urchin, handsome in its light-brown, yellow-striped skin. The young boys found five of these cucumbers lying in a crooked row on the sand, all put there by a vine which had mostly died and shrivelled away. We picked them and ate them. They have a watery green flesh which looks just like the flesh of a cucumber as we know it but which is sweet.

Witabe, noting the direction of the vine by the way it had deposited its cucumbers, traced it to its source and found a bit of it left above the ground, below the branches of a white-thorn bush. He said there would be an edible root there, and when he dug, there was.

Meanwhile, Gai had found a solid, stiff vine like a stalk among the roots of a grey bush which was the home of a small flock of birds. Just for fun, Gai chased the birds out; they would have gone anyway, but, frightened by him, they flew like little pellets in every direction, leaving behind a pale, soft grass nest blowing in the wind. Gai sat down facing the bush with the branch shadows all over him and dug with a digging-stick in the sand between his legs. The branches around his head got in his way, tickling his ears, causing him to slash impatiently at them with his digging-stick, and when this did no good he endured the nuisance for a moment, then flung himself down on his back, put up his long legs like a fighting cock, and kicked the branches down.

Nigel Barley

(1947–)

Barley is a British anthropologist who did two years of fieldwork in West Africa among the Dowayos, indigenous people of the Cameroon. 'Feeling a little like a ball in a pinball machine, I set off in quest of the Dowayos,' he commented. *The Innocent Anthropologist* is a very funny account of his experiences.

A beauty contest in Cameroon

The beauty contest had been organized by the simple expedient of sending official letters to all chiefs instructing them to send a certain number of young women to town on a certain day. Quite what was made of this in the hills, I shudder to think. The Fulani, in former times, were in the habit of levying slaves and concubines from these people; perhaps they feared the resumption of this system. Whatever the precise interpretation, the women had a uniformly oppressed look. Many had doubtless been made to walk long distances and were decidedly travel-stained. The Fulanis of course disdained to exhibit their own women in this fashion, but were delighted at the opportunity to view the women of other races. The ladies were obliged to walk, or in most cases slouch, past the spectators in a wide circle. They had the resentful air of goods at a slave market and stared tearfully down at the ground or glared and hissed at their tormentors. The spectators rose to the occasion admirably with hoots of derision mingled with enthusiastic offers of all manner of unions short of marriage. A minor dispute broke out between those invited and the throng that pressed in upon them. Some had climbed into the trees for a better view; these fell to the lot of the party officials who shook the trunks until they came tumbling out to tears of popular approval. After some discussion, Miss Poli was announced – alongside her Miss Poli Two and Miss Poli Consolation. The *sous-préfet*'s new young assistant was delegated to present each with

84

a prize, embrace them modestly and dance with the winner. The winner was clearly from way out in the hills and terrified of the whole proceeding. She recoiled in horror when the noble young assistant offered his chaste embrace. When urged to dance, she clenched her fists tearfully and refused. Embarrassed smiles gave way to whispered threats. She stamped her feet in their new blue plastic shoes. Two gendarmes swooped down on her and threw her out. The crowd cheered. The aptly named Miss Consolation stepped into the breach. The party had begun.

Michael Haag

(1943–)

Traveller, writer and publisher, in particular about things and peoples Egyptian. His *Discovery Guide to Egypt* is required reading.

A guide to Egypt

In pharaonic times the people of Egypt believed the sun was daily born of the goddess Nut and travelled westwards across the heavens until swallowed by her at day's end, to be born once more the following dawn. And they believed the waters of the Nile rose from beneath the firmament, flowed through their country and out beyond the Delta where they sank to their source and then rose to run their course again.

The cycle and continuity of natural events was translated into the philosophical basis of ancient Egyptian politics and religion. In hieroglyphics the name of a pharaoh or god always appeared within a cartouche, an oval ring that represented the unbroken, unending, unchanging power of ruler or deity. The order of natural events in Egypt continues to impress a sense of timelessness upon the country.

Herodotus described Egypt as 'a gift of the river', and Egypt's gift, like a great river of time, has been to carry within it the presence of the pharaonic, Hellenistic, Christian and Islamic periods, all embraced by the cartouche of the fellahin's millennial toil. Egypt's endurance and stability in a region of conflict, flux and immense creativity has been its outstanding contribution to the world. Egypt itself has not been exceptionally innovative; it did not give mankind mathematics, philosophy, science, medicine, Judaism, Christianity or Islam. But Egypt was essential to each, offering an impetus or a home, sometimes stamping them with the shape by which we know them today.

Egypt's sense of permanence and duration makes it par excellence the land of the past, and it is for this that the traveller usually comes, too often ignoring its living present. But for all the spectacle over the millennia of migrations and invasions, probably 90 per cent of its population are the descendants of its ancient inhabitants, and they will not be ignored. I first came to Egypt to see the Pyramids, but what I met with greater force were the Egyptian people. It was because of them that I cared enough to explore as best I could the totality of their history and their experience. They are a warm, friendly and generous people; ambitious, intelligent and proud; naïve, religious and fatalistic; and also the most indefatigable hustlers on earth. They are all these things in such an open and sometimes importunate way that the novice visitor is likely to find himself swinging from one extreme reaction to another within minutes. But it is only their vitality you are reacting to, for though their conditions are extreme they are not an extreme people. If you enjoy people, you will enjoy the Egyptian people especially.

Ryszard Kapuscinski

(1932–)

A remarkable Polish journalist who has spent much of his career in Africa, 'avoiding official routes, palaces, important personages and high level politics', and travelling at a more grass-roots level, which was often all his employers could afford.

The Serengeti

We drove onto the enormous plain of the Serengeti, the largest concentration of wild animals on earth. Everywhere you look, huge herds of zebras, antelopes, buffalo, giraffes. And all of them are grazing, frisking, frolicking, galloping. Right by the side of the road, motionless lions; a bit farther, a group of elephants; and farther still, on the horizon, a leopard running in huge bounds. It's all improbable, incredible. As if one were witnessing the birth of the world, that precise moment when the earth and sky already exist, as do water, plants, and wild animals, but not yet Adam and Eve. It is this world barely born, the world without mankind and hence also without sin, that one can imagine one is seeing here.

The Monastery of Debre Libanos, Ethiopia

Near this same road – but one must walk down, deep into a nearly impenetrable cleft between two steep mountain slopes – lies the monastery of Debre Libanos. Inside, the church is dark and cool. After hours of driving in blinding sun, the eyes must adjust to this place, which at first impression seems submerged in total darkness. After a time you begin to discern frescoes on the walls, and see Ethiopian pilgrims dressed in white lying facedown on the mat-covered floor. In one corner an old monk is chanting a psalm in a drowsy voice, which periodically dies away altogether, in the already dead language of Ge'ez. In this atmosphere replete with a concentrated and quiet mysticism, everything seems beyond time; beyond measure and weight, beyond life.

Who knows how long these pilgrims lay there, for I walked in and out of the church several times in the course of that day, and each time they were still resting motionless on the mats.

All day? A month? A year? Eternity?

Redmond O'Hanlon

(1947–)

English scholar, naturalist, and author of very funny but
erudite books about his intrepid travels. *Congo Journey* is
the story of his search for the Mokélé-mbembé, the Congo
dinosaur. It begins with an unpromising visit to a *féticheuse*
or sorceress in Brazzaville.

Meeting a féticheuse, Brazzaville

'Please!' said the *féticheuse*, tossing her head right back and pressing her
palms into her eyes. 'You must be quiet. If you talk one to the other I
cannot see. And if I cannot see I cannot help you.' And then, 'Here,
take these,' she said, opening her eyes, reaching forward, gathering up
the shells and giving us three each. 'Hold these against a banknote and
breathe your desires into them.'

With my free hand I drew two 1000 CFA (two pound) notes out of
my leg-pocket, gave one to Lary, and crumpled the other over the shells
in my cupped palm.

'Now,' she said, 'who is responsible for all this?'

'I am,' I said, puffing out my chest.

'Then tell me – what is it that you really want? What is it that
you want most when you are quiet inside? – and don't bother me
with anything else, don't tell me the story you prepared for your
wives.'

'I hope to go on a great journey through the far northern forests', I
said, liking the sound of the words, 'by dugout to the headwaters of the
Motaba where we'll abandon the boats, walk east through the swamp
jungle and across the watershed to the Ibenga, take a chance on finding
another canoe, and then, if we're lucky, paddle down to the Likouala
aux Herbes and walk to the hidden lake, Lake Télé, where Mokélé-
mbembé, the Congo dinosaur, is said to live.'

'No! No! No!' sang the féticheuse.

'What's wrong? You think the army won't let us go? You think we'll never get out of Brazzaville?'

'You are not an educated man,' she said, exasperated, rattling the shells in her hand like dice in a box. 'You don't speak your desires. You think them. *I see everything.*'

She snatched my shells and the banknote and threw them hard across the mat; the note spun down like a sycamore seed.

'Your children love you,' she intoned, glancing with contempt at the scatter. 'Your wife loves you.'

I thought: I'll double her fee.

'If you stay for two months,' she said, already turning to Lary, 'the spirits of the forest will not harm you. But if you stay for two months and one day, you will die.'

'But I'm staying for six months!'

'Then you will die,' she said, fixing her attention on Lary with indecent haste and closing her eyes.

He held his shells and 1000 CFA note in the approved manner and bowed his head. A drop of sweat fell from the end of his nose to the floor. His lips moved.

Louis Sarno

(1954–)

Sarno heard pygmy music playing on Amsterdam radio, and bought a one-way ticket for the Central African Republic. He moved in with a group of Ba-Benjellé pygmies. His book tells the story.

A pygmy dance

The next night another *eboka* was held. It lacked the intimate chamber-music quality of the previous night dance – in fact, it was the biggest dance I had yet seen at Amopolo. Practically everyone except Simbu took part. The women sat in a large circle, an unusual arrangement, and the singing had a vast, vigorous oratorical sound. It was impossible to record it all at once, so for each song I moved to a different location. Yet as the music grew increasingly intense, with a polyphony of stunning complexity, my mind wandered to thoughts of Mbina. Earlier in the day, when everyone was off in the forest and camp seemed empty, I had played through the songs of the night before. Mbina's splendid singing had filled me with a soaring sense of optimism. Then suddenly Mbina herself had appeared and sat down in my hut. During the play-back she looked at me steadily and so intently that I could only sneak an occasional glance back at her. At the end of the tape she simply got up and left.

Now I couldn't help but wonder: had Mbina been trying to tell me that she was a woman now, no longer a girl? That had been my distinct impression. But maybe I was deluding myself, reading significance into meaningless incidents. The subtlety of Mbina's message argued against its being intentional. What did I know of the intimate undercurrents of daily life among the Bayaka? I should concentrate on the music, write my diary, and mind my own business.

Eventually a single large bush broke through the circle of singers, scattering them before it, and began to spin right and left, pausing occasionally to beat the earth rapidly. Men and women regrouped and danced slowly around it. Doko, usually restrained in his dancing, was plastered on *mbaku* and danced like a man thirty years younger, shaking his behind, swivelling his hips, and in general causing such hilarity among the women that his presence was almost a disruption. But the *eboka* had an irrepressible energy and focus that overrode even Doko's wild antics, swallowing them into itself.

Then I noticed her – the fabulous flirtatious dancer. The moon had risen, and as she danced, her necklace and her underpants, bright in the moonlight, marked her every move. I couldn't take my eyes off her. Her energy was magnetic, and I marvelled that everyone else wasn't looking at her, she seemed so obviously the centre of attraction. As if in response to my thoughts, Doko made a lunge for her. She ran away, her underpants bobbing off and finally merging into the distant shadows. But she was soon back and bolder than ever, dancing right up to me, then retreating into the circle of singers.

At the height of the *eboka* the bush spirit suddenly split into two, and during the remainder of the night's celebration the two halves seemed to grow bigger and bushier with each song. The dance was still going strong when there came a burst of light from a far corner of camp. Huge flames shot up. A hut had caught fire. There was a moment of confused wonder. Then, with cries of excitement, everyone sprinted off. The girl with the pink necklace, I fondly noted, was an incredibly fast runner.

Justin Marozzi

(1970–)

A professional journalist whose career has also involved selling tobacco to Libya. *South From Barbary* describes a journey he made from Tripoli across the Libyan Sahara, following the old slave routes and travellers with camels rather than the four-wheel drive vehicles. Marozzi did this with the help of a succession of Tuareg and Tubbu guides.

Getting under way in Libya

Before we left for Jerma, Salek was anxious for us to check in with the local police. We were keen to have as little to do with them as possible. 'If you go to desert, you must see police, or Salek in trouble,' he explained. We set off in first gear and remained stuck in first gear for the several kilometres to the police station. A group of officers was sitting round a table in the sun playing cards, each man immaculately dressed in navy blue uniform with white flashes. It seemed a shame to disturb this scene. Salek told the senior officer about our plans.

'Where are your passports?' he asked shortly.

'They're in Tripoli with a travel agent,' I replied. 'We were advised to leave them with him.'

'You cannot leave Idri until you show me your passports,' the policeman continued.

'That's not possible. They've just been taken to Tripoli,' I repeated, thinking dark thoughts of Taher.

'Then you cannot go.' He was admirably direct.

Salek remonstrated with him. The officer looked over to the game of cards he was missing and weighed the two alternatives. Take the foreigners to task for this breach of protocol – which would doubtless prove tedious – or get on with the game and pretend he had never seen us. He gave us to understand he had chosen the latter option and saved face by not waving goodbye to us as we shot off in first gear.

All that remained for us to do was fill the water bidouns and stock up on more tins of tuna fish and any other supplies we could get our hands on. In the 'market', which consisted of three or four poorly stocked general grocery stores, hardly more than holes in the wall, the shopkeepers, who had heard of our trip on the Idri grapevine, were ready with a myriad questions.

'Why are travelling by camel?'

'Where are you from?'

'Do you like Libya?'

'Where are you going?'

'Do you like camels?'

'Do you have a desert in Britain?'

'How much did your camels cost?'

Initial disbelief was their first reaction (was this due to our choice of guide?), followed soon after by a chorus of '*wallahi*' and '*alhamdulillah*'. It was good to travel in the Sahara, they said. It was the most beautiful place on earth. We struggled through our shopping under this good-natured inquisition. Tuna fish, perhaps unsurprisingly, proved easy to find, as were Sando chocolate bars (made in Egypt), later to become one of our most cherished staples. Garlic and onions, however, proved elusive.

Back at Salek's house, I snatched a quick makeshift shower from a bucket inside a filthy cubicle that served as the family bathroom. Peering out of the prison cell window I was met with a nose and a pair of flashing eyes. It was Khalil, staring in with undimmed curiosity.

'What are you doing in there?' he asked imperiously.

'Bugger off,' I replied.

There was no escaping this infuriating man. Wherever we went, he was always only a few steps behind, prying into whatever it was we were doing. He would accompany us into shops, follow us from room to room in Salek's house, ask what we were doing, recommend alternatives, upset the camels by handling them too roughly and generally get in the way.

Europe

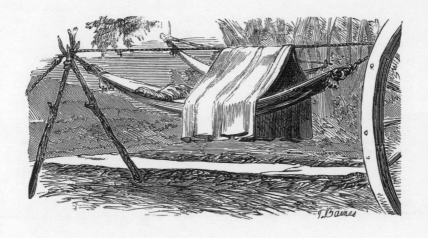

RUSSIA

Voronezh •

Danzig

POLAND

Berlin •
• Dessau
Halle
• Leipzig
• Weissenfels

Vienna

Danube

Budapest

MOLDAVIA

l p s

Trieste
Venice

Rimini

Black Sea

Danube

P e n n i n e s

Rome

ITALY

Tirana

Livadia

• Constantinople

• Naples

*Mt
Olympus*

*Mt
Athos*

Lake Yanina

Messina

Missolonghi

Delphi

• Athens

Kastráki

GREECE

CRETE

Mediterranean Sea

Herodotus

(c. 485–425 BC)

Greek historian, born in Asia Minor. Herodotus travelled widely in the Mediterranean, North Africa and Near East, collecting information for his *Histories of the Wars between the Greeks and the Barbarians*, i.e., the Persians. It was the most complete synthesis of information about the world at the time; besides history the *Histories* cover geography, natural history, ethnography and just about everything.

The geography of Europe

With Europe, however, the case is different; for no one has ever determined whether or not there is sea either to the east or to the north of it; all we know is that in length it is equal to Asia and Libya combined. Another thing that puzzles me is why three distinct women's names should have been given to what is really a single land-mass; and why, too, the Nile and the Phasis – or, according to some, the Maeotic Tanais and the Cimmerian Strait – should have been fixed upon for the boundaries. Nor have I been able to learn who it was that first marked the boundaries, or where they got the names from. Most Greeks assume that Libya was so called after a native woman and that Asia was named after the wife of Prometheus; the Lydians, however, claim the latter name for themselves, and say that Asia was named not after the wife of Prometheus, but after Asies, the son of Cotys and grandson of Manes, who passed it on besides to the tribe called Asias in Sardis. As for Europe, nobody knows if it is surrounded by sea, or where it got its name from, or who gave it, unless we are to say that it came from

Europa, the Tyrian woman, and before that was nameless like the rest. This, however, is unlikely; for Europa was an Asiatic and never visited the country which we now call Europe, but only sailed from Phoenicia to Crete and from Crete to Lycia. But that is quite enough on this subject.

Strabo

(c. 63 BC – after AD 21)

Greek historian and geographer. Strabo, 'the squint-eyed', travelled from the Black Sea to Ethiopia and Arabia, explored the Nile and finally settled in Rome. He wrote forty-seven history books and seventeen of geography, not all of which survive.

The end of the habitable earth

We will now commence our detailed account, beginning from the Sacred Promontory. This is the most western point not only of Europe, but of the whole habitable earth. For the habitable earth is bounded to the west by two continents, namely, the extremities of Europe and Libya, which are inhabited respectively by the Iberians and the Maurusians. But the Iberian extremity, at the promontory we have mentioned, juts out beyond the other as much as 1500 stadia.

Edward Barton

(c. 1563–98)

Barton was the second English ambassador at Constantinople; he accompanied the Turkish army in their campaign against the Emperor Maximilian, and died of the plague.

The court of Constantinople

They went into the innermost court passing by the window of that roome, where the grand Signior sate, who, as it went by to be laid up in certaine roomes adjoining, tooke view of all. Presently after the present followed the ambassador with his gentlemen; at the gate of which court stoode 20 or 30 Agaus which be eunuchs. Within the court yard were the Turkes Dwarfes and Dumbe men, being most of them youths. At the doore of his roome stood the Bustangibassa, with another Bassa to lead the ambassador and his followers to the grand Signior who sate in a chaire of estate, apparelled in a gowne of cloth or silver. The floore under his feete, which part was a foote higher then the rest, was covered with a carpet of green sattin embrodered most richly with silver, orient perles & great Turkeses; ye other part of the house was covered with a carpet of Carnation sattin imbrodered wt gold, none were in the roome with him, but a Bassa who stood next the wall over against him hanging down his head, & looking submissively upon the ground as all his subjects doe in his presence. The ambassador thus betwixt two which stood at the doore being led in, either of them taking an arme, kissed his hand, and so backward with his face to the Turke they brought him nigh the dore againe, where he stood untill they had likewise done so with all the rest of his gentlemen. Which ended, the ambassador, according as it is the custome when any present is delivered, made his three demaunds, such as he thought most expedient for her majesties honor, & the peaceable traffique of our nation into his dominions.

Fynes Moryson

(1566–1630)

English traveller and academic, a fellow of Peterhouse, Cambridge. He visited much of Europe and the Levant during six years of constant wandering. Moryson was interested in everything that caught his eye. In France he was assailed by robbers, who took off him the doublet in which he had quilted his gold, and particularly peeving, exchanged his hat with a 'deepe greasie French hat'. Having anticipated such an event, Moryson had put the rest of his 'French Crownes' in a wooden box, and 'covered them with a stinking ointment for scabs'; so that the robbers were repelled by the 'stinke'. He later used the greasy hat as a drinking vessel, 'but three daies sicknesse of vomiting and looseness made me repent this intemperance'.

The howling of woolves

In this passage of the Alpes, I did many times observe mountaines of snow to fal from the high mountaines into the vallies, with such noise as if it had thundered: and this noise many times preserves passengers from being overwhelmed with the same, falling many times into the very high waies.

Out of the wood neere Lanzi, in the twilight of the evening; I did heare more then a hundred Woolves howling, and because it was towards night, I had hired a Countrey Churle to guide me unto the Towne, who trembled for feare, and desired me to make ready my Carbiner to shoot at them: for hee said nothing terrified them more then the smell of powder; I wished him to be of good cheare, because the Woolves seemed busie about a prey, and the Towne was neere at hand, promising that I would not forsake him, but if need were, let him ride behind me: but feare giving him wings, so as he went as fast as my horse could trot; within short space we came to Lanzi, where I paid sixteene batzen for my supper, breakfast, and horse-meat.

Thomas Coryate

(c. 1577–1617)

English eccentric and traveller, born at Odstock Rectory in Somerset. Coryate became an unofficial jester at the court of James I. In 1608 he set off on a 1975-mile walk across Europe, described in his book, *Coryat's Crudities, Hastily gobled up in Five Moneths Travelles in France . . . Newly digested in the hungry aire of Odcombe in the County of Somerset and now dispersed to the nourishment of the travelling members of this Kingdome.* On his return to Odstock, he hung up the shoes in which he had walked back from Venice in the village church. In 1612 he set off again in an easterly direction via Greece and Constantinople. He died at Surat on the west coast of India five years later, presumably worn out himself.

The baths of Baden

Most of the private bathes are but little, but very delicate and pleasant places, being divided asunder by certaine convenient partitions wherein are contrived divers windowes, to the end that those in the bathes may have recourse to each other, and mutually drinke together. For they reach out their drinking glasses one to another through the windowes. The roomes over head are lodgings for the strangers. Here I have observed the people in the bathes feede together upon a table that hath swimmed upon the superficies of the water. Also I have noted another strange thing amongst them that I have not a little wondred at. Men and women bathing themselves together naked from the middle upward in one bathe: whereof some of the women were wives (as I was told) and the men partly bachelers, and partly married men, but not the husbands of the same women.

Here also I saw many passing faire yong Ladies and Gentlewomen naked in the bathes with their wooers and favorites in the same. For at this time of the yeare many woers come thither to solace themselves with their beautifull mistresses. Many of these yong Ladies had the haire of their head very curiously plaited in locks, & they wore certaine pretty garlands upon their heads made of fragrant and odoriferous flowers. A spectacle exceeding amorous.

William Lithgow

(1582–1645)

Scottish traveller from Lanark. He may have left home as a result of having his ears cut off by his brothers after they found him with their sister. By 1610, he had been to the Shetlands and parts of Europe. He then set off on foot from Paris for the Near East and Egypt. By 1629 he claimed to have walked over 36,000 miles through Europe, Asia and Africa. Prone to 'painefull' experiences, Lithgow was tortured by the Inquisition at Malaga, attacked in Libya and Moldavia, and on his return was put in Marshalsea Prison after a contretemps with the Spanish ambassador. His memoirs, published in 1632, were appropriately entitled *The Totall Discourse of Rare Adventures and Painefull Peregrinations of long nineteen yeares travayles*.

The most melancholy city of Europe

In Padua I stayed three moneths learning the Italian tongue, and found there a Countrey Gentleman of mine. Doctor John Wedderburne, a learned Mathematician, but now dwelling in Moravia, who taught me well in the language, and in all other respects exceeding friendly to me. Padua is the most melancholy City of Europe, the cause onely arising of the narrow passage of the open streets, and of the long galleries and dark-ranges of pillars, that goe alwhere on every hand of you, through the whole streets of the Towne: The Schollers here in the night commit many murthers against their privat adversaries, and too often executed upon the stranger and innocent, and all with gun-shot or else stilettoes: for beastly Sodomy, it is as rife here as in Rome, Naples, Florence, Bullogna, Venice, Ferrara, Genoa, Parma not being exempted, nor yet the smallest Village of Italy. A monstrous filthinesse, and yet to them a pleasant past-time, making songs, and singing Sonets of the beauty and pleasure of their Bardassi, or buggerd boyes.

I commend the devotion of Venice and Genua, beyond all the other Cities of Italy; for the Venetians have banished the Jesuites out of their Territories and llands: And the Genueses have abandoned the society of Jewes, and exposed them from their jurisdiction. The Jewes and the Jesuites are brethren in blasphemies; for the Jewes are naturally subtill, hatefull, avaritious, and above all the greatest calumniators of Christs name: and the ambitious Jesuites, are flatterers, bloudy-gospellers, treasonable tale-tellers, and the onely railers upon the sincere life of good Christians. Wherefore I end with this verdict, the Jew and the Jesuite, is a Pultrone and a Parasite.

Thomas Dallam

(c. 1599–1615)

English organ builder, who made instruments for King's College, Cambridge, and Worcester Cathedral. In 1599 Queen Elizabeth I sent an organ to Sultan Mehmet III as a gift. The organ was itself a wonderful thing topped by 'a holly bushe full of blacke birds and thrushis, which at the end of the musick did singe and shake theire wynges'. Dallam went to install it in the Topkapi Palace at Constantinople, a hazardous place. He found that in the little house where he was to set up the 'instramente', the sultan 'had nynteene brotheres put to death in it, and it was bulte for no other use but for the stranglinge of everie emperors bretherin'.

Nessecaries for my voyage into Turkie, 1599

In this Book is the Account of an Organ Carryed to the Grand Seignor and Other Curious Matter.

Nessecaries for my voyege into Turkie, the which I bought upon a verrie short warninge, havinge no frend to advise me in any thing.

	£	s	d
Imprimis for one sute of sackcloth to weare at sea	1	2	0
Item for another sute of Carsaye	1	18	0
Item for two wastcotes of flanell	0	8	0
Item for one hatt	0	7	6
Item for an arminge sorde	0	6	0
Item for a chiste	0	9	8
Item for 3 shirtes	0	18	6
Item for one doson of bandes	0	12	8
Item for half a doson of bandes	0	10	0
Item for one bande	0	2	6
Item for six shirtes more	1	14	0
Item for one doson of hand chirthers (handkerchiefs)	0	10	0
Item for one pare of garters	0	4	0
Item for one doson of poyntes	0	1	0
Item for another doson	0	2	0
Item for 2 pare of stockins	0	12	0
Item for one pare of lininge britchis	0	1	4
Item for one pare of pumpes and pantables	0	3	6
Item for 3 pare of showes	0	7	0
Item for a girdle and hangers	0	2	8
Item for a gowne	1	10	0
Item for a pare of virginals	1	15	0
Item for a pare of fustion britchis	0	2	6
Item for a hatbande	0	4	2
For a seller and glassis	0	11	6
Item for Rosa solis and a compostie	0	6	0
Item for oyle and vineger	0	2	0
Item for prunes	0	1	3
Item for Resons of the son (sun-dried raisins)	0	1	4
Item for cloves, mace, and peper	0	1	6
Item 2 pounde of suger	0	3	0
Item for nutmuges	0	1	0
Item for gloves	0	3	0
Item for knives	0	5	0
Item for 30" of tin in bars	0	18	0
Item for a grose of Spownes (spoons)	0	9	0

	£	s	d
Item for otemeale	0	0	10
Item for carreing my chiste to Blacke wale	0	1	6
Item for my passige to Graves end	0	0	6
Item for my staying there 4 days – it coste me	0	12	0
Item at Deale Castell	0	1	0
Item at Dartmouthe	0	4	0

A souvenir of Troy

Also thare we saw more at large the rewins of the wales and housis in Troye, and from thence I broughte a peece of whyte marble piller, the which I broke with my owne handes, havinge a good hmer, which my mate Harvie did carrie a shore for the same purpose; and I broughte this peece of marble to London.

A close thing in the Seraglio

By chance I caled to my drugaman and asked him the cause of theire runinge awaye; than he saide the Grand Sinyor and his Conquebines weare cominge, we muste be gone in paine of deathe; but they run all away and lefte me behinde, and before I gott oute of the house they weare run over the grene quit out at the gate, and I runn as faste as my leggss would carried me aftere, and 4 neageres or blackamoors cam runinge towardes me with their semetaries drawne; yf they could have catchte me theye would have hewed me all in peecis with there semeteris. When I cam to the wickett or gate, thare stood a great number of jemoglanes, praying that I myghte escape the handes of those runninge wolves; when I was got out of the gate they weare verrie joyfull that I had so well escaped their handes. I stayed not thare, but touke boate and went presently to my Lord and tould him how I had run for my life.

Robert Withers

(fl. 1620)

Withers visited Constantinople in the early seventeenth
century and wrote a vivid and detailed eyewitness account
of everything from court protocol to the royal kitchens
where food was 'dressed by Agicmolans, brought up to
Cookerie'. He also describes the life of women in the
harems, the 'guelding' of Eunuchs, and the cost of court
garments, and was shown round the 'backward roomes,
divers bagnioes, and many other very curious and delightful things' of the Sultan, when he was away hunting.

Capoochee-Bashees of the Seraglio

The aforesaid chiefe and common Gate, is in the day time guarded by
a great companie of Capoochees, which change their watch by turnes;
and in the night likewise by others; all which Capoochees are under the
command of a Capoochee-Bashee, which Capoochee-Bashees being sixe
in number, are bound that every weeke one of them lie within the
Serraglio, for the securitie and safeguard of the same. And without the
Gate, about ten or twelve paces off, there stands a little House made of
boords, upon wheeles, in which every night a Companie of Janizaries
doe watch, who upon any occasion are ready to awake those within,
and to give them notice of whatsoever sudden accident may happen
without.

The Sultan's audience chamber

There is amongst the aforesaid Roomes, the Chamber into which the
Grand Signior repaireth, when he is to give audience to Ambassadors;
to the Bashawes on the dayes of publique Divan, and to those who
being to depart upon any weighty service or employment, are to take
their leave of him; as also to such as are returned from their places of

government and charge which was before given unto them: This Roome standeth in a fine little Court adorned with many very delicate Fountaines, and hath within it a Sofa spread with very sumptuous Carpets of Gold, and of crimson Velvet embroydered with very costly Pearles, upon which the Grand Signior sitteth; and about the Chamber in stead of hangings, the walls are covered with very fine white stones, which having divers sorts of leaves and flowers artificially wrought upon them, doe make a glorious shew. There is also a little Roome adjoyning unto it, the whole inside whereof is covered with Silver plate hatcht with Gold, and the ground is spread with very rich Persian Carpets of Silke and Gold.

Within the harem

First, I say that all they which are in the Serraglio, both men and women, are the Grand Signiors slaves, and so are all they which are subject to his Empire: for, as hee is their onely Soveraigne, so they doe all of them acknowledge, that whatsoever they doe possesse or enjoy, proceedeth meerely and simply from his goodwill and favour.

This Serraglio may rightly bee termed the Seminarie or Nurcerie of Subjects; for, in it all they have their bringing up, which afterward become the principall Officers, and subordinate Rulers of the state and affaires of the whole Empire.

They which are within the third Gate, called the Kings gate, are about two thousand persons men and women, whereof the women (old and young one with another, what with the Kings Concubines, old women, and women servants) may bee about eleven or twelve hundred. Now, those which are kept up for their beauties, are all young Virgins taken and stollen from forren Nations, who after they have beene nurtured in good manners, and can play on Instruments, sing, dance, and sew curiously, they are given to the Grand Signior as Presents of exceeding great value; and the number of these encreaseth daily.

These Virgins, immediately after their comming into the serraglio ... are placed in a Roome with the others of the same age, spirit, and inclination, to dwell and live together. Now, in the Womens lodgings, they live just as the Nunnes doe in their great Monasteries; for, these Virgins have very large Roomes to live in, and their Bed-chambers will hold almost a hundred of them a piece: they sleepe upon Sofaes, which are built long wise on both sides of the Roome, so that there is a large space in the midst for to walke in. Their Beds are very course and hard, and by every ten Virgins there lies an old woman: and all the night long there are many lights burning, so that one may see very plainely throughout the whole Roome; which doth both keepe the yong Wenches from wantonnesse.

Women of the Seraglio

The Women of the Serraglio, are punished for their faults very severely, and extreamely beaten by their Overseers: and if they prove disobedient, incorrigible and insolent, they are by the Kings order and expresse commandment, turned out and sent into the old Serraglio, as being rejected and cast off, and most part of that they have is taken from them. But if they shall be found culpable for Witchcraft: or any such hainous offence, then are they tyed and put into a Sacke, and in the Night cast into the Sea: so that by all meanes it behooveth them to bee very obedient, and containe themselves within the bounds of honestie and modestie, if they meane to come to a good end.

Now it is not lawfull for any one to bring ought in unto them, with which they may commit the deeds of beastly uncleannesse; so that if they have a will to eate Cucumbers, Gourds, or such like meates, they are sent in unto them slice, to deprive them of the meanes of playing the wantons; for, they all being young, lustie, and lascivious Wenches, and wanting the societie of Men (which would better instruct them) are doubtlesse of themselves inclined to that which is naught, and will be possest with unchast thoughts.

John Evelyn

(1620–1706)

Writer, diarist and public figure, Evelyn turned his attention to many subjects from coins to trees. His advocacy
of reforestation in *Sylva* guaranteed the future of the
British Navy. He travelled abroad during the English Civil
War, carrying ciphered messages for the Royalists, and
marrying the ambassador's daughter in Paris. He became
a public servant at the Restoration, and the first secretary
of the Royal Society. His property at Sayes Court was
ravaged by his tenant Peter the Great who came to inspect
the shipyards at Deptford. One of the world's great diarists,
he witnessed the Plague, the Great Fire of London, and
claimed to have discovered the master woodcarver Grinling Gibbons.

The slave market at Livorno

Just before the sea is an ample Piazza for the Market, where are erected
those incomparable Statues, with the fowre slaves of Copper much
exceeding the life for proportion; and in the judgment of most Artists
one of the best pieces of modern Worke that was ever don.

Here is in Ligorne, and especially this Piazzo, such a concourse of
Slaves, consisting of Turks, Mores and other Nations, as the number
and confusion is prodigious; some buying, others selling; some drinking,
others playing, some working, others sleeping, fighting, singing, weeping
and a thousand other postures and Passions; yet all of them naked, and
miserably Chayn'd, with a Canvas onely to hide their shame: Here was
now a Tent erected, where any idle fellow, weary of that trifle, might
stake his liberty against a few Crownes; which if lost (at Dice or other
hazard) he was immediately chayned, and lead away to the Gallys, where
he was to serve a tearme of Yeares, but whence they seldome returnd;
and many sottish persons would in a drunken bravado trye their fortune.

Madame de Sévigné

(1626–96)

French aristocrat and woman of letters. Marie de Rabutin-Chantal married a wicked marquis who was killed in a duel. Over twenty-five years she wrote a series of brilliant letters, mostly to her daughter, who married the Comte de Grignan and lived in a huge castle in southeastern France. The Marquise de Sevigné eventually died there of smallpox, but left a superb record of her life and times at the French court.

Travel on the Loire

17 September 1675

For the river is so low that we run aground every few yards, and well may I regret my carriages and horses, which travel fast and without delays. It is tedious to travel alone by boat, and the need of a little Comte des Chapelles and a little Mlle de Sévigné to distract me is greatly felt. In short to embark at Orleans, or at Paris, for that matter, is really an act of madness. I can only suppose one does it to be obliging, and as at Chartres we feel [constrained] to purchase rosaries, so at Orleans we hire boatmen.

Nantes is thirty leagues distant from Saumur, we were resolved to accomplish the distance in two days, arriving at Nantes today. With this purpose in mind we travelled for two hours in the dark, ran aground irrevocably, found ourselves a hundred yards from our Inn and with no possibility of landing ... When finally we did so it was midnight and we took shelter in a miserable hovel where three old hags sat spinning. There was a little clean straw on the ground on which we threw ourselves fully dressed; I should have laughed at our plight, had it not been for my discomfiture at exposing the Abbé to such fatigue. We re-embarked at dawn and were still so firmly grounded that it took us a full hour to resume the thread of our discourse, but so determined were we to reach Nantes, against wind and tide, that every man jack of us took to the oars. I hope to find your letters awaiting me there, and shall leave this missive where a mailcoach is expected to call. I am well, but thirst for good conversation. Farewell, dearest and most cherished one, you are my very dear child. A peck for the "curmudgeon".

Nantes, Friday 20 September [1675]

I have just received your letter in which you picture me as a wanderer on the ocean's brink, which conclusions are more than justified. I wrote from the boat whenever possible. At nine o'clock of the evening I arrived at the foot of this great castle which you know so well and from which our Cardinal made his escape. The sound of oars was heard it seems, and a faint "Who goes there?" reached us over the water. I was about to give an answering call, when the figure of M. de Lavardin appeared at the small gate preceded by six torch-bearers and accompanied by several noblemen desirous of greeting me, which they did with the utmost courtesy. The scene from the river was, I am told, picturesque in the extreme, and greatly enhanced me in the eyes of my boatmen. I supped well, not having eaten or slept for twenty-four hours. I lay at M. d'Harouys' and took part in the festivities both there and at the château.

Hair fashions

24 September 1677

I do wish you were here to see the effect produced by the presence of de Termes and Flamarens on the hairdressing modes of the local beauties. From six o'clock of the morning everyone and everything is up in the air, headdresses erect, powdered and frizzed, bonnets wagging, rouge and patches applied, wigs half-way down the back, fans waving, long tight petticoats adjusted: you would die of laughing, and yet the poor dears are forced to drink the waters which they shortly regurgitate from the mouth as well as from elsewhere.

John Covel

(1638–1722)

English natural scientist and cleric. Covel became Chaplain to the Levant Company, 1669–70, and subsequently served at the Sublime Porte, Constantinople, 1670–7. He published illustrated journals of his travels.

Beneath Santa Sofia

We went to see the vaults under Sta Sophia; they were full of water, then 17 ft deep, and overhead from the water up to the top of the arch, about 2 yards and 6 inches. Every pillar is square 4½ feet, and distant one from another just 12 feet. The bricks very broad, thin, wel baked; not playstered within; the mortar very hard. They say it goes under Atmaidan; we could not enter it. The wast water of the aquaeduct enters into it and out of it, passing through the Seraglio goes into sea by the dunghill. Severe punishment to have houses with offices into it, or throw any filth into it; the well of Sta Sophia runs into it, and many wells in the Seraglio, etc.

Lady Mary Wortley Montagu

(1689–1762)

Poet, essayist and brilliant conversationalist. She eloped at twenty-three with Edward Wortley Montagu who became an MP and Ambassador at the Sublime Porte at Constantinople, where she learned Turkish and wrote many entertaining and observant letters. Lady Mary also brought home the smallpox inoculation from Turkey; the disease had marked her own beauty. She lived alone in Italy from

1739–61; her husband became a miser but left her his huge fortune, which she did not live to enjoy.

Turkish dress

The first piece of my dress is a pair of drawers, very full, that reach to my shoes, and conceal the legs more modestly than your petticoats. They are of a thin rose-coloured damask, brocaded with silver flowers, my shoes of white kid leather, embroidered with gold. Over this hangs my smock, of a fine white silk gauze, edged with embroidery. This smock has wide sleeves, hanging half way down the arm, and is closed at the neck with a diamond button; but the shape and colour of the bosom very well to be distinguished through it. The *antery* is a waistcoat, made close to the shape, of white and gold damask, with very long sleeves falling back, and fringed with deep gold fringe, and should have diamond or pearl buttons. My *caftan*, of the same stuff with my drawers, is a robe exactly fitted to my shape, and reaching to my feet, with very long strait falling sleeves. Over this is the girdle of about four fingers broad, which all that can afford have entirely of diamonds or others precious stones; those who will not be at that expense, have it of exquisite embroidery on satin, but it must be fastened before with a clasp of diamonds. The *curdee* is a loose robe they throw off or put on according to the weather, being of a rich brocade (mine is green and gold), either lined with ermine or sables; the sleeves reach very little below the shoulders. The head-dress is composed of a cap, called *talpock*, which is in winter of fine velvet embroidered with pearls or diamonds, and in summer of a light shining silver stuff. This is fixed on one side of the head, hanging a little way down with a gold tassel, and bound on, either with a circle of diamonds (as I have seen several) or a rich embroidered handkerchief. On the other side of the head, the hair is laid flat; and here the ladies are at liberty to shew their fancies; some putting flowers, others a plume of heron's feathers, and, in short, what they please; but the most general fashion is a large *bouquet* of jewels, made like natural flowers; that is, the buds of pearl; the roses, of different coloured rubies; the jessamines, of diamonds; jonquils, of topazes, &c, so well set and enamelled, 'tis hard to imagine any thing of that kind so beautiful. The hair hangs at its full length behind, divided into tresses braided with pearl or ribbon which is always in great quantity.

I never saw in my life so many fine heads of hair. I have counted a hundred and ten of these tresses of one lady's all natural; but it must be owned, that every beauty is more common here than with us. 'Tis surprising to see a young woman that is not very handsome. They have naturally the most beautiful complexions in the world, and generally large black eyes. I can assure you with great truth, that the court of England (though I believe it the fairest in Christendom) cannot shew so many beauties as are under our protection here. They generally shape their eyebrows; and the Greeks and Turks have a custom of putting round their eyes (on the inside) a black tincture, that, at a distance, or by candle-light, adds very much to the blackness of them. I fancy many of our ladies would be overjoyed to know this secret; but 'tis too visible by day. They dye their nails a rose-colour. I own, I cannot enough accustom myself to this fashion to find any beauty in it.

Tobias Smollett

(1721–71)

Scottish surgeon and writer of picaresque novels. He sailed away from financial desperation to Jamaica as assistant ship's surgeon, returning with a wealthy heiress from Jamaica as his wife. Satirised as 'Smelfungus' by Laurence Sterne, he was also described as a 'human porcupine in his social relations'. His writing is most entertaining, however.

Boulogne

The poorest tradesman in Boulogne has a napkin on every cover, and silver forks with four prongs, which are used with the right hand, there being very little occasion for knives; for the meat is boiled or roasted to rags. The French beds are so high, that sometimes one is obliged to mount them by the help of steps; and this is also the case in Flanders.

They very seldom use feather-beds; but they lie upon a *paillasse*, or bag of straw, over which are laid two, and sometimes three mattrasses. Their testers are high and old-fashioned, and their curtains generally of thin bays, red, or green, laced with taudry yellow, in imitation of gold. In some houses, however, one meets with furniture of stamped linen; but there is no such thing as a carpet to be seen, and the floors are in a very dirty condition. They have not even the implements of cleanliness in this country. Every chamber is furnished with an *armoire*, or clothes-press, and a chest of drawers, of very clumsy workmanship. Every thing shews a deficiency in the mechanic arts. There is not a door, nor a window, that shuts close. The hinges, locks, and latches, are of iron, coarsely made, and ill contrived. The very chimnies are built so open, that they admit both rain and sun, and all of them smoke intolerably. If there is no cleanliness among these people, much less shall we find delicacy, which is the cleanliness of the mind. Indeed they are utter strangers to what we call common decency; and I could give you some high-flavoured instances, at which even a native of Edinburgh would stop his nose.

Foreign habits

There are certain mortifying views of human nature, which undoubtedly ought to be concealed as much as possible, in order to prevent giving offence: and nothing can be more absurd, than to plead the difference of custom in different countries, in defence of those usages which cannot fail giving disgust to the organs and sense of all mankind. Will custom exempt from the imputation of gross indecency a French lady, who shifts her frowsy smock in presence of a male visitant, and talks to him of her *lavement*, her *medicine*, and her *bidet*! An Italian *signora* makes no scruple of telling you, she is such a day to begin a course of physic for the *pox*. The celebrated reformer of the Italian comedy introduces a child befouling itself on the stage, OE, NO TI SENTI? BISOGNA DESFASSARLO, (*fa cenno che sentesi mal odore*). I have known a lady handed to the house of office by her admirer, who stood at the door, and entertained her with *bons mots* all the time she was within. But I should be glad to know, whether it is possible for a fine lady to speak and act in this manner, without exciting ideas to her own disadvantage in the mind of every man who has any imagination left, and enjoys the intire use of his senses, howsoever she may be authorised by the customs of her country? There is nothing so vile or repugnant to nature, but you may plead prescription for it, in the customs of some nation or other. A Parisian likes mortified flesh: a native of Legiboli will not taste his fish till it is quite putrefied: the civilized inhabitants of Kamschatka get drunk with the urine of their guests, whom they have already intoxicated: the Nova Zemblans make merry on train-oil: the Groenlanders eat in the same dish with their dogs: the Caffres, at the Cape of Good Hope, piss upon those whom they delight to honour, and feast upon a sheep's intestines with their contents, as they greatest dainty that can be presented. A true-bred Frenchman dips his fingers, imbrowned with snuff, into his plate filled with ragout: between every three mouthfuls, he produces his snuff-box, and takes a fresh pinch, with the most graceful gesticulations: then he displays his handkerchief, which may be termed the *flag of abomination*, and, in the use of both, scatters his favours among those who have the happiness to sit near him. It must be owned, however, that a Frenchman will not drink out of a tankard, in which, perhaps, a dozen of filthy mouths have slabbered, as is the custom in England. Here every individual has his own gobelet, which stands before him, and he helps himself occasionally with wine, or water, or both, which likewise stand upon the table. But I know no custom more beastly than that of using water-glasses, in which polite company spirt, and squirt, and spue the filthy scourings of their gums, under the eyes of each other. I knew a lover cured of his passion, by seeing this nasty cascade discharged from the mouth of his mistress.

Edward Gibbon

(1737–94)

British historian with five brothers all named Edward; he was the only survivor. Gibbon converted to Catholicism at Oxford; this upset his father who sent him to Calvinist Switzerland to recover his senses. Visiting Rome, he had the idea for *The Decline and Fall of the Roman Empire*, which monumental work once reputedly prompted a Duke of Gloucester to remark, 'Always scribble, scribble, scribble' to produce 'another damned thick book'.

My final deliverance

I have presumed to mark the moment of conception: I shall now commemorate the hour of my final deliverance. It was on the day, or rather night, of the 27th of June, 1787, between the hours of eleven and twelve, that I wrote the last lines of the last page, in a summer-house in my garden. After laying down my pen, I took several turns in a *berceau*, or covered walk of acacias, which commands a prospect of the country, the lake, and the mountains. The air was temperate, the sky was serene, the silver orb of the moon was reflected from the waters, and all nature was silent. I will not dissemble the first emotions of joy on the recovery of my freedom, and, perhaps, the establishment of my fame. But my pride was soon humbled, and a sober melancholy was spread over my mind, by the idea that I had taken an everlasting leave of an old and agreeable companion, and that whatsoever might be the future date of my History, the life of the historian must be short and precarious. I will add two facts, which have seldom occurred in the composition of six, or at least five quartos. 1. My first rough manuscript, without any intermediate copy, has been sent to the press. 2. Not a sheet has been seen by any human eyes, excepting those of the author and the printer; the faults and the merits are exclusively my own.

James Boswell

(1740–95)

Scottish lawyer, and man of letters. His biography of Dr Johnson ensured their mutual place in history. Boswell toured the Hebrides with Johnson, and the Continent, where he met Voltaire and Rousseau. His wonderful, outrageous but honest journals were not discovered until the twentieth century at Malahide Castle in Ireland.

Girls at Naples: devotions in Rome

[Letter to J.J. Rousseau, Lucca, 3 October 1765]
I went little into company at Naples, and remember solely that the Neapolitan ladies resembled country chamber-maids. I was there during Lent when there are no public entertainments. During my stay at Naples I was truly libertine. I ran after girls without restraint. My blood was inflamed by the burning climate, and my passions were violent. I indulged them; my mind had almost nothing to do with it. I found some very pretty girls. I escaped all danger. I have nothing to say about this period; I merely describe it for you as it occurred.

I returned to Rome for Holy Week. I grew calm. The solemn services of the Roman Catholic Church made a serious impression on me. I began to be a little melancholy and I recalled with religious regret how I had once been, like you, in the bosom of the faithful. But your Savoyard doctrines came to my aid and made me see a church even more catholic that that which I revered: the entire Universe, all souls being emanations of the Eternal Being. On Easter I was in St Peter's, and in that superb temple I saw noble and mystical adorations offered to the Supreme Being. I was penetrated with devotion. I was sure that the revelation given by Jesus was true; and when I saw the Christian High Priest with venerable magnificence elevate before the Eternal Justice a Sacrifice for the sins of the whole world, I fell to my knees among the throng of my fellow men who remained fixed in respectful silence; I struck my breast, and with all the ardour of which my soul was capable I prostrated myself at the feet of my Father "who is in Heaven", convinced that, by varied ways of which we know nothing clearly, he would one day lead all his creatures to happiness. Let cold beings sneer; I was never more nobly happy than on that day.

The Alps machine

[Letter to J.J. Ronsseau, 6 January 1765]
At six I mounted the Alps machine, which consisted of two trees between which were twisted some cords on which I sat. There was also a kind of back and arms, and a board hung before on which I put my feet. In this machine did four fellows (six I should say), changing two and two, carry me over the *saevas Alpes*. I drank some of the snow, that I might say, "I have climbed the rudest heights – and drunk the Alpine snow." The prospect was horridly grand. The snow was sometimes six foot deep, but the road had been well hardened by passengers. I saw the chamois at a distance, of whose skins is made the shambo or shammy leather. I then came to the plain which is upon the mountain, and to the Hôpital de Pèlerins, which the worthy King of Sardinia maintains. There is here a church with a good bold bells, and a priest, who lives as a kind of hermit, takes care of the pilgrims and says mass.

Johann Wolfgang von Goethe

(1749–1832)

German poet, novelist, dramatist, natural scientist and
official at the Court of Weimar. He went to Italy in 1786–
88 and 1790, visiting Florence, Venice and Naples. His
Italiensche Reise (*Italian Journey*), based on his journals
and numerous letters, is one of the great works of travel
literature.

High mass in the church of St Justina, Venice, October 1786

This morning I was present at high mass, which annually on this day the Doge must attend, in the church of St Justina, to commemorate an old victory over the Turks. When the gangways covered with carpet are placed from the vessels to the shore, and first the full violent dresses of the Savii, next the ample red robes of the Senators are unfolded upon the pavement, and lastly when the old Doge adorned with his golden Phrygian cap, in his long golden *talar* and his ermine cloak, steps out of the vessel – when all this, I say, takes place in a little square before the portal of a church, one feels as if one were looking at an old worked tapestry, exceedingly well designed and coloured. To me, northern fugitive as I am, this ceremony gave a great deal of pleasure. With us, who parade nothing but short coats in our processions of pomp, and who conceive nothing greater than one performed with shouldered arms, such an affair might be out of place. But these trains, these peaceful celebrations are all in keeping here.

The Doge is a well-grown and well-shaped man, who, perhaps, suffers from ill health, but, nevertheless, for dignity's sake, bears himself upright under his heavy robe. In other respects he looks like the grandpapa of the whole race, and is kind and affable. His dress is very becoming, the little cap, which he wears under the large one, does not offend the eye, resting as it does upon the whitest and finest hair in the world.

About fifty *nobili*, with long dark-red trains, were with him. For the most part they were handsome men, and there was not a single uncouth figure among them. Several of them were tall with large heads, so that the white curly wigs were very becoming to them. Their features are prominent; the flesh of their faces is soft and white, without looking flabby and disagreeable. On the contrary, there is an appearance of talent without exertion, repose, self-confidence, easiness of existence, and a certain joyousness pervades the whole.

When all had taken their places in the church, and mass began, the fraternities entered by the chief door, and went out at the side door to the right, after they had received holy water in couples, and made their obeisance to the high altar, to the Doge, and the nobility.

A wet day in Venice, October 1786

When a rainy day comes, the filth is intolerable; every one is cursing and scolding. In ascending and descending the bridges one soils one's mantle and great coat (*Tabarro*) which is here worn all the year long, and as one goes along in shoes and silk stockings, one gets splashed, and then scolds for it is not common mud.

Mary Wollstonecraft

(1759–1797)

The English author of *Vindication of the Rights of Man* (1790) and of *Vindication of the Rights of Woman* (1792), an exposition of equality of the sexes. In Paris 1792, to research a book on the French Revolution, Wollstonecraft witnessed the 'Terror'. She also met an American timber-merchant and writer, Captain Gilbert Imlay with whom she had a daughter, Fanny. When Imlay left her, Mary attempted suicide from Putney Bridge. She later married William Godwin, but died as complication of the birth of their daughter Mary Shelley (**q.v.**).

The King of France goes to his death

About nine o'clock this morning, the king passed by my window, moving silently along (excepting now and then a few strokes on the drum, which rendered the stillness more awful) through empty streets, surrounded by the national guards, who, clustering round the carriage, seemed to deserve their name. The inhabitants flocked to their windows, but the casements were all shut, not a voice was heard, nor did I see any thing like an insulting gesture. For the first time since I entered France, I bowed to the majesty of the people, and respected the propriety of behaviour so perfectly in unison with my own feelings. I can scarcely tell you why, but an association of ideas made the tears flow insensibly from my eyes, when I saw Louis sitting, with more dignity than I expected from his character, in a hackney coach going to meet death, where so many of his race have triumphed ... Not the distant sound of a footstep can I hear. My apartments are remote from those of the servants, the only persons who sleep with me in an immense hotel, one folding door after another. I wish I had even kept the cat with me! – I want to see something alive; death in so many frightful shapes has taken hold of my fancy. I am going to bed – and, for the first time in my life, I cannot put out the candle.

William Beckford

(1760–1844)

Beckford was a precocious and eccentric writer and collector. He inherited estates in the West Indies and an enormous fortune at the age of ten. He travelled extensively
in Europe from 1777, and bought artworks, including Gibbon's library. In 1793 he settled near Cintra in Portugal
for a time. At Fonthill, Wiltshire, where he was born,
Beckford consumed much of his fortune in rebuilding the
family house into a Gothic fantasy incorporating a tower
three hundred feet high. This fell down and had to be
rebuilt. Eventually forced to sell the estate, Beckford
moved to Bath and built another tower at Lansdown,
where his dwarf manservant, Porro, is buried in the
garden.

The Queen comes to Cintra

10 September 1787

Adieu to the tranquillity of Cintra, we shall soon have nothing but
hubbub and confusion. The Queen is on the point of arriving with all
her maids of honour, secretaries of state, dwarfs, negresses and horses,
white, black and pie-bald. Half the quintas around will be dried up,
military possession having been taken of the aqueducts, and their waters
diverted into new channels for the use of an encampment.

I was walking in a long arched bower of citron-trees, when M-
appeared at the end of the avenue, accompanied by the Duke d'Alafoins.
This is the identical personage well-known in every part of Europe by
the appellation of Duke of Braganza. He has no right, however, to wear
that illustrious title, which is merged in the crown. Were he called
Duchess Dowager, of anything you please, I think nobody would dispute
the propriety of his style, he being so like an old lady of the bed-chamber,
so fiddle-faddle and so coquettish. He had put on rough and patches,

and though he has seen seventy winters, contrived to turn on his heel and glide about with juvenile agility.

I was much surprised at the ease of his motions, having been told that he was a martyr to the gout. After lisping French with a most refined accent, complaining of the sun, and the road, and the state of architecture, he departed, (thank heaven!) to mark out a spot for the encampment of the cavalry, which are to guard the Queen's sacred person during her residence in these mountains.

Robert Southey

(1774–1843)

English writer and poet. He was expelled from Westminster School for subversive contributions to the school magazine. His sister-in-law married the poet Coleridge whose political ideas he admired as a young man. Southey became Poet Laureate in 1813, although his prose is now considered better than his verse. He wrote mainly about historical subjects such as Nelson, Joan of Arc and John Wesley. Southey visited Lisbon twice.

Next to a nunnery

There is a large Nunnery* near us, where we have heard the Nuns sing. The chapel grating is by no means close, and when the service was over they came close to it, probably to gratify their own curiosity as well as ours. Some of them were handsome, and I saw none who either by their size of their countenance indicated austerity. This is a beautiful

---

* The Infanta D. Sancha, sister of Alfonso VII funded this Cistercian monastery 1152. In 1530, the Nuns of S. Guillermo de Villabuena, three leagues off, upon the Cua, being washed out by the floods, were incorporated with this Convent. Villabuena was also a royal foundation. It had been a palace of the kings of Leon. Bermudo II resided and was buried there. Alfonso IX gave it to his first wife, Queen S. Teresa, daughter of Sancho I of Portugal, and she erected it into a Cisterican monastery, in which two of her daughters professed. Both endowments being thus incorporated, S. Miguel de las Duenas is a wealthy convent, and in high estimation.

spot. The room I am in commands a tranquil and pleasing view: a little stream, the Bueza, flows near the house; the convent lies to the right, and we look over a rich valley to the high mountains near us. Where we are to sleep I know not, for our host's daughter and her husband sleep in the kitchen, and in this, the only other room, the barber, his wife, and child!

The only face for which I have conceived any affection in Spain, is a dried pig's, in the kitchen below; and, alas! this is a hopeless passion!

William Hazlitt

(1778–1830)

English essayist, critic and failed artist. Hazlitt claimed to have 'done nothing' for eight years, although in reality he had been educating himself and honing his talent for devastating criticism. His *Liber Amoris*, the account of a love affair with a young woman for whom he divorced his wife, created a scandal, but his writing was otherwise concerned with literature, politics and ethics. He lacked social finesse and his marriages were short-lived, but intellectually, his life was a success. In 1824–5 Hazlitt did a tour of France, Italy and Switzerland, visiting the Rhine and Holland on the return journey.

The palaces of Venice

I never saw palaces anywhere but at Venice. Those at Rome are dungeons compared to them. They generally come down to the water's edge, and as there are canals on each side of them, you see them *four-square*, the views by Canaletti are very like, both for the effect of the buildings and the hue of the water. The principal are by Palladio, Longhena, and Sansovino. They are massy, elegant, well-proportioned, costly in materials, profuse of ornament. Perhaps if they were raised above the water's edge on low terraces (as some of them are), the appearance of comfort and security would be greater, though the architectural daring, the poetical miracle would appear less. As it is, they seem literally to be suspended in the water. The richest in interior decoration that I saw, was the Grimani Palace, which answered to all the imaginary conditions of this sort of thing. Aladdin might have exchanged his for it, and given his lamp into the bargain. The floors are of marble, the tables of precious stones, the chairs and curtains of rich silk, the walls covered with looking-glasses, and it contains a cabinet of invaluable antique sculpture, and some of Titian's finest portraits. The rooms were not too large for comfort neither; for space is a consideration at Venice. All that it wanted of an Eastern Palace was light and air, with distant vistas of hill and grove.

Stendhal

(1783–1842)

Pseudonym of Marie Henri Beyle, French writer and soldier under Napoleon. Stendhal fought in the Russian campaign in 1812, which devastated the French army. Afterwards he spent six years in Italy, writing his great masterpieces, *Le Rouge et le Noir* and *La Chartreuse de Parme*. After the 1830 Revolution he was made consul first at Trieste, then in Civitavecchia. Stendhal's *Journal*, published posthumously, covers the period 1801–15.

Canonica

At Canonica, a village twenty miles from Milan and ten from Bergamo, situated on the Adda, there's one of the most beautiful views possible. The one from the town of Bergamo is less attractive and infinitely more extensive. From the Casa Terzi, where General Michaud is staying, the Apennines, twenty-five leagues away, can be seen quite clearly. The details can be made out very well with a twenty-inch Ramsden spyglass which the general has. There are two theatres here, a splendid one in the Borgo, which is the part of the town situated on the plain, the other, built of wood, in the square of the old town. We go to the latter every night, as it's quite near the place where we're staying. The other is a half hour away. Signora Nota has the reputation of being the prettiest woman in town, and really she's not bad; they say she has an income of 60,000 livres, she has a *cavaliere servente*, a fine-looking man who spends a great deal on her; she's consequently unattackable. We might – two countesses who are staying near us, but they are twenty-eight or thirty years old and have a dirty look which is repellent.

Washington Irving

(1783–1859)

American writer, barrister, officer in the 1812 war. Irving travelled in Europe and became Ambassador to Spain, 1842–6. He wrote prodigiously. *Tales of the Alhambra* is a highly romantic account of his stay in the then neglected palace at Granada.

The Alhambra by night

A vague and indescribable awe was creeping over me. I would fain have ascribed it to the thoughts of robbers awakened by the evening's conversation, but I felt that it was something more unreal and absurd. In a word, the long-buried impressions of the nursery were reviving and asserting their power over my imagination. Everything began to be affected by the working of my mind. The whispering of the wind among the citron-trees beneath my window had something sinister. I cast my eyes into the garden of Lindaraxa; the groves presented a gulf of shadows; the thickets, indistinct and ghastly shapes. I was glad to close the window, but my chamber itself became infected. A bat had found its way in and flitted about my head and athwart my solitary lamp; the grotesque faces carved in the cedar ceiling seemed to mope and mow at me.

Rousing myself and half smiling at this temporary weakness, I resolved to brave it and, taking lamp in hand, sallied forth to make a tour of the ancient palace. Notwithstanding every mental exertion, the task was a severe one. The rays of my lamp extended to but a limited distance around me. I walked as it were in a mere halo of light and all beyond was thick darkness. The vaulted corridors were lost in gloom; what unseen foe might not be lurking before or behind me! My own shadow playing about the walls, and the echoes of my own footsteps, disturbed me.

In this excited state, as I was traversing the great Hall of Ambassadors there were added real sounds to these conjectural fancies. Low moans and indistinct ejaculations, seemed to rise as it were beneath my feet. I paused and listened. They then appeared to resound from without the tower. Sometimes they resembled the howlings of an animal, at others they were stifled shrieks, mingled with articulate ravings. The thrilling effect of these sounds, in that still hour and singular place, destroyed all inclination to continue my lonely perambulation.

Benjamin Robert Haydon

(1786–1846)

English painter of ambitious historical subjects. Never a great success as an artist, Haydon was imprisoned for debt twice. He did better as a lecturer, and campaigned successfully for the British government to buy the Elgin Marbles. Embittered by his failures, and by the death of five of his children, however, he went to his studio and shot himself, after making a final entry in his journal. Despite this, the *Autobiography* derived from the twenty-seven volumes of his journals makes excellent reading.

News of the Battle of Waterloo, 23 June 1815

I had spent the evening with John Scott who lived in the Edgware Road. I had stayed rather late, and was coming home to Great Marlborough Street, when in crossing Portman Square a messenger from the Foreign

Office came right up to me and said: 'Which is Lord Harrowby's? The Duke has beat Napoleon, taken one hundred and fifty pieces of cannon and is marching to Paris.' 'Is it true?' said I, quite bewildered. 'True!' said he; 'which is Lord Harrowby's?' Forgetting in my joy this was not Grosvenor Square, I said: 'There,' pointing to the same point in Portman Square as Lord Harrowby's house occupies in Grosvenor Square, which happened to be Mrs Boehm's where there was actually a rout. In rushed the messenger through servants and all, and I ran back again to Scott's. They were gone to bed but I knocked them up and said: 'The Duke has beat Napoleon, taken one hundred and fifty pieces of cannon, and is marching to Paris.' Scott began to ask questions. I said: 'None of your questions; it's a fact,' and both of us said 'Huzza!'

Lord Byron

(1788–1824)

English romantic poet, aristocrat and revolutionary. Byron made the Grand Tour in 1809. His poetry brought him enormous fame and he was lionised by society. He later left England in disgrace, however, under suspicion of an incestuous relationship with his half-sister. Byron spent two years in Venice, preoccupied with writing and love affairs. In Italy he developed a taste for revolution, and in 1823 went to Greece to help the Greek struggle for independence. He took his own uniforms with specially made helmets, but he died of fever at Missolonghi. His letters are both entertaining and of the greatest interest.

A list of wants

[to John Murray, Venice, 15 May 1819]
PS – I petition for tooth-brushes – powder – Magnesia – Macassar oil – (or Russia) *the* Sashes – and Sir N[athanie]l Wraxall's memoirs of his own times – I want besides a Bulldog – a terrier – and two Newfound-

land dogs – and I want (is it Buck's?) a life of *Richard 3d.* advertised by Longman *long long long* ago – I asked you for it at least three years since.

Settled like a sausage

[To Richard Belgrave Hoppner, Bologna, 6 June 1819]
Dear Hoppner – I am at length joined to Bologna – where I am settled like a Sausage – and shall be broiled like one if this weather continues.

A tempest in Venice

[To John Murray, Ravenna, 1 August 1819]
In the autumn one day going to the Lido with my Gondoliers – we were overtaken by a heavy Squall and the Gondola put in peril – hats blown away – boat filling – oar lost – tumbling sea – thunder – rain in torrents – night coming – & wind increasing. – On our return – after a tight struggle: I found her on the open steps of the Mocenigo palace on the Grand Canal – with her great black eyes flashing through her tears and the long dark hair which was streaming drenched with rain over her brows & breast; – she was perfectly exposed to the storm – and the wind blowing her hair & dress about her tall thin figure – and the lightning flashing round her – with the waves rolling at her feet – made her look like Medea alighted from her chariot – or the Sibyl of the tempest that was rolling around her – the only living thing within hail at that moment except ourselves.

Percy Bysshe Shelley

(1792–1822)

English poet, who eloped with Mary, daughter of William Godwin, the political philosopher who greatly influenced him. From 1818 the Shelleys lived in Italy, where much of his great work was produced. In Venice, Shelley met

Byron; in the Gulf of La Spezia he met his death by drowning while caught in a storm in a small boat.

On river travel

[To Thomas Love Peacock, Geneva, 17 July 1816]
If possible, we think of descending the Danube in a boat, of visiting
Constantinople and Athens, then Rome and the Tuscan cities, and
returning by the south of France, always following great rivers, the
Danube, the Po, the Rhone, and the Garonne: rivers are not like roads,
the work of the hands of man; they imitate mind, which wanders at
will over pathless deserts, and flows through Nature's loveliest recesses,
which are inaccessible to anything besides. They have the viler advantage
also of affording a cheaper mode of conveyance.

Herodotus on the rocks, Bagni di Lucca

[To Thomas Love Peacock, Bagni di Lucca, 25 July 1818]
In the middle of the day, I bathe in a pool or fountain, formed in the
middle of the forests by a torrent. It is surrounded on all sides by
precipitous rocks, and the waterfall of the stream which forms it falls
into it on one side with perpetual dashing. Close to it, on the top of
the rocks, are alders, and, above, the great chestnut trees, whose long
and pointed leaves pierce the deep blue sky in strong relief. The water
of this pool, which, to venture an unrhythmical paraphrase, is "sixteen
feet long and ten feet wide", is as transparent as the air, so that the
stones and sand at the bottom seem, as it were, trembling in the light
of noonday. It is exceedingly cold also. My custom is to undress and
sit on the rocks, reading Herodotus, until the perspiration has subsided,
and then to leap from the edge of the rock into this fountain – a practice
in the hot weather exceedingly refreshing. This torrent is composed, as
it were, of a succession of pools and waterfalls, up which I sometimes
amuse myself by climbing when I bathe, and receiving the spray all over
my body, whilst I clamber up the moist crags with difficulty.

Edward John Trelawny

(1792–1881)

Trelawny was an adventurer and writer who joined the navy aged eleven but deserted at Bombay. He met Shelley at Pisa in 1821; he helped to burn the poet's body after he drowned, snatched his heart from the cremation pyre and prepared his tomb at Rome, where he was later buried beside him. Trelawny went to Greece with Byron to join the independence struggle; there he married Tersitza, sister of Odysseus, one of the Greek leaders. Later he eloped with Lady Vane Goring, who became his fourth wife and bore him four children. Trelawny also travelled in America in 1833–5; he paid for the liberation of a negro slave and swam across the river at Niagara, between the river and the falls.

Death had closed the door on Byron, Missolonghi, 1824

So I was not surprised at seeing Missolonghi, situated as it is on the verge of the most dismal swamp I had ever seen. The marvel was that Byron, prone to fevers, should have been induced to land on this mud-bank, and stick there for three months shut in by a circle of stagnant pools which might be called the belt of death ... It was the 24th or 25th of April when I arrived; Byron had died on the 19th. I waded through the streets, between wind and water, to the house he had lived in; it was detached, and on the margin of the shallow slimy sea-waters. For three months this house had been besieged, day and night, like a bank that has a run upon it. Now that death had closed the door, it was as silent as a cemetery. No one was within the house but Fletcher, of which I was glad. As if he knew my wishes, he led me up a narrow stair into a small room, with nothing in it but a coffin standing on trestles. No word was spoken by either of us; he withdrew the black pall and the white shroud, and there lay the embalmed body of the Pilgrim – more beautiful in death than in life. The contraction of the muscles and skin had effaced every line that time or passion had ever traced on it; few marble busts could have matched its stainless white, the harmony of its proportions, and perfect finish; yet he had been dissatisfied with that body, and longed to cast its slough. How often I had heard him curse it!

... he wore steel splints, which so wrenched the sinews and tendons of his leg, that they increased his lameness; the foot was twisted inwards, only the edge touched the ground, and that leg was shorter than the other. His shoes were peculiar – very high heeled, with the soles uncommonly thick on the inside and pared thin on the outside – the toes were stuffed with cotton-wool, and his trousers were very large below the knee and strapped down so as to cover his feet. The peculiarity of his gait was now accounted for.

Lady Burghersh

(1793–1879)

Born Priscilla Ann Wesley-Pole, Lady Burghersh was well born and well educated. Her father was an influential statesman, her uncle the future Duke of Wellington; she married a diplomat who accompanied Napoleon to Elba. Travelling with her husband in Europe during the Napoleonic campaigns under conditions of some difficulty, and often without him, Lady Burghersh wrote vivid letters home from the cities and war-ravaged countryside. As France had been effectively closed to the British for twenty years, her observations were of particular interest. She subsequently accompanied her husband on postings in Florence, Berlin and Vienna. Her letters were edited for publication by one of her twelve children.

Berlin, 1813

I went out and walked all over the town, which is the most beautiful I ever saw. The buildings are quite magnificent, and not one or two of them, but at every step the most beautiful palaces and buildings of all kinds. The gate which leads to Charlottenburg is the finest thing I ever saw. The Linden, where we live, is a long double alley of trees, with this gate at the end and very fine houses on each side. The King's palace, the arsenal, the churches, &c, are superb. You see but few equipages, but quantities of soldiers of all kinds and Cossacks in plenty, both officers and men, and all the greatest beasts I ever saw! The ladies walk a great deal in the Linden with bonnets that you must *see* to conceive, for they are really a mile high and ten miles round, and many of them with ten and twelve feathers on the top! They either wear these bonnets or go without anything at all on their heads, which is quite astonishing, for the intense cold here is beyond anything I ever felt. I have been obliged to take to worsted stockings.

I went yesterday to the theatre. It is about the size of Covent Garden, perhaps rather bigger. It is reckoned the best-lighted theatre in Germany, but it appeared to me wretchedly dark, having only one large lustre hanging in the centre and one small one in the Royal box, which was in the middle of the house.

French devastation near Leipzig

We have come all along the line of the French retreat, and it is not a month since they passed, the roads are covered with dead horses and remains of dead men. The latter, I am told, we shall see many of between this and Frankfurt, particularly at Hanau, where Wrede fought his sanguinary battle a fortnight ago. No language can describe the horrible devastation these French have left behind them, and without seeing it no one can form an idea of the country through which such a retreat as theirs has been made. Every bridge blown up, every village burnt or pulled down, fields completely devastated, orchards all turned up, and we traced their bivouaques all along by every horror you can conceive. None of the country people will bury them or their horses, so there they remain lying all over the fields and roads, with millions of crows feasting – we passed quantities, bones of all kinds, hats, shoes, epaulettes, a surprising quantity of rags and linen – every kind of horror.

At Dessau, and below, we crossed on bridges of boats (rather nervous work), and at Weissenfels we went over a bridge of rafts only, which was thrown over a very wide river, the Saale, in three hours' time, for General Blücher to pursue the French, who had hardly time to get out of the town, and Buonaparte hid himself in the mill. They told us that the French soldiers were in such a state of starvation that they took the earrings from their ears and implored for bits of bread, which none of the inhabitants would give them. The consequence is the river is full of bodies; we found Halle full of wounded; there being 14,000 in that town.

Richard Ford

(1796–1858)

English author and critic. Ford trained for the bar but never practised. After spending three years riding around Spain on horseback, he wrote two encyclopaedic and unbeatable works on that country and also brought the artists Velasquez and Murillo to the attention of the British public.

Spain on horseback

As a pedestrian tour for pleasure is a thing utterly unknown in Spain, except in the northern provinces, *excursions on horseback* are truly national and preferable, and bring the stranger in close contact with Spanish man and nature. Horses or mules may be hired in most large cities, or the traveller to whom time is no object may join the caravans of the regular muleteers and carriers, who ply from fixed places to others. Those who can only ride on an English saddle should procure one before starting, and every man will do well to bring out a good pair of English spurs, with some spare sets of rowels, and attend to their efficient sharpness, for the hide of a Spanish beast is hard and unimpressionable.

Ladies must not expect to find English saddles in any but the large towns. The native saddles used by women, *hamugas*, are comfortable; they consist of a sort of chair, with a footboard to rest the feet.

It cannot be said that the animals owned by Spanish muleteers are pleasant to ride, nor indeed are the hacks (*hacas*) and cattle usually let for hire much better; to those, therefore, who propose making an extensive riding tour, especially in the provinces of Galicia, Estremadura, and Aragon, the better plan is to perform it on their own animals, the masters on horses, the attendants on mules. The chief points in such journeys are to take as few things as possible: trunks – the impedimenta of travellers – are thorns in their path, who pass more lightly and pleasantly by sending the heavier luggage on from town to town; "attend also to the provend," as the commissariat has even been *the* difficulty in hungry and thirsty Spain. Each master should have his own *Alforjas* or saddle-bags, in which he will stow away whatever is absolutely necessary for his own immediate wants and comforts, strapping his cloak or *manta* over it. The servant should be mounted on a stout mule, and provided with strong and capacious *capachos de esparto*, or peculiar baskets made of this useful Spanish grass; one side may be dedicated to the wardrobe, the other to the larder; and let neither master nor man omit to take a *bota*, or leather wine-bottle, or forget to keep it full; spare sets of shoes for horses and mules, with nails and hammer, are also essential. When once off the beaten tracks, those travellers who make up their minds to find *nothing* on the road but discomfort will be the least likely to be disappointed, while by being prepared and forearmed they will overcome every difficulty – *hombre prevenido, nunca fué vencido*, a little foresight and provision gives small trouble and ensures great comfort.

An india-rubber bath

It is desirable for the traveller to carry with him some simple medicines. English prescriptions are not readily made up in Spain. For dysentery the usual Spanish remedy is rice-water, which sometimes stops the diarrhœa. It is well also to have a supply of tea and French brandy, and small metal teapot, neither of these being procurable except in the larger towns. An india-rubber bath will be found a great comfort.

Spanish robbers and the Guardia Civil

Undoubtedly on the long highways of a thinly-peopled land, accidents may occur; but the regular and really formidable robbers have almost disappeared on the high roads, in consequence of the institution of a body of well-armed men, admirably disciplined (part mounted) as Gens-d'armes, who are stationed on the principal routes as escorts and patrols. They are called *Guardias civiles*, to distinguish them from *military* and *rural* guards. This noble body of men is composed of 20,000 Foot and 5000 Horse Guards, or Gendarmerie, first organised 1844–45: they are dressed in black tunic and trousers of the same colour, with light buff-coloured belts. The *Guardias civiles* are under military law; their punishments and penalties exceptionally severe. Their *esprits de corps* is good. Their ranks are composed of the high-character and long-service men of the Spanish army; and of cadets from the College, near Madrid, where all the orphan children of Civil Guards who have died in the pursuance of their duty are educated, free of expense, for the force. The duties of the Civil Guards are much the same as those of the Irish Constabulary, whom they greatly resemble in organisation. They are stationed, in *couples*, in every town and small village, and in small barracks along every frequented high-road, and in squads of 25 to 50 in Spain's larger cities. They are *police*, without being spies; *soldiers*, without being liable to be called on for service beyond the Peninsula. They perform their duties as police most effectively. Two of them meet every train at every station, and check everything that is wrong, as well by their presence and *morale* as by the strong arm of the law. They escort prisoners from one prison to another, and, knowing how uncertain in its action is Spanish law, they constantly shoot down a murderer, taken red-handed, or trying to escape when on the march with them from prison to prison. They have done more to establish order in Spain than any other body. The men are 5 feet 8 inches in stature, well-set and powerful. Their head is a General in the army, living in Madrid, with the title of Director-General. All members of the force *must read and write*. Promotion from the ranks is the rule, not the exception. They live in barracks, mess together, and associate but little with the outer world. The force supports a weekly periodical, called *Boletin oficial de la Guardia Civil*, first started in 1858. The rules of the corps are arranged in the Cartilla, gambling being entirely prohibited. "The couples engaged in patrolling the roads must walk twelve paces apart from one another, so as not to be both surprised at once." The cavalry carry heavy dragon swords of Toledo make, and revolvers and short carbines; the foot-soldiers Remington rifle and bayonet, and sometimes revolvers. The safety of property in Spain may, without exaggeration, be said to depend on this most excellent force. No Civil Guard is allowed to accept a reward, however great be his service to you. In cases of difficulty, the traveller should inquire for the *Casa Cuartel de la Guardia Civil*, and there make his report to some responsible official.

Mary Shelley

(1797–1851)

English writer. Mary Shelley was the daughter of William Godwin, social reformer, and Mary Wollstonecroft (**q.v.**) who died soon after the birth of her daughter. Brought up by a stepmother she disliked, at sixteen Mary eloped with the poet Shelley (**q.v.**). At nineteen, she wrote the influential novel, *Frankenstein*. Mary continued writing furiously after Shelley's death in Italy in order to support herself and their son, Percy, with whom she later travelled in Europe.

The Ligurian coast

The lanes are filled with fire-flies; they dart between the trunks of the trees and people the land with earthstars. I walked among them to-night and descended towards the sea. I passed by the ruined church, and stood on the platform that overlooks the beach. The black rocks were stretched out among the blue waters, which dashed with no impetuous motion against them. The dark boats with their white sails glided gently over its surface, and the star-enlightened promontories closed in the bay; below, amid the crags, I heard the monotonous, but harmonious voices of the fishermen.

"How beautiful these shores, and this sea! Such is the scene – such the waves within which my beloved vanished from mortality.

"The time is drawing near when I must quit this country. It is true that in the situation I now am, Italy is but the corpse of the enchantress that she was."

Paris coiffures

When at Paris I will tell you more what I think of the French. They still seem miracles of quietness in comparison with Marianne's noisy friends; and the women's dresses afford the drollest contrast with those in fashion when I first set foot in Paris in 1814. Then their waists were between their shoulders, and as Hogg observed they were rather curtains than gowns. Their hair too dragged to the top of their head, and then lifted to its height, appeared as if each female wished to be a Tower of Babel in herself. Now their waists are long (not so long, however as the Genoese), and their hair flat at the top, with quantities of curls on the temples. I remember in 1814, a Frenchman's pathetic horror at my appearance in the streets of Paris, in Oldenburg (as they were called) hats: now they all wear machines of that shape, and a high bonnet would of course be as far out of the right road, as if the earth were to take a flying leap to another system.

Robert Curzon

(1810–73)

English scholar and traveller. Curzon (14th Baron Zouche of Harringworth) travelled in Egypt and Palestine in search of early manuscripts which were being treated in a careless manner in the monasteries of the Near East. He visited Mount Athos and made dramatic ascents to the rock mon-asteries of Meteora, in Albania. Curzon was also attaché at the embassy at Constantinople and involved in defining

the boundary between Turkey and Persia, for which service
he was decorated by the Turkish Sultan.

In Albania

6 November – I had engaged a tall, thin, dismal-looking man, well
provided with pistols, knives, and daggers, as an additional servant, for
he was said to know all the passes of the mountains, which I thought
might be a useful accomplishment in case I had to avoid the more
public roads – or paths, rather – for roads there were none. I purchased
a stock of provisions, and hired five horses – three for myself and my
men, one for the muleteer, and the other for the baggage, which was
well strapped on, that the beast might gallop with it, as it was not very
heavy. They were pretty good horses – rough and hardy. Mine looked
very hard at me out of the corner of his eye when I got upon his back
in the cold grey dawn, as if to find out what sort of a person I was. By
means of a stout kourbatch – a sort of whip of rhinoceros hide which
they use in Egypt – I immediately gave him all the information he
desired; and off we galloped round the back part of the town, and,
unquestioned by any one, we soon found ourselves trotting along
the plain by the south end of the lake of Yanina. Here the waters from
the lake disappear in an extraordinary manner in a great cavern, or
pit full of rocks and stones, through which the water runs away into
some subterranean channel – a dark and mysterious river, which the
dismal-looking man, my new attendant, said came out into the light
again somewhere in the Gulf of Arta. Before long we got upon the
remains of a paved road, like a Roman way, which had been made by
Ali Pasha. It was, however, out of repair, having in places been swept
away by the torrents, and was an impediment rather than an assistance
to travellers.

Edward Lear

(1812–88)

English artist. Lear is remembered principally for the wonderful nonsense verse that he wrote for the children of his patron, the Earl of Derby, but his own epitaph read, 'A landscape Painter in Many Lands'. He lived in Rome for ten years and wandered through Europe and the Middle East, leaving a legacy of superb topographical paintings.

Are there not Banditti?

Thus, and in such a groove, did the machinery of thought go on, gradually refusing to move otherwise than by jerky spasms, after the fashion of mechanical Ollendorff exercises, or verb-catechisms of familiar phrases –

Are there not Banditti?
Had there not been Vendetta?
Were there not Corsican brothers?
Should I not carry clothes for all sorts of weather?
Must *thou* not have taken a dress coat?
Had *he* not many letters of introduction?
Might *we* not have taken extra pairs of spectacles?
Could *you* not have provided numerous walking boots?
Should *they* not have forgotten boxes of quinine pills?
Shall *we* possess flea-powder?
Could *you* not procure copper money?
May *they* not find cream cheeses?
Should there not be innumerable moufflons?
Ought not the cabin lamps and glasses to cease jingling?
Might not those poodles stop worrying?

Thus and thus, till be reason of long hours of monotonous rolling and shaking, a sort of comatose insensibility, miscalled sleep, takes the place of all thought, and so the night passes.

Castles in the air

We arrived at Kastráki, a village nestled immediately below these gigantic crags, at sunset. I do not think I ever saw any scene so startling and incredible; such vast sheer perpendicular pyramids, standing out of the earth, with the tiny houses of the village clustering at the roots.

With difficulty – for it is the time when silk-worms are being bred in the houses, and the inhabitants will not allow them to be disturbed – Andréa procured a lodging for me in the upper part of a dwelling, formed as are most in the village, like a tower, the entrance to which, for the sake of defence, was by a hole three feet high. Here, after having gazed in utter astonishment at the wild scenery as long as the light lasted, I took up my abode for the night. The inhabitants of this place, as well as of Kalabáka (or Stagús), are Christians, and every nook of the village was swarming with pigs and little children. 'Πολλα πιδλια,' said an old man to me, as the little creatures thronged about me, 'δια τον νερόν χαλόν'. What a contrast there is between the precipices, from five to six hundred feet high, and these atoms of life playing at their base! Strange, unearthly-looking rocks are these, full of gigantic chasms and round holes, resembling Gruyère cheese, as it were, highly magnified, their surface being otherwise perfectly smooth. Behind the village of Kastráki, the groups of rock are more crowded, and darkened with vegetation; and at this late hour a sombre mystery makes them seem like the work of some genii, or enchanter of Arabian romance. Before the dwellings, a slope covered with mulberry trees descends to the river, and grand scenes of Thessalian plain and hill fill up the southern and eastern horizon.

I went very early with a villager to visit and sketch the monasteries. Truly they are a most wonderful spectacle; and are infinitely more picturesque than I had expected them to be. The magnificent foreground of fine oak and detached fragments of rock struck me as one of the peculiar features of the scene. The detached and massive pillars of stone, crowned with the retreats of the monks, rise perpendicularly from the sea of foliage, which at this early hour, 6 a.m., is wrapped in the deepest shade, while the bright eastern light strikes the upper part of the magic heights with brilliant force and breadth. To make any real use of the most exquisite landscape abounding throughout this marvellous spot, an artist should stay here for a month: there are both the simplest and most classic poetries of scenery at their foot looking towards the plain and mountain; and when I mounted the cliffs on a level with the summit of the great rocks of Metéora and Baarlám, the solitary and quiet tone of these most wonderful haunts appeared to me inexpressibly delightful. Silvery white goats were peeping from the edge of the rocks into the deep, black abyss below; the simple forms of the rocks rise high in air, crowned with church and convent, while the eye reaches the plains of Thessaly to the far-away hills of Agrafa. No pen or pencil can do justice to the scenery of Metéora. I did not go up to any of the monasteries. Suffering from a severe fall in the autumn of last year, I had no desire to run the risk of increasing the weakness of my right arm, the use of which I was only now beginning to regain, so the interior of these monkish habitations I left unvisited; regretting that I did so the less, as every moment of the short time I lingered among these scenes, was too little to carry away even imperfect representations of their marvels.

I had been more than half inclined to turn back after having seen the Metéora convents, but the improvements in the weather, the inducement of beholding Olympus and Tempe, and the dread of so soon re-encountering the gloomy Pass of Métzovo, prevailed to lead me forward.

A Madras Officer

An anonymous East India Company officer, who described his return journey to England by sea and over land in vivid detail.

Capuchin vaults at Messina, Sicily

The guide crossed himself, as his imagination pictured to his own mind himself similarly situated. On entering the little chapel on the right hand side, I observed the Friar take something off the altar table, and throw it on the ground; it fell heavily, and as the room was dark, I could not then distinguish what it was; but as I became accustomed to the light, I saw, to my great horror, a dead child! A lady who was with me almost fainted at the sight; the dead infant's mother was standing outside looking at the corpse with perfect coolness and nonchalance. I asked the guide what was going to be done with the body? He informed me, that it would be kept there for a day or two, whilst the priests offered up prayers in its behalf; and then it would be thrown into a grave or pit, where other dead bodies are cast. I believe they have a curious mode of sepulture here, for the poorer classes of inhabitants; all dead bodies which cannot be interred in coffins, are cast promiscuously into the same pit, devoid even of clothes or covering of any sort – a most disgusting and unchristian-like practice, which savages even are not guilty of. The old Friar led us down a flight of worn-out stone steps, into the vaults; and here a most revolting sight met our view; worse ten thousand times than the corpse of the poor little child; which, they are taken up, and placed as above described. I have heard that the soil in which they are interred, has some peculiar property in drying up dead bodies, without putrefaction; so that, although life is extinct, the features are preserved for some time: those I saw, were, however, fast crumbling into dust . . .

Robert Louis Stevenson

(1850–94)

Scottish writer, from a family of lighthouse builders. This extract is from his first book, *An Inland Voyage*, was the story of a canoe journey through France and Belgium. The same year, he did his *Travels with a Donkey in the*

Cévennes. Hampered throughout his life by tuberculosis, Stevenson, his wife and stepson eventually settled in Samoa, where the writer is buried at the foot of Mount Vaea. *In the South Seas* is an account of two cruises in the Marquesas, Paumotus and Gilbert Islands in 1889.

A night chez Bazin

It faired as the night went on, and the moon came out of the clouds. We sat in front of the door, talking softly with Bazin. At the guardhouse opposite, the guard was being for ever turned out, as trains of field artillery kept clanking in out of the night, or patrols of horsemen trotted by in their cloaks. Madame Bazin came out after a while; she was tired with her day's work, I suppose; and she nestled up to her husband and laid her head upon his breast. He had his arm about her and kept gently patting her on the shoulder. I think Bazin was right and he was really married. Of how few people can the same be said!

Little did the Bazins know how much they served us. We were charged for candles, for food and drink, and for the beds we slept in. But there was nothing in the bill for the husband's pleasant talk; nor for the pretty spectacle of their married life. And there was yet another item uncharged. For these people's politeness really set us up again in our own esteem. We had a thirst for consideration; the sense of insult was still hot in our spirits; and civil usage seemed to restore us to our position in the world.

How little we pay our way in life! Although we have our purses continually in our hand the better part of service goes still unrewarded. But I like to fancy that a grateful spirit gives as good as it gets. Perhaps the Bazins knew how much I liked them? Perhaps, they also, were healed of some slights by the thanks that I gave them in my manner?

Sir James George Frazer

(1854–1941)

Scottish anthopologist. In his book, *The Golden Bough: a Study in Comparative Religion*, Frazer evokes an Arcadian picture of pagan Italy.

By the waters of Lake Nemi

Diana and Virbius. Who does not know Turner's picture of the Golden Bough? The scene, suffused with the golden glow of imagination in which the divine mind of Turner steeped and transfigured even the fairest natural landscape, is a dream-like vision of the little woodland lake of Nemi – "Diana's Mirror", as it was called by the ancients. No one who has seen that calm water, lapped in a green hollow of the Alban hills, can ever forget it. The two characteristic Italian villages which slumber on its banks, and the equally Italian palace whose terraced gardens descend steeply to the lake, hardly break the stillness and even the solitariness of the scene. Dian herself might still linger by this lonely shore, still haunt these woodlands wild.

In antiquity this sylvan landscape was the scene of a strange and recurring tragedy. On the northern shore of the lake, right under the precipitous cliffs on which the modern village of Nemi is perched, stood the sacred grove and sanctuary of Diana Nemorensis, or Diana of the Wood. The lake and the grove were sometimes known as the lake and grove of Aricia. But the town of Aricia (the modern La Riccia) was situated about three miles off, at the foot of the Alban Mount, and separated by a steep descent from the lake, which lies in a small crater-like hollow on the mountain side. In this sacred grove there grew a certain tree round which at any time of the day, and probably far into the night, a grim figure might be seen to prowl. In his hand he carried a drawn sword, and he kept peering warily about him as if at every instant he expected to be set upon by an enemy. He was a priest and a murderer; and the man for whom he looked was sooner or later to murder him and hold the priesthood in his stead. Such was the rule of the sanctuary. A candidate for the priesthood could only succeed to the office by slaying the priest, and having slain him, he retained the office till he was himself slain by a stronger or a craftier.

The post which he held by this precarious tenure carried with it the title of king; but surely no crowned head ever lay uneasier, or was visited by more evil dreams, than his. For year in year out, in summer and winter, in fair weather and foul, he had to keep his lonely watch, and whenever he snatched a troubled slumber it was at the peril of his life. The least relaxation of his vigilance, the smallest abatement of his strength of limb or skill of fence, put him in jeopardy; grey hairs might seal his death-warrant. To gentle and pious pilgrims at the shrine the sight of him might well seem to darken the fair landscape, as when a cloud suddenly blots the sun on a bright day.

Edith Wharton

(1862–1937)

American writer. Best known for her novels unwrapping *fin de siècle* New York society, Wharton wrote prolifically, lived in France for several years, and was well travelled in Europe and Morocco, about which she wrote a guidebook. She was awarded the *Légion d'Honneur* for her war work in France.

The landscape of a sanatorium prospectus

For ten days we had not known what ailed us. We had fled from the August heat and crowd of the Vorderrheinthal to the post-inn below the Splügen pass; and here fortune had given us all the midsummer tourist can hope for – solitude, cool air and fine scenery. A dozen times a day we counted our mercies, but still privately felt them to be insufficient. As we walked through the larch-groves beside the Rhine, or climbed the grassy heights above the valley, we were oppressed by the didactic quality of our surroundings . . . We seemed to be living in the landscape of a sanatorium prospectus . . . One can forgive a place three thousand miles from Italy for not being Italian; but that a village on the very border should remain stolidly, immovably Swiss was a constant source of exasperation. Even the landscape had neglected its opportunities. A few miles off it became the accomplice of man's most exquisite imaginings; but here we could see in it only endless material for Swiss clocks and fodder.

German manners

Certain forms and titles are also prefixed on the address of a letter: thus a Count of the high nobility and ancient empire must be addressed *Erlaucht* (Illustrious); a Count of the lesser noblesse, *Hochgeborener Herr* (High-born Sir); a baron and a minister, even though not of a noble birth, is called *Hochwohls geboren*; a merchant or roturier must content himself with being termed *Wohl-* (well) *geboren*; while *Hochedel* (high noble) is ironically applied to tradesmen.

> In one respect, in Germany, I think politeness is carried too far – I mean in the perpetual act of pulling off the hat. Speaking ludicrously of it, it really becomes *expensive*, for, with a man who has a large acquaintance in any public place, his hat is never two minutes at rest. – NIMROD'S *Letters from Holstein*.

A curious instance of the extent to which this practice of bowing is carried occurred to the writer in a small provincial town in the S. of Germany. At the entrance of the public promenade in the Grande Place he observed notices painted on boards, which at first he imagined to contain some police regulations, or important order of the magistracy of the town; upon perusal, however, it proved to be an ordonnance to this effect: – "For the convenience of promenaders, it is particularly requested that the troublesome custom of saluting by taking off the hat should here be dispensed with." It is not to friends alone that it is necessary to doff the hat, for, if the friend with whom you are walking meets an acquaintance to whom he takes off his hat, you must do the same, even though you never saw him before.

German entertainment

These places of amusement do not open till after the hours of morning service in the churches, and most of the persons who resort to them have previously attended a church. A large portion are tradesmen who have been shut up in their shops, and artisans who have been working hard, all the week. They come in their best clothes, and accompanied by wives and children, who, be it observed, are always made parties in these amusements; they content themselves with coffee, beer, or wine, in moderate quantities; spirits are never seen, and instances of noisy turbulence and drunkenness are almost unknown on these occasions. Such recreation, even with the mirthful exercise of dancing superadded, is surely harmless in comparison with the solitary orgies of the pot-house and gin-shop, to which the same class of persons but too often devote their Sundays in our country, squandering in loathsome intemperance the earnings of the week, which ought to be devoted to the wants of the starving and neglected wife and family, who are left behind in their close and miserable home.

Norman Douglas

(1868–1952)

Scottish writer, linguist and zoologist. Douglas spent much of his life on Capri, which he immortalised in *South Wind* (1917). His other remarkable travel books are *Siren Land* (1911), *Fountains in the Sand* (1912) and *Old Calabria* (1915), quoted here. Reported missing in 1940, Douglas returned to London across Europe with great difficulty.

How much to Catanzaro?

With the improvidence of the true traveller I had consumed my stock of provisions ere reaching the town of Taverna after a march of nine hours or thereabouts. A place of this size and renown, I had argued, would surely be able to provide a meal. But Taverna belies its name.

The only tavern discoverable was a composite hovel, half wine-shop, half hen-house, whose proprietor, disturbed in his noonday nap, stoutly refused to produce anything eatable. And there I stood in the blazing sunshine, famished and unbefriended. Forthwith the strength melted out of my bones; the prospect of walking to Catanzaro, so alluring with a full stomach, faded out of the realm of possibility; and it seemed a special dispensation of Providence when, at my lowest ebb of vitality, a small carriage suddenly hove in sight.

"How much to Catanzaro?"

The owner eyed me critically, and then replied in English:

"You can pay twenty dollars."

Twenty dollars – a hundred francs! But it is useless trying to bargain with an *americano* (their time is too valuable).

"A dollar a mile?" I protested.

"That's so."

"You be damned."

"Same to you, mister." And he drove off.

Erskine Childers

(1870–1922)

The son of a civil servant in Ceylon, Childers served in the South African War and the First World War. He became dedicated to the cause of Irish independence, carrying arms from Europe to Ireland with his American wife in their yacht. He was later court-martialled and executed by the Irish Free State authorities for refusing to agree to a treaty he had helped negotiate. Childers shook hands with every man in the firing squad before they shot him. *The Riddle of the Sands* was the outcome of a yachting expedition to the German coast in 1903. The story is about an English civil servant and his friend, cruising the Baltic in a small yacht, the *Dulcibella*. They discover a German plan for the invasion of England under escort of the German Imperial Navy.

Kitting out for the Baltic

At Lancaster's I inquired for his gun, was received coolly, and had to pay a heavy bill, which it seemed to have incurred, before it was handed over. Having ordered the gun and No. 4's to be sent to my chambers, I bought the Raven mixture with that peculiar sense of injury which the prospect of smuggling in another's behalf always entails; and wondered where in the world Carey and Neilson's was, a firm which Davies spoke of as though it were as well known as the Bank of England or the Stores, instead of specializing in "rigging-screws", whatever they might be. They sounded important, though, and it would be only politic to unearth them. I connected them with the "few repairs", and awoke new misgivings. At the Stores I asked for a No. 3 Rippingill stove and was confronted with a formidable and hideous piece of ironmongery, which burned petroleum in two capacious tanks, horribly prophetic of a smell of warm oil; I paid for this miserably, convinced of its grim efficiency, but speculating as to the domestic conditions which caused it to be sent for as an afterthought by telegram. I also asked about rigging-screws in the yachting department, but learnt that they were not kept in stock; that Carey and Neilson's would certainly have them, and their shop was in the Minories, in the far east, meaning a journey nearly as long as to Flensburg, and twice as tiresome. They would be shut by the time I got there, so after this exhausting round of duty I went home in a cab, omitted dressing for dinner (an epoch in itself), ordered a chop up from the basement kitchen, and spent the rest of the evening packing and writing with the methodical gloom of a man setting his affairs in order for the last time.

For the eleven-shilling oilskins I was referred to a villainous den in a back street, which the shopman said they always recommended, and where a dirty and bejewelled Hebrew chaffered with me (beginning at 18s) over two reeking orange slabs distantly resembling moieties of the human figure. Their odour made me close prematurely for 14s, and I hurried back (for I was due there at 11) to my office with my two disreputable brown-paper parcels, one of which made itself so noticeable in the close official air that Carter attentively asked if I would like to have it sent to my chambers, and K – was inquisitive to bluntness about it and my movements. But I did not care to enlighten K –, whose comments I knew would be provokingly envious or wounding to my pride in some way.

I remembered, later on, the prismatic compass, and wired to the Minories to have one sent at once, feeling rather relieved that I was not present there to be cross-examined as to size and make. The reply was, "Not stocked: try surveying-instrument maker" – a reply both puzzling and reassuring . . .

Luigi Barzini

(1874–1947)

Italian writer, journalist and former editor of the *Corriere Della Sera*. Barzini reported on an expedition to China against the Boxers in 1900, the beginning of the Russo–Japanese War in 1904 and the 1906 San Francisco earthquake. He wrote a classic account of Prince Borghese's Great Horseless Race, a journey by car from Peking to Paris in 1907. They achieved the then unheard-of speed of sixty miles per hour across the Gobi desert.

To Paris from Peking

At four o'clock a strange kind of car appears from Paris and puts itself at the head of our procession. It is one of those gigantic motor-cars for twenty or thirty passengers, used to take tourists round Paris when they desire to see the town in a few hours. In this car are some bandsmen armed with trumpets and trombones, and the car is decked out with trophies and numerous French and Italian flags. It looks a little like a carnival show, but it seems indispensable to the due solemnisation of our arrival. The band strikes up with the triumphal march out of *Aïda*. This is the entry of Radames, in Paris!

We continue our progress. It is now 4.15.

We come out on to the Avenue du Trône, between the two gigantic columns of Philip Augustus, half hidden by a crowd of people. Before us, veiled by the rain, we see the dim outline of the Tour Eiffel. It looks like some gigantic lighthouse – the great lighthouse of our journey's harbour.

The cheering becomes clamorous, intense, continuous. Whenever it abates for a moment we hear the ringing voices of the street-vendors offering souvenir post-cards for sale, with cries of: "LE PRINCE BORGHESE, QUATRE SOUS! QUATRE SOUS, LE PRINCE BORGHESE!"

Lady Lina Duff Gordon

(1874–1964)

English journalist who interviewed Mussolini for the *Observer* in 1922, and was later arrested for 'intriguing' with socialists. Lady Duff Gordon inherited a fourteenth-century Italian castle, Poggio Gherardo, from her aunt, Janet Ross, the daughter of Lady Lucie Duff Gordon (**q.v.**). *Home Life in Italy* describes the life and neighbours she enjoyed there for fifty years with her artist husband, Aubrey Waterfield. In 1899, Janet Ross published a book of recipes used at the castle, *Leaves from our Tuscan Kitchen*.

A country fair in the Apennines

The chief business of the Fair was the selling of cattle and sheep. The animals were herded together in the dry river-bed close to the village, where poplars, growing on the bank high above it, cast down a slender shade. The oxen turned weary eyes upon the peasants, who pushed and pressed among them, and filled the air with a buzz of talk. A bargain is rarely concluded upon an empty stomach; the crafty peasant, especially when he has a poor animal to dispose of, drags on the bargaining until the magic hour of twelve.

We glanced into the *trattoria* as it began to fill. The long vaulted room, with thick pillars supporting the barrel-shaped roof, looked like some cavernous retreat of Bacchic followers. The walls gleamed white, and the men sat at little tables plying freely at the golden wine and twisting yards of *maccheroni* round their forks from a plate piled high. There were the usual bargainers, and the beggar eating heartily after a successful morning; the sporting priest, who never misses a Fair, the prosperous bailiff, pulling his money out of a greasy pocket-book, and contentedly counting it in a quiet corner; and the bearded peasant from the higher Apennines come to sell cheeses, in buskins, with a gourd for water slung over his shoulder and a pointed hat stuck on at an angle.

Xavier Marcel Boulestin

(1878–1943)

French chef. He spent much time in London as a young man, and opened a renowned French restaurant in the city in the 1920s. Boulestin also became a cookery writer and teacher and was the first television chef; he even made cookery records on which his commentary could be heard above a background of sizzling noises. *Myself, My Two Countries* is his engaging early autobiography.

Troop train

The train stopped. The shadow began to lift silently and presently the landscape appeared in that dim atmosphere which is not yet day and which is night no longer. All things remained so for a little time in a state of expectation, once or twice torn by the whistling of the engine; then the sky began to change colour gradually, and all of a sudden life awoke; mysterious noises arose from the grass and from the trees, from the insects and the birds; the first flush of pink appeared in the pale grey sky; and then a sunrise of such colour I had not seen for years.

I turned to my companions; how ghastly they looked in that light.

Knowing military life, I had taken with me, in a small attaché case, only one shirt, a few collars, two pairs of socks, a few handkerchiefs, a book and my toilet things. That was at present all my possessions, but in my toilet things was a little manicure set, because I never believed in what is known as "pigging it" if it could be helped. So I took my nail file and I started doing my nails, which, lit by the rays of the rising sun, appeared abnormally pink. Manicuring one's nails is an absorbing and soothing occupation, a relaxation of a good quarter of an hour. I washed my face and my hands with Eau de Cologne, combed my hair and felt ready for a cup of coffee at the next station.

Janet Flanner

(1892–1978)

An American writer; Flanner was the Paris correspondent of the *New Yorker*, 1925–75, with the nom de plume, Genêt. She wrote a lively fortnightly 'Letter from Paris'; and sent reports on European life and culture with great documentary value. She was at the centre of an intellectual and largely lesbian circle in Paris.

There isn't a cat in Paris

As the French phrase goes, "There isn't a cat in Paris," meaning it is empty – is emptied utterly by the holiday. The August holiday here is like a milk sleeping sickness; the city seems drowsy, somnolent, recumbent. It is no time to be hungry for fine food, because the restaurants are mostly closed; no time to have a toothache, because your dentist is on his Normandy farm; no time to be ill, because your doctor has gone to Norway, no time to twist your sacroiliac, because your osteopath is climbing mountains in Switzerland. A vacation is a time for resting. The capital of France itself seems to be resting, sprawling indolently beside the Seine.

Aldous Huxley

(1894–1963)

English writer, born into the distinguished clan of Huxleys
and Arnolds, scientists and writers. As a young man Huxley suffered from blindness; he wrote his first novel on a
Braille typewriter. He recovered his vision, but turned to
writing instead of medicine. In the 1920s, Huxley lived
in Italy with his wife and son, and continued to travel
throughout his life, eventually moving to California.

In Rimini with the thaumaturgical arm of St Francis Xavier

Rimini was honoured, that morning, by the presence of three distinguished visitors – ourselves and the Thaumaturgical Arm of St Francis
Xavier. Divorced from the rest of the saint's remains, whose home is a
jewelled tabernacle in the church of Jesus at Old Goa, the Arm, like
ourselves, was making an Italian tour. But while we poor common
tourists were spending money on the way, the Thaumaturgical Arm –
and this was perhaps its most miraculous achievement – was raking it
in. It had only to show itself through the crystal window of the reliquary
in which it travelled – a skeleton arm, with a huge amethyst ring still
glittering on one of the fingers of its bony hand – to command the
veneration of all beholders and a copper collection, thinly interspersed
with nickel and the smallest paper. The copper collection went to the
foreign missions: what happened to their veneration, I do not venture
to guess. It was set down, no doubt, with their offered pence, to the
credit of those who felt it, in the recording angel's book.

I felt rather sorry for St Francis Xavier's arm. The body of the saint,
after translation from China to Malacca and from Malacca to India,
now reposes, as I have said, in the gaudy shrine at Goa. After a life so
extraordinarily strenuous as was his, the great missionary deserves to
rest in peace. And so he does, most of him. But his right arm has had
to forgo its secular quiet; its missionary voyages are not yet over. In its

gold and crystal box it travels indefatigably through catholic Christendom collecting pence – 'for spoiling Indian innocence,' as Mr Matthew Green tersely and rather tartly put it, two hundred years ago. Poor Arm!

We found it, that morning, in the church of San Francesco at Rimini. A crowd of adorers filled the building and overflowed into the street outside. The people seemed to be waiting rather vaguely in the hope of something thaumaturgical happening. Within the church, a long queue of men and women shuffled slowly up into the choir to kiss the jewelled bone-box and deposit their *soldi*. Outside, among the crowd at the door of the church, stood a number of hawkers, selling picture postcards of the Thaumaturgical Arm and brief but fabulous biographies of its owner . . .

During the lunch hour the Arm was taken for a drive round Rimini. Red and yellow counterpanes were hung out of all the windows in its honour; the faithful waited impatiently. And at last it came, driving in a very large, very noisy and dirty old Fiat, accompanied, not, as one might have expected, by the ecclesiastical dignitaries of the city, but by seven or eight very secular young men in black shirts, with frizzy hair, their trouser pockets bulging with automatic pistols – the committee of the local fascio, no doubt.

The Arm occupied the front seat, next the driver; the fascists lolled behind. As the car passed, the faithful did a very curious thing; mingling the gestures of reverence and applause, they fell on their knees and clapped their hands. The Arm was treated as though it were a combination of Jackie Coogan and the Host. After lunch, it was driven rapidly away to Bologna.

Cyril Connolly

(1903–74)

English man of letters. He founded the literary magazine *Horizon* in 1940, and recorded many of his inter war travels in his book *The Unquiet Grave*, written under the nom de plume, Palinurus.

Early morning on the Mediterranean

Early morning on the Mediterranean: bright air resinous with Aleppo pine, water spraying over the gleaming tarmac of the Route Nationale and darkly reflecting the spring-summer green of the planes; swifts wheeling round the oleanders, waiters unpiling the wicker chairs and scrubbing the café tables; armfuls of carnations on the flower-stalls, pyramids of aubergines and lemons, *rascasses* on the fishmonger's slab goggling among the wine-dark urchins; smell of brioches from the bakeries, sound of reed curtains jingling in the barber shops, clang of the tin kiosk opening for *Le Petit Var*. Rope-soles warming up on the cobbles by the harbour where the *Jean d'Agrève* prepares for a trip to the Islands and the Annamese boy scrubs her brass. Now cooks from many yachts step ashore with their market-baskets, one-eyed cats scrounge among the fish-heads, while the hot sun refracts the dancing sea-glitter on the café awnings, and the sea becomes a green gin-fizz of stillness in whose depth a quiver of sprats charges and counter-charges in the pleasure of fishes.

Sir Cecil Beaton

(1904–80)

British photographer, stage designer and traveller. He kept the most piquant of diaries.

Noël's Swiss retreat

Montreux: September 1972
I had heard about Noël's Swiss retreat. 'It's very typical of him, lots of signed photographs, a house that might have been brought from Eastbourne.' It is true the house suits Noël perfectly. It has no real character, is ugly, is decorated in the typical theatre-folk style, but it is warm and comfortable and it works.

I found Noël in a scarlet jacket hunched and crumpled in a chair, looking very old and resigned and fatter. He seemed a bit surprised to see me although, no doubt, as he later said, he had been looking forward to my visit. A glass of brandy and ginger-ale was within reach and the cigarettes at hand. Noël is only a bit more than seventy. He suffers from a bad leg; the circulation cannot be relied upon and if he walks he can be in great pain. As a result, he doesn't walk, and spends most of his time in bed. This is not good for anyone. But Noël has aged into a very nice and kind old man. He is really a darling, so trim and neat, his memory unfailing. His intelligence was as quick as ever and within a few moments we were enjoying each others' jokes and laughing a lot.

Robert Byron

(1905–41)

English historian, art critic and traveller. His *Road to Oxiana*, a search for the origins of Islamic architecture in Persia and Afghanistan in 1932, is a classic of travel writing. Byron travelled as far as China and Tibet and wrote four other books. He was killed when his ship was torpedoed in the Mediterranean in 1941.

A weird little town in Greece

6 August 1926, The Holy Mountain
At last, after a year's planning, I am here, and the suitcase. It is too wonderful for words – this long narrow peninsula – and a single wooded range of mountains stretching out into the sea – and ending suddenly in a terrific peak, six thousand feet high – with clouds wreathing round it – all around the fresh green of the gardens of the monasteries, the woods of planes and Spanish chestnut – and the sea, an ethereal silvery blue, like the wing of a butterfly, always visible.

Hay has met us. We arrived at Daphni, the little port, at six this morning – and were greeted by Peter Bonifacious, formerly Archimandrite of Jerusalem, who has a divorced wife in Athens, whom he visits now and then. Our breakfast consisted of liqueurs like fire, watermelon and tea – which he had already sugared! Then we got three mules, heaved the suitcases and the Gladstone bag – containing insect spray, 8 tins of sardines, 2 of tongue, 2 of paté de foie gras, marching chocolate, cooking stove etc. on to it – and getting on the others set off on a 3 hour ride to Caryes, the capital. A weird little town with beggars and half-witted monks lying about the tiny streets – one or two shops kept by monks, and not a woman or a child, not a hen, a cow, a dog nor female cat to be seen.

Lunch with an Abbot

Grace completed, we sat down. The abbot took the head of the table opposite Father Stephen. On his left was myself, followed by Mark and David; on his right an *epitropos* and Father Barlaam, between whom were placed a priest from the mainland and a layman, plump and moustached. The assistant guest-master, towering over the table with eyes lifted in eternal protestation, waited. The light was localised by two lamps, one warm and incompetent, the other cold and bright, which cast the farther side of the room into total blackness.

A certain stiffness pervaded the meal. The abbot, though human and pleasantly inclined, was none the less an abbot. Each dish was placed before him first, with a bow. Once in five minutes he addressed a remark to the company. After an attempt to initiate conversation by remarking, in the voice of a practised *raconteur*, that we had been to the top, I thought it better to wait till I was spoken to. The layman attempted to fill the gap. But, having learnt his English in the United States, was troubled by our inability to understand it.

"You pronounce different," he said.

"Yes, we do."

"I ran over Canada once. Friend mine had lill mo'-cycle. Fine place. Now do business here – buy wood from monks. Make no money in Greece"; and he shrugged his shoulders and jerked down the corners of his mouth as Greeks do to denote disgust. He was a pleasant example of a type which, being compounded of the most conceited mentality and the most democratic manners on earth, is as repulsive as anything that humanity has yet achieved.

Edmund d'Auvergne

(fl. 1909)

French writer. *The Nightside of Paris* is a delightful evo-
cation of Paris in its *fin-de-siècle* heyday.

The Can-Can at Bullier's

The students still dance at Bullier's. That far-famed dancing-hall is at
the far end of the Boul' Miche, in the Avenue de l'Observatoire, opposite
the Closerie des Lilas, where they danced in Albert Smith's day. The
exterior is like that of a country circus, gaudily painted with representations of the joys awaiting you within. You may shake a leg here on
Thursdays, Saturdays and Sundays – the first day preferably, when the
femmes chics of the Quartier appear to advantage in the mazy dance.
They don't come the other days, being too busy with their rich patrons
from the Rive Droite at the Harcourt and Panthéon. You drive up to
the entrance and find a crowd collected who will audibly criticise your
appearance and especially that of your lady friend with candour and
vivacity. You may be surprised to find that the delightful little lady who
has honoured you with her company is hailed by name as a well-known
personage by the bystanders. "There's Berthe!" they will exclaim, "and
what's that she has got with her?" Berthe, annoyed by these indiscretions,
will hurry you into the hall, where you pay your two francs and surrender
your stick or umbrella to the harpies in attendance, you need not trouble
to remove your hat. The rather low hall is divided lengthwise by a row
of columns; on one side is the orchestra, on another the usual terrace
for those taking refreshments; on a third side the open arcades give
directly on the garden. Crossing the floor you find yourself in a whirling,
screaming, kicking mass of humanity. Who are these people – students?
Well, only a minority. A great number of the men are clearly of the
clerk and shop-assistant types. Still the student element gives a *cachet*
to the place. Among them we notice an American who does not speak
a word of French, but makes himself quite at home. You engage him

in conversation. He arrived only an hour ago from Rome, he tells you, and came here right away without troubling to look for rooms. He guesses he'll find some after the show anyway, and – "Say! what fine girls these are anyhow!" They are, indeed, and among them we recognise several familiar faces from the cafés down the road. But mingled with these are the *demi-semi-mondaines* – shop-girls and clerks in search of profitable adventures, but not yet having acquired the bold allures of their professional rivals. As at the Tabarin a great many of the girls are dancing together, lifting their skirts higher and higher, and drawing them closer and closer, till you are forcibly reminded of the hosiers' advertisements in the ladies' papers.

James Cameron

(1911–85)

British journalist. Cameron travelled widely as a foreign correspondent reporting on events such as the Chinese invasion of Tibet, the atomic bomb tests on the Bikini Atoll in 1946 and the Vietnam War. Despite these experiences, his memoirs remain vivid and amusing.

The Daiti Hotel, Tirana

The hotel in Tirana stood off the main boulevard behind a belt of evergreens. It was unexpectedly grand. Like almost everything else of any pretension in town, it had clearly been built by the Italians in an expansive mood, but it had long ago acquired the colourless antiseptic cheerlessness of all Popular Democratic hotels. This is very difficult to define; it has something to do with a dim economy of underpowered electric bulbs, and immobility of elevators, a dusty emptiness of show-cases, a greyness of table linen, an absence of servants, and a super-fluity of unidentifiable shadowy functionaries who are clearly neither staff nor guests. These characteristics are, in my experience, shared by all hotels in the Communist economy, and are explicable in the simple fact that, as befits their function in societies where people circulate only on specific instructions, they have long since changed from hotels to institutions.

However, the Daiti Hotel in Tirana put on as fair a show of hospitality as was permitted by its manifest lack of practice. To deny by implication the travellers' tales that Albania is a country of unexampled filthiness, the place reeked of floor polish and germicide. I was given a large, dispiriting, but spotless room with a most elaborate bathroom, complete with bidet, most certainly a memento of the Italian occupation. The profusion of taps and faucets emitted a series of hollow clanks and groans, but no water. Of the set of five wall switches, one alone was operational, producing a thin subaqueous light.

It was unfair to blame Albania, of all places, for an inadequacy with tourists – even tourists as spurious as we. And yet the peculiar fact was that Albania really did affect to believe that it *was* a tourist centre. The bleak lobby of the hotel was littered with leaflets and brochures extolling the virtues of its *richesses archéologiques*, its *culture artistique*, its *vie sociale*, its *traditions etynographiques*. Some of them looked as though they had been there for centuries. They were printed in several languages – German, French, Russian, Italian. To produce an English version was presumably pointless. Americans are neither sought nor, indeed, permitted, and there have been no relations whatever with Britain since 1946, when Albania inconsiderately mined a couple of British destroyers in the Corfu Channel.

Lawrence Durrell

(1912–90)

Writer and poet. Worked as a press attaché in Greece, Cairo, Alexandria and Cyprus, and travelled widely. His *Alexandria Quartet* evoked life in Egypt under British rule.

Delphi

Among these ancient sites Delphi is the most grandiose, as well as the most sphingine; the long winding roads leading away north from Livadia coil like the sacred serpent. The landscape, curled inwards upon itself, reveals itself only in snatches; the mountain ranges come up and recede, recline and rise up. It is almost as if the dose had been one measured by ancient physicians who built this road towards the centre of the earth – towards that mysterious omphalos which I first found as a boy, lying in an open field above the road. I still have an impertinent picture of myself, leaning negligently against it as if at a bar . . . But among so many visits to Delphi I have never found the slightest variation in the impression it makes on me; the latest was last year, after an absence from Greece of nearly twenty years. What is this strange impression? As I have said, each site in Greece has its singular emanation: Mycenae, for example, is ominous and grim – like the castle where Macbeth is laid. It is a place of tragedy, and blood. One doesn't get this from its history and myths – they merely confirm one's sensation of physical unease. Watch the people walking around the site. They are afraid that the slightest slip and they may fall into a hole in the ground, and break a leg. It is a place of rich transgressions, tears, and insanity. A few miles away lies dream-saturated Epidaurus, so lax and so quiet; one would not dare to be ill for long if one lived there. Its innocence is provoking. But Delphi . . . The heart rises as the road rises and as the great scarps of mountain rise on either side; the air becomes chill. Finally, round the last corner, there she is in her eyrie like a golden eagle, her claws clamped around the blood-coloured rock which falls away with vertiginous certainty to the dry bed of the Pleistos. The long thrilling sweep of the olive groves – greener than anywhere in Greece – is like the sudden sweep of strings in some great symphony.

Hilary Sumner-Boyd

(1913–76) and John Freely (1926–)

Academics from the University of the Bosphorus at Istanbul, and writers on Turkey, its history and monuments. Published in 1972, *Strolling Through Istanbul* was the first portable guide to the city. Only the most vigorous of guide book compilers would face up to the mountainous task of carrying out what they threatened to do – uncover the city from the Galata Bridge to the last stroll, at the fishing village of Kumkapi. There are twenty-three itineraries, taking from an hour or two to a day to complete.

The ancient hans of Istanbul

A little farther up Çakmakçilar Yokuşu and on the opposite side we come to the entrance to the grandest and most interesting of all the hans in the city, the Valide Hani. This han was built by the Sultan Valide Kösem shortly before her death in 1651, apparently on the site of an older palace founded by Cerrah Mehmet Paşa. We enter through a great gateway into the first courtyard, small and irregularly shaped because of the alignment of the han relative to the street outside. From there we pass into the main court a vast area 55 metres square surrounded by a double-tiered arcade, the innumerable chambers of which are now given over to every conceivable form of industry and commerce. Although the entire han is now in a state of appalling squalor and dilapidation, it is nonetheless still impressive and extremely colourful. In the centre of the courtyard there is a little mosque (recently rebuilt) which for many years has been the property of Persians of the Shiite sect of Islam. (The Turks are Sunni Moslems.) The Valide Hani has for long been the headquarters for Persians living in Istanbul, and indeed, many of them still have shops in the han itself. Each year, on the twenty-third day of the month Muharrem, the Persians used to congregate in the Valide Hani in mournful commemoration of the battle of Kerbala in the year

638, weeping and flagellating themselves while the imam recites to them the tragic story of the martyrdom of Hüseyin, grandson of the Prophet.

A vaulted tunnel leads from a corner of the main court into the inner court, which because of the lie of the land is set at a lower level than the rest of the han. This court now houses a weaving-mill. At the back of this courtyard we see the remains of a Byzantine tower which is built into the structure of the han. This has traditionally been called the Tower of Eirene and is thought to date from the middle Byzantine period, but the evidence for this is very uncertain. This tower appears as a prominent feature of the city skyline in the drawing made by Melchio Lorichs in 1559, where it is shown much taller than it is at present. The lower room of the tower is part of the weaving mill which occupies this part of the han, while the upper room is fitted out as a mosque with a pretty ribbed dome; the mosque is now disaffected and serves as a storage room.

It was in this han, or rather in the palace which preceded it on the same site, that was established one of the first printing presses in the city. This was set up in 1567 by one Apkar from Sivas, who went to Venice to procure type in the Armenian script. This was not *the* first printing press in the city, however, for the local Jews had a press as early as 1494, the Greeks not till 1624, the Turks only in 1727, although books in Turkish had been printed long before this time in western Europe.

Once past the church we turn right and take the road which leads down toward the sea. As we do so we are confronted almost immediately with an interesting view of a vast double hamam. It is astonishing how many domes of all sizes and arranged apparently at random these hamams have, and it is not often that one can get a good view of them from above. This one is called Ağa Hamami and is a work of Sinan. It is unfortunately disaffected and ruinous, used partly as a storage depot, partly as a workshop for tempering copper. The workshop is installed in what was once the hararet of the bath, a typical cruciform room with cubicles in the corners, now much blackened by the smoke of the furnace; but it is interesting to watch the great sheets of red-hot copper being taken from the furnace and immersed in a pool of cool water.

Norman Lewis

(1908–2003)

English writer and traveller who has covered most of the globe, and written many very fine travel books. *A Dragon Apparent* is about Indo-China before its devastation by decades of war. *Naples '44* is considered one of the best books about the Second World War.

The Catacombs of San Gennaro, Naples

Of the two networks of catacombs under Naples, the principal one, which concerned us, is entered from the back of the church of San Gennaro. These catacombs are believed to date from the first century, and consist of four galleries, excavated one below the other, each gallery having numerous ramifications and lateral passages. The two nethermost galleries having partially fallen in, they have not been accessible in modern times.

It was decided to enter the catacombs shortly after dawn, and we arrived at the church in a dozen jeeps, lavishly equipped with gear of the kind used in cave-exploration, as well as all the usual weaponry. The monks in charge were already up and about, and showed us extreme hostility. One monk who planted himself, arms outstretched, at the entrance to the catacombs had to be removed by force, and then, when we went in, followed us, keeping up a resounding denunciation of our desecration of a holy place.

The Americans had equipped themselves with lamps like miniature searchlights; these shone on the walls of the ante-rooms through which we passed to reach the galleries, showing them to be so closely covered with frescoes – mostly in excellent condition after sixteen centuries – as to give the impression of colossal ikons. We were instantly confronted with the purpose for which the catacombs had been designed. Rows of niches forming burial chambers had been cut one above the other in the walls, and all these were crammed with skeletons, many said to have been plague victims of the sixteenth century. When somebody picked up a skull to examine it the angry monk trudging at our heels roared at him to put it back. Questioned about the possibility of Germans being in the catacombs, this man answered in an evasive and suspicious way.

It soon became clear that we were looking for a needle in a haystack. We were in narrow, bone-choked streets, with innumerable side turnings to be explored, each with its many dark chambers in any one of which our quarry could have hidden, or from which they could have suddenly sprung out to ambush us, if they were still alive. These men, had they gone into the catacombs – and we were all still convinced they had – must have been in the darkness for nearly a fortnight since their torch batteries had finally given out. After which, groping their way, or crawling about among the bones, they would have encountered terrible hazards. Even in the second gallery we came suddenly to a black chasm. In the depths of this, where the whole roadway from wall to wall had caved in, the lights showed us a pile of dust from which protruded a few ancient rib-bones. We dangled a microphone into this pit and listened while the monk muttered at our backs, but the silence below was absolute.

Patrick Leigh Fermor

(1915–)

English writer and traveller who has spent much of his life living in the Balkans and the Greek archipelago. At the age of eighteen, he walked from Holland to Constantinople, and wrote about the experience in *A Time of Gifts* and *Between the Woods and the Water*, quoted here. During the Second World War he helped to organise the Greek resistance in Crete, and afterwards travelled to the Caribbean and produced his classic book, *The Traveller's Tree*.

The Marches of Transylvania

When the evening train from Budapest arrived, I had been hanging about the station platform at Lökösháza since noon and by the time I had climbed in and the red-white-and-green Hungarian flag had disappeared, night had fallen.

This borderland was the most resented frontier in Europe and recent conversations in Hungary had cloaked it with an added shadow of menace. Well, I thought, at least I have nothing to declare . . . I sat up with a jerk in the corner of the empty carriage: what about that automatic pistol? Seeing myself being led to a cell, I dug the little unwanted weapon out of the bottom of my rucksack and undid the flap of the leather case; the smallness, the lightness and the mother-of-pearl-plated stock made it look like a toy. Should I steal away from these bare wooden seats and hide it in the first-class upholstery next door? Or slip it behind the cistern in the lavatory? Or simply chuck it out into No-Man's-Land? In the end I hid it in a thick fold in the bottom corner of my greatcoat, fixed it there with three safety-pins, put the guilty garment on the rack and sat underneath with pounding heart as the train crawled through the moonlight.

In a few miles we reached the border and the blue-yellow-and-red flag of the Rumanian frontier post. Above the desk inside hung a photograph of King Carol in a white-plumed helmet, a steel breastplate and a white cloak with a cross on the shoulder. Another frame showed Prince Michael, a nice-looking boy in a white jersey with large, soft eyes and thick, neatly brushed hair; he had also been a king during a three years' abdication by his father. It was a relief and rather an anticlimax when the yawning official stamped my passport without a single glance at my stuff. The battered document still shows the date: *Curtici 27 April 1934*, the sixth frontier of my journey.

John Horne Burns

(1916–53)

American writer and teacher. His book *The Gallery* is an
account of life in Naples in 1944–5, after the Italian collapse.

The Galleria

There's an arcade in Naples that they call the Galleria Umberto Primo. It's
a cross between a railroad station and a church. You think you're in a
museum till you see the bars and the shops. Once this Galleria had a dome
of glass, but the bombings of Naples shattered this skylight, and tinkling
glass fell like cruel snow to the pavement. But life went on in the Galleria.
In August, 1944, it was the unofficial heart of Naples. It was a living and
subdividing cell of vermouth, Allied soldiery, and the Italian people.

Everybody in Naples came to the Galleria Umberto. At night the flags,
the columns, the archangels blowing their trumpets on the cornices, the
metal grids that held the glass before the bombs broke it heard more
than they saw in the daytime. There was the pad of American combat
boots on the prowl, the slide of Neapolitan sandals, the click of British
hobnails out of rhythm from vermouth. There were screams and coos
and slaps and stumbles. There were the hasty press of kisses and sibilance
of urine on the pavement. By moonlight, shadows singly and in pairs
chased from corner to corner.

David James

(1919–86)

During the Second World War, James served in naval motor
torpedo boats. He was captured and imprisoned at Marlag
near Hamburg. He wrote an exciting account of his escape.

Danzig, spring 1944

Danzig in the spring of 1944 had an atmosphere quite unlike that of any other German town I visited. It was not unlike that of Edinburgh, for both had been left untouched by the destruction of war. Like Edinburgh, Danzig had been, during the course of five years' hostilities, the recipient of about four bombs, of which the inhabitants were inordinately proud. There was just that little bit more in the shop windows, too, and an outward air of prosperity, though in the case of Danzig this was largely fictitious, for their wares were only for display.

As I walked up the broad, cobbled streets, with their set-back painted facades and with trams squeezing under the low brick arches, I found it hard to believe that this was the match that had set Europe alight. The only reminder of war was the current anti-espionage campaign. In every shop window, on every page of every paper, was the silhouette of a sinister figure in black. These were displayed throughout the whole of Germany and afforded me particular pleasure, for I, too, was dressed completely in black, and hitherto nobody had attempted to stop me.

Near the station I found a very nice little restaurant. My beer was brought to me in a litre mug instead of the usual tooth-glass, and a waiter in tails showed me with deference to a sofa table. There were well-dressed people about, including girls with make-up. All this was quite unlike anything else I had seen in Germany, and even the bowl of *Stamm* tasted better. If anyone cares to spend a week travelling third class, sleeping every night in the Paddington waiting-room, and then goes to, say, Claridges, he will readily understand my sudden upwelling of spirits.

In the afternoon I resolved to carry my search farther afield. Walking down to the docks I overtook a French POW in a comparatively empty street. I stopped him and asked for a match. While he was producing it I told him hurriedly who I was and asked his advice on where I should find a ship. He showed no surprise, but directed me to the French stevedores' camp some two miles distant. He said they would put me up, feed me, and find me a suitable ship in due course. Then, with a "*Vive les Alliés!*" he was gone.

Walking to the camp, my feet grew increasingly sore. It needed a great effort of will not to limp, but I thought it might cause suspicion.

Nearing the French camp I fell in with two more Frenchmen. Their welcome was less friendly. They assured me that it was impossible to keep me in their camp for things had been tightened up. As for Swedish ships – that, too, was very difficult. No, they knew of none at that minute. Had I tried the workmen in the goods yard? Perhaps they could help. Where could I sleep? There was a good hay-barn down the road, about a mile away, on the left-hand side.

Suddenly I realised that I was almost beyond making it. I had enough money left for one meal. I could go to the barn hungry and have a feed next morning, or I could have a hot dinner that evening and look forward to nothing later. It was well below freezing-point again, so it was doubtful whether I could last longer than one more day. It seemed highly doubtful whether this extra day would materially alter the shipping situation. But I could reasonably expect help aboard one of the Danish ships, and there was no logical reason why they should not be going to Sweden. I decided it would be better to board one that evening, while I still had sufficient reserves of strength, rather than to wait an extra day, when fatigue and cold might well reduce me below the level of taking adequate precautions.

Tony Davies

(1920–)

English writer and general practitioner. He served in the Honourable Artillery Company during the Second World War and was captured in North Africa. Davies made a daring jump from a train at night on his way to a prison camp in Italy, but was recaptured. At the Armistice, he and two companions walked the entire length of the Apennines before being captured a third time. He and I met in a prison camp in Italy, and again in Germany and Czechoslovakia.

A daring escape

This waiting was the worst part of the whole business, and as I sat in my corner with as much composure as I could muster, my knees felt like water and my stomach quite hollow. Time and again I was convinced that the ideal spot had arrived and was just tensing myself to leap when with a 'woosh' and a sigh the train plunged under a bridge or into a tunnel. After each of these episodes I had a distinct vision of my body hurtling against the bridge parapet, or falling like a sack into the river bed hundreds of feet below. Eventually I was sweating with apprehension and could happily have called the whole thing off.

All this time the train had been climbing into the mountains at a steady thirty miles an hour; but now, to our horror, we felt her start to accelerate. That could only mean we were on a down gradient. If we were going to jump at all, now was the time. I kicked the chap next to me, who was in on the plan. He rose and offered the sentry a cigarette. Standing with his back to us, he struck a match and shielded it in his cupped hands while he and the sentry lit up. Mike tapped my boot, and, in one movement, pulled down the window and was gone. I followed. As I heaved myself over the window and hung there by my hands for a second, I had a momentary view of the sentry's face as the match illuminated it. Then, pushing hard with my legs against the side of the carriage, I dropped. In the next few seconds I hit the ground at least twice, rolled over and over and eventually came to rest in the middle of a small road that ran beside the track. I picked myself up and tore up the hillside – scrambling over rocks and falling through bushes – and even as I did so I heard the scream of the wheels on metal as the engine braked, and the shots from the sentries. The soldiers on the flat van at the rear of the train must have seen us go.

Frank Tatchell

(*fl.* 1920)

English clergyman, the Vicar of Midhurst, Sussex. His charming book *The Happy Traveller: A Book for Poor Men*, published in 1923, suggests that he must have been something of an absentee vicar. His book was one of the inspirations of my own youth and must have lured innumerable Britons from their hearths in search of new horizons.

France

Few men are more to be envied than a young and eager traveller, just landed in France with the summer before him and no need to worry about his tiny share of the world's money. He will not need very much, owing to the thriftiness of the people and the cheapness of living. The price of a bed at an *auberge*, the village inn with the familiar sign *Ici on loge à pied et à cheval*, is very cheap (before the War it was 75c.), and though the sheets may be a little rough, they are usually spotlessly clean. The welcome at these natty inns is warm and pleasing once the *patronne* has looked you up and down and satisfied herself as to your respectability; the excellence of the cooking is proverbial, and I know no country where a poor man has better fare at so small a cost. If you are at a loss where to eat in a town, follow some decent-looking workman, about noon, and lunch at the little restaurant which he patronizes. The French are experts at serving meals at odd hours at very short notice, and, failing an omelette and a cutlet, an emergency meal of bread and white wine can be had anywhere. I usually buy the little cheeses sold at the country markets and like to have a pocketful of raisins (*mendiants*) to munch on the road. In the autumn you can pick as many blackberries as you like, since the French do not care for them and leave them for the birds and wasps.

A walk in Touraine

From Blois, a picturesque old city with steep and narrow streets cut into innumerable steps and with a famous bridge, take the road to Cheverny, a village with a delightful castle. Go by train to Onzaine and stroll through the park to Chaumont and Amboise, where you best realize the grandeur of the Loire. Walk along the river to Tours (where you should drink *Vouvray*, a white, sparkling wine) and notice the jumble of old houses and the painted glass in the Cathedral. The patterns of the windows here and at Chartres are thought to have been copied from the carpets which the Crusaders brought home. The way which I suggest now goes to Langeais, where you should sit at the little Café Rabelais and admire the old fortifications, then across the river to Azay le Rideau, one of the prettiest places in France, and so to Chinon.

A walk in Provence

Go in April when the orchards and water-meadows are carpeted with narcissi, and irises cumber the roadside with their purple masses. The roads in this part of France have not the usual bordering of grass and avenues of poplars, but are *provençal*, with a canal at the side and many plane trees. The towns have narrow streets of high houses, shutting out the fierce sun, and the scenery is wild and melancholy. There is occasionally a vile wind from the North called the *Mistral*, or *vent magistral*, because it makes you turn round. Try a glass of *Armagnac*, the "cognac" of the country south of the Garonne.

Start from Tarascon, and go east to St Rémy-en-Provence, a very jolly little town with a market on Wednesdays. Now turn south and go up five miles through fine gorges to Les Baux, a "dead" town with a handful of Greek-blooded inhabitants, the very scene of Dante's "Inferno". A straight desolate road of twenty-five miles goes down the south slope of the Alpilles to Arles (market day Saturday), south-west of which city there is a sandy marsh, the haunt of flamingoes and water fowl, of which stretch a mere glimpse is sufficient. Go by train from Arles to Martigues, have a dish of *bouillabasse* at the hotel, which was once a convent, and walk along the charming corniche road to

Marseilles. Another time start from Aix en Provence and take the delightful road through Trets to Brignoles. It runs amid pines and little friendly mountains, and ends at Fréjus. You should also walk along the *Corniche d'Esterel* between Agay (east of St Raphael) and Le Trayas and along the *corniche* road between Nice and Menton. On the rest of the French Riviera the sea-front is in most places obstructed by dog-in-the-manger villas, but the hinterland from Fréjus to Grasse is unspoilt.

Jan Morris

(1926–)

Welsh writer, historian of the British Empire, and world traveller. She accompanied the successful 1953 expedition to Everest as a *Times* reporter, and subsequently wrote a superb book about Venice. There have been numerous works on travel and history since then.

Seen from the Lagoon

Silent islands lie all about, lapped in marsh and mud-bank. Here is a glowering octagonal fort, here a gaunt abandoned lighthouse. A mesh of nets patterns the walls of a fishermen's islet, and a restless covey of boats nuzzles its water-gate. From the ramparts of an island barracks a listless soldier with his cap over his eyes waves half-heartedly out of his sentry-box. Two savage dogs bark and rage from a broken villa. There is a flicker of lizards on a wall. Sometimes a country smell steals across the water, of cows or hay or fertilizer: and sometimes there flutters in the wake of the boat, not an albatross, but a butterfly.

Presently this desolate place quickens, and smart white villas appear upon the reef. The hump of a great hotel protrudes above the trees, gay parasols ornament a café. A trim passenger steamer flurries southward, loaded deep. A fishing flotilla streams workmanlike towards the open sea. To the west, beneath a smudge of mountains, there is a thin silver gleam of oil drums, and a suggestion of smoke. A yellow barge, piled

177

high with pop bottles, springs from a landing-stage like a cheerful dove from an ark. A white yacht sidles indolently by. Three small boys have grounded their boat on a sand-bank, and are throwing slobbery mud at each other. There is a flash of oxy-acetylene from a dark shed, and a barge stands on stilts outside a boat yard. A hooter sounds; a bell booms nobly; a big white seabird settles heavily upon a post; and thus the navigator, rounding a promontory, sees before him a city.

It is very old, and very grand, and bent-backed. Its towers survey the lagoon in crotchety splendour, some leaning one way, some another. Its skyline is elaborate with campaniles, domes, pinnacles, cranes, riggings, television aerials, crenellations, eccentric chimneys and a big red grain elevator. There are glimpses of flags and fretted rooftops, marble pillars, cavernous canals. An incessant bustle of boats passes before the quays of the place; a great white liner slips towards its port; a multitude of tottering palaces, brooding and monstrous, presses towards its waterfront like so many invalid aristocrats jostling for fresh air. It is a gnarled but gorgeous city: and as the boat approaches through the last church-crowned islands, and a jet fighter screams splendidly out of the sun, so the whole scene seems to shimmer – with pinkness, with age, with self-satisfaction, with sadness, with delight.

The navigator stows away his charts and puts on a gay straw hat: for he has reached that paragon among landfalls, Venice.

Bruce Chatwin

(1940–89)

English traveller and writer. Chatwin made his name with *In Patagonia* (1977), and went on to write books set in Africa, Australia, Wales, and in Prague; some were fact, some fiction, others somewhere between the two. All reflected the esoteric range of his interests.

Madeleine Vionnet

Madeleine Vionnet is an alert and mischievous old lady of ninety-six with eighty-six years of practical experience in the art of dressmaking . . .

Today she lives in the Seizième Arrondissement, in a street top-heavy with apartment buildings from the Belle Epoque. The facade of her house is adorned with swags of fruit and metal balconies in the heaviest bourgeois taste. Once through the door, however, you enter a world of aluminium grilles, sand-blasted walls, mirror glass and sleek lacquer surfaces: an interior as clean-cut and unsentimental as Madame Vionnet herself.

'I have nothing old in my house. Everything is modern. I did it all myself.'

Like a Vionnet dress, this is spareness achieved expensively. When she moved here in 1929 the rooms were quickly purged of meaningless ornament. Even the sepia family photographs were ripped from their frames, sandwiched between sheets of plate-glass, and hung on walls that were otherwise free of pictures.

Squares of natural parchment line the salon. 'Each one a sheepskin!' she laughs. 'You see, I am a shepherdess.' The room is said to be the most exceptional art deco interior in Paris to have survived – with its owner – intact. There are fur-covered sofas, chromium chairs up-holstered in white leather and tables of scarlet lacquer, the colour of Buddhist temples in Japan. The fireplace is of sheet copper, silvered. On it stands a photo of the Parthenon: a talismanic photo, for Madame Vionnet has always turned to Classical Greece for inspiration. Her portrait, resting on an easel, was painted by Jean Dunand, the 'lacquer master' of the 1920s. The face is made from a mosaic of the minutest chips of eggshell.

Philip Mansel

(1951–)

English historian of the historic courts of Europe.

Janissaries

Constantinople was a battleground not only between different embassics, nationalities and religions, but also between the Sultan and his guard. Between them was a shifting balance of fear and need, power and weakness, blood and gold – until, at the end of the empire, the last Sultan fled under protection of a foreign guard. The cause of the soldiers' power was the absence of independent civilian institutions. In an absolute monarchy barriers against political intervention by the armed forces are weakened. As Suetonius wrote of the Praetorian Guard: '*Quis custodiet ipsos custodes?*' ('Who is to guard the guards themselves?') On eight occasions in Russia between 1725 and 1825, units in the Imperial Guard decided who should rule as monarch or regent. Napoleon also felt the danger. He said: 'Palace troops are terrifying and become more dangerous as the sovereign becomes more autocratic,' and advised other monarchs to avoid them.

The principal military force in Constantinople were the janissaries. The janissaries were composed of 196 *ortas*, or units, in theory of 100 men each. In the sixteenth century they formed one of the most effective armed forces in Europe, and certainly the best fed, enjoying regular rations of soup, mutton and rice. Food played such a central part in their life that the commander of each *orta* had the title *corbaci*, or soup cook, and as a sign of his rank wore a soup ladle hanging from his belt. Each *orta* had its own flag, displaying such symbols as a lion, a mosque, a pulpit or a ship. Janissaries wore uniforms of blue cloth and a majestic pleated white head-dress like a giant sleeve, sometimes decorated with plumes and jewels. When janissaries bowed their heads at the same time, they were compared to a field of ripe corn rippling in the breeze.

The sixtieth, sixty-first, sixty-second and sixty-third *ortas* composed the Sultan's personal bodyguard, known as *solaks*. Their ample plumed head-dresses made the Sultan appear to be floating on clouds as he road to mosque. Other *ortas* also had specific palace duties. The sixty-fourth was responsible for the Sultan's hunting dogs, the sixty-ninth for his greyhounds and falcons. Janissaries also, with the Bostancis, acted as the policemen, fire watchers and customs officials of the capital. They were responsible for checking the identity of immigrants coming into the city, or expelling recent immigrants when the Sultan considered the city overcrowded. The complex of janissary barracks between the Suleymaniye mosque and the Golden Horn was one of the power-centres of the city, together with the palace, the Porte, the mosques, the patri-archate and the embassies. Their supreme commander, the Aga of the janissaries, lived there in a palace so splendid that Suleyman the Magnificent once sighed: 'If I could be the Aga of the Janissaries for just forty days!'

Charlotte Hobson

(1970–)

English writer. She spent a year as a student in the town of Voronezh, 500 kilometres south east of Moscow, while the Soviet Union collapsed around her. *Black Earth City* recounts her experiences.

Hobson's choice

The hostel had a well-deserved reputation for low morals. In its defence, however, it must be said that a sexual revolution was taking place all over Russia. The Communist regime was prudish in the extreme. Of course men had affairs, that was normal, but women were expected to behave nicely – not smoke in public, for example, or wear short skirts. As for any hint of open licentiousness, despite what went on behind the scenes in Party dachas – it was considered antisocial and dealt with severely.

Now, suddenly, the controls disappeared and seventy years of pent-up desire burst onto the streets. Voronezh at that time was far more liberal than London. Pornographic magazines and crotchless knickers were for sale at every bus stop. The morning news programme might show a woman giving birth, and soft porn dominated the airwaves in the evening. Even the babushkas exchanged their string shopping bags for new, Polish-made plastic with naked lovelies on each side.

The Proletariat cinema on Revolution Prospect, meanwhile, revelling in its new freedom, dug out all the films it had not been allowed to show and billed them as 'classics' and 'great entertainment for all'. The selection was unpredictable. *Night Porter*, in a fuzzy seventies print that made Dirk Bogarde's face look orange, caused its final sensation here in Voronezh where it was advertised on a huge hand-painted board as 'New! Shocking! Erotica!' One week there would be a season of Fellini or Buñuel; the next you might find yourself watching *Caligula*, probably the only movie that Sir John Gielgud made in association with Penthouse Films. I was left with the distinct feeling that Sir John had not been shown this version of the film, in which chunks of soft porn had been spliced alongside the cinematic Ancient Rome that is familiar to us all. Billed as 'educational' and screened by the Proletariat at seven o'clock on a weekday, it played to the usual crowd of middle-aged couples on an evening out. Half an hour into the film, there were so many people walking out that you couldn't see the screen. Not everybody approved of the new climate.

In the Voronezh papers there was an air of bewilderment. Where had all this filth sprung from? How was it that a poll of teenage girls, who five years previously had held only one ambition – to be Lenin's little helper – now answered overwhelmingly that when they were grown up, they wanted to be a hard-currency prostitute? For the time being, however, even the most choleric voices tailed away into resignation. It was inevitable, after all, that Western decadence would arrive along with glasnost, said the pessimistic characters in the butter queue. They're only young, rejoined others comfortably. Let them enjoy themselves while they can. Lord knows we did just the same, although it was all a secret back then.

Great Britain and Ireland

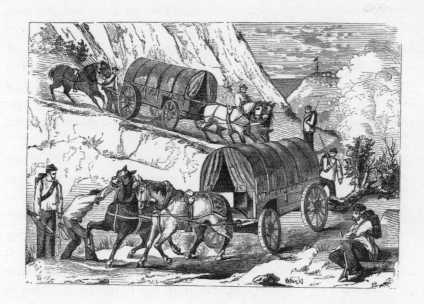

Peter Mundy

(fl. 1600–67)

English traveller of indefatigable curiosity who travelled
all over Europe and the Far East.

A camera obscura on the Strand, 1636

Alsoe att Sir Henry Moodies, lyeing in the Strand, one of his gentlemen
shewed mee divers conceipts [devices, inventions] of his Masters.
Amonge the rest, the roome being made quite darke, only one little
hole in it with a glasse through which a light strooke to the opposite
side, where was placed white paper, and thereon was represented, as in
a glasse, all that was without, as Boates roweing on the Thames, men
rideinge on the other side, trees, etts., but all reversed or upside downe,
in their true Collours.

A snail storm at Weymouth, 1635

Weymouth Snailes.
When I came over to Weymouth side, I found on the grass a multitude
of small Coulord shells ½ as bigg as pease. The people report they dropp
out of the Ayre, findeing them on their hatts as they walke the fields.
The like is reported of the raineing of small froggs in the Isle of Jersy
(where I had formerly bene). My brother also told mee that neere
Weymouth hee himselfe saw one of theis walking Fires called Ignis
fatuus, which only Crosse[d] his way without any more hurt. The naturall Cawses of theis things must be left to the decision of the Learned,
as also of that light which is reported to appear on Shipps in or after

stormes, termed by the Spaniard St Elmo; heere being of our Company that have seene them, gon to them and found a Jelly or froth, which soe shined by night, stickinge on their Mast Yards, etts.

John Evelyn

(1620–1706)

Writer, diarist and public figure, Evelyn turned his attention to many subjects from coins to trees. His advocacy of reforestation in *Sylva* guaranteed the future of the British Navy. He travelled abroad during the English Civil War, carrying ciphered messages for the Royalists, and marrying the ambassador's daughter in Paris. He became a public servant at the Restoration, and the first secretary of the Royal Society. His property at Sayes Court was wrecked by his tenant Peter the Great who came to inspect the shipyards at Deptford. One of the world's great diarists, he witnessed the Plague, the Great Fire of London, and claimed to have discovered the master woodcarver Grinling Gibbons.

The Thames frozen

[1684. January 1] My Daughter Susan had some few small pox come forth on her, so as I sent her out of the Family; The Weather continuing intollerably severe, so as streetes of Boothes were set up upon the Thames etc: and the aire so very cold and thick, as of many yeares there had not ben the like: The small pox being very mortal, many feared a worse Contagion to follow etc:

2 I dined at Sir St: Foxes, after dinner came a fellow that eate live charcoale glowingly ignited, quenching them in his mouth, and then champing and swallowing them downe: There was a dog also that seemed to do many rational actions. . .

6 i went home to Says-Court to see my Grandson, it being extreame

hard weather, and return'd the next-day by Coach the river being quite frozen up:

9 I went crosse the Thames upon the Ice (which was now become so incredibly thick, as to beare not onely whole streetes of boothes in which the[y] roasted meate, and had divers shops of wares, quite crosse as in a Towne, but Coaches and carts and horses passed over): So I went from Westminster stayers to Lambeth and dined with my L. Archbishop, where I met my Lord Bruce, Sir Geo. Wheeler, Coll: Coock and severall Divines; after dinner, and discourse with his Grace 'til Evening prayer, Sir Geo: and I returnd, walking over the Ice from Lambeth stayres to the Horse Ferry, and thence walked on foote to our Lodgings: 10: I visited Sir Rob: Reading, where after supper we had musique, but none comparable to that which Mrs Bridgeman made us upon the Gittar, which she master'd with such extraordinary skill, and dexterity, as I hardly ever heard any lute exceede for sweetnesse.

Bull-baiting on Ice

24 The frost still continuing more and more severe, the Thames before London was planted with bothes in formal streets, as in a Citty, or Continual faire, all sorts of Trades and shops furnished, and full of Commodities, even to a Printing presse, where the People and Ladys tooke a fansy to have their names Printed and the day and yeare set downe, when printed on the Thames: This humour tooke so universaly, that 'twas estimated the Printer gained five pound a day, for printing a line onely, at six-pence a name, besides what he gott by Ballads etc: Coaches now plied from Westminster to the Temple, and from severall other staires too and froo, as in the streets; also on sleds, sliding with skeetes; There was likewise Bull-baiting, Horse and Coach races, Pupet-plays and interludes, Cookes and Tipling, and lewder places; so as it seem'd to be a bacchanalia, Triumph or Carnoval on the Water, whilst it was a severe Judgement upon the Land: the Trees not onely splitting as if lightning-stock, but Men and Cattell perishing in divers places, and the very seas so locked up withyce, that no vessells could shirr out, or come in: The fowle Fish and birds, and all our exotique Plants and Greenes universaly perishing; many Parks of deere destroied, and all sorts of fuell so deare that there were great Contributions to preserve

the poor alive; nor was this severe weather much lesse intense in most parts of Europe even as far as Spaine, and the most southern tracts: London, by reason of the excessive coldnesse of the aire, hindring the ascent of the smoke, was so filld with the fuliginous streame of the Sea-Coale, that hardly could one see crosse the streete, and this filling the lungs with its grosse particles exceedingly obstructed the breast, so as one could scarce breath: There was no water to be had from the Pipes and Engines, nor could the Brewers, and divers other Tradesmen work, and every moment was full of disastrous accidents etc.

John Aubrey

(1626–1697)

Aubrey was a lawyer and antiquary who recognised the megalithic remains at Avebury in Wiltshire while out hunting in January 1649. By his own account, as a boy he 'did ever love to converse with old men as Living Histories', and fortunately kept up the habit throughout his life. His inimitable, gossipy anecdotes about contemporary celebrities were not published until 1813; the complete collection included four hundred and twenty-six Lives in fifty volumes.

Edmund Halley

Mr Edmund Halley, Artium Magister, the eldest son of Edmund Halley, a Soape-boyler, a wealthy Citizen of the City of London, of the Halleys, of Derbyshire, a good family. He was born in Shoreditch parish, at a place called Haggerston, the backside of Hogsdon.

At 9 yeares old, his father's apprentice taught him to write, and arithmetique. He went to Paule's schoole to Dr Gale: while he was there he was very perfect in the caelestiall Globes in so much that I heard Mr Moxton (the Globe-maker) say that if a star were misplaced in the Globe, he would presently find it. He studyed Geometry, and at 16 could make a dyall, and then, he said, thought himselfe a brave fellow.

At 16 went to Queen's Colledge in Oxon, well versed in Latin, Greeke, and Hebrew: where, at the age of nineteen, he solved this useful Probleme in Astronomie, never donne before, viz. *from 3 distances given from the sun, and Angles between, to find the Orbe,* for which his name will be ever famous.

He went to Dantzick to visit Hevelius. December 1st, 1680, went to Paris: Cardinal d'Estrée caressed him and sent him to his brother the Admirall with a lettre of Recommendation. He hath contracted an acquaintance and friendship with all the eminentst Mathematicians of France and Italie, and holds a correspondence with them.

He gott leave and a *viaticum* of his father to goe to the Island of *Sancta Hellena,* purely upon account of advancement of Astronomy, to make the globe of the Southern Hemisphere right, which before was very erroneous, as being donne only after the observations of ignorant seamen. There he stayed some moneths. There went over with him (amongst others) a woman, and her husband, who had no child in several yeares; before he came from the Island, she was brought to bed of a Child. At his returne, he presented his Planisphere, with a short description, to his Majesty who was very well pleased with it; but received nothing but Prayse.

Francis Bacon's garden

The garden is large, which was (no doubt) rarely planted and kept in his Lordship's time. Here is a handsome Dore, which opens into Oake-wood; over his dore in golden letters on blew are six verses.

The Oakes of this wood are very great and shadie. His Lordship much delighted himselfe here: under every tree, he planted some fine flower, or flowers, some whereof are there still (1656) viz. Paeonies, Tulips.

From this Wood a dore opens into a place as big as an ordinary Parke, the west part whereof is Coppice-wood, where are Walkes cut-out as straight as a line, and broad enough for a coach, a quarter of a mile long or better. Here his Lordship much meditated, his servant Mr Bushell attending him with his pen and inke horne to sette down his present Notions.

The cast of this Parquet was heretofore, in his Lordship's prosperitie, a Paradise; now is a large ploughed field. The walkes, both in the Coppices and other Boscages, were most ingeniosely designed: at severall good Viewes, were erected elegant Sommer-howses well built of Roman-architecture, well wainscotted and cieled; yet standing, but defaced, so that one would have thought the Barbarians had made a Conquest here.

Celia Fiennes

(1662–1741)

English traveller. Fiennes's father was a Colonel in Cromwell's army, and she perpetuated his nonconformism. She toured Britain on horseback between 1685 and 1710, keeping a detailed account of her journeys, and leaving us a vivid picture of English life at the time.

The grottoe at Wilton

The Gardens are very fine, with many gravel walkes with gras squaires set with fine brass and stone statues, with fish ponds and basons with figures in the middle spouting out water, dwarfe trees of all sorts and a fine flower garden, much wall fruite: the river runns through the garden that easeily conveys by pipes water to all parts. Grottoe is at the end of the garden just the middle off the house, its garnished with many fine figures of the Goddesses, and about 2 yards off the doore is severall pipes in a line that with a sluce spoutts water up to wett the Strangers; in the middle roome is a round table, a large pipe in the midst, on which they put a crown or gun or a branch, and so it spouts the water through the carvings and poynts all round the roome at the Artists pleasure to wet the Company; there are figures at each corner of the roome than can weep water on the beholders, and by a straight pipe on the table they force up the water into the hollow carving of the rooff like a crown or coronet to appearance, but is hollow within to retaine the water forced into it in great quantetyes, that disperses in the hollow cavity over the roome and descends in a shower of raine all about the

roome; on each side is two little roomes which by the turning their
wires the water runnes in the rockes you see and hear it, and also it is
so contrived in one room that it makes the melody of Nightingerlls and
all sorts of birds which engaged the curiosity of the Strangers to go in
to see, but at the entrance off each room, is a line of pipes that appear
not till by a sluce moved it washes the spectators, designed for diversion.

Purbeck

From thence by boate we went to a little Isle called Brownsea 3 or 4
leagues off, where there is much Copperice made, the stones being found
about the Isle in the shore in great quantetyes, there is only one house
there which is the Governours, besides little fishermens houses, they
being all taken up about the Copperice [Copperas] workes; they gather
the stones and places them on ground raised like the beds in gardens,
rows one above the other, and are all shelving so that the raine disolves
the stones and it draines down into trenches and pipes made to receive
and convey it to the house; that is fitted with iron panns foursquare
and of a pretty depth at least 12 yards over, they place iron spikes in
the panns full of branches and so as the liquor boyles to a candy it
hangs on those branches: I saw some taken up it look't like a vast bunch
of grapes, the coullour of the Copperace not being much differing, it
looks cleare like sugar-candy, so when the water is boyled to a candy
they take it out and replenish the panns with more liquor; I do not
remember they added anything to it only the stones of Copperice dis-
olved by the raine into liquour as I mention'd at first; there are great
furnaces under, that keepes all the panns boyling; it was a large room
or building with severall of these large panns; they do add old iron and
nailes to the Copperass Stones. This is a noted place for lobsters and
crabs and shrimps, there I eate some very good.

From Merly we went to the Isle of Purbeck. At Warrum [Wareham]
we passed over a bridge where the sea flowed in and came by the ruines
of Corffe Castle, which stands on a hill yet surrounded by much higher
hills that might easily command it, and so in the Civil warrs was batter'd
down with Granadeers, thence you rise a great ascent of hills called the
Linch [Lynch], or rather the ridge, being so for 3 or 4 miles, rideing to

Quare [Quar] which was 16 miles from Merly to a relations house Cos'n Colliers.

From this ridge you see all the Island over, which lookes very fruitfull, good lands meadows woods and inclosures; there are many quarys in these hills of that which is called the free stone, from hence they digg it. The shores are very rocky all about the Island, we went 3 miles off to Sonidge [Swanage] a sea faire place not very big; there is a flatt sand by the sea a little way; they take up stones by the shores that are so oyly as the poor burn it for fire, and its so light a fire it serves for candle too, but it has a strong offensive smell. At a place 4 mile off called Sea Cume [Seacombe] the rockes are so craggy and the creekes of land so many that the sea is very turbulent, there I pick'd shells and it being a springtide I saw the sea beat upon the rockes at least 20 yards with such a foame or froth, and at another place the rockes had so large a cavity and hollow that when the sea flowed in it runne almost round, and sounded like some hall or high arch. In this Island are severall pretty good houses though not very large, att Kingston Sir William Muex [Meux] has a pretty house, and att Income [Encombe] Mr Coliffords. . .

César de Saussure

(b. 1705–?)

Swiss traveller. He travelled for eleven years, spending five of them in England. He developed a sort of circular letter system, so that some two hundred people in Switzerland read them, among them Voltaire. In 1730, he joined the British Embassy in Constantinople.

Water in London

The amount of water English people employ is inconceivable, especially for the cleansing of their houses. Though they are not slaves to cleanliness, like the Dutch, still they are very remarkable for this virtue. Not a week passes by but well-kept houses are washed twice in the seven days, and that from top to bottom; and even every morning most kitchens, staircase, and entrance are scrubbed. All furniture, and especially all kitchen utensils, are kept with the greatest cleanliness. Even the large hammers and the locks on the door are rubbed and shine brightly.

Would you believe it, though water is to be had in abundance in London, and of fairly good quality, absolutely none is drunk? The lower classes, even the paupers, do not know what it is to quench their thirst with water. In this country nothing but beer is drunk, and it is made in several qualities. Small beer is what everyone drinks when thirsty; it is used even in the best houses, and costs only a penny the pot. Another kind of beer is called porter, meaning carrier, because the greater quantity of this beer is consumed by the working classes. It is a thick and strong beverage, and the effect it produces, if drunk in excess, is the same as that of wine; this porter costs threepence the pot. In London there are a number of alehouses, where nothing but this sort of beer is sold. There are again other clear beers, called ale, some of these being as transparent as fine old wine, foreigners often mistaking them at first sight for the latter. The prices of ales differ, some costing one shilling the bottle, and others as much as eighteenpence. It is said that more grain is consumed in England for making beer than for making bread.

All dressed up to kill

The day I went to see the gladiators fight I witnessed an extraordinary combat, two women being the champions. As soon as they appeared on the stage they made the spectators a profound reverence; they then saluted each other and engaged in a lively and amusing conversation. They boasted that they had a great amount of courage, strength, and intrepidity. One of them regretted she was not born a man, else she would have made her fortune by her powers; the other declared she beat her husband every morning to keep her hand in, etc. Both these women were very scantily clothed, and wore little bodices and very short petticoats of white linen. One of these amazons was a stout Irishwoman, strong and lithe to look at, the other was a small Englishwoman, full of fire and very agile. The first was decked with blue ribbons on the head, waist, and right arm; the second wore red ribbons. Their weapons were a sort of two-handed sword, three or three and a half feet in length;

the guard was covered, and the blade was about three inches wide and not sharp – only about half a foot of it was, but then that part cut like a razor. The spectators made numerous bets, and some peers who were there some very large wagers. On either side of the two amazons a man stood by, holding a long staff, ready to separate them should blood flow. After a time the combat became very animated, and was conducted with force and vigour with the broad side of the weapons, for points there were none. The Irishwoman presently received a great cut across her forehead, and that put a stop to the first part of the combat.

Peter Kalm

(1716–79)

A Swedish botanist, sent by Linnaeus on a botanical expedition to America. He spent three years there. Kalm also spent six weeks in England; his book of *Travels* was published in 1772, and records his unbounded curiosity about everything, from how the English heated their houses to their method of planting radishes.

A snake handler

We saw to-day as well as on the previous days a common man clad in rags, who had a large collection of living Vipers and snakes . . . which he went and carried about in the streets . . . to show to folk for money . . . He could handle them with his hands quite quietly, and without the snakes offering in the least to bite him . . . He had a bag, in which he laid them, and when anyone gave him "en *halfpence*", he took them out with his hands, either one after another or also by the handfull, as many as he could hold. Often to awaken more astonishment, he stuffed either a viper or a snake whole into his mouth . . . and kept his mouth shut for a little while, and then opened his mouth and let the snake crawl out of it. When he slipped them on the ground they sought to run away. He said he had sometimes been bitten in the thumb by them when he had caught them; but he knew such an antidote for it . . . that it could not do him any harm; yet he would not make known what it consisted in. That the *snakes* did not do him any harm was no wonder, but how he managed it with the vipers . . . I know not. This I saw, that they not only did not offer to bite him but also when a stick was pointed . . .

Tobias Smollett

(1721–71)

Scottish surgeon and writer of picaresque novels. He sailed away from financial desperation to Jamaica as assistant ship's surgeon, returning with a wealthy heiress from Jamaica as his wife. Satirised as 'Smelfungus' by Laurence Sterne, he was also described as a 'human porcupine in his social relations'. His writing is most entertaining, however.

The worst road in England

I need not tell you this is the worst road in England, with respect to the conveniencies of travelling, and must certainly impress foreigners with an unfavourable opinion of the nation in general. The chambers are in general cold and comfortless, the beds paultry, the cookery execrable, the wine poison, the attendance bad, the publicans insolent, and the bills extortion; there is not a drop of tolerable malt liquor to be had from London to Dover . . .

Dover is commonly termed a den of thieves; and I am afraid it is not altogether without reason, it has acquired this appellation. The people are said to live by piracy in time of war; and by smuggling and fleecing strangers in time of peace: but I will do them the justice to say, they make no distinction between foreigners and natives. Without all doubt a man cannot be much worse lodged and worse treated in any part of Europe nor will he in any other place meet with more flagrant instances of fraud, imposition, and brutality. One would imagine they had formed a general conspiracy against all those who either go to, or return from the continent.

Dorothy Wordsworth

(1771–1855)

English writer, the younger sister of the poet William Wordsworth. Dorothy lived with her brother and his family in the Lake District. In 1803 she went on a walking tour in Scotland with William and the poet Coleridge with whom they had a close friendship, until opium got the better of him. The last years of Dorothy's life were saddened by her loss of reason and memory; her *Journals* remain her great legacy.

The death of Lord Nelson as heard at Ullswater

10th November Saturday. A beautiful morning. When we were at breakfast heard the tidings of Lord Nelson's death and the victory of Trafalgar. Went to the inn to make further inquiries. I was shocked to hear that there had been great rejoicings at Penrith. Returned by William's rock and grove, and were so much pleased with the spot that William determined to buy it if possible, therefore we prepared to set off to Park House that Wm. might apply to Thomas Wilkinson to negotiate for him with the owner. We went down that side of the lake opposite to Stybarrow Crag. I dismounted, and we sate some time under the same rock as before, above Blowick. Owing to the brightness of the sunshine the church and other buildings were even more concealed from us than by the mists of two days before. It had been a sharp frost in the night, and the grass and trees were yet wet. We observed the lemon-coloured leaves of the birches in the wood below, as the wind turned them to the sun, sparkle, or rather flash, like diamonds. The day continued unclouded to the end.

John James Audubon

(1785–1851)

Born in Santo Domingo, Audubon was the illegitimate son of a Creole woman and a French sailor who took him back to France where he studied painting under the artist David. Returning to America, he married and tried to become a merchant. He made a living by painting portraits while making illustrations of birds as he travelled in America, charming society with his somewhat wild appearance. After exhibitions in Britain, he published *Birds of America* at vast expense in 1827–8; it consisted of eighty-seven portfolios containing 1065 coloured, life-sized depictions of birds. A more manageable seven-volume edition was successfully published. This was followed by a work on quadrupeds, completed by his sons.

Reminiscences of Thomas Bewick

The old gentleman and I stuck to each other, he talking of my drawings, I of his wood-cuts. Now and then he would take off his cap, and draw up his grey worsted stockings to his nether clothes; but whenever our conversation became animated, the replaced cap was left sticking as if by magic to the hind part of his head, the neglected hose resumed their downward tendency, his fine eyes sparkled, and he delivered his sentiments with a freedom and vivacity which afforded me great pleasure. He said he had heard that my drawings had been exhibited in Liverpool, and felt great anxiety to see some of them, which he proposed to gratify by visiting me early next morning along with his daughters and a few friends. Recollecting at that moment how desirous my sons, then in Kentucky, were to have a copy of his works on Quadrupeds, I asked him where I could procure one, when he immediately answered "Here," and forthwith presented me with a beautiful set.

The tea-drinking having in due time come to an end, young Bewick, to amuse me, brought a bagpipe of a new construction, called the

Durham Pipe, and played some simple Scotch, English and Irish airs, all sweet and pleasing to my taste. I could scarcely understand how, with his large fingers, he managed to cover each hole separately. The instrument sounded somewhat like a hautboy, and had none of the shrill war-like notes of booming sound of the military bagpipe of the Scotch Highlanders. The company dispersed at an early hour, and when I parted from Bewick that night, I parted from a friend.

Richard Ayton

(1786–1823) and William Daniell (1769–1837)

Ayton was a writer, who trained for the bar but did not practise. Instead he wrote and adapted plays for the stage. William Daniell was a landscape painter, nephew of the artist Thomas Daniell with whom he spent nearly ten years making topographical paintings and prints in India, travelling there and back via China. They covered thousands of miles on foot, on horseback, boats and carts, carrying all their equipment for making drawings, paintings and engravings.

The north coast of Cornwall

There is no part of the English coast where the ocean can be seen in such grandeur as on the north coast of Cornwall, which is entirely open to the whole sweep of the Atlantic. In most of the land-locked channels round our coast, the waves, in consequence of frequent sands and shoals, are short and broken, but here, the huge, round billows come rolling on, each a mountain, which you have time to gaze and ponder on, while you may distinctly see the immense chasm which separates each from that which follows, and thus pursue in detail the march of the mighty sea, as it moves along with majestic regularity. In the calmest weather there frequently rise up 'ground-swells', which are extremely dangerous for all open boats, and which, not being to be foreseen or provided against, make the life of a fisherman on this coast as precarious as his sport. I endeavoured to ascertain the causes of these ground-swells, but could learn nothing satisfactory respecting them. Some assured me, that they were the forerunners of an approaching gale, and others, that they were in consequence of a gale that was passed; but all agreed, that they were more to be dreaded than a gale, as they came on without warning. They occur only along shore, as their name imports, and beyond them, the sea is frequently quite calm. In this case the effect is very singular; for the space of a quarter of a mile, the sea, without wind, is tossed, as if by a hurricane, into the wildest uproar and confusion, while beyond, as far as the eye can see, it is one still surface as smooth as glass.

Bathing at Bude

The village of Bude is very small, but has some neat houses in it, which are let out in lodgings to visitors, who go thither for the benefit of sea-bathing, though the place is not supplied with any conveniences that can render the act of bathing either comfortable or decent, particularly to the ladies. No bathing machines are employed, and consequently, the ladies are reduced to the necessity of undressing themselves in the dark and dismal caverns hollowed out in the cliffs by the sea, and of parading into the water not unseen. At the precise moment which they choose for their dip, some male starers are certain to be picking up shells at the water's edge, who, under this pretence, have an opportunity of seeing the whole exhibition.

There is no circulating library or trinket shop at Bude, where the visitors can spend their money and their mornings, so that, in spite of the bracing effects of the cold bath, I think I discovered some symptoms of flaccidity about them, and a certain anxiety in their countenances which declared that they were seeking more than they could find. I have heard some seamen say that they preferred a storm to a calm, and I confess that beating hemp would be more to my taste than waiting three and twenty hours every day for a plunge in the sea.

Harriet Martineau

(1802–76)

An English writer of Huguenot origin, Martineau was driven to writing through financial necessity. She wrote economic and social works, travel books and novels. Martineau was very hard of hearing from the age of eighteen and five years of her life were spent as an invalid; she claimed to have been cured by Mesmerism. Despite this she travelled widely, notably in America, Egypt and Palestine.

The Wilds of Erris

11 September 1852

We have crossed the wilds of Erris – the wildest district of Ireland, and the scene of the worst horrors of the famine. Of the horrors of the famine we shall say nothing here. It is more profitable to look at the present state of the district, to see if future famines cannot be avoided.

The district of Erris extends north of a line drawn from the two great mountains, Nephin and Croagh Patrick, or the Reek – a holy mountain, to which the people make pilgrimages. Few but sportsmen and poor-law officials know much about Erris. Snipe and trout abound among its blue lakes and ponds, and grouse among the heather, which extends as far as the eye can reach. Police barracks, brilliantly white-washed, glitter here and there; and near them may be seen a shooting-box, a public-house, and a few cottages. But in one place, at least, and probably more, the high road passes through wilds where no dwelling is seen for miles. The traveller must amuse himself with the vegetation, the various heaths, the exquisite ferns, the marsh willows, the bog-cotton waving in the wind, and the bog myrtle; or with the cranes, fishing from a stone; or with the moor game, poking up their heads from the heather; or with the snipe, swinging on a bulrush; or he may feast his eyes on the outlines and shadowy hollows of the distant mountains; for of human beings he will see none for miles together.

George Henry Borrow

(1803–81)

English writer and master of numerous languages. Borrow roamed England for seven years, often in the company of gypsies; *Lavengro* and *The Romany Rye* were the outcome. As an agent of the British and Foreign Bible Society, his first assignment was to translate the Bible into Manchu. He learned the language in nineteen weeks, but had to go to Russia to do it. Failing to gain entry to Tibet in order to convert the Dalai Lama to Christianity, Borrow went to Spain, where he spent five years selling bibles. He retired to his wife's estate in Suffolk, where, always hospitable, he allowed gypsies to camp on his land.

The road from Capel Curig

The road to Bangor from Capel Curig is almost due west. An hour's walking brought me to a bleak moor, extending for a long way amidst wild sterile hills.

The first of a chain on the left, was a huge lumpy hill with a precipice towards the road probably three hundred feet high. When I had come nearly parallel with the commencement of this precipice, I saw on the left-hand side of the road two children looking over a low wall behind which at a little distance stood a wretched hovel. On coming up I stopped and looked at them; they were a boy and girl, the first about twelve, the latter a year or two younger; both wretchedly dressed and looking very sickly.

"Have you any English?" said I, addressing the boy in Welsh.

"Dim gair," said the boy; "not a word, there is no Saesneg near here."

"What is the name of this place?"

"The name of our house is Helyg."

"And what is the name of that hill?" said I, pointing to the hill of the precipice.

"Allt y Gôg – the high place of the cuckoo."

"Have you a father and mother?"

"We have."

"Are they in the house?"

"They are gone to Capel Curig."

"And they left you alone?"

"They did. With the cat and the trin-wire."

"Do your father and mother make wire-work?"

"They do. They live by making it."

"What is the wire-work for?"

"It is for hedges to fence the fields with."

"Do you help your father and mother?"

"We do; as far as we can."

"You both look unwell."

"We have lately had the cryd" (ague).

"Is there much cryd about here?"

"Plenty."

"Do you live well?"

"When we have bread we live well."

"If I give you a penny will you bring me some water?"

"We will, whether you give us a penny or not. Come, sister, let us go and fetch the gentleman water."

They ran into the house and presently returned, the girl bearing a pan of water. After I had drunk I gave each of the children a penny, and received in return from each a diolch or thanks.

"Can either of you read?"

"Neither one nor the other."

"Can your father and mother read?"

"My father cannot, my mother can a little."

"Are there books in the house?"

"There are not."

"No Bible?"

"There is no book at all."

"Do you go to church?"

"We do not."

"To chapel?"

"In fine weather."

"Are you happy?"

"When there is bread in the house and no cryd we are all happy."

"Farewell to you, children."

"Farewell to you, gentleman!" exclaimed both.

"I have learnt something," said I, "of Welsh cottage life and feeling from that poor sickly child."

I had passed the first and second of the hills which stood on the left, and a huge long mountain on the right which confronted both, when a young man came down from a gully on my left hand, and proceeded in the same direction as myself. He was dressed in a blue coat and corduroy trowsers, and appeared to be of a condition a little above that of a labourer. He shook his head and scowled when I spoke to him in English, but smiled on my speaking Welsh, and said: "Ah, you speak Cumraeg: I thought no Sais could speak Cumraeg."

Alphonse Esquiros

(1814–76)

French poet and politician, who escaped to England for political reasons in 1851. He wrote three books about England and the English, making the sort of observations that only a foreigner could.

The English costers

The costermongers of London belong to two distinct races, the English and Irish. The English costers reside in courts and alleys in the vicinity of the various London markets, and those localities in which a colony of street-sellers is established are known to themselves by the name of the coster districts. Their domicile generally consists of a room in which they boil their shell-fish, smoke sprats, steam oranges, trim apples, and sleep all together – men, women, and children. Such a place offers, as may be supposed, but slight attractions, and hence their home is the street, the beer-shop, and the market. It is calculated that only one-third of the costers have a capital of their own; some borrow the money to buy their daily stock, others the stock itself; many, again, hire their basket shallows, truck, or donkey-cart, while some even hire their weights and scales. The interest of money lent generally amounts to twenty per cent per week. The most sad thing is, that this iniquitous tax does not fall only on the street-sellers, but also on the poor classes whom the costers supply with provisions: the public food is, therefore, in great measure tributary to the usurers. Taken as a body, the nomadic dealers form an ignorant class, and only one in ten can read. A child is hardly able to walk ere it follows its father's or mother's truck: these children grow old quickly, and by the age of seven are thorough business people. You are amazed to find in them, by the side of the deepest ignorance, great readiness of mind, judgment, and a marvellous trade knowledge in a certain line. The English costers do not avowedly belong to the English Church, or any sect, but it must not be concluded from this that they are utter strangers to religious sentiment. What touches them most in the Gospels – of which they know very little, however – is the history of Our Saviour feeding so many poor people, and giving each of them a barley-loaf and two small fishes. "That proves," they add simply, "that he was a thorough gentleman."

Queen Victoria

(1819–1901)

'Homely accounts of excursions near home,' was how the Queen described her *Journal of Our Life in the Highlands*. There are mountain tours, pony riding, children sitting on wasps' nests and damp picnics. The *Journal* delights in things ordinary but new: 'porridge', 'Finnan haddies' and 'Scotch mist'. We also share vicariously the Royal experience of tours and holidays. 'Innumerable little pleasure steamboats have been following us covered with people.' We hear 'the cheers of the numberless crowds, guns firing and bands playing'.

A picnic on Cairn Turc

We sat on a very precipitous place, which made one dread any one moving backwards; and here, at a little before two o'clock, we lunched. The lights were charmingly soft, and, as I said before, like the bloom on a plum. The luncheon was very acceptable, for the air was extremely keen, and we found ice thicker than a shilling on the top of Cairn Turc, which did not melt when Brown took it and kept it in his hand. Helena was so delighted, for this was *the only really great* expedition in which she had accompanied us.

Hippolyte Taine

(1828–93)

French philosopher, writer and critic. *Notes on England* was written after a ten-week stay.

A wet Sunday in London

Sunday in London in the rain: the shops are shut, the streets almost deserted; the aspect is that of an immense and a well-ordered cemetery. The few passers-by under their umbrellas, in the desert of squares and streets, have the look of uneasy spirits who have risen from their graves; it is appalling.

I had no conception of such a spectacle, which is said to be frequent in London. The rain is small, compact, pitiless; looking at it one can see no reason why it should not continue to the end of all things; one's feet churn water, there is water everywhere, filthy water impregnated with an odour of soot. A yellow, dense fog fills the air, sweeps down to the ground; at thirty paces a house, a steam-boat appear as spots upon blotting-paper. After an hour's walk in the Strand especially, and in the rest of the City, one has the spleen, one meditates suicide. The lofty lines of fronts are of sombre brick, the exudations being encrusted with fog and soot. Monotony and silence; yet the inscriptions on metal or marble speak and tell of the absent master, as in a large manufactory of bone-black closed on account of a death.

W.H. Hudson

(1841–1922)

Hudson was an author and naturalist. Born in Buenos Aires; he grew up on ranches on Rio de la Plata. He returned to England in 1869 on account of a weak heart; and lived in dreary boarding houses. Things improved when he moved to Hampshire, a life recounted in *Hampshire Days*, 1903. He wrote beautifully about the natural history of both South America and England.

Old Sarum

Old Sarum stands over the Avon, a mile and a half from Salisbury; a round chalk hill about 300 feet high, in its round shape and isolation resembling a stupendous tumulus in which the giants of antiquity were buried, its steeply sloping, green sides ringed about with vast, concentric earth-works and ditches, the work of the "old people", as they say on the Plain, when referring to the ancient Britons, but how ancient, whether invading Celts or Aborigines – the true Britons, who possessed the land from neolithic times – even the anthropologists, the wise men of to-day, are unable to tell us. Later, it was a Roman station, one of the most important, and in after ages a great Norman castle and cathedral city, until early in the thirteenth century, when the old church was pulled down and a new and better one to last for ever was built in the green plain by many running waters. Church and people gone, the castle fell into ruin, though some believe it existed down to the fifteenth century; but from that time onwards the site has been a place of historical memories and a wilderness. Nature had made it a sweet and beautiful spot; the earth over the old buried ruins was covered with an elastic turf, jewelled with the bright little flowers of the chalk, the ramparts and ditches being all overgrown with a dense thicket of thorn, holly, elder, bramble, and ash, tangled up with ivy, briony, and traveller's-joy. Once only during the last five or six centuries some slight excavations were made when, in 1834, as the result of an excessively dry summer, the lines of the cathedral foundations were discernible on the surface. But it will no longer be the place it was, the Society of Antiquaries having received permission from the Dean and Chapter of Salisbury to work their sweet will on the site. That ancient, beautiful carcass, which had long made their mouths water, on which they have now fallen like a pack of hungry hyenas to tear off the old hide of green turf and burrow down to open to the light or drag out the deep, stony framework. The beautiful surrounding thickets, too, must go, they tell me, since you cannot turn the hill inside out without destroying the trees and bushes that crown it. What person who has known it and has often sought that spot for the sake of its ancient associations, and of the sweet solace they have found in the solitude, or for the noble view of the sacred city from its summit, will not deplore this fatal amiability of the authorities, this weak desire to please every one and inability to say no to such a proposal!

Henry James

(1843–1916)

American novelist and critic. As a young man he travelled a great deal, but settled in England in 1869, living in London and at Rye, in Kent. James became a British citizen in 1915. Many of his novels have a particular preoccupation with the meeting of the cultures of the Old and New worlds.

A rustic walk through London

It takes London to put you in the way of a purely rustic walk from Notting Hill to Whitehall. You may traverse this immense distance – a most comprehensive diagonal – altogether on soft, fine turn, amid the song of birds, the bleat of lambs, the ripple of ponds, the rustle of admirable trees. Frequently have I wished that, for the sake of such a daily luxury and of exercise made romantic, I were a government-clerk living, in snug domestic conditions, in a Pembridge villa.

London's neglected river front

The way that with her magnificent opportunity London has neglected to achieve a river-front is, of course, the best possible proof that she has rarely, in the past, been in the architectural mood which at present shows somewhat inexpensive signs of settling upon her. Here and there a fine fragment apologises for the failure which it doesn't remedy. Somerset House stands up higher, perhaps, than anything else on its granite pedestal, and the palace of Westminster reclines – it can hardly be said to stand – on the big parliamentary bench of its terrace. The Embankment, which is admirable if not particularly interesting, does what it can, and the mannered houses of Chelsea stare across at Battersea Park like eighteenth-century ladies surveying a horrid wilderness. On the other hand, the Charing Cross railway-station, placed where it is, is a national crime; Millbank prison is a worse act of violence than any it was erected to punish, and the water-side generally a shameless renunciation of effect. We acknowledge, however, that its very cynicism is expressive; so that if one were to choose again – short of there being a London Louvre – between the usual English irresponsibility in such matters and some particular flight of conscience, one would perhaps do as well to let the case stand. We know what it is, the stretch from Chelsea to Wapping, but we know not what it might be. It doesn't prevent my being always more or less thrilled, of a summer afternoon, by the journey on a penny-steamer to Greenwich.

Tomás Ó'Crohan

(1856–1937)

Ó'Crohan (Gaelic spelling Ó Criomthain) was a master of the Irish language and wrote in Gaelic. *The Islandman*, first published in 1937, is a remarkable account of life on the Great Blasket Islands off the West Coast of Ireland. He was born and died there, living in a rustic cottage with his family of ten children.

Islandman

I knew perfectly well that I'd cut my last sod of turf that day when I saw the mop head of the first of them coming between me and the daylight. For the gang of girls we had in the Island in those days were next door to being half wild. And, though I was pretty tired before they came, sure it was they that finished me altogether. And no wonder – six girls, just about beginning to ripen, running over with high spirits, whatever sort of food and drink they had. It's easy baking when you have meal to hand, and so it was with them: stout, strong hoydens, as healthy as the fish in the sea; it made no odds to them what sort of food they had on the table, and they didn't care.

Hilaire Belloc

(1870–1953)

The son of a French barrister and English mother, Belloc was educated in England but served in the French army. He was elected as a Liberal MP for one term, but is best known as a writer, particularly of children's verse and travel books. One of the best known is *The Old Road* in which Belloc revisited the Pilgrim's Way from Winchester to Canterbury.

Journey to Canterbury

It was as though a shaft of influence had risen enormous above the shrine: the last of all the emanations which the sacred city cast outwards just as its sanctity died. That tower was yet new when the commissioners came riding in, guarded by terror all around them, to destroy, perhaps to burn, the poor materials of worship in the great choir below: it was the last think in England which the true Gothic spirit made. It signifies the history of the three centuries during which Canterbury drew towards it all Europe. But it stands quite silent and emptied of every meaning, tragic and blind against the changing life of the sky and those activities of light that never fail or die as do all things intimate and our own, even religions. I received its silence for an hour, but without comfort and without response. It seemed only an awful and fitting terminal to that long way I had come. It sounded the note of all my road – the droning voice of extreme, incalculable age.

As I had so fixed the date of this journey, the hour and the day were the day and hour of the murder. The weather was the weather of the same day seven hundred and twenty-nine years before: a clear cold air, a clean sky, and a little wind. I went into the church and stood at the edge of the north transept, where the archbishop fell, and where a few Norman stones lend a material basis for the resurrection of the past. It was almost dark ... I had hoped in such an exact coincidence to see the gigantic figure, huge in its winter swaddling, watching the door from the cloister, watching it unbarred at his command. I had thought to discover the hard large face in profile, still caught by the last light from the round southern windows and gazing fixedly; the choir beyond at their alternate nasal chaunt; the clamour; the battering of oak; the jangle of arms, and of scabbards trailing, as the troops broke in; the footfalls of the monks that fled, the sharp insults, the blows and Gilbert groaning, wounded, and à Becket dead. I listened for Mauclerc's mad boast of violence, scattering the brains on the pavement and swearing that the dead could never rise.

John Millington Synge

(1871–1909)

Irish playwright and director of the Abbey Theatre from 1904. Synge lived in Paris and later, inspired by W.B. Yeats, made several visits to the Aran Islands. Of Inishmaan, the middle island, he wrote, 'the life is perhaps the most primitive that is left in Europe'. Synge learned the Irish language there. The life inspired many of his plays including *The Playboy of the Western World* (1907).

What the Aran Islanders wore

The simplicity and unity of the dress increases in another way the local air of beauty. The women wear red petticoats and jackets of the island wool stained with madder, to which they usually add a plaid shawl twisted round their chests and tied at the back. When it rains they throw another petticoat over their heads with the waistband round their faces, or, if they are young, they use a heavy shawl like those worn in Galway. Occasionally other wraps are worn, and during the thunderstorm I arrived in I saw several girls with men's waistcoats buttoned round their bodies. Their skirts do not come much below the knee, and show their powerful legs in the heavy indigo stockings with which they are all provided.

The men wear three colours: the natural wool, indigo, and a grey flannel that is woven of alternate threads of indigo and the natural wool. In Aranmor many of the younger men have adopted the usual fisherman's jersey, but I have only seen one on this island.

As flannel is cheap – the women spin the yarn from the wool of their own sheep, and it is then woven by a weaver in Kilronan for fourpence a yard – the men seem to wear an indefinite number of waistcoats and woollen drawers one over the other. They are usually surprised at the lightness of my own dress, and one old man I spoke to for a minute on the pier, when I came ashore, asked me if I was not cold with 'my little clothes'.

Tom Longstaff

(1875–1964)

A doctor and mountaineer, Longstaff climbed in the Caucasus, Himalayas, Karakorum and Canadian Rockies. He spent long periods at high altitudes, once surviving fifty-four days at between 16,000 and 21,000 feet in the Himalayas and spent one night on a snow crest at 23,000 feet without a tent. He also served in India, 1914–18, went on expeditions to Spitsbergen, Greenland, and joined the 1935 attempt on Everest. Longstaff became Honorary Secretary and then Vice President of the Royal Geographical Society and President of the Alpine Club.

An enchanted land; beyond the Great Glen

Here our mountains are small, but they are steep-sided, individual in colour, form and texture. They stand proudly in their own right. Clouds sweep over them. Snow turns them white. In fact as I see it they are true mountains. Half an hour's walk up the hill-side and we change the world about us in all its perspective. Seaward the Summer Isles are spread like a chart below. Away to the west across the Minch lies the long horizon of the Hebrides. On a clear day the peaks of the Cuillin can be picked out seventy miles to the south-west. The whole eastern sky-line is of mainland mountains. They start with the rugged sandstone bosses of Torridon: then Slioch, over against Loch Maree: and above Gruinard Bay rise the spikes of An Teallach. The five tops of Coigach build a massy block in the south-east. Then comes Stac Polly with its cockscomb crest and strange lobster claws of rock; the crown of Cul Mor and the massive Atlantic watch-tower of Suilven. These peaks guard a wide sanctuary of moor and loch of which over 100 square miles is uninhabited. No man sleeps there. Beyond Edrachillis Bay rise the hills behind Scourie; and beyond those we can see nearly to Cape Wrath. And then behold the sky, an hundred miles of it. So many things going on at once: clouds of every pattern with play of colour on sea and land; here bright sunlight, there a black storm. An enchanted land.

So I have come back there to live.

Sir Osbert Sitwell

(1892–1969)

English writer and traveller. His brother was the writer Sacheverell, his sister Edith, the poet. He was educated 'during the holidays from Eton' at home, Renishaw Hall in Derbyshire. Sitwell travelled grandly in the 1930s and was a prolific writer. The Sixth Baronet, he inherited the family title in 1942.

The Guard at the Bank of England

After the business of the day had been finished, at the hour at which we arrived, this one-storey building, emptied altogether of life, and with its garden-courts and cloisters, resembled a monastery or a deserted temple rather than the most famous financial institution in the world. By one of the passionate paradoxes of its creator – surely the most original of all English architects – it seemed to offer a quiet, leafy, well-kept retreat from the world. And, to one on guard, the most striking feature of it was the absolute silence, even deeper than that of St James's, that prevailed during the hours of duty. At dusk, it was true, there would be the chirruping of thousands of starlings who dunly sprinkled the branches of the trees, temporarily communicating to them the liveliness and mobility of watch-springs: but, after darkness had penned these flocks, there would be no sound, except the very distant rumble of traffic, and the dragging footsteps, from time to time, of the peripatetic night watchman ... Officers and men received a special fee for duty here, and the Ensign was allowed to have two guests to dine with him. The serving of dinner, the silver and linen, were just what they should have been; grilled sole, and fillet of beef to eat, and rats'-tail spoons and eighteenth-century forks with curving ends, to eat them with; all sound, unadventurous, irreproachable – safe, in fact, as the Bank of England. But in the space of a year or two, this atmosphere was to be destroyed, and a top-heavy Tower of Babel, perhaps typifying post-war insecurity and the instability of its finances, was designed by Sir Herbert Baker to blot out Sir John Soane's restrained courts and screens, and to extinguish the peace of its cloisters by the substitution of heavy stonework for fresh air.

Sacheverell Sitwell

(1897–1988)

English poet, writer and architectural historian, brother of Edith, the poet, and the writer Osbert Sitwell of Renishaw, Derbyshire. After Eton he joined the Guards and he served in the First World War. Afterwards he travelled abroad with his brother. *Splendours and Miseries* depicts a somewhat apocalyptic picture of the world.

Storm at Sea

The howling of the storm is let loose as though to the lifting of a hand.

It is as if, coming round the corner of a street down by the harbour, we are hit by its full, mad force, shrieking and raving in from sea. Doors and wooden shutters are wrenched open. The windows are pointed arches, or the bifora, of a pair of lights with a stone pillar in between. And the street, all of stone houses, leads down into the gale.

The long clouts of rain beat like the ends of ropes. Listen to the roar of the wind! It could be the wailing of seabirds flying, in their millions, inland from the storm. Great bodies of them could be passing overhead. That might be the beating of their wings. It blows through the flesh and bones. It is a storm in ten thousand: in a lifetime. And a night when much will happen. Not yet sunset: but the livid evening.

But the rain has stopped. You can hear nothing but the wind and waves. A pause, as though for living things to hide themselves. Suddenly, lightning flickers like fire set to the entire firmament. There is utter silence. A rushing, tearing sound. Then a wild leaping, and one tremendous boom of thunder. It hits, at the end of that, like a whip that lashes upon metal. The next moment striking full upon that, shuddering and shrinking, while it rolls in triumph and booms above our heads.

Growing darker, ever darker. It could be something animal and gigantic. But it rises into a wild and endless shrieking. A huge engine or machinery is working in the storm. Or a rhythm. For it is blowing in from sea. And no one has run for shelter. A crowd of persons is waiting on the quay. As though their help will be needed. They have hurried out from their houses because, storm or no storm, the hour has come. For all we know it may have been delayed for weeks. But now it is imminent.

The whole air is shaken and beaten in the gale. But there has been a message: or some signal has been seen. It grows dark and darker; and still the howling of the storm. Those low clouds could be seabirds flying south out of the white or polar darkness. The lightning plays again upon the leaden waters. Thunder booms and rattles: and then hits with all its force, close by, as though some building has been struck. Dry thunder, now, without a drop of rain. So that the emptiness is sinister and lies like tinder for the fire to fall. Imagined lightning flares every way you look, as those eyes of fire within the eyelids upon the middle of the night. The leaden air is incandescent and could be lit with flame.

John Piper

(1903–92)

English artist, who also designed stained glass windows, tapestries and sets for the theatre and opera. Known for his modern romantic paintings of English landscape and architecture, Piper also wrote and took photographs for some of the *Shell Guides* to Britain published in the 1930s, and other British guidebooks.

Portland

Great rectangular blocks, with cutting marks in regular rows, lie about everywhere, weathering in the rain and wind and odd unrectangular but still angular blocks have been thrown aside, blocks whose stratification has defeated the expert quarryman; other blocks wait to be shipped from the low cliffs, and now wait for ever, for the shipping of stone from the shore near the Bill ceased about fifty years ago and the moss and wind and lichen have had their way with them. In the quarries yet more stone lies half cut, surprised by the light, with the straight strata joints exposed as if it had all been cut and packed away and hidden there by men in the first place, and has been waiting all this time for other men to unpack it and take it out again. And among the debris of the whole island, among the half-humanized blocks thrown about, stand the equally miraculous-looking consolidations of blocks into neat dwellings, low and solid among the strips of common land, with new crazy-paved villas here and there, and newer collections of pre-fabs and concrete and brick houses, and another crazy tangle of electricity wires overhead, the skyline cut by television aerials, and by more distant derricks and radar masts . . .

Cornwall, 1943

July 5 1943 Talland. Tangle of seaweed on the beach; tangle of hedgeflowers in the banks. The pinkish, short, round-leafed seaweed, and the vivid green ribbon-like kind – both, held up to the sun, show an enriched stained glass light. The pink has an inner tree-like veining in darker tone. Clouds on hills. Warm drizzle and clammy air. Hedgeflowers dangling uncut in deep lane. Tansy, burdock, hemp agrimony, sea-pea, mugwort, profuse bedstraw – dimmed rich colours and thick pale tones.

Uphill to church in high terraced churchyard, long-grassed with slate tombstones. Lichen on pale Cornish granite; grows slowly at first, but finally takes with vigour, producing whites, pale Naples, blue-greys in round overlapping spots and scabs. Good effect of sound holes in belfry, east side; quatrefoils, spades, diamonds, loopholes, date (1834) and so on all pierced in thick slabs of slate. Interior dark and spacious in late, cloud darkened twilight. (Subdued detail of dark old bench ends, and lack of detail in Cornish window tracery.)

Farm opposite with palest blue-washed wall and wet slates reflecting sky of identical colour and tone. Barn on left, and yard with stream, straw and dung of good levels and curves.

Maurice O'Sullivan

(1904 50)

> Born on Great Blasket, Muiris Ó' Súileabháin (Gaelic spelling) returned there at the age of seven, learned the Irish language and stayed for the next twenty years. He became a soldier, and wrote his book about growing up on the Blaskets in Gaelic. Ironically for an island man, he drowned while bathing in Connemara.

My first suit

A nun was standing before us in the doorway. She gave my father a welcome and questioned him about me kindly and courteously. When she had left us, I saw a parcel on the table and I thought at once of the new suit. I kept watching until my father opened it. He took out a pair of breeches and a jacket, then a shirt, a collar, a cap, slippers and a pair of black stockings.

'Now,' said he, 'cast off your child's clothes.'

When I was ready, my father looked at me laughing. 'Faith, you are a grown man, God bless you. Turn round till I see the back. They fit you as well as if the tailor had made them. Wait till I get you the looking-glass. Look at yourself now,' said he.

When I saw the form in which I was, all thought of Mickil and of everything else went out of my mind. 'Oh, dad,' said I, 'I am a great sport to look at.'

Sir Cecil Beaton

(1904–80)

British photographer, stage designer and traveller. He kept
the most piquant of diaries.

On the road with Cecil Beaton

On to Perth Castle. This was just what we were looking for – a riot
of stuffed stags' heads, antlers, weapons of aggression, guns, spears, all
displayed with the tasteless meticulousness that is really an art in itself.
Tartan beds, four-posters with mad ostrich feathers, Victoriana, early
photographs, good and bad collections of every sort all jumbled together.
The crowds were so delighted to find no guides to keep them in control
that they ran in every direction, up and down polished staircases, in
and out of bedrooms and bathrooms. The white pebble-dash with which
the castle is covered is better than the usual cream, and the black roofs
and turrets give the wild impression of Scotland that we have so far
missed.

Early departure for a hell of a drive – Scottish holiday over – now
down to Durham at rush-hour in time to see the cathedral and the
Venerable Bede's tomb. The scale is tremendous – marvellous proportions, thick arches, decorated with the simple, crude design cut into
the stone. The best cathedral in England.

To step into Bindie Lambton's world of children and dogs was quite
a shock. We ate marrow bones for dinner in a room with the beautifully
brought-up dogs asleep in niches, each with their brass plates on them,
under the china cabinets.

Long drive on main roads, including the M1, at tremendous speed.
King's Lynn for lunch at the delightful eighteenth-century hotel in the
main square; delight at Norfolk Dutch atmosphere; pretty gabled houses;
no Woolworths, no new building. A Festival of Constable, Henry Moore
and Sybil Cholmondeley.

'Why didn't you let me know before. All I can offer you is tea at five o'clock with the Queen Mother and twelve guests from Sandringham.' In fact we welshed. We were too ragged in body and mind to make the necessary readjustment. But we did go to see Sybil, and as we were going down the tall avenue on our way to her glorious house we were so impressed that we got out of the car and changed our trousers.

The house and its furnishings are superb. Sybil, calm and funny, well-informed and no-nonsense, showed us all.

My last Ascot

The colour of Royal Ascot has changed – Edwardian Ascot must have been entirely pastel coloured. But this was a transformation that I enjoyed. Everywhere there were large touches of brilliant magenta, orange and viridian. The Maharaja of Jaipur in a marvellous turban of ochre and scarlet. Yet the retina-irritant mutation of the plastic and the nylon looked crummy in the outdoors; the crocheted shift, the mini skirts and little-girl fashions were hardly right. But then I was not right.

James Lees-Milne

(1908–97)

English writer and architectural historian. As country houses secretary of the National Trust, Lees-Milne spent many years visiting country houses, some of them cold and decrepit. He helped to save many stately homes from destruction and decay. His diaries are witty and full of chic gossip.

With the Hinchingbrookes at Huntingdon, January, 1946

I reached Huntingdon and Hinchingbrooke at one o'c. What a contrast to the Hollywood Anglesey Abbey. No answer from the front door bell, so I drove round to the back. Walked in and wound my way through a labyrinth of passages, finally emerging into the square oak room at the corner where Hinch was squatting over an inadequate fire. He greeted me with 'My dear Jimmie, has no one helped you find the way in?' He and Rosemary most welcoming. Gave me sherry and a rabbit pie cooked by Rosemary, for the staff consists of army batmen and wives, not trained servants at all, and no cook. The Hinchingbrookes are picnicking in the house, still full of hospital beds and furniture. The hospital has only just vacated. Hinch took me round the outside and inside of the house. The gatehouse and nunnery, with gables, and the large 1602 bay window are the best features. Hinch has contracted for £400 to have the 1880 wing of red brick pulled down; also the ugly pepper-box tower of that date. This will make the house far more manageable and improve its appearance. It will also reveal the nunnery from the gardens, all sloping gently down to a lake with fine elm trees close to the house. The raised terrace overlooking the road is a Jacobean conceit. There is absolutely nothing to see inside the house, apart from the Charles II dado of the staircase.

At 3.30 I found Rosemary on hands and knees scrubbing the kitchen floor, and I helped her swab it over. We went to tea with the Sandwiches, now living in the dower house. Lady S. of enormous girth. Lord S. very distinguished with two prominent wall eyes. He showed me his pictures, ranging from Etty down to present times. Really a superb collection of French Impressionists and English school. We got on well. He rather disapproves of Hinch's intention to make over the place to the NT under the 1939 Act.

The kind Hinchingbrookes made me stay the night in the house, so I cancelled my room at the George Inn. Very cold and most primitive bathroom with no bath mat, no soap, etc. Rosemary a true bohemian, untidy and slapdash; and for this reason admirable, and tough. She is like a very jolly able-bodied seaman. Has four children and intends to have lots more. After dinner she showed me the contents of the crops of three pigeons shot that afternoon. Gave a precise anatomical lecture as she tore open their guts, squeezing out undigested acorns and berries. Then started on the gizzards and stomachs, by which time I felt rather sick and turned away. She has studied medicine and wanted to become a qualified doctor, but Hinch put a stop to that. She is robust, intelligent and affectionate.

Birds fly over her bed (Arlington Court, Somerset, May 1946)

Arlington Court is plain to ugliness. Of a dark, hard ironstone, the old part is severe Greek Regency, featureless. Unappetising annexe built on *c.* 1875 by Miss Chichester's father. The park untidy and overrun with rabbits, the whole estate no more remarkable than the country round it. Miss Chichester very old, white haired and dropsical, the last of her line. Looked after by a gentle, fawn-like young man from Shaftesbury Avenue. Her museum, made by herself, is a nightmare of model ships, shells and New Zealand Maori headdresses. She lives and sleeps in her drawing-room which is made into an aviary. Birds fly over her bed and perch on a clutter of bric-à-brac and masses of flowers. In the church is a memorial tablet to Mr John Meadows, architect from London who died in 1791. The Rectory, which Mr Meadows may have built (if he was still alive) is a very satisfactory building, with four projecting rounded bays. It has the minimum of ornamentation and relies upon line and curve. A pure architectural abstraction. I was riveted. The Holnicote agent, with the most sympathetic attention, could see nothing in it at all.

L.T. Rolt

(1910–74)

British mechanical engineer who became a dedicated historian of the Industrial Revolution and its monuments, particularly the waterways.

Sheepwash Staunch to Baitsbite Sluice

A large-scale map of the canal system hung on the wall of my bedroom, and I would lie abed planning imaginary journeys.

I had also acquired a second-hand copy of a book which is indispensable to any canal traveller, *Bradshaw's Guide to the Canals and Navigable Rivers of England and Wales*, by the late Mr Rodolph de Salis. This may sound dry reading, but I pored over it by the hour. Perhaps it was the names which appeared in the distance tables which fascinated me most and made the page live. Sheepwash Staunch, Maids Moreton Mill and Wainlode Honeystreet, Rushey Lock, Freewarrens and Stoke Bardolph Foxhangers, Sexton's Lode, Offord D'Archy and Withybed Green – these names had for me the power of poetry to conjure beauty in my imagination. Others stirred me no less by their oddity: Bumblehole Bridge, Popes Corner and Nip Square; Plucks Gutter, Stewponey Wharf and Blunder Lock; Old Man's Footbridge and Guthram Gout; Baitsbite Sluice, Dog-in-a-Doublet, Twentypence Ferry and Totterdown. What a wealth of history and legend spoke here and clamoured to be explored! Honeystreet and Wainlode had all the languorous scents and sounds of summer in them, while surely foxes barked in the dark coverts of Fox-hangers under the harvest moon. Did fishermen flock to Baitsbite Sluice? Who was Guthram, and did they brew strong ale at Totterdown? I was resolved to find out.

Barbara Jones

(1912–)

English artist and author with an interest in follies, grot-toes, fairgrounds, funerary monuments and other eccen-tricities of English culture.

Some follies

The cone stands on its peg leg at the western boundary; the south mark is a thin, thin needle of random rubble above the trees, bent at the top, an obelisk like a scream, a look-out post for the owls' army.

To the north is a calmer boundary called the Fish Tower, an untapered column about 50 feet high on a square plinth, again of random rubble except for a Ham stone, almost art-nouveau, well-head at the top, above whose iron cage was once fixed a fish weathervane. The well-head, a cylindrical cap to the column, is divided vertically by odd little mouldings that make palm trees or ogival arches, according as one looks at stem or space. The Tower is like an Edwardian factory chimney, slightly comic in this setting. There is a door in the north side of the base, and the hollow shaft is irregularly lit by rough slits to show the footholds that go up to the light. The local story is merely that it was built by the Romans; all the love and skill that make folly-stories have been reserved for the fourth folly, 'Jack the Treacle Eater'. This name is not as one might suppose a corruption of some Latin inscription, but refers to Jack, a celebrated local runner who took messages to and from London for the Messiters. He trained on treacle. The Hermes on top of the folly is Jack himself, waiting for midnight before he comes down to the lake by the house to quench the treacle thirst.

John Hillaby

(1917–)

English naturalist and prolific walker. His walk from Land's End to John O'Groats brought him public attention, and he has also walked, often alone, in Africa, from the North Sea to the Mediterranean, and from Kenya to Lake Rudolf, a journey recounted in his *Journey to the Jade Sea*.

Preparations for a Walk Through Britain

Somewhere up in the high forests between England and Wales I had been walking for hours and, not for the first time, I had lost my way. All tracks seemed to lead west when it was clear from map and compass that I should be heading north. Down in the valley an old man explained in elaborate detail how I'd strayed miles off course. In any case, he said, there wasn't much worth seeing even had I got to where I intended to spend the night. A thoroughly dispiriting old man. From time to time you meet them. I thanked him and began to move off.

'Where've you come from?' he asked. Not wishing to go into the history of a walk scarcely begun, I named the last town I had passed through. But he wasn't to be put off that easily. He wanted to know how I had got *there*? With a touch of pride, I said I had walked from Bristol. He looked adequately surprised. Had I started from Bristol?

'No,' I said. Truth must out. Why not relate all? I told him I'd walked from Cornwall. He looked astonished. For the first time in days I felt rather pleased with myself.

'From Cornwall?' he said. 'Do you mean to tell me you've walked *all* the way here?'

I nodded. Shaking his head sadly, he said: 'Then all I can say is it's a pity you couldn't be doing something useful.'

You can't win. Go to deserted parts of Africa and walk round some lake or other and people say you were darned lucky to get the chance. It looks like an exotic stunt. They reckon it's just a matter of being able to raise the cash. Some point out you could have hired a Land-Rover instead of camels and get there in a tenth of the time.

If, on the other hand you decide, as I did, to walk across your own, your native land they tell you its been done many times before. Men have set off on foot, on bicycles, on tricycles. Somebody, I heard, had even pushed a pram from Land's End to John O'Groats. But all this of course was done on the roads I tried to avoid.

For me the question wasn't whether it could be done, but whether I could do it. I'm fifty. I'm interested in biology and pre-history. They are, in fact, my business. For years I've had the notion of getting the feel of the whole country in one brisk walk: mountains and moorlands, downlands and dales. Thick as it is with history and scenic contrast, Britain is just small enough to be walked across in the springtime. It seemed an attractive idea. There was a challenge in the prospect. But to see the best of what's left I knew I should have to set off pretty soon. Each year the country in every sense of the word gets a bit smaller. Already there are caravans in some of the most improbable places. Long-distance walkers are becoming rare. You can regard what follows as the lay of one of the last.

I set off with the intention of avoiding *all* roads. I meant to keep to cross-country tracks and footpaths all the way. In places this turned out to be practically impossible for notwithstanding what's been written about the ancient by-ways, many of them are now hopelessly overgrown; others have been enclosed, ploughed up, or deliberately obstructed in one way or another. As far as I know, you can't get into the Midlands from the Welsh border or cross the Lowlands of Scotland without making use of country lanes, derelict railway tracks or, in places, the towpaths of the old canals. I did my best to keep out of the public arteries, but I sometimes got squeezed into the little capillaries of transport. Otherwise I kept to the out-of-the-way places, especially the highlands and moors.

From Land's End I followed the cliff-top paths of Cornwall for sixty or seventy miles and then struck east into Devon, crossing the centre of Dartmoor and reaching Bristol by way of the airy uplands of north Somerset. Then up the Wye valley through the Forest of Dean, perhaps the most beautiful woodland in Britain. A roundabout route through the Black Mountains, Shropshire and industrial Staffordshire led me into Derbyshire and the foot of the Pennine Way. From there north a high track along the spine of England extends as far as the Scottish border. In the West Highlands I used what are called the drove roads, the old cattle-tracks that wind through the deserted glens. In all I did about 1100 miles in fifty-five walking days. It may have been much more; it may have been a little less. The calculation is based on map-miles which means I haven't taken into account innumerable forays in wrong directions.

As for trappings, I carried the basic minimum, including a tent that eliminated the need to look for lodgings at nightfall. This gives you a comforting sense of independence. I don't mean I'm over-fond of the Spartan life. If I found a pub or a hotel at dusk, I went in, gratefully. But I had no need to rely on static shelter.

Looking back on all the stuff I bought, tried out and discarded, I don't think there's much I could have done without. I managed to reduce clothing and the contents of a rucksack to about thirty-five pounds. If I did the trip again, I should take the same gear with, perhaps, the addition of something easier to handle than a tin can to brew tea in.

Clothing is a simple matter. The trick is to wear as little as possible without becoming even a fraction too cold or too hot. The important thing is to feel comfortable throughout the whole day. I bought a light windproof anorak with a zip-fastener down the front that could be easily adjusted. I zipped it up tightly when I set off in the morning and gradually increased aeration when I began to generate my own heat. On wet days I put on one of two pairs of skin-thin bits of protective clothing, made of artificial fibre, that were supposed to be waterproof. They gradually leaked. I never got very wet and certainly never wet and cold, which I had been told is fatal. For this reason I covered my light-weight cotton tent with an outer fly sheet made of Terylene that was wholly waterproof. When things got really bad, even during the day, I crawled inside. At night I slept in a bag quilted with what the salesman said were feathers from Chinese eider ducks. It felt like heaven, weighed three pounds and cost a lot of money.

Footwear is tricky. I treat my feet like premature twins. The moment I feel even a slight twinge of discomfort I stop and put it right. Most people advocate stout boots and thick socks. I know of nothing more uncomfortable. They give you a leaden, non-springy stride. You can't trot along in boots. I bought two pairs, broke them in and eventually threw them aside. On a trip across the desert some years ago I wore tennis shoes, but these, I found, are useless in Britain for they become sodden. After trying various kinds of shoes, I settled for an expensive Italian pair with light commando-type soles. They weighed about fifteen ounces each and, when oiled, fitted me like gloves. I had no trouble with shoes. Certainly not from blisters, although in the last stages of the journey some of my toe-nails dropped off. In places I went bare-footed through bogs, and on warm days in deserted country I sometimes wore only a pair of shorts.

Eric Newby

(1919–)

English traveller and writer, formerly an apprentice on a four-masted barque, a soldier and a buyer in the fashion trade.

Branscombe

Behind the Mason's Arms, the pub which stood next door to the cottage my father had taken for the summer and of which it formed a part, there was a yard surrounded by various dilapidated buildings and a piece of ground overgrown with grass and nettles which concealed various interesting pieces of rusted, outmoded machinery, the most important of which was an old motor car smelling of decayed rubber and dirty engine oil. The stuffing of what was left of its buttoned leather upholstery was a home for a large family of mice. This yard was to be the scene of some of the more memorable games I played with my best friend in the village, Peter Hutchings, whose mother kept a grocery, confectionery and hardware shop on the corner opposite Mr Hayman, the butcher's. It was from Peter Hutchings, who was killed while serving as a soldier in the Second World War, and whose name is inscribed with the names of fourteen other village boys who died in the two great wars on the war memorial at the entrance to Branscombe churchyard, that I learned the broad local dialect which was so broad that by the end of that first summer at Branscombe no one except a local inhabitant could understand what I was saying. "Sweatin' like a bull 'er be," was how Peter Hutchings described to me one day the condition of his sister Betty, confined to bed with a temperature, and it was in this form that I passed on this important piece of news to my parents.

There in the inn yard, in the long summer evenings, we used to sit in the old motor car, either myself or Peter at the wheel, taking it in turn, the driver making BRRR-ing noises, the one sitting next to him in the front making honking noises – the horn had long since ceased to be – as we roared round imaginary corners, narrowly missing imaginary vehicles coming in the opposite direction, driving through an imaginary world to an imaginary destination on an imaginary road, a pair of arm-chair travellers. In the back we used to put Betty Hutchings, if she was available, who wore a white beret, was placid, said nothing, apart from an occasional BRR, and was in fact an ideal back-seat passenger. Sometimes, if we felt like doing something 'rude', we used to stop the car and pee on the seats in the back, and Betty would pee too. This gave us a sense of power, at least I knew it did to me, as I would not have dared to pee on the upholstery of a real motor car belonging to real people.

Dervla Murphy

(1931–)

Irish travel writer. Fearless and ubiquitous, Murphy has travelled almost everywhere, often on a bicycle, and has dealt with many of the crises that travellers fear but do not actually encounter.

Into town

Beyond the sheep farm a little lonely road climbed high between small emerald rock-flecked fields. Low rounded mountains overlooked green valleys dotted with neat white dwellings. The turf-cutters on the dark-brown bogs straightened up to wave and sometimes marshy land glistened black and silver. Along high steep banks grew vivid clusters of pink and purple bog-flowers and the may and gorse were still blooming great clouds of white and gold resting on the fields. There was no traffic until I had free-wheeled down and down to level, rich farmland, sheltered by many stands of beeches, elms and chestnuts.

The North's towns and villages seem unnaturally subdued. There are so few cars, so many lines of concrete-filled barrels down the main streets to prevent parking near shops, so few people about and such grim police barracks fortified, inside giant wire cages, against bombs and machine-guns. These jolt one, in prim-looking little towns, after cycling for hours through tranquil countryside. We are used to thinking of the village police-station or gardai-barracks as a place into which anyone can wander at any hour, without even knocking, for advice and sympathy about a lost cat or a stolen bicycle.

Pavement games in Belfast

A filthy four- or five-year-old boy was playing all alone on a broken pavement with a length of stick; it was his gun and he was aiming at us. One wouldn't even notice him in London or Dublin but in Belfast I wondered, "How soon will he have the real thing?" Already, in his little mind, possession of a gun is equated with bravery and safety, with having the will and ability to defend his own territory against 'the Oranges'. Around the next corner two slightly older children were carefully placing cardboard cartons in the middle of the narrow street. "Are these pretend bombs?" I asked, appalled. "They might not be pretend," replied Jim, driving onto the pavement to avoid one. Even more appalled, I said nothing. Jim looked at me and laughed. "You'll get used to it!" he said. "Almost certainly they are pretend. But hereabouts sensible people don't take chances."

Everywhere stones and broken bricks were available to be thrown at passing army vehicles. Jagged broken bottles lay in gutters flashing as they caught the strong sunlight. We passed an elaborately fortified barracks and then a famous "confrontation spot". "In the afternoons," explained Jim, "you get the locals out here stoning the troops. And the same evening the same people will run across to the sentry-box and ask could they ever use the 'phone to ring the aunt in Armagh."

Bruce Chatwin

(1940–89)

English traveller and writer. Chatwin made his name with *In Patagonia* (1977), and went on to write books set in Africa, Australia, Wales, and in Prague; some were fact, some fiction, others somewhere between the two. All reflected the esoteric range of his interests.

At dinner with Diana Vreeland

Her glass of neat vodka sat on the white damask tablecloth. Beyond the smear of lipstick, a twist of lemon floated among the ice-cubes. We were sitting side by side, on a banquette.

'What are you writing about, Bruce?'

'Wales, Diana.'

The lower lip shot forward. Her painted cheeks swivelled through an angle of ninety degrees.

'Whales!' she said. 'Blue whales! ... Sperrrm whales! ... THE WHITE WHALE!'

'No ... no, Diana! Wales! Welsh Wales! The country to the west of England.'

'Oh! Wales. I *do* know Wales. Little grey houses ... covered in roses ... in the rain ...'

Paul Theroux

(1941–)

American writer of travel books and fiction often set in the exotic places where he has lived. His *Great Railway Bazaar* is a memorable account of a circum-locomotion of the world by train; *The Kingdom by the Sea* is the account of a journey through Britain.

Cape Wrath

Some fantasies prepare us for reality. The sharp steep Cuillins were like mountains from a story-book – they had a dramatic, fairy-tale strangeness. But Cape Wrath was unimaginable. It was one of those places where, I guessed, every traveller felt like a discoverer who was seeing it for the first time. There are not many such places in the world. I felt I had penetrated a fastness of mountains and moors, after two months of searching; and I had found something new. So even this old, over-scrutinized kingdom had a secret patch of coast! I was very happy at Cape Wrath. I even liked its ambiguous name. I did not want to leave.

There were other people in the area: a hard-pressed settlement of sheep farmers and fishermen, and a community of drop-outs making pots and jewellery and quilts at the edge of Balnakiel. There were anglers and campers, too, and every so often a brown plane flew overhead and dropped bombs on one of the Cape Wrath beaches, where the army had a firing range. But the size of the place easily absorbed these people. They were lost in it, and as with all people in a special place they were secretive and a little suspicious of strangers.

Gwyn Headley

(1946–) and Wim Meulenkamp (1946–)

Headley spent thirty-four years collecting follies for his book. Meulenkamp, a writer born and educated in Holland, wrote a thesis on the follies of Mad Jack Fuller.

Northamptonshire Follies

In this shoemakers' county the follies are far from pedestrian. There are relatively few, but while Sir Thomas Tresham's buildings at Rushton and Lyveden may not be the oldest British follies, his Triangular Lodge of 1597 has a strong claim to be the purest in the country. With Tresham, building loses all pretence of function; it is a means of expressing an idea, an obsession . . .

Sir Thomas Tresham himself spent the best part of his life in gaol. Nominally brought up in the Church of England – it was a criminal offence not to be – he became a recusant at the age of 15, and for the rest of his life, though fiercely loyal to the Crown as head of state, waged an unyielding battle against the religious intolerance of that time. Roman Catholicism was the passion of the Treshams; Sir Thomas transmuted that passion into stone . . .

In 1581 . . . he was sentenced to seven years' imprisonment, first at Fleet Prison, then under house arrest at Hoxton Hall, and finally at Ely Prison. Here, on the walls of his cell, he worked out the mottoes, emblems and symbols that were to result in his magnum opus, the Rushton Triangular Lodge . . .

The format is quite simple – as soon as one overcomes the initial shock of seeing what is unquestionably the oddest building of its period

233

in the country. The brick building has three sides, each measuring 33 feet; three storeys; three gables on each side; and a total of nine gargoyles. In addition, the exterior is littered with trefoils, three to a row, and the crowning (solitary) central chimney has, inevitably, three sides. All this stands for the Trinity, but Tresham himself also comes into it: above the door (only one door) and below the Tresham coat-of-arms is a text reading:

TRES · TESTI

MONIVM · DANT

This is a biblical quotation (1 John, 5:7): 'For there are three that bear record [in heaven]'. The 'TRES' stands for Tresham as well, a wordplay quite acceptable to Elizabethans. Biblical quotations are carried on as a frieze along the outside walls of the lodge; each text consisting of 33 letters. They can be interpreted to reflect on the persecution of Catholics in England:

QVIS · SEPARABIT · NOS · A · CHARITATE · CHRISTI

CONSIDERAVI · OPERA · TUA · DOMINE · ET · EXPAVI

APERIATVR · TERRA · ET · GERMINET · SALVATORUM

'Who will part us from the love of Christ?' 'I have looked on thy works Lord and am afraid.' 'Let the earth open and bring forth a saviour.' There are still more mottoes on the walls, gables and chimney, together with some singular ciphers that have been attributed to a presumed interest in the Cabbala and Black Magic. However, the ciphers also prove to be biblical in content. Above the door, for example, is the number 5555. If one puts the date of the Creation at 3962 BC (as more than one 16th-century cleric did) the date turns out to be 1593 AD. The other numbers, 3098 and 3509, are important Old Testament dates: the Deluge and the Call of Abraham.

Nick Danziger

(1958–)

English film-maker. *Danziger's Travels* is about the author's reckless journey along the Silk Route from Istanbul to Peking, including a two-month stay with Afghan guerrillas en route. Danziger hitch-hiked most of the way, crossing six frontiers, mostly without visas. This is what happened when he got home after eighteen months on rough roads.

Home sweet home

I suppose I ought to have abandoned my Afghan clothes, but I found wearing them in London most educational. Everywhere I went I was either shunned or regarded with undisguised suspicion. But the biggest shock came on my second day back. I was walking down an empty John Islip Street in Westminster when suddenly I heard the sound of a van approaching me from behind. I knew it was a van because I used to drive one and the engine has an unmistakable sound. It slowed slightly as it drew level with me. A red Post Office van. The man in the passenger seat was sliding his door open. He was looking at me. The look wasn't friendly.

'You fucking nignog,' he yelled. Then the van sped off.

I was home.

Near Asia

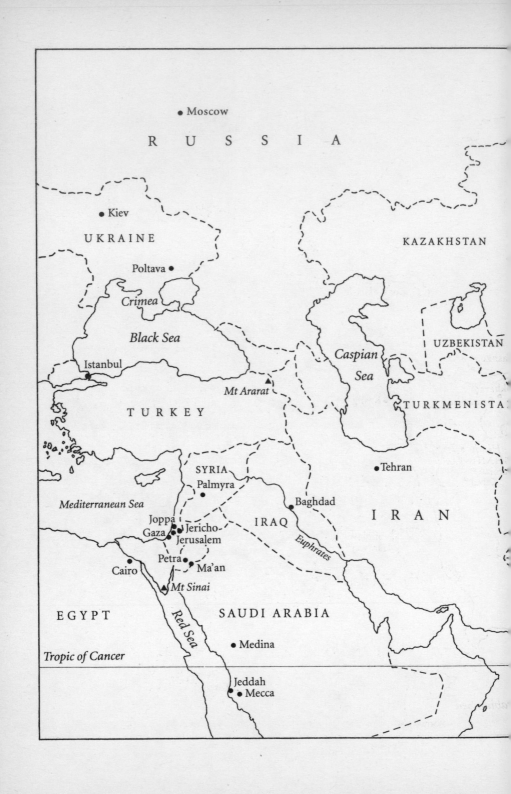

RUSSIA

Moscow

Kiev

UKRAINE

Poltava

KAZAKHSTAN

Crimea

Black Sea

Caspian
Sea

UZBEKISTAN

Istanbul

Mt Ararat

TURKEY

TURKMENISTAN

Mediterranean Sea

SYRIA

Palmyra

Tehran

Baghdad

IRAN

Joppa

Gaza

Jericho-
Jerusalem

IRAQ

Euphrates

Cairo

Petra

Ma'an

Mt Sinai

EGYPT

SAUDI ARABIA

Red Sea

Tropic of Cancer

Medina

Jeddah
Mecca

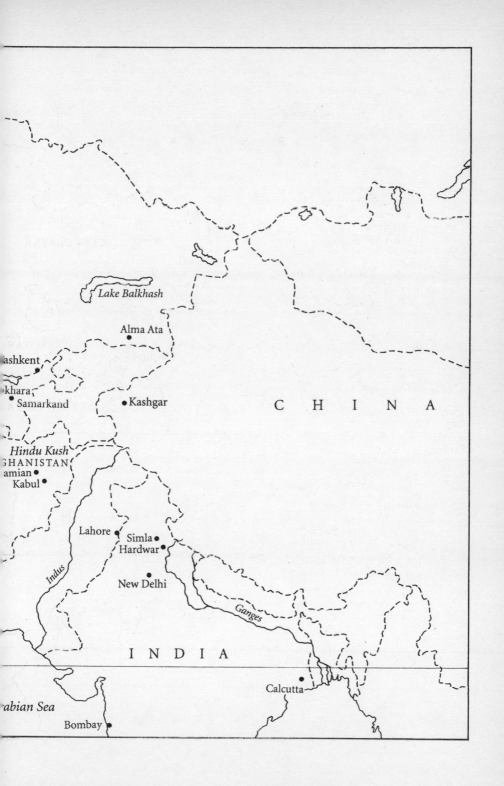

Strabo

(*c.* 63 BC – after AD 21)

Greek historian and geographer. Strabo, 'the squint-eyed', travelled from the Black Sea to Ethiopia and Arabia, explored the Nile and finally settled in Rome. He wrote forty-seven history books and seventeen of geography, not all of which survive.

Fish and turtle eaters of the Arabian Gulf

Above these people is situated a desert tract with extensive pastures. It was abandoned in consequence of the multitudes of scorpions and tarantulas, called tetragnathi (or four-jawed), which formerly abounded to so great a degree as to occasion a complete desertion of the place long since by its inhabitants.

Next to the harbour of Eumenes, as far as Deire and the straits opposite the six islands, live the Icthyophagi, Creophagi, and Colobi, who extend into the interior.

Many hunting-grounds for elephants, and obscure cities and islands, lie in front of the coast.

The greater part are Nomades; husbandmen are few in number. In the country occupied by some of these nations styrax grows in large quantity. The Icthyophagi, on the ebbing of the tide, collect fish, which they cast upon the rocks and dry in the sun. When they have well broiled them, the bones are piled in heaps, and the flesh trodden with the feet is made into cakes, which are again exposed to the sun and used as food. In bad weather, when fish cannot be procured, the bones of which they have made heaps are pounded, made into cakes and eaten, but they suck the fresh bones. Some also live upon shell-fish, when they are fattened, which is done by throwing them into holes and standing pools of the sea, where they are supplied with small fish, and used as food when other fish are scarce. They have various kinds of places for preserving and feeding fish, from whence they derive their supply . . .

The Chelonophagi (or Turtle-eaters) live under the cover of shells (of turtles), which are large enough to be used as boats. Some make of the sea-weed, which is thrown up in large quantities, lofty and hill-like heaps, which are hollowed out, and underneath which they live. They cast out the dead, which are carried away by the tide, as food for fish.

Arrian

(c. AD/BC 95–180)

Flavius Arrianus, Greek officer in the Roman army who became Prefect of Cappodocia, and a historian, principally of the campaigns of Alexander the Great, conqueror of the Persian Empire.

Alexander's army at the Rock of Chorienes

When Alexander had secured his conquests in Sogdia, by his obtaining possession of this rock, he led his army against the Paraetacae, because he had received intelligence that there was another fort erected upon a rock in that country, into which abundance of the inhabitants had retired. This was named the Rock of Chorienes; and Chorienes himself, and other great men in vast numbers, had chosen that place for their safety. The slant height of this rock was about twenty stadia, and the circuit thereof near sixty, every were steep and craggy. There was only one ascent leading to the summit, hewn out by art, and purposely made so extremely narrow as not to admit of two men to ascend abreast. The foot of this rock was also surrounded with a deep ditch, so that whosoever would lead an army to it must of necessity reduce some part of the ditch to a level before he could bring his forces to a convenient station for an assault.

Alexander, however, in spite of all these difficulties, resolved to under-take the task, as deeming no place inaccessible, or impregnable against such an assailer; so great a confidence did he place in the continued course of his successes, having therefore ordered a vast number of fir-trees, which grew every where near this mountain, to be cut down, he commanded ladders to be made of them, whereby his soldiers might descend to the bottom of the ditch, which they could do by no other contrivance. All day long Alexander employed the half of his army upon this task; and in the night time, Perdiccas, Leonatus, and Ptolemy the son of Lagus, having divided the other half into three parts, took care to see the work carried on, which was of so great difficulty, by reason of the extraordinary hardness of the rock, that they finished no more than twenty cubits in a whole day, and in a night much less, though the whole army laboured therein by turns. However, descending into the ditch, and forcing large wooden piles into the bottom, at such a convenient distance from each other as to be able to bear a certain proposed weight; upon the tops of these piles they laid vast hurdles of osiers, or other twigs bound together, and those they covered with earth, that the army might pass over the ditch as upon a bridge.

Saewulf

(fl. 1101–3)

Twelfth century German or British monk who spent the best part of a year travelling from Apulia in Italy to the Holy Land, returning via Constantinople.

The perils of pilgrimage

What is the use of saying how sadly the sailors and pilgrims – some in boats, some clutching to masts or to yards or to cross-members – had all hope of escape gone. That's that. Some people were consumed with terror and drowned there and then. Some people were – as seemed unbelievable to many – clutching to the wooden parts of the ship, but as I saw they were cut to pieces or, being snatched off the timber of the ship, were taken off to deep water. Some people who knew how to swim took the chance of trusting to the waves, and many of them died, but just a few, trusting in their own strength, reached the shore safely.

So of thirty big ships, some known as Dormundi, others Gulafri and others Cats, all of them laden with palmers and merchandise, before I left the shore only a mere seven remained unharmed. Of human beings of either sex more than a thousand died that day.

No eye has seen greater misery in one day. But from all these things the Lord by his grace has saved me, to whom be honour and glory through innumerable ages. Amen.

So we climbed up from Joppa into the city of Jerusalem. The journey lasted two days and it was by a very hard mountain road. It was very dangerous too, because the Saracens, who are continually plotting an ambush against Christians, were hiding in the caves of the hills and among rocky caverns. They were awake day and night, always keeping a look-out for someone to attack, whether because he had not enough people with him, or because he was fatigued enough to leave a space between himself and his party. Sometimes the Saracens could be seen everywhere in the neighbourhood, and sometimes they disappeared.

Anyone who has taken that road can see how many human bodies there are in the road and next to the road, and there are countless corpses which have been torn up by wild beasts. It might be questioned why so many Christian corpses should lie there unburied, but it is in fact no surprise. There is little soil there, and the rocks are not easy to move. Even if the soil were there, who would be stupid enough to leave his brethren and be alone digging a grave!

Abbott Daniel

(*fl.* 1106–8)

A Russian abbot who travelled to the Holy Land and wrote an account of his observations which became a guidebook for other pilgrims.

The way to the River Jordan

The way from Jerusalem to the Jordan runs past the Mount of Olives to the north-east, and it is a very difficult road and dangerous and waterless, for the hills are high and rocky and there are many brigands in those fearful hills and valleys . . . From Choziba to Jericho is 5 versts and from Jericho to the Jordan 6 long versts over a plain in the sand, a very difficult road; here many choke from the heat and die of thirst; and the Sea of Sodom is near the road and it gives off a hot and stinking vapour and the heat burns up the whole of the area. Here, near the road, before you reach the Jordan, is the monastery of St John the Baptist, built high on a hill . . .

From the place where Christ was baptized to the Jordan itself is as far as a man can throw a small stone.

There is a pool in the Jordan and here all the Christians come to bathe; and there is a ford here across the Jordan into Arabia; here of old the Jordan parted for the sons of Israel and the people passed through on dry land. There too Elisha struck the water with the mantle of Elijah and they crossed the Jordan on dry land; and at the same pool Mary the Egyptian crossed the waters to Father Zosimus to receive the body of Christ and, crossing the waters again, went back into the desert.

The river Jordan flows rapidly; its bank is steep on the far side but gently sloping on the near side. Its water is very muddy but sweet to drink and one can never drink too much of this holy water and it will not make you ill or upset a man's stomach. In every way the River Jordan is like the river Snov, both in width and depth, and it flows very quickly and twists in its course like the river Snov. It is 4 fathoms deep at the middle of the bathing place, as I measured and tested myself, for I have crossed to the far side of the Jordan and have travelled much along its bank. The Jordan is as wide as the Snov at its mouth. There is on this side of the Jordan at the bathing-place a sort of wood of small trees like the willow. Further up the Jordan from the pool there are many osiers but not like our osiers, but rather like *silyazhi* and there are many reeds, and it has marshy areas like the river Snov. There are many wild beasts here, wild pigs without number and many panthers and lions. On the far side of the Jordan and some way off there are high rocky mountains and at the foot of these mountains there are other mountains nearer the Jordan and they are white. And there on the other side of the Jordan is the land of Zebulon and Naphtali.

Giovanni de Piano Carpini

(c. 1182–1253)

Italian Franciscan monk from Umbria; a friend of St Francis of Assisi. At over sixty years of age, Carpini was sent as an ambassador to the Mongol Khans sent by Pope Innocent IV, who feared the threat to Christendom from the Mongol hordes, the demons of their age. After fifteen months travel, three thousand miles on horseback through foul and freezing weather, Carpini's party reached the imperial encampment near Karakorum, where preparations were in progress for the enthronement of the Great Khan Guyuk, attended by four thousand noblemen from all over the empire. The Khan's eventual, blasphemous reply to the Pope was that he must come and submit personally to the 'Son of God and Lord of the World, the Great Khan'.

The great tent of the Tartars

And when we had been there five or six days, he sent us to his mother, where the solemn court was being held. When we got there they had already erected a great tent made of white purple, which in our opinion was large enough to hold more than two thousand persons; and around it a wooden paling had been made, and it was ornamented with divers designs.

On the second or third day we went with the Tartars who had been assigned to guard us (to this tent); and all the chiefs met there, and each one was riding around in a circle over hill and dale with his men. On the first day they were all dressed in white purple; on the second day, and then it was that Cuyuc came to the tent, they were dressed in red (purple); on the third day they were all in blue purple, and on the fourth day in the finest baldakins. In the paling near the tent were two big gates: one through which only the Emperor could pass, and at which there was no guard though it was open, for no one would dare to go in or out by it; and the other way by which all those who had admittance went in, and at this one were guards with swords, bows and arrows, and if anyone came near the tent outside of the set bounds, he was beaten if caught, or shot at with headless arrows if he ran away. The horses were kept at about two arrow-flights, I should say, from the tent. The chiefs went about everywhere with a number of their men all armed; but nobody, unless a chief, could go to the horses, without getting badly beaten for trying to do so. And many (of the horses) there were which had on their bits, breast-plates, saddles and cruppers quite twenty marks worth of gold I should think. And so the chiefs held counsel beyond the tent, and discussed the election, while all the rest of the people were far away from the tent. And there they remained till about noon, when they began drinking mare's milk, and they drank till evening so plentifully that it was a rare sight.

William of Rubruck

(1215–70)

Franciscan monk from Flanders. Like his predecessor, Carpini, he was sent as an ambassador to the Mongol court, but by King Louis IX of France. He found 'Turkie full of Christians' and describes everything from mare's milk and 'men milkers' to idolotary, soothsayers, Scythian tents, a 'Counterfeit Armenian Monke' a 'Coozening Clerke' and 'Manichean Blasphemie'. He was greatly surprised at the cosmopolitan entourage of the Khan, which he observed, 'wavers betwixt Ethnikes, Saracens and Christians'.

Mount Ararat

Near this city are mountains in which they say that Noah's ark rests; and there are two mountains, the one greater than the other; and the Araxes flows at their base; and there is a town there called Cemanum, which interpreted means "eight", and they say that it was thus called from the eight persons who came out of the ark, and who built it on the greater mountain. Many have tried to climb it, but none has been able. This bishop told me that there had been a monk who was most desirous (of climbing it), but that an angel appeared to him bearing a piece of the wood of the ark, and told him to try no more. They had this piece of wood in his church they told me. This mountain did not seem to me so high, that men could not ascend it. An old man gave quite a good reason why one ought not to try to climb it. They call the mountain Massis, and it is of the feminine gender in their language. "No one," he said, "ought to climb up Massis; it is the mother of the world."

Ibn Battuta

(c. 1304–77)

An Arab, born at Tangier, Ibn Battuta was perhaps the greatest traveller in world history. His travels started in 1325 with a pilgrimage to Mecca and Medina, via the North African coast, Egypt, the Nile and the Levant. He did not stop there but continued through the Near East, returning to Mecca to spend three years studying law, before sailing as a trader from Yemen to Somalia and on to Mombasa. He eventually reached Hangchow and the China Sea via Constantinople, Afghanistan, India, and the Maldive Islands, where he took an official position and four wives, eventually moving on to Ceylon with one of them. Battuta covered some 75,000 miles in thirty years of travel in Asia and Africa, not including detours. He settled in Fez to dictate the account of his journeys; this took thirty years.

Afterwards he travelled across the Atlas Mountains and the Sahara to Timbuktu.

The Sultan's meteorite

In the course of this audience the sultan asked me this question: 'Have you ever seen a stone that fell from the sky?' I replied, 'I have never seen one, nor ever heard tell of one.' 'Well,' he said, 'a stone did fall from the sky outside this town of ours,' and then called some men and told them to bring the stone. They brought in a great black stone, very hard and with a glitter in it – I reckoned its weight to amount to a hundredweight. The sultan ordered the stonebreakers to be summoned, and four of them came and on his command to strike it they beat upon it as one man four times with iron hammers, but made no impression on it. I was astonished at this phenomenon, and he ordered it to be taken back to its place.

Edward Daniel Clarke

(1769–1822)

English minerologist and traveller. As tutor to the sons of noblemen, Clarke travelled widely in Britain, Europe and the Near East. His book of *Travels* was very popular, no doubt on account of his great enjoyment of the world he witnessed. He later became the first professor of mineralogy at Cambridge.

Barbarous decorations at Tsarskoselo

The gardens of Tsarskoselo are laid out in the English taste; and therefore the only novelty belonging to them is their situation, so far removed from the nation whose customs they pretend to represent.

The interior of the building presents a number of spacious and gaudy rooms, fitted up in a style combining a mixture of barbarism and magnificence hardly to be credited. The walls of one of the rooms are entirely covered with fine pictures, by the best of the Flemish, and by other masters. These are fitted together, without frames, so as to cover, on each side, the whole of the wall, without the smallest attention to disposition or general effect. But, to consummate the Vandalism of those who directed the work, when they found a place they could not conveniently fill, the pictures were cut, in order to adapt them to the accidental spaces left vacant. The soldiers of Mummius, at the sacking of Corinth, would have been puzzled to contrive more ingenious destruction of the Fine Arts. Some of Ostade's best works were among the number of those thus ruined. We were also assured, by authority we shall not venture to name, that a profusion of pictures of the Flemish School were then lying in a cellar of the palace . . . the most extraordinary apartment, and that which usually attracts the notice of strangers more than any other, is a room, about thirty feet square, entirely covered, on all sides, from top to bottom, with amber; a lamentable waste of innumerable specimens of a substance which could nowhere have been so ill employed. The effect produces neither beauty nor magnificence. It would have been better expended even in ornamenting the heads of Turkish pipes; a custom which consumes the greatest quantity of this beautiful mineral. The appearance made by it on the walls is dull and heavy. It was a present from the King of Prussia. In an apartment prepared for Prince Potemkin, the floor was covered with different sorts of exotic wood, interlaid; the expense of which amounted to an hundred roubles for every squared archine. A profusion of gilding appears in many of the other rooms. The ball-room is an hundred and forty feet long by fifty-two feet wide, and two stories high. The walls and pilasters of another apartment were ornamented with lapis-lazuli, as well as the tables it contained.

Johann Ludwig Burckhardt

(1784–1817)

Swiss explorer. Appointed by the African Association to explore the Niger, he prepared himself by studying Arabic and Islamic law in Syria for two and a half years, in local guise. While in the Middle East he discovered the ruined Nabatean city of Petra and visited Palmyra. It was not until 1812 that he felt ready to set off for the Niger, still disguised as an Arab. Travelling southwards down the Nile, he made another great discovery, the rock temple of Abu Simbel. He then decided to complete his Arab alibi by visiting Mecca and Medina. Burckhardt died of dysentery at Cairo while waiting for a caravan to join across the Sahara and was buried under his Muslim name.

A sight of the Hadj

From the summit of Arafat, I counted about three thousand tents dispersed over the plain, of which two thirds belonged to the two Hadj caravans, and to the suite and soldiers of Mohammed Aly; the rest to the Arabs of the Sherif, the Bedouin hadjys, and the people of Mekka and Djidda. These assembled multitudes were for the greater number, like myself, without tents. The two caravans were encamped without much order, each party of pilgrims or soldiers having pitched its tents in large circles of *dowars*, in the midst of which many of their camels were reposing. The plain contained, dispersed in different parts, from twenty to twenty-five thousand camels, twelve thousand of which belonged to the Syrian Hadj, and from five to six thousand to the Egyptian; besides about three thousand, purchased by Mohammed Aly from the Bedouins in the Syrian Deserts, and brought to Mekka with the Hadj, to convey the pilgrims to this place, previously to being used for the transport of army-provisions to Tayf.

The Syrian Hadj was encamped on the south and south-west side of the mountain; the Egyptian on the south-east. Around the house of the

Sherif, Yahya himself was encamped with his Bedouin troops, and in its neighbourhood were all the Hedjaz people. Here it was that the two Yemen caravans used formerly to take their station. Mohammed Aly, and Soleyman Pasha of Damascus, as well as several of their officers, had very handsome tents; but the most magnificent of all was that of the wife of Mohammed Aly, the mother of Tousoun Pasha, and Ibrahim Pasha, who had lately arrived from Cairo for the Hadj, with a truly royal equipage, five hundred camels being necessary to transport her baggage from Djidda to Mekka. Her tent was in fact an encampment consisting of a dozen tents of different sizes, inhabited by her women; the whole enclosed by a wall of linen cloth, eight hundred paces in circuit, the single entrance to which was guarded by eunuchs in splendid dresses. Around this enclosure were pitched the tents of the men who formed her numerous suite. The beautiful embroidery on the exterior of this linen palace, with the various colours displayed on every part of it, constituted an object which reminded me of some descriptions in the Arabian Tales of the Thousand and One Nights. Among the rich equipages of the other hadjys, or of the Mekka people, none were so conspicuous as that belonging to the family of Djeylany, the merchant, whose tents, pitched in a semicircle, rivalled in beauty those of the two Pashas, and far exceeded those of Sherif Yahya. In other parts of the East, a merchant would as soon think of buying a rope for his own neck, as of displaying his wealth in the presence of a Pasha; but Djeylany has not yet laid aside the customs which the Mekkawys learned under their old government, particularly that of Sherif Ghaleb, who seldom exercised extortion upon single individuals; and they now rely on the promises of Mohammed Aly, that he will respect their property . . . I estimated the number of persons assembled here at about seventy thousand. The camp was from three to four miles, and between one and two in breadth. There is, perhaps, no spot on earth where, in so small a place, such a diversity of languages are heard; I reckoned about forty, and have no doubt that there were many more.

David Roberts

(1796–1864)

Scottish topographical painter. The son of a shoemaker, Roberts began his career as a house decorator, becoming a scene painter for travelling shows and later at Covent Garden. He eventually travelled and painted extensively in Europe, North Africa, the Near East and Egypt, where he claimed to have been the first artist to draw the Pyramids, in 1838. As well as paintings, Roberts published numerous lithographs.

'What an Eastern monarch I am'

31st January 1839, from a letter to his daughter Christine
I am so completely transmogrified in appearance that my dear old mother would never know me. Before I could get admission to the mosques, I had to transfer my whiskers to my upper lip, and don the full Arab costume, since which I have been allowed to make sketches, both in oil and water colours, of the principal mosques, etc.

I have provided everything requisite for my journey. A tent (a very gay one, I assure you), skins for carrying water, pewter dishes, provisions of all sorts, not forgetting a brace of Turkish pistols, and a warm covering for night. Imagine me mounted on my camel, my black servant on another, and two men with my tent and luggage; the other two gentlemen similarly furnished and accoutred, surrounded by a host of the children of the desert – the wild Arabs; and you will have an idea of what an Eastern monarch I am.

William Henry Bartlett

(1809–54)

English topographical draughtsman. Bartlett then visited
Europe, and made three journeys to the Middle East. Over
a thousand of his drawings were published in numerous
books of engravings. He died on the way home from Egypt
and was buried at sea, somewhere between Malta and
Marseilles. Here, he prepares for *Forty Days in the Desert*,
a journey from Cairo to Petra in 1845.

Setting out

To provision ourselves was the next point; and as I was desirous of
hitting, if possible, the *juste milieu* between starvation and prodigality,
we repaired to the shop of old Carlo Peni, near the consulate, and there,
in conclave, decided on the following articles, the quantity of which
served well for the entire tour to Petra, though of six weeks' duration,
and, in realty, calculated at the time as for a far shorter period. I give
the list, hoping it may save some trouble to future travellers, and amuse
the general reader with a picture of Desert housekeeping.

September 27. – 1845

	Piastres
2 okas Lump Sugar, at 6 piastres (100 piastres equal £1. sterling)	12
40 Biscuits, (instead of bread,) at 2 piastres	80
4 Soap, (none in the Desert, nor washerwomen) at 7 piastres	26
10 Rice, at 3 piastres	30
20 rotl., each 2lbs., Coffee. (A very large supply is needful, as nothing is done without it,) at 3 piastres	60
3 okas Tobacco, at 15 piastres	45
1 bag for ditto	5
Onions, (very desirable for stewing)	10
Lentiles, (for soup, similar to peas)	12

Charcoal. (A small quantity is needful for occasional use, when no brush-wood can be had)	10
12 okas Potatoes, (invaluable)	18
Dates	10
3 okas Dried Apricots, (delicious and refreshing when stewed)	18
2 packets Wax Candles	20
An Arab Paper Lantern for ditto	5
12 okas Chocolate	24
1 " Salt	1
1 box Pepper	4
3 bottles Cognac, (more desirable than wine or beer, on account of the bad water, but must be temperately used)	42
1 Cantine, with lock, (a box of palm-sticks, made expressly for carrying various small necessary articles)	25
5 okas Liquid Cooking-butter and Pot	38
Matches	6
8 Nets for the camels, complete, (to sling small packages in)	50
3 Water-Skins, complete, (Much care is requisite to get them, not *new*, but sufficiently seasoned not to flavour the water, and they never should be laid on the *sand*, but on the nets. *A filler is highly desirable*)	90
2 Zemzemie, or leathern Drinking-bottles	30
1 Large Cooking-Pot	5
Cords, Thread, Needles, &c., (A few extra pegs too, for the tent, are very necessary, of iron if possible)	16
2 common Pipes, (for Arabs;) Umbrella of double Cotton; double Straw, or *light* Hat, well lined	10
12 Fowls, Cafass, (or coop,) and Corn. (We did not find any of them die, as often reported; but they require care.)	25
3 Camp Stools, (broad and low – *very useful*)	60
Some pieces of Oilcloth to spread under, or put over the tent, in case of rain, when on the march.	
Tea.	
Curry-Powder, (desirable for seasoning a tough fowl occasionally.)	
Marmalade, (very refreshing and easily carried.)	
Lemons, (a good supply.)	

Eau de Cologne which should be put in a stone bottle.
All these arrange in the cafasses, or in loose bags.

Departure by camel

At length, everything being ready, the camels blockading the door, and
the usual clamour of the Arabs filling the street, I left the hotel to pay
one or two farewell visits, and joined my little caravan in the cemetery
outside the Bab-en-Nusr, or Gate of Victory, where the splendid domes
of the tombs of the Memlook sultans – the perfection of Arabian architecture – rise like an exhalation from the lonely waste. By unusually good
management the camels, often reloaded here, were already provided with
their respective burdens, and I had nothing to do but to start. It was
so much earlier than I had expected to be ready, that no one was found
to give me a parting convoy; and I stood in the dead, oppressive heat
of noon, alone on the verge of the Desert. The hot film trembled over
the far-stretched and apparently boundless sands; and though I had
looked forward with delight to the time of setting off, the journey now
for the first time seemed formidable; and with not even a friendly shake
of the hand, or a parting God-b'w'ye – within a stone's throw too of
the grave of poor Burckhardt, I could not repress a feeling of melancholy.
But the Arabs cut this short, by suddenly leaping up out of the shade
of a ruined tomb, and mechanically bringing forward my dromedary.

Alexander Kinglake

(1809–91)

English historian, lawyer and traveller. In 1835 he made a
journey to the Levant and Near East, described in his very
successful book, *Eothen*, in which he describes 'the splendour and havoc of the East'. In 1854 Kinglake went to the
Crimea and later, at the invitation of Lady Raglan, wrote the
official history of the campaign at enormous length.

Lady Hester Stanhope

One favoured subject of discourse was that of "race", upon which she was very diffuse, and yet rather mysterious; she set great value upon the ancient French (not Norman blood, for that she vilified), but did not at all appreciate that which we call in this country, "an old family". She had a vast idea of the Cornish miners, on account of their race, and said, if she chose, she could give me the means of rousing them to the most tremendous enthusiasm.

Such are the topics on which the Lady mainly conversed, but very often she would descend to more worldly chat, and then she was no longer the prophetess, but the sort of woman that you sometimes see, I am told, in London drawing-rooms, cool – decisive in manner – unsparing of enemies – full of audacious fun, and saying the downright things that the sheepish society around her is afraid to utter. I am told that Lady Hester was in her youth a capital mimic, and she shewed me that not all the queenly dullness to which she had condemned herself, not all her fasting, and solitude, had destroyed this terrible power. The first whom she crucified in my presence, was poor Lord Byron; she had seen him, it appeared, I know not where, soon after his arrival in the East, and was vastly amused at his little affectations; he had picked up a few sentences of the Romaic, with which he affected to give orders to his Greek servant; I can't tell whether Lady Hester's mimicry of the bard was at all close, but it was amusing; she attributed to him a curiously coxcombical lisp.

Another person, whose style of speaking the Lady took off amusingly, was one who would scarcely object to suffer by the side of Lord Byron, I mean Lamartine, who had visited her in the course of his travels; the peculiarity which attracted her ridicule was an over-refinement of manner: according to my Lady's imitation of Lamartine (I have never seen him myself), he had none of the violent grimace of his countrymen, and not even their usual way of talking, but rather bore himself mincingly, like the humbler sort of English dandy.

Lady Hester seems to have heartily despised every thing approaching to exquisiteness; she told me, by the by (and her opinion upon that subject is worth having) that a downright manner, amounting even to brusqueness, is more effective than any other with the Oriental; and that amongst the English, of all ranks, and all classes, there is no man so attractive to the Orientals – no man who can negotiate with them half so effectively, as a good, honest, open-hearted, and positive naval officer of the old school . . .

The Secretary told me that his Mistress was greatly disliked by the surrounding people, whom she oppressed by her exactions, and the truth of this statement was borne out by the way in which my Lady spoke to me of her neighbours. But in Eastern countries, hate and veneration are very commonly felt for the same object, and the general belief in the superhuman power of this wonderful white lady – her resolute and imperious character, and above all, perhaps, her fierce Albanians (not backward to obey an order for the sacking of a village) inspired sincere respect amongst the surrounding inhabitants.

Evariste Regis Huc

(1813–60)

French Catholic missionary. Disguised as Tibetan lamas, he and a colleague, Father Gabet set off from their Lazarist mission in China to convert Tibet. After an extraordinary and hazardous two-year journey, they reached Lhasa but two months later were expelled on the initiative of a Chinese resident. He eventually returned to France, his health broken by his ordeals.

Eating sheeps' tails at the Mongol Festival of the Moon

The family being assembled round the table, the chief drew a knife from his girdle, severed the sheep's tail, and divided it into two equal pieces, which he placed before us.

With the Tartars, the tail is considered the most delicious portion of their sheep, and accordingly the most honourable. These tails of the Tartarian sheep are of immense size and weight, the fat upon them alone weighing from six to eight pounds.

The fat and juicy tail having thus been offered a homage to the two stranger guests, the rest of the company, knife in hand, attacked the four quarters of the animal, and had speedily, each man, a huge piece before him. Plate or fork, there was none, the knees supplied the absence of the one, the hands of the other, the flowing grease being wiped off, from time to time, upon the front of the jacket. Our own embarrassment was extreme. That great white mass of fat had been given to us with the best intentions, but, not quite clear of European prejudices, we could not make up our stomachs to venture, without bread or salt, upon the lumps of tallow that quivered in our hands. We briefly consulted, in our native tongue, as to what on earth was to be done under these distressing circumstances. Furtively, to replace the horrible masses upon the table would be imprudent; openly to express to our Amphytrion our repugnance to this *par excellence* Tartarian delicacy, was impossible, as wholly opposed to Tartar etiquette. We devised this plan: we cut the villanous tail into numerous pieces, and insisted, in that day of general rejoicing, upon the company's partaking with us of this precious dish.

Roger Fenton

(1819–69)

English photographer who trained as painter in Paris. He went to Russia in 1852 to photograph the construction of the new suspension bridge in Kiev. Three years later he went to Crimea as one of the world's first war photographers. He travelled in the Crimea with two assistants, three horses and a small converted wine-merchant's vehicle serving as caravan and darkroom. Glass plates had to be coated with wet collodion in the most difficult conditions; the plates had to be exposed while still damp, and heat haze was as much of a problem as smoke from the battles. The van came under Russian fire on more than one occasion. Fenton returned to England after contracting cholera; his remarkable photographs were exhibited and published. Fenton also introduced the Royal family to

photography and was one of the founders of the Photo-
graphic Society, but in 1862 he gave up photography and
became a lawyer.

The valley of Inkerman

Yesterday was May day, and a lovely day we had. I got Sir George Brown
to sit with me; he was very amiable, put on his uniform and a cocked
hat and did just as I wished him. He asked me to dine with him at
seven.

In the afternoon I rode with Hallewell to Inkerman, got halfway
down the slope, took the bridles off our horses, let them graze, and we
lay basking in the sun and looking through the glass at a piquet of
Cossacks along the Tchernaya and a regiment of infantry being drilled
about two miles off, in front of the lines which the Russians have made
across the country where the Mackenzie farm road comes down.

Wherever the ground is not quite safe to go on (where it is commanded by Russian batteries) it is quite surprising to see the mass of
wild flowers with which the ground is covered; all over the steep sides
of the Inkerman the grass and flowers are gradually budding; the pieces
of torn cloth, ragged caps, shoes without soles, now form the principal
indications of the struggles which took place there. I have been there
now three times, and with people who were in the battle, and none of
them can tell me where any of the principal incidents took place. Everybody was busy about what immediately concerned their own corps or
department, and saw nothing of the general action. I was told a new
version of the French attack on the Russian flank. It was said that a
French regiment mounted the hill to meet the Russians and was observed
at once when on the top to turn right about face and come down again.
An ADC rode up to the Colonel and said, "*Mais monsieur*, are you
retreating?" The answer was, "*Voilà les Ruses!*"

On our return just before dinner Sir George Brown sent for Hallewell
and told him something that made him come home dancing and kicking
and emptying a tumbler of champagne, when he grew able to inform
us that an expedition was to start off the next day [3rd May] by sea
somewhere or other.

Sir Richard Francis Burton

(1821–1890)

English explorer. Burton started travelling with his parents; he learned five languages as a boy. He joined the Bombay Native Infantry and spent three years studying Indian life and oriental languages, posing as a wealthy merchant. In 1853 he visited Mecca and Medina in oriental disguises, and then went to Harar, a forbidden city in Somalia. Four years later he was sent by the Royal Geographical Society with John Hanning Speke to find Lake Nyanza and the sources of the Nile. After 900 miles, and half dead, they found Lake Tanganyika, before falling out and going their separate ways. Burton's later travels were in North America, and as consul at Fernando Po, Santos in Brazil, Damascus and Trieste, where he died. Burton was also the translator of sixteen volumes of *The Arabian Nights*, *The Perfumed Garden* and the *Kama Sutra*. The prurient Lady Burton burned many of his manuscripts.

The Road to Mecca

At three p.m. we left Al-Zaribah, travelling towards the South-West, and a wondrously picturesque scene met the eye. Crowds hurried along, habited in the pilgrim-garb, whose whiteness contrasted strangely with their black skins; their newly shaven heads glistening in the sun, and their long black hair streaming in the wind. The rocks rang with shouts of *Labbayk! Labbayk!* At a pass we fell in with the Wahhabis, accompanying the Baghdad Caravan, screaming 'Here am I'; and, guided by a large loud kettle-drum, they followed in double file the camel of a standard-bearer, whose green flag bore in huge white letters the formula of the Moslem creed. They were wild-looking mountaineers, dark and fierce, with hair twisted into thick Dalik or plaits: each was armed with a long spear, a matchlock, or a dagger. They were seated upon coarse wooden saddles, without cushions or stirrups, a fine saddle-cloth alone denoting a chief. The women emulated the men; they either guided their own dromedaries, or, sitting in pillion, they clung to their husbands; veils they disdained, and the counternances certainly belonged not to a 'soft sex'. These Wahhabis were by no means pleasant companions. Most of them were followed by spare dromedaries, either unladen or carrying water-skins, fodder, fuel, and other necessaries for the march. The beasts delighted in dashing furiously through our file, which being lashed together, head and tail, was thrown each time into the greatest confusion. And whenever we were observed smoking, we were cursed aloud for Infidels and Idolaters.

Looking back at Al-Zaribah, soon after our departure, I saw a heavy nimbus settle upon the hill-tops, a sheet of rain being stretched between it and the plain. The low grumbling of thunder sounded joyfully in our ears. We hoped for a shower, but were disappointed by a dust-storm, which ended with a few heavy drops. There arose a report that the Badawin had attacked a party of Meccans with stones, and the news caused men to look exceeding grave.

William Gifford Palgrave

(1826–88)

English diplomat and traveller. After serving in the Bombay Light Infantry, Palgrave became a Jesuit and went on a mission to Syria and Arabia. He often travelled disguised as a Syrian doctor. In 1865 he left the Jesuits and became a British diplomat in Abyssinia, Trebizond, Turkish Georgia, Upper Euphrates, West Indies, Manila, Bulgaria, Bangkok and Uruguay.

Dress and equipment for Arabian travel

Myself and my companion were dressed like ordinary middle-class travellers of inner Syria; an equipment in which we had already made our way from Gaza on the sea coast to Ma'an without much remark or unseasonable questioning from those whom we fell in with, while we traversed a country so often described already by Pococke, Laborde, and downwards, under the name of Arabia Petræa, that it would be superfluous for me to enter into any new account of it in the present work. Our dress then consisted partly of a long stout blouse of Egyptian hemp, under which, unlike our Bedouin fellow-travellers, we indulged in the luxury of the loose cotton drawers common in the East, while our coloured head-kerchiefs, though simple enough, were girt by 'akkals or head-bands of some pretension to elegance; the loose red leather boots of the country completed our toilet.

But in the large travelling-sacks at our camels' sides were contained suits of a more elegant appearance, carefully concealed from Bedouin gaze, but destined for appearance when we should reach better inhabited and more civilized districts. This reserve toilet numbered articles like the following: coloured overdresses, the Syrian combaz, handkerchiefs where silk stripes relieved the plebeian cotton, and girdles of good material and tasteful colouring; such clothes being absolutely requisite to maintain our assumed character. Mine was that of a native travelling doctor, a quack if you will; and accordingly a tolerable dress was indispensable for the credit of my medical practice. My comrade, who in a general way passed for my brother-in-law, appeared sometimes as a retail merchant, such as not unfrequently visit these countries, and sometimes as pupil or associate in my assumed profession.

Our pharmacopœia consisted of a few but well selected and efficacious drugs, inclosed in small tight-fitting tin boxes, stowed away for the present in the ample recesses of our travelling-bags about fifty of these little cases contained wherewithal to kill or cure half the sick men of Arabia. Medicines of a liquid form had been as much as possible omitted, not only from the difficulty of ensuring them a safe transport amid so rough a mode of journeying, but also on account of the rapid evaporation unavoidable in this dry and burning climate. In fact two or three small bottles, whose contents had seemed to me of absolute necessity, soon retained nothing save their labels to indicate what they had held, in spite of air-tight stoppers and double coverings. I record this, because the hint may be useful to any one who should be inclined to embark in similar guise on the same adventures.

Viscount James Bryce

(1838–1922)

Scottish historian, lawyer, statesman and mountaineer. In 1876 he visited Russia, Caucasus and Armenia; and wrote a charming book about his travels around Mount Ararat.

To the summit of Mount Ararat

At length the rock-slope came suddenly to an end, and I stepped out upon the almost level snow at the top of it, coming at the same time into the clouds, which naturally clung to the colder surfaces. A violent west wind was blowing, and the temperature must have been pretty low, for a big icicle at once enveloped the lower half of my face, and did not melt till I got to the bottom of the cone, four hours afterwards. Unluckily, I was very thinly clad, the stout tweed coat reserved for such occasions having been stolen on a Russian railway. The only expedient to be tried against the piercing cold was to tighten in my loose light coat by winding round the waist a Spanish *faja*, or scarf, which I had brought up to use, in case of need, as a neck wrapper. Its bright purple looked odd enough in such surroundings, but as there was nobody there to notice, appearances did not much matter. In the mist, which was now thick, the eye could pierce only some thirty yards ahead; so I walked on over the snow five or six minutes, following the rise of its surface, which was gentle, and fancying there might still be a good long way to go. To mark the backward track, I trailed the point of the ice-axe along behind me in the soft snow, for there was no longer any landmark: all was cloud on every side. Suddenly, to my astonishment, the ground began to fall away to the north; I stopped, a puff of wind drove off the mists on one side, the opposite side to that by which I had come, and showed the Araxes plain at an abysmal depth below. It was the top of Ararat.

From this tremendous height it looked more like a broken obelisk than an independent summit 12,800 feet in height. Clouds covered the farther side of the great snow basin, and were seething like waves about the savage pinnacles, the towers of the Jinn palace, which guard its lower margin, and past which my upward path had lain. With mists to the left and above, and a range of black precipices cutting off all view to the right, there came a vehement sense of isolation and solitude, and I began to understand better the awe with which the mountain silence inspires the Kurdish shepherds. Overhead the sky had turned from dark blue to an intense bright green, a colour whose strangeness seemed to add to the weird terror of the scene. It wanted barely an hour to the time when I had resolved to turn back; and as I struggled up the crumbling rocks, trying now to right and now to left, where the foothold looked a little firmer, I began to doubt whether there was strength enough to carry me an hour higher.

Wilfred Scawen Blunt

(1840–1922)

English traveller, politician, poet and writer. Between 1858–69, Blunt was a diplomat, but became fiercely anti-imperialist and was imprisoned in Ireland for his activities.

A true wilderness, Siwah, 1897

Of birds I saw only three, mourning chats, black with white beaks and rumps – nothing else alive. The depth of the oasis puzzled my barometer. It must be about 150 feet below the sea. From the bottom the track led up by some clumps of palms, where I am sure there must be water underground, across deep *nefuds* to the opposite *nukbe* marked by some wonderful rocks – one quite square, white as marble, and with curious architectural markings, another like a tall chessman, both 100 feet high at least, their tops level with the plain above, a splendid hermitage where one might find shade and shelter at all hours and in every weather. They are geologically of limestone, with layers of shells, their tops black, like lava. One layer of the chessman, one of those round white flakes,

Suliman calls *dirahem* (money). This place was the wildest, the most romantic, the most supernatural in its natural structure I have ever seen, an abode of all the *jan*.

Frederick Burnaby

(1842–85)

English professional soldier and traveller, who journeyed in Central and South America, Spain and Tangier. He achieved fame with his astonishing account of his *Ride to Khiva*, on horseback. Burnaby died in the Sudan, while ostensibly on General Gordon's mission to relieve Khartoum, but secretly joined Sir Herbert Stewart's Nile expedition and was killed by a native spear. He had earlier crossed the English Channel in a balloon. A splendid painting of him hangs in the National Portrait Gallery, London.

Conversation with a Turkish porter

I had ordered a porter at my hotel to call me early on the following morning, as the train started at seven, and it was quite half an hour's walk to the station. Luckily I awoke myself, and on looking at my watch, found it was about half-past six. Hastily dressing, I hurried downstairs, and found the individual whose business it was to awake me, fast asleep under a billiard table in the café belonging to the hotel. He grumbled at being disturbed, and did not fancy the idea of carrying my box to the station. It was necessary to use a little persuasive force, so, seizing a billiard cue, I gave him a violent poke in the side.

"Get up directly! I shall miss the train!"

"Please God you will not," replied the Turk, with a yawn.

I had no time to lose, so, taking the recumbent man by the collar, I lifted him bodily on his legs, put my bag in his hand, and, with another push from the billiard cue, precipitated him down the steps into the street.

"You want me to go to the station, Effendi!" said the fellow, now thoroughly aroused.

"Yes."

"But the train will be gone."

"Not if we run."

"Run!" replied the porter, very much astonished, "and what will the Effendi do?"

"Run too."

And with another thrust from the billiard cue, I started him down Pera.

Charles Montagu Doughty

(1843–1926)

English traveller, writer and poet. In 1870 he spent two years wandering in Arabia. Tall and with a red beard, he followed the *Haj* or pilgrimage to Mecca, giving himself away when he entered the mosque in the closed city of Keybar with his shoes on. He spent four months in prison. He then went into the desert and travelled among the Bedu, often in conditions of the greatest hardship. His *Travels in Arabia Deserta*, written in archaic language evoking the Golden Age of English, that of Chaucer and Spenser, is a masterpiece of travel literature.

In the deserts of Nejd

At daybreak we departed from Gofar: this by my reckoning was the first week of April. Eyâd loosed out our sick *thelûl* to pasture; and they drove her slowly forward in the desert plain till the sun went down behind Ajja, when we halted under bergs of grey granite. These rocks are fretted into bosses and caves more than the granite of Sinai: the heads of the granite crags are commonly trap rock. Eyâd, kindling a fire, heated his iron ramrod, and branded their mangy *thelûl*. I had gone all day on foot; and the Ageylies threatened every hour to cast down my bags, though now light as Merjàn's *temmn*, which she also carried. We marched four miles further, and espied a camp fire; and coming to the place we found a ruckling troop of camels couched for the night, in the open *khála*. The herd-lad and his brother sat sheltering in the hollow bank of a *seyl*, and a watch-fire of sticks was burning before them. The hounds of the Aarab follow not with the herds, the lads could not see beyond their fire-light, and our *salaam* startled them: then falling on our knees we sat down by them, – and with that word we were acquainted. The lads made some of their *nâgas* stand up, and they milked full bowls and frothing over for us. We heard a night-fowl shriek, where we had left our bags with the *thelûl*: my *rafiks* rose and ran back with their sticks, for the bird (which they call *sirrûk*, a thief) might, they said, steal something. When we had thus supped, we lay down upon the pleasant *seyl* sand to sleep.

Anton Chekhov

(1860–1904)

Russian doctor, and writer of plays and stories. Suffering from tuberculosis, Chekhov lived mostly abroad or in the Crimea after 1857, but had earlier undertaken an extremely demanding journey through Siberia. *Saghalien Island*, his account of a Siberian penal colony, had a mitigating effect on Russian penal laws.

An estate at Sorotchintsi

To A.N. Pleshtcheyev

SUMY, *June* 28, 1888.

We have been to the province of Poltava. We went to the Smagins', and to Sorotchintsi. We drove with a four-in-hand, in an ancestral, very comfortable carriage. We had no end of laughter, adventures, misunderstandings, halts, and meetings on the way . . . If you had only seen the places where we stayed the night and the villages stretching eight or ten versts through which we drove! . . . What weddings we met on the road, what lovely music we heard in the evening stillness, and what a heavy smell of fresh hay there was! Really one might sell one's soul to the devil for the pleasure of looking at the warm evening sky, the pools and the rivulets reflecting the sad, languid sunset . . .

. . . The Smagins' estate is "great and fertile", but old, neglected, and dead as last year's cobwebs. The house has sunk, the doors won't shut, the tiles in the stove squeeze one another out and form angles, young suckers of cherries and plums peep up between the cracks of the floors . . . At the beehouse there is an old grandsire who remembers King Goroh and Cleopatra of Egypt.

Everything is crumbling and decrepit, but poetical, sad, and beautiful in the extreme.

Meteors in my cabin

To his Sister

The Steamer "Muravyov", *June* 29, 1890.

Meteors are flying in my cabin – these are luminous beetles, that look like electric sparks. Wild goats swim across the Amur in the day-time. The flies here are huge. I am sharing my cabin with a Chinaman – Son-Luli – who is constantly telling me how in China for the merest trifle it is "off with his head". Last night he got drunk with opium, and was talking in his sleep all night and preventing me from sleeping. On the 27th I walked about the Chinese town Aigun. Little by little I seem gradually to be stepping into a fantastic world. The steamer rocks, it is hard to write.

To-morrow I shall reach Habarovsk. The Chinaman began to sing from music written on his fan.

David George Hogarth

(1862–1927)

English scholar, archaeologist and traveller. Director of the British School at Athens, he also joined Sir Arthur Evans as he began the excavation of Knossos in Crete. He worked and travelled in the Middle East and as Director of the Arab Bureau in Cairo, 1915–18, was one of the architects of the Arab Revolt. Hogarth was Keeper of the Ashmolean Museum in Oxford from 1909 until his death.

A Central Asian breakfast

The horses were brought out, the saddle-bags packed, and, after much opium and scalding milk, I was lifted into the saddle, with a rug and an overcoat rolled before and behind for support. At first we proceeded but uncertainly, but, as the town was left behind, something in the pure morning air, something in the sense of motion and escape put heart into me again, and I kept on. The farther we went, the better I became; and indeed I suppose my malady must have been largely nervous, for in the end, with the exception of a short halt at a bridge, into whose balustrade a Roman milestone and a Greek inscription were built, I sat in the saddle for five hours, and at midday reached Felleli, a large half-deserted Turk village of the plain. I could eat nothing, but I slept, and so pulled myself round sufficiently to copy in the afternoon the few inscribed stones reported by the villagers.

Gertrude Bell

(1868–1926)

English traveller. Bell was also a writer, mountaineer, archaeologist and member of the British Secret Service; she was also the first woman to take first class honours in modern history. She made a fourteen-day crossing of the Syrian Desert in 1911 as part of her intrepid explorations of Persia, Anatolia and Syria. Bell also helped to establish the museum in Baghdad, the city where she died.

Excursion to Palmyra, 1900

At 3 we were off again, and down into the plain, and then straight east at the foot of the hills. It had never been really hot all day, fortunately; the sun set without a cloud and it began to be very cold. We rode till 7 and then stopped for the animals to eat, and for us to eat too. I put on gaiters, a second pair of knickerbockers and a covert coat under my thick winter coat, rolled myself up in a blanket and a cape and went to sleep, all the men following my example, rolled up in their long cloaks.

The cold and the bright moon woke me at midnight and I roused all my people (with some difficulty!) and at one we were off. Again, you see, we had to reach our water as soon as possible after the sun, so that the animals might not suffer too much from thirst. We went on and on; the dawn came and the sun rose – the evening and the morning of the second day, but I seemed to have been riding since the beginning of time. At sunrise, far away in the distance, on top of one of a group of low hills, I saw the castle of Palmyra. We were still five hours away. They were long hours. Except Petra, Palmyra is the loveliest thing I have seen in this country, but five hours away. They were long hours. The wide plain gradually narrowed and we approached the W. belt of hills, rocky, broken and waterless. It's a fine approach, the hills forming a kind of gigantic avenue with a low range at the end behind which Palmyra stands, and the flat desert, very sandy here, running up to them. My horse was very tired, and I was half dazed with sleep. As we drew near Palmyra, the hills were covered with the strangest buildings, great stone towers, four stories high, some more ruined and some less, standing together in groups or bordering the road. They are the famous Palmyrene tower tombs. At length we stood on the end of the col and looked over Palmyra. I wonder if the wide world presents a more singular landscape. It is a mass of columns, ranged into long avenues, grouped into temples, lying broken on the sand or pointing one long solitary finger to heaven. Beyond them is the immense Temple of Baal; the modern town is built inside it and its rows of columns rise out of a mass of mud roofs. And beyond all is the desert, sand and white stretches of salt and sand again, with the dust clouds whirling over it and the Euphrates five days away. It looks like the white skeleton of a town, standing knee deep in the blown sand.

T.E. Lawrence

(1888–1935)

English adventurer, soldier and scholar. Lawrence worked on digs with distinguished archaeologists, including David Hogarth (q.v.) in Syria where he learned Arabic, Flinders Petrie in Egypt, and Sir Leonard Woolley. In 1914 he joined the intelligence section of the British Army in Egypt, and, supported by Emir Feisal, became a leader of the Arab Revolt against the Turks in a partisan war in the desert. His *Seven Pillars of Wisdom*, of which most of the first manuscript was lost at Reading Station, was eventually published by subscription. It became a classic. In 1922, Lawrence joined the RAF and then the Royal Tank Corps under pseudonyms. He was killed as the result of a motor cycle accident near his home in Dorset where he lived frugally.

Lost in the Bisaita

There was no one behind, so I rode forward wishing to see how his camel was: and at last found it, riderless, being led by one of the Howeitat. His saddle-bags were on it, and his rifle and his food, but he himself was nowhere; gradually it dawned on us that the miserable man was lost. This was a dreadful business, for in the haze and mirage the caravan could not be seen for two miles, and on the iron ground it made no tracks: afoot he would never overtake us.

Everyone had marched on, thinking him elsewhere in our loose line; but much time had passed and it was nearly midday, so he must be miles back. His loaded camel was proof that he had not been forgotten asleep at our night halt. The Ageyl ventured that perhaps he had dozed in the saddle and fallen, stunning or killing himself: or perhaps someone of the party had borne him a grudge. Anyway they did not know. He was an ill-natured stranger, no charge on any of them, and they did not greatly care . . .

Without saying anything, I turned my unwilling camel round, and forced her, grunting and moaning for her camel friends, back past the long line of men, and past the baggage into the emptiness behind . . .

Before twenty minutes, the caravan was out of sight, and it was borne in on me how really barren the Bisaita was. Its only marks were the old sanded samh pits, across all possible of which I rode, because my camel tracks would show in them, and be so many blazes of the way back. This samh was the wild flour of the Sherarat; who, poor in all but camel-stocks, made it a boast to find the desert sufficient for their every need. When mixed with dates and loosened with butter, it was good food . . .

The pits, little threshing floors, were made by pushing aside the flints over a circle of ten feet across. The flints, heaped up round the rim of the pit, made it inches deep, and in this hollow place the women collected and beat out the small red seed. The constant winds, sweeping since over them, could not indeed put back the flint surface (that would perhaps be done by the rain in thousands of winters), but had levelled them up with pale blown sand, so that the pits were grey eyes in the black stony surface.

I had ridden about an hour and a half, easily, for the following breeze had let me wipe the crust from my red eyes and look forward almost without pain: when I saw a figure, or large bush, or at least something black ahead of me. The shifting mirage disguised height or distance; but this thing seemed moving, a little east of our course. On chance I turned my camel's head that way, and in a few minutes saw that it was Gasim.

Bertram Thomas

(1892–1950)

English explorer of Arabia and English political officer. Thomas made the first crossing of the Empty Quarter, the Rub'al-Khali, in 1930–31, beating Harry St John Philby by a year. Thomas reached Doha on the Persian Gulf, sixty-seven days after leaving Salala, accompanied by a party of Rashid Bedouin. On seeing the desert, Thomas noted the 'dunes of all sizes, unsymmetrical in relation to one another, but with the exquisite roundness of a girl's breasts, rise tier upon tier like a mighty mountain system'.

Badawin bedding

We camped in Umm al Hait at a point where Nukhdat Waraiga, a distributary, takes off on a north-easterly bearing. A twin Nukhdat Hishman lying to the north-west has a more northerly course, both penetrating into these southern sands for a distance of a day and a half's march to embrace a region called Umm Dharta.

The temperature fell to 47°F that night, and we felt the cold bitterly as we were sleeping in the open after a hot day in the saddle, and on waking my hands were too numbed with cold to do much note-taking. For the next six nights the temperature fell about as low. My two blankets made it endurable for me, wearing all my clothes as well, but for my companions it meant wretchedness. The Badawin sleep on the sands, which are very hot by day and very cold by night; they have no other clothes than the cotton rags they wear by day; no bedding, which would be a nuisance, anyhow, and be thought effeminate. They collect a night's store of brushwood for the campfire, and curl up before it, naked but for a loin-cloth, for their other garment, a shirt, is doffed and used as a sheet. So also the women folk, though they have 'tents of hair' in the sands for a shelter, and a rug to sleep upon, wear only their trousers by night, their outer garment – except in case of the well-to-do – serving again as sheet. By day nearly all go barefoot; but if the sands are very hot, both sexes may use a roughly knitted sock. Excessive indulgence is, however, deprecated.

Our course for the next five days skirted this southern fringe of the great sands, first west-north-west, then gradually veering to west. The altitude remained fairly constant at about 950 feet, though the fall of wadi courses made me think that higher ground lay to the west. The afternoon march was unpleasant, as we were marching into the sun's eye. I had experienced this in former journeys, when long marches into the sun turned my face first lobster colour, then blistering raw; but now I had learnt the secret of swathing my head in the full wraps of an Arab head-dress and so saved all but my nose and lips.

Lesley Blanch

(1907–)

Romantic writer. Her book *The Wilder Shores of Love* describes the lives of four women who adopted an Arab way of life: Isabel Burton, Jane Digby El Mezrab, Aimée Dubecq de Rivery and Isabelle Eberhardt.

Jane Digby el Mezrab: love in the desert

She had become a deeply cultivated woman. The manner of her living had not affected the quality of her thinking. She was musical; she painted; and her sculpture was said to be remarkable; she followed the intellectual developments in Europe closely, and she spoke and read eight languages: later, she was to add Arabic to the list . . .

Less than a month after she left Athens she was involved with an Arab of surpassing attractions. Not much is known about Sâlih. He was young, handsome, lusty, and as conscious of her charms as she of his. There is no suggestion that he was the sort of opportunist dragoman who could be hired out by any lonely lady. He appears to have been a splendid creature, very possessive, who swept her off her feet and into the black Bedouin tents of his encampment out in the desert. Jane was enraptured. The Pallikares paled. When Sâlih's tribe entertained her with the traditional and picturesque Arab hospitality, she was lost . . . All at once she discovered the living East, and it went to her head.

Wilfred Thesiger

(1910–)

English soldier, explorer, writer and photographer. Thesiger was born at the British Legation in Addis Ababa, and, having completed his formal education in England, returned to travel through the Sultanate of Aussa, inhabited by the Danakil, a tribe prone to doing very unpleasant things to people they did not like. He joined the Sudan political service in 1935, spending five years in remote areas of the Sudan, Libya and French Sahara. Between 1946–9, Thesiger twice crossed the Empty Quarter of Arabia, the Rub'al-Khali, on foot, with local Bedu. He also lived among the Marsh Arabs of Southern Iraq, whose homeland has since been flooded, travelled in remote parts of Asia, and lived for many years among the Samburu in Kenya. He has published many accounts of his travels, and books of photographs of now vanished ways of life.

The marshes of southern Iraq

We rounded a promontory of rushes and there, on a shining expanse, just rippled by the breeze, was the village, the houses reflected in the water. A haze of white smoke merged into the pale blue sky above them and a wall of yellow rushes lay beyond. Scattered about the lagoon were sixty-seven houses. From a distance they appeared to be actually in the water but each was in fact constructed on a soggy pile of rushes like a giant swan's nest, just large enough for the building and a space in front where the buffaloes rested at night. The houses, like those on the mainland, were of mats fastened over a framework of *usab*. The newer ones were the colour of fresh straw but most had weathered to a dirty grey.

Everywhere people climbed in and out of canoes to get from one house to another. Sadam's *mudhif* was the largest building in the village and the only one on dry ground, being built on a small island, evidently an ancient site, for brickwork showed near the water-level. Sadam, a tall lean man with a lightly pock-marked face, received me cordially. After we had fed, the canoe-men rose to leave. 'What? You are going? Nonsense, spend the night.' 'No, we have work to do, we must get back.' 'I beg you to stay.' 'No, really we must go. Remain in the safe-keeping of God.' Sadam said, 'All right; go in peace'. And I added, 'Give my salutations to Falih.'

That evening, back in Sadam's *mudhif* after visiting the village, I watched the sun go down behind reed-beds that stretched to the world's end. High overhead banks of cirrus cloud, blown to tattered streamers, ranged from ebony to flaming gold and the colour of old ivory against a background of vermilion, orange, violet and palest green. From all around, as if the Marshes breathed, came the massed voices of frogs, an all-pervading pulse of sound, so sustained that the mind soon ceased to take note of it. More than any other, even than the crying of geese in winter, this was the sound of the Marshes. A dog barked; a buffalo grunted; a man called out a long and to me unintelligible message; a pause, and someone answered. Buffaloes swam across the open water towards the village, only their heads showing, each leaving a wake. A boy, late back from the reed-beds, paddled down a waterway, a path of shining gold leading to the setting sun. He sang softly as he came towards me, the notes lingering in the air.

Sir Fitzroy Maclean

(1911–)

British diplomat, born in Cairo; soldier, politician and
traveller. In 1943–4, he was commander of a military mission to assist the Jugoslav partisans. His books, *Eastern
Approaches* (1949), *A Person From England* (1958), and *Back
from Bokhara* (1959), all explore his interest in central Asia
and the people who have travelled there.

In Central Asia

All day we trundled across the desert towards those distant peaks. Then,
suddenly in the early afternoon, we found ourselves once again amid
cultivation: apple orchards, the trees heavily laden with fruit; golden
fields of Indian corn ripening in the sun; plantations of melons; rows
of tall poplars growing by the side of canals and irrigation ditches. After
the desert the foliage seemed lusciously, exuberantly green. We were
nearing Alma Ata. Already we could see the white houses of the town.
Beyond it the tree-covered foothills of the Tien Shan rose steeply towards
the snow-covered peaks behind them.

I was in Central Asia.

Alma Ata lies ten miles from the railway. After an interminable wait,
followed by a sharp melee, I succeeded in securing myself a place in
a lorry that was going there. Next to me was a grubby but cheerful
individual, with a snub nose, a mouthful of irregular, broken teeth and
a shock of tangled hair, who told me that he had just completed five
years in a penal settlement. Life there, he said, had not been so bad,
though to this day he did not know why he had been sent there. Perhaps
it was because he was a Pole. But now, although he had never applied
for them, he had been given Soviet papers, so things would perhaps be
easier for him. Before being deported he had been a barber by profession;
now he hoped to make a living by picking apples. He seemed a happy-go-
lucky sort of fellow, ready to take things as he found them.

After a fierce jolting down long dusty roads lined with poplars, we passed through a colony of dilapidated Kazakh *yurts* on the outskirts and almost immediately found ourselves in the centre of the town.

Alma Ata must be one of the pleasantest provincial towns in the Soviet Union. In character it is purely Russian, being one of the first Russian settlements in Central Asia.

Baedeker's Guide Books

Karl Baedeker (1810–59) started his publishing business in Germany in 1827 and, with the English firm of John Murray, dominated the production of nineteenth and early twentieth-century travel books. Baedeker was more or less totally devoted to the production of his famous *Guide Books*, whose detail filled even the most experienced travellers with awe. Speaking to the publisher on the telephone in Germany after the Second World War, I remarked that, 'Even your maps of Dover look as if they were drawn by spies, for spies.' 'I never thought of that,' he replied. The last of the great Baedeker cartographers only died relatively recently.

Bokhara

Bokhara contains 364 mosques and 109 medresehs or theological colleges, which, however, lack the architectural interest possessed by similar buildings in Samarkand.

The chief sight of the town is the very extensive and richly stocked Bazaar. The narrow covered passages in the various sections (*tims*) of the bazaar are thronged by Persians, Kirghizes, Hindoos, Armenians, Tartars, Afghans, Turcomans, Uzbeks, and Tajiks, most of them wearing light-coloured garments. As in all Oriental towns the various industries are separately grouped in the bazaar, while manufacturing and sale are (when possible) carried on at the same spot. To give some protection against the burning rays of the sun, the streets are either arched over or covered in with mats, linen, or canvas. Among the most attractive goods in the bazaar are the carpets, the fine silks, the copper and other metal wares, and the black lambskins known as *karákul*, good specimens of which cost at least 6 rb. The spacious points of intersection of the bazaar streets are covered with domes and are called *tchar-su*. The frequent shout of '*posht, posht*' means 'look out!' Tea-booths are numerous; and a large platform has been built out over the canal in front of the gate to provide a place for the tea-drinkers. Purchases of any extent should not be made without the assistance of an intelligent resident. The shopkeepers, with the exception of the Jews, seldom understand Russian. The Bokhara *tenga* is a silver coin worth about 15 cop., while the brass *puhl* is worth only ¼ copeck.

Preparations for travelling in the Caucasus

The title of prince [Russian text] has been granted by Russia to all the former feudal lords of Georgia, great and small; and it is advisable for the traveller to have as many *Introductions* as possible to influential members of this class as well as a letter of recommendation [Russian text] from the Viceroy of the Caucasus, addressed to the Russian provincial officials. Such introductions, however, will not always avail in helping him to surmount the difficulties that arise; many of these can be successfully met only by a resolute bearing on his own part. The Caucasian idea of the value of time is still hazier than that of the Russian: hence patience is the first requisite. The traveller must take care to conceal the fact that he is pressed for time, as otherwise the demands for porters and horses will at once be raised. A bargain should never be concluded until personal inspection has proved everything to be as stated. – *Public Safety* is on a somewhat unstable footing, and it is as well to avoid travelling alone or the exhibition of much money . . . It is advisable to keep a sharp look-out on one's belongings, as the natives are not averse from picking up unconsidered trifles.

Philip Glazebrook

(1937–)

English writer with a penchant for travelling in remote places, particularly the wilder parts of what were large slices of Russian Central Asia.

Thirty miles from Bokhara

We were about thirty miles from Bokhara before the cultivation of the landscape into cottonfields began to falter. The soil grew sandier, waste patches more extensive, the face of nature harsher. Groves of silver-leafed poplars were left behind, and the road was no longer lined by mulberry and elm. Without altering its structure the landscape shrugged off the works of man. It became again its primitive self, level and dim wastes of sand, a hard reddish granular surface tufted with spiny shrubs, which reached to every horizon. The sand formed low undulations, or occasionally hillocks enclosing the road, and a rare pool amid marsh grass flashed gunmetal water at the cloudy, hurrying sky. In such a pool I glimpsed a pair of tufted ducks swimming, and once an ash-coloured bird of prey drifted low over the sand; but across the desert the road lay straight and empty into infinite distance, the occasional black dot on the horizon enlarging itself into a truck we met with a rush, its slip-stream clapping into ours and shuddering the car like the lance of a jousting horseman shivering on plate armour.

About eight o'clock, three hours on our way, Anatoly pulled off the road into a hollow and stopped the car. We got out and met the desert. It was cold, the sands swept by a north wind pushing bruise-coloured clouds overhead . . .

He laid out a delicious meal. There was bread and cold mutton, there was yoghurt in one jar, sour cream in another, there was fruit and handfuls of raisins, and raw carrots which Anatoly had sliced up with the sheath knife which was always in his hand. Whilst he carefully snapped the *saksaoul* and built the fire into a crackling pyramid he told me (through Alex) of the journeys he had made by car through Russia: to Odessa, once to Moscow itself . . .

When I had eaten all I wanted I climbed the slope out of our sheltered hollow. Near and far the desert was infinitely dreary under a sky of rapidly moving clouds. Again I was cold. The cheerless scene, the emptiness, the knowledge that these wastes of gravel extend to distances vast even by Russia's vastness – this was just the point of view I'd hoped for, to look into a wind singing drearily over the sands which have over centuries swallowed up much blood and treasure from Russia's many expeditions sent to capture Khiva.

Middle Asia

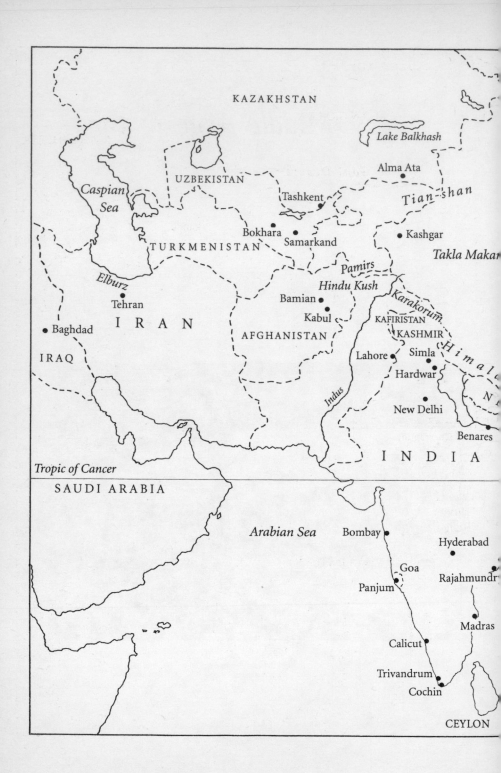

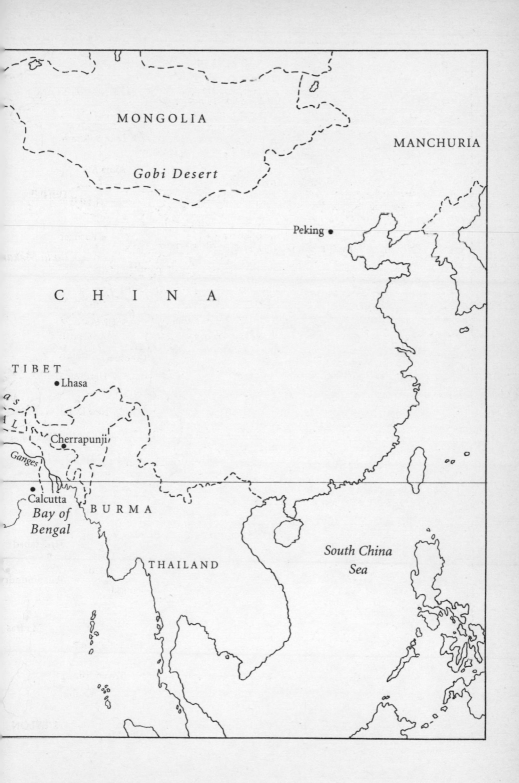

Arrian

(c. 95–180)

Flavius Arrianus, Greek officer in the Roman army who
became Prefect of Cappodocia, and a historian, principally
of the campaigns of Alexander the Great, conqueror of
the Persian Empire.

Alexander crosses the Indus

He, in the mean time, directed his march towards the river Acesines.
Ptolemy the son of Lagus has given us a description of this river, and
indeed it is the only one throughout all India he has taken the pains to
describe. He tells us that the current in that part thereof where Alexander
ferried over his army with his hides and his vessels, was fierce and rapid,
and the channel full of large and sharp rocks, which, beating the waters
back, and wheeling them about, caused vast boilings and eddies; that
its breadth was about fifteen furlongs; that those who were placed upon
the hides found a safe and easy passage; but many of those who embarked
on board the vessels were wrecked, by striking against the rocks, and
lost their lives. From the description of this river, it is no hard matter
to gather that those authors err not much, who give us an account of
the breadth of the river Indus, namely, that it is forty furlongs where
widest, but in the narrowest and deepest parts thereof not above fifteen;
and that this is the general breadth all along. I am of opinion that
Alexander chose that part of the river Acesines where the channel was
widest, and consequently stillest, for the transportation of his army.

287

Marco Polo

(c. 1254–1324)

Venetian traveller and merchant. Marco Polo's father and uncle had found their way to China, known as Cathay. They met the great Kublai Khan, who sent them home with a petition to the Pope for European scientists and artists. They had to wait for the election of Gregory X, whom they met at Acre. Marco accompanied them on their second journey, with two Dominican monks who took fright in Armenia and returned home, a letter from the Pope, and a flask containing oil from the Holy Sepulchre. The party took a roundabout route overland, with an eye open for trading opportunities, through the Middle East, across the Hindu Kush and the Pamirs, Kashgar and the Gobi desert. The Great Khan was eventually found at his summer place at Shangtu. He took a liking to Marco who remained twenty years in Cathay as his roving ambassador in Asia and for three years was Governor of Yang Chow province. The Polos returned to Venice in 1295, laden with treasures. The next year Marco was captured at sea by the Genoese, and recounted his stories to a fellow prisoner, Rusticiano of Pisa. Even without embellishment his tale was wonderful, but he became known 'Messer Marco Millioni' on account of his habit of exaggeration.

Indian Yogis

Among them are certain men living under a rule who are called Yogis. They live even longer than the others, as much as 150 or 200 years. And their bodies remain so active that they can still come and go as they will and perform all the services required by their monastery and their idols and serve them just as well as if they were younger. This comes of their great abstinence and of eating very little food and only what is wholesome. For it is their practice to eat chiefly rice and milk. Let me tell you also of a special food they eat, which I am sure will strike you as remarkable. For I assure you that they take quicksilver and sulphur and mix them together and make a drink of them, which they then drink. They declare that this prolongs life, and so they live all the longer. They drink this mixture twice a month, and make a practice of it from childhood in order to live longer. And certainly those who live to such a great age are habituated to this drink of sulphur and quicksilver.

There is a regular religious order in this kingdom of Maabar, of those who are called by this name of Yogi, who carry abstinence to the extremes of which I will tell you and lead a harsh and austere life. You may take it for a fact that they go stark naked, wearing not a stitch of clothing nor even covering their private parts or any bodily member. They worship the ox, and most of them carry a little ox made of gilt copper or bronze in the middle of the forehead. You must understand that they wear it tied on. Let me tell you further that they burn cow-dung and make a powder of it. With this they anoint various parts of their body with great reverence, no less than Christians display in the use of holy water. If anyone does reverence to them while they are passing in the street, they anoint him with this powder on the forehead in token of blessing. They do not eat out of platters or on trenchers; but they take their food on the leaves of apples of paradise or other big leaves – not green leaves, but dried ones; for they say that the green leaves have souls, so that this would be a sin.

Friar Jordanus

(fl. 1320–30)

French Dominican priest who was driven onto the Malabar coast of India by a storm on his way to Cathay with four Franciscan missionaries. He became Bishop of Columbum (probably Quilon, in Kerala). His account of the 'Wonders of the East', *Mirabilia Descripta*, is fascinating, even when truth and hearsay overlap.

Wonders of India

In this India be many islands, and more than 10,000 of them inhabited, as I have heard; wherein are many world's wonders. For there is one called Silem, where are found the best precious stones in the whole world, and in the greatest quantity and number, and of all kinds.

Between that island and the main are taken pearls of marguerites, in such quantity as to be quite wonderful. So indeed that there are sometimes more than 8000 boats or vessels, for three months continuously, [engaged in this fishery]. It is astounding, and almost incredible, to those who have not seen it, how many are taken.

Of birds I say this: that there be many different from those of Lesser India, and of different colours, for there be some white all over as snow; some red as scarlet of the grain; some green as grass; some particoloured; in such quantity and delectability as cannot be uttered. Parrots also, or popinjays, after their kind, of every possible colour except black, for black ones are never found; but white all over, and green, and red, and also of mixed colours. The birds of this India seem really like the creatures of Paradise.

There is also told a marvellous thing of the islands aforesaid, to wit that there is one of them in which there is a water and a certain tree in the middle of it. Every metal which is washed with that water becomes gold; every wound on which are placed the bruised leaves of that tree is incontinently healed.

In this India, whilst I was at Columbum, were found two cats having wings like the wings of bats; and in Lesser India there be some rats as big as foxes, and venomous exceedingly.

Ruy Gonzales de Clavijo

(d. 1412)

Spanish diplomat and traveller. Clavijo was sent as an ambassador to the court of Timur Leng (or Tamerlane) by the King of Castile in 1403. His description of Samarkand and its wealth is still astonishing. A hundred and

fifty thousand people had assembled for the marriage of
Timur's eleven-year-old son: 'Turks, Arabs, Moors, Christian Armenians, Greek Catholics, and Jacobites, and those
who baptize with fire in the face.' Twenty thousand tents
had been pitched, some of them lined with sable. Still there
were so many people that many camped in trees and caves.

The Amazons of Samarcand

Fifteen days journey from the city of Samarcand, in the direction of
China, there is a land inhabited by Amazons, and to this day they
continue the custom of having no men with them, except at one time
of the year; when they are permitted, by their leaders, to go with their
daughters to the nearest settlements, and have communication with
men, each taking the one who pleased her most, with whom they live,
and eat, and drink, after which they return to their own land. If they
bring forth daughters afterwards, they keep them; but they send the
sons to their fathers. These women are subject to Timour Beg; they
used to under the emperor of Cathay, and they are Christians of the
Greek Church. They are of the lineage of the Amazons who were at
Troy, when it was destroyed by the Greeks.

Ludovico di Varthema

(c. 1465–1517)

Italian traveller from Bologna, who saw an opportunity
to establish himself by 'bringing men new knowledge
about the great world in which we live'. He was probably
the second non-Muslim ever to enter Mecca, dressed as
an Arab pilgrim. Remaining in disguise, Varthema travelled in the Indian Ocean, did well in the spice trade and
became involved in political intrigue. He was imprisoned
as a Christian spy at Aden where the Sultan's wife saved
his life, though almost sacrificed it to her own lustfulness.
Varthema appeared to be rather prone to such adventures.

The king of Calicut's wife

The king of the said city does not cause his wife's virginity to be taken by the Brahmins as the king of Calicut does, but he causes her to be deflowered by white men, whether Christians or Moors, provided they be not Pagans. Which Pagans also, before they conduct their wives to their house, find a white man, of whatever country he may be, and take him to their house for this particular purpose, to make him deflower the wife. And this happened to us when we arrived in the said city. We met by chance three or four merchants, who began to speak to my companion in this wise: "*Langalli ni pardesi,*" that is, "Friend, are you strangers?" He answered: "Yes." Said the merchants: "*Ethera nali ni banno,*" that is, "How many days have you been in this country?" We replied: "*Mun nal gnad banno,*" that is, "It is four days since we arrived." Another one of the said merchants said: "*Biti banno guan pigamanthon ondo,*" that is, "Come to my house, for we are good friends of strangers;" and we, hearing this, went with him. When we had arrived at his house, he gave us a collation, and then he said to us: "My friends, *Patanci nale banno gnan penna periti in penna orangono panna panai cortu,*" that is, "Fifteen days hence I wish to bring home my wife, and one of you shall sleep with her the first night, and shall deflower her for me." We remained quite ashamed at hearing such a thing. Then our interpreter said: "Do not be ashamed, for this is the custom of the country." Then my companion hearing this said: "Let them not do us any other mischief, for we will satisfy you in this;" but we thought that they were mocking us. The merchant saw that we remained undecided, and said: "*O langal limaranconia ille ocha manezar irichenu,*" that is, "*Do not be dispirited, for all this country follows this custom.*"

Vasco da Gama

(c. 1469–1524)

Portugese navigator who pioneered the sea route to the India via the Cape of Good Hope, discovered by Diaz ten years earlier. His second journey, as admiral of a fleet of twenty-one armed ships, punitively enforced the Portugese presence in the East Indies. After doing nothing for twenty years, in 1524 da Gama was made sixth Viceroy of India, but died when he reached Cochin.

A bloodthirsty arrival at Calicut

On the 20th day of October we went to the country of Cannaer, and bought there all kinds of spices, and the king came in great state, bringing with him two elephants and several strange animals which I cannot name.

On the 27th day of October we failed thence, and arrived in a kingdom called Calcoen, which is 40 miles from Cannaer, and we mustered our forces before the town, and we fought with them during three days, and we took a great number of people, and we hanged them to the yards of the ships, and taking them down, we cut off their hands, feet, and heads; and we took one of their ships and threw into it the hands, feet, and heads, and we wrote a letter, which we put on a stick, and we left that ship to go a-drift towards the land. We took there a ship which we put on fire, and burnt many of the subjects of the king.

Ferdinand Magellan

(c. 1480–1521)

Portugese navigator. After taking part in the conquest of Malacca and the search for the Moluccas, or Spice Islands, Magellan fell out with the King of Portugal and entered the service of Charles V of Spain. He persuaded him of the existence of a South-West Passage. His expedition sailed down the coast of Patagonia, and, 'On the day of the Eleven Thousand Virgins', found the 'Strait of all the Saints' (Strait of Magellan). This was after a near mutiny among the captains of his five ships which caused him to execute two of them; a third was later left ashore with a priest. He reached the ocean that he named the Pacific. His ship, the *Victoria*, was the only one to reach the Philippines, but Magellan was fatally wounded there. The skeleton crew took the ship back to Spain, thus completing the first circumnavigation of the world.

The people of Palaoan

The people of Palaoan go naked like the other islanders, they almost all till their own fields. They have blow-pipes, with thick arrows more than a span in length, with a point like that of a harpoon; some have a point made with a fish bone, and others are of reed, poisoned with a certain herb; the arrows are not trimmed with feathers, but with a soft light wood. At the foot of the blow-pipe they bind a piece of iron, by means of which, when they have no more arrows, they wield the blow-pipe like a lance. They like to adorn themselves with rings and chains of gimp and with little bells, but above all they are fond of brass wire, with which they bind their fish hooks. They have some rather large domestic cocks, which, from some superstition, they do not eat, but they keep them for fighting; on such occasions they make bets and offer prizes, which are acquired by the owner of the conquering cock.

Going from Palaoan towards the south-west, after a run of ten leagues, we reached another island. While coasting it, it seemed in a certain manner to go forward; we coasted it for a distance of fully fifty leagues, until we found a port. We had hardly reached the port when the heavens were darkened, and the lights of St Elmo appeared on our masts.

Sir Thomas Roe

(c. 1580–1644)

English ambassador, soldier and Member of Parliament. Roe was sent by Henry Frederick, Prince of Wales, on three expeditions to search for gold in the West Indies and South America. He was subsequently sent as ambassador to the court of Jehangir, Mogul Emperor of Hindustan, to arrange a commercial treaty, from 1615–18. His efforts assisted the foundation of the British power in India. On the return journey he visited Persia and later became ambassador at Sublime Porte, Constantinople, and then Vienna. His journals give a remarkable and vivid account of his experiences.

A woman taken in some action with an Eunuch

This day a gentellwoeman of Normalls was taken in the kings house in some action with an Eunuch. Another Capon that loued her kylld him. The Poore Woeman was sett up to the Arme pitts in the Earth hard ramed, her feete tyde to a stake, to abyde 3 dayes and 2 nights without any sustenance, her head and armes bare, exposed to the sunns violence: if shee died not in that tyme she should bee pardoned. The Eunuch was Condemned to the Eliphantes. This damsell yeelded in Pearle, Jewelles, and ready mony 160,000 *rupias*.

The Moghul is weighed

In the midst a Pinacle, where was prepared the scales, being hung in large tressels, and a crosse beame plated on with Gold thinne, the scales of massie Gold, the borders set with small stones, Rubies and Turkey, the Chaines of Gold large and massie, but strengthened with silke Cords. Here attended the Nobilitie, all sitting about it on Carpets, vntill the King came; who at last appeared clothed, or rather loden with Diamonds,

Rubies, Pearles, and other precious vanities, so great, so glorious! his Sword, Target, Throne to rest on correspondent; his head, necke, breast, armes, aboue the elbowes, at the wrists, his fingers euery one with at least two or three Rings, fettered with chaines, or dyalled Dyamonds, Rubies as great as Wal-nuts (some greater), and Pearles such as mine eyes were amazed it. Suddenly hee entered into the scales, sate like a woman on his legges, and there was put in against him many bagges to fit his weight, which were changed sixe times, and they say was silver, and that I vnderstood his weight to be nine thousand *rupias*, which are almost one thousand pound sterling. After with Gold and Iewels, and precious stones, but I saw non; it beeing in bagges might bee Pibles. Then against Cloth of Gold, Silke, Stuffes, Linnen, Spices, and all sorts of goods, but I must beleeue, for they were in fardles. Lastly, against Meale, Butter, Corne, which is said to be giuen to the *Baniani*, and all the rest of the Stuffe; but I saw it carefully carryed in, and none distributed. Onely the siluer is reserued for the poore, and serues the ensuing yeare, the King vsing in the night to call for some before him, and with his owne hands in great familiaritie and humilitie to distribute that money. The scale he sate in by one side, he gazed on me, and turned me his stones and wealth, and smiled, but spake nothing, for my Enterpreter could not be admitted in. After he was weighted, he ascended his Throne, and had Basons of Nuts, Almonds, Fruits, Spices of all sort, made in thinne siluer, which he cast about, and his great men scrambled prostrate vpon their bellies; which seeing I did not, hee reached one Bason almost full, and powred into my Cloke. His Noblemen were so bold as to put in their hands, so thicke that they had left me none if I had not put a remayner vp. I heard he threw Gold till I came in, but found it siluer so thinne, that all I had at first, being thousands of seuerall pieces, had not weighed sixtie *Rupias*. I saued about twentie *Rupias* weight, yet a good dishfull, which I keepe to shew the ostentation; for by my proportion he could not that day cast away aboue one hundred pound sterling. At night he drinketh with all his Nobilitie in rich Plate. I was inuited to that, but told I must not refuse to drinke, and their waters are fire. I was sicke and in a little fluxe of bloud, and durst not stay to venture my health.

Edward Terry

(1590–1660)

English chaplain to the East India Company, and to Sir
Thomas Roe, ambassador to the Mogul court.

Pests in Paradise

But lest this remote Countrey should seeme like an earthly Paradise
without any discommodities: I must needes take notice there of many
Lions, Tygres, Wolves, Jackals (which seeme to be wild Dogs) and many
other harmefull beasts. In their Rivers are many Crocodiles, and on
the Land over-growne Snakes, with other venimous and pernicious
Creatures. In our houses there we often meete with Scorpions, whose
stinging is more sensible and deadly, if the patient have not presently
some Oyle that is made of them, to anoint the part affected, which is
a present cure. The aboundance of Flyes in those parts doe likewise
much annoy us, for in the heate of the day their numberlesse number
is such as that we can be quiet in no place for them, they are ready to
cover our meate as soone as it is placed on the Table, and therefore
wee have men that stand on purpose with Napkins to fright them away
when as wee are eating: in the night likewise we are much disquieted
with Musquatoes, like our Gnats, but somewhat lesse: and in their great
Cities, there are such aboundance of bigge hungrie Rats, that they often
bite a man as he lyeth on his bed.

Peter Mundy

(fl. 1600–67)

English traveller of indefatigable curiosity who travelled
all over Europe and the far East.

The River Ganges

The River Ganges (vulgarly called Gonga, by somme of the better sort,
Ganghem), soe famous in auntient tymes and att present, and noe lesse
honoured by the Hindooes, Had att this place (3 course [from Kar-
anbās]) and tyme noe more water then runneth before Blackwall att
full Sea (it beinge now out of the raynes); neither were the Bancks much
more then ½ a mile from side to side hereabouts, although both above
and belowe it the Channell appeares to be above 2 miles in breadth,
which is full of great shelves and bancks of verie white sand, amonge
which the water runneth heere and there. Att the place where I passed
over is about 7 or 8 fathome deepe, the water of somewhat a darke
Greene. In tyme of Raines it overflowes the Bancks the distance of 8 or
9 miles, the banck of the hither side somewhat highe, and the Countrie
for 10 or 12 course verie fruitefull, pleasant, peaceable, and well governed,
being in the Jaggueere of Raja Aneera aforesaid. Of Ganges I can say
noe more att present, although the superstitious Hindoos reporte a
thousand fables of it, and come as many miles almost to wash themselves
in it cleane of all their sinns, it being accompted most sacred amongst
them. I passed to the farther side in a small boate, but swamme back,
it being not very broad, as afore mentioned.

Jean Lacombe de Quercy

(c. 1640–?)

A French soldier in Louis XIV's army, and a traveller.
Lacombe went to England, to Quebec and along the coast
of the Americas as far as Brazil. He travelled via the Cape
of Good Hope to Batavia in Java, probably with the Dutch
East India Company. He spent three years in Ceylon where
he claims to have seen the tombs of Adam and Eve, which
he describes in great detail. He went to Medina and Mecca,
and was arrested at the twenty-ninth gate in Peking, while
attempting to catch sight of the Imperial Throne.

Ear stretching in Ceylon

They greatly deform their ears by generally making them hang down as
far as their breasts by means of a big pebble or some other heavy weight,
which they keep always attached to the bottom of each from their earliest
years to an advanced age, having them first pierced for this purpose.
The continual weight borne by the lower part of the ear has the effect
to make them grow bit by bit as extraordinarily against Nature as those
little vessels of porcelain which (also against Nature) hinder the growth
of the feet of Chinese women. When the time comes for them to be
freed from their weight and their ears have descended sufficiently to
their taste, they pierce them for the whole length of their outer edge,
making a row of thirty or forty little holes, and in each one they thrust
a tiny quill as far as the cartilage before the ear-hole. Next they have
several diamonds and other precious stones set in the end of certain
little pieces of silver and sometimes also gold, which are fashioned in
the manner of cloves, the surface of the stone forming the head. They
put one of these clove-pins in each little hole, turning the stone to the
outside; and as they place them they fix small pieces of the same stuff
as the pins, flat, round or square and as big as a denier, but thicker,
which are pierced in the middle with a hole the same width as the pin's

shank; and they put one of these in each hole at the back of the ear as deep as they can so that they shall not lose them and the pins are held firmly in their holes on each side. These jewels are as great a weight to the ears as the pebbles or shot which were used before, extending them even more after they have been freed from the first. The rich and wealthy furnish themselves magnificently in this manner.

George Forster

(d. 1792)

East India Company servant, traveller and writer.

Ague in Afghanistan

By sleeping in the open air, I imagine, and on nitrous ground, a fever, accompanied with an ague, seized me a few days after my arrival at Kabul, the effects of which were singularly violent. The fever, during its continuance, caused a delirious stupefaction, and created an insatiable thirst, which frequently relieving by draughts of extremely cold water, it seemed at once to gush from every pore, and drenched me in profuse perspirations. When the fit of ague commenced, my bed-clothes, with those of Bagdasir, and all the horse-covering that could be procured, were heaped on me, but to little purpose; for I lay in the state of the damned, if such can be formed by human idea, until the paroxysm had wreaked its vengeance. My body was filled with spots of a very bright colour, shaded between purple and crimson, which I should have beheld with pleasure, thinking that such eruption would diminish the disease, had not an Armenian pronounced them a symptom of the plague. This opinion gave a common alarm; and though no alteration appeared in the conduct of Bagdasir, it operated strongly on the fears of my neighbours, and they were disposed to exclude me from their quarter, when I confidently asserted, that the fever of the plague always produced its crisis in three days. Seeing that I had endured seven, and preserved a brisk flow of spirits, their apprehension was much allayed, and the scene of banishment set aside.

In the course of my illness I was visited by many of the Armenians, and one of them, a zealous devotee, desired me to swallow some small rolls of paper on which were written certain mysterious words, infallible, he said, in their effects, upon the bodies of pious Christians.

I expressed my thanks to this dealer in spells, and readily agreed to take his dose, should Bagdasir, who was my absolute director, give assent. On an investigation into their virtue, he permitted me, though with reluctance, for he abhorred the Armenian sect, to eat them, at the same time expressing strong doubts of their efficacy. But whether from not being a member of the orthodox faith, as the Armenian urged, or according to the Georgian, from the heretical preparation of the charm, I received no benefit; indeed I grew daily worse, as the sickness was then in its progressive stage.

Emily Eden

(1797–1869)

English writer and traveller and amateur artist, the twelfth of fourteen children of Baron Auckland. In 1835, Eden abandoned her position as an eligible political hostess in London, and went off to India for six years with her sister Fanny, as companion to their brother George, the new Governor-General of India. Based in Calcutta, they travelled extensively in India, by barge, palanquin, horse, elephant, and other means besides, usually with a vast entourage – their caravan could be ten miles long. In many ways a benevolent Governor, George Eden initiated the catastrophic First Afghan War. Emily Eden's observant and compassionate letters cover the whole panoply of their life in India, from life among the Maharajahs, their horses bedecked with emeralds, to weeks spent under canvas, and the pains of famine.

Camping at Benares

We landed at five, and drove four miles through immense crowds and much dust to our camp. The first evening of tents, I must say, was more uncomfortable than I had ever fancied. Everybody kept saying, 'What a magnificent camp!' and I thought I never had seen such squalid, melancholy discomfort. G., F., and I have three private tents, and a fourth, to make up the square, for our sitting-room, and great covered passage, leading from one tent to the other.

Each tent is divided into bed-room, dressing-room, and sitting-room. They have covered us up in every direction, just as if we were native women; and, besides that, there is a wall of red cloth, eight feet high, drawn all round our enclosure, so that, even on going out of the tent, we see nothing but a crimson wall.

Inside each tent were our beds – one leaf of a dining-table and three cane chairs. Our pittarahs and the camel-trunks were brought in; and in about half an hour the nazir came to say they must all, with our books, dressing-cases, &c., be carried off to be put under the care of a sentry, as nothing is safe in a tent from the decoits; so, if there were anything to arrange, there would be no use in arranging it, as it must all be moved at dusk. The canvas flops about, and it was very chilly in the night, though that is the only part I do not object to, as when we get our curtains that will be merely bracing; but it feels *open-airish* and unsafe. They say everybody begins by hating their tents and ends by loving them, but at present I am much prepossessed in favour of a house. Opposite to our private tents is the great dining-tent, and the durbar tent, which is less shut up, and will be less melancholy to live in. God bless you, dearest! When I am tired, or *tented*, or hot, or cold, and generally when I am in India, I have at least the comfort of always sitting down to tell you about it, and 'There is no harm in *that*,' as the man says in 'Zohrab.'

Julia Charlotte Maitland

(fl. 1830s)

Spent the years 1836–9 in India with her husband, an East India Company lawyer who became a district judge. Julia Maitland wrote very lively and observant letters home, far preferring rural India to the rather stuffy social life of Madras, although they did travel with a retinue of over 150 attendants.

Ladies of Madras

It is wonderful how little interested most of the English ladies seem by all the strange habits and ways of the natives; and it is not merely that they have grown used to them all, but that, by their own accounts, they never cared more about what goes on around them than they do now. I can only suppose they have forgotten their first impressions. But this makes me wish to try and see everything that I can while the bloom of my Orientalism is fresh upon me, and before this apathy and listlessness have laid hold on me, as no doubt they will.

I asked one lady what she had seen of the country and the natives since she had been in India. "Oh, nothing!" said she: "thank goodness, I know nothing at all about them, nor I don't wish to: really I think the less one sees and knows of them the better!"

Our establishment in South India

Rajahmundry, 3 October
Servants are expensive altogether, though cheap individually; but we are obliged to have such a number of them that their pay mounts up. We keep fewer than many people, because we wish to be economical. Here is our establishment: one butler, one dress-boy, one matee, two ayahs, one amah, one cook, one tunnicutchy, two gardeners, six bearers, one water-carrier, two horse-keepers, two grass-cutters, one dog-boy, one

poultry man, one washerman, one tailor, one hunter, and one amah's cook – altogether twenty-seven: and this is reckoned few; and it is as much as ever they can do to get through their little work in their lazy dawdling way. If anybody comes to dinner, the cook sits down and cries for a cook's maty or helper, and I am obliged to hire one for him. They all find their own food themselves, and the Caste people would not touch any of our food; but the maties and under-servants are generally Pariahs, and are very glad to eat up anything they can lay their hands on. The amah is a Caste woman, and her whims are the plague of my life: I am obliged to keep a cook on purpose for her, because her food must all be dressed by a person of her own caste; and even then she will sometimes starve all day rather than eat it, if she fancies anybody else has been near it: she has a house built of cocoa-nut leaves in the compound, on purpose to cook her food in. I am also obliged to keep a separate nurse for her baby, and see after it regularly myself, because they are so careless about their own children when they are nursing other people's, that she and her husband would let the poor little creature die from neglect, and then curse us as the cause of it.

Think of the amah's being caught drinking rack and eating opium! She used to go out and howl so that the servants were afraid to come near her, saying she made "one *pishashi* (devil) noise." When she had cleared the coast with her *pishashi*-ing, her own people crept out from their hiding-holes, and brought her rack and bang (that is, spirits and opium).

You ask what shops we have. None at all: the butler buys everything in the bazaar or market, and brings in his bill every day. One of the Court native writers translates it into English, and very queer articles they concoct together! such as, "one beef of rump for biled;" – "one mutton of line beef for *alamoor estoo*," meaning *à-la-mode stew*; – "mutton for curry pups" (puffs); – "durkey for stups" (stuffing for turkey); "eggs for saps, snobs, tips, and pups" (chops, snipes, tipsycake, and puffs); – "mediation (medicine) for ducks;" – and at the end "*ghirand totell*" (grand total), and "howl balance".

Sir George Scott Robertson

(1852–1916)

British agent in Gilghit. Robertson went to the Astor Valley
in Kashmir in 1888, 'that strange and enticing dreamland'.
He was only the second European to travel in the remote
area of Kafiristan in the 1880s, before its population was
converted to Islam.

Death among the Káfirs

The funeral ceremonies of the Káfirs are curious and fantastic. I have
only witnessed those of the Kám tribe, but probably all the Siáh-Posh
have similar observances . . .

In December 1890 I witnessed the ceremonies observed on the death
of the old wife of Torag Merak. The dead woman had occupied the
highest position among the women of the village. On adjacent house-
tops nearly all the notables of Kámdesh assembled. In the centre of the
concourse, on a bed supported at each corner by a slave, lay the body
of the deceased, covered over with bright-coloured turbans. The head
was adorned with a kind of crown of sprigs of juniper-cedar, and monstrous imitations of feathers made by fastening bits of red cotton round
sticks. The eyebrows, closed lids, and grey cheeks were exposed to view.
The blinker silver ornaments were placed one on each side of the head,
as with the body in a lying posture they could not be fixed as they
would be worn during life. On the feet were dancing shoes fringed at
the top with markhor hair. At the foot of the bed were a second pair
of dancing-boots of similar make. Festoons of wheat hanging from the
bed proclaimed to all that the deceased during her life had given freely
of her substance. Underneath the bed several women of the house
were seated weeping and wailing, while many more surrounded the bier,
circling slowly round it. One of the women, the deceased's daughter, stood
on the left of the corpse, holding the bedframe with both hands. She
appeared to be the chief mourner. In the intervals of the music she

addressed her dead mother in accents of shrill praise and lament, often without paying the slightest heed to the formal speeches presently to be referred to. None of the women wore their horned head-dresses or other ornaments. As the feeble pipes and drums marked the time, the throng of women moved slowly round the bier sideways from left to right, their hands uplifted to the level of their shoulders. With outspread fingers they incessantly turned the palm first towards themselves then towards the corpse, a gesture supposed to indicate "she has gone from us". Beyond the circle of women were a few women closely related to the dead woman. They also edged round sideways, and made a similar gesture to that of the women, except that the hands were twisted at the level of the brows, and the action was much more energetic. Outside these men a few couples danced round merrily in the usual stamping way. In the intervals of the music the bed was placed on the ground, and some one of the spectators, usually Samatu Malik, declaimed short staccato sentences praising the virtues of the deceased, her lavish feasts, and extolling her family and kindred.

Lord Curzon of Kedleston

(1859–1925)

English statesman. *George Nathaniel Curzon* was made Viceroy of India at the age of thirty-nine, and was British Foreign Secretary, 1919–24. He was a brilliant but difficult man, who suffered from a demonic father and from curvature of the spine. A controversial Viceroy, he was responsible for the establishment of the North-West Frontier Province and the partition of Bengal. As a young man he travelled widely in the East, and wrote entertainingly about his experiences.

The Amir of Afghanistan

He confided to an Englishman at Kabul that he had put to death 120,000 of his own people. After one unsuccessful rebellion he had many thousands of the guilty tribesmen blinded with quicklime, and spoke to me of the punishment without a trace of compunction. Crimes such as robbery or rape were punished with fiendish severity. Men were blown from guns, or thrown down a dark well, or beaten to death, or flayed alive, or tortured in the offending member. For instance, one of the favourite penalties for petty larceny was to amputate the hand at the wrist, the raw stump being then plunged in boiling oil. One official who had outraged a woman was stripped naked and placed in a hole dug for the purpose on the top of a high hill outside Kabul. It was in mid-winter; and water was then poured upon him until he was converted into an icicle and frozen alive. As the Amir sardonically remarked, "He would never be too hot again."

A woman of his harem being found in the family way, he had her tied up in a sack and brought into the Durbar hall, where he ran her through with his own sword . . .

His cruelty even extended to punishing acts, however innocent, which had not been authorised by himself or which seemed to trench upon his prerogative. Though I was his guest and he sincerely desired to do me honour, and did so, he could not tolerate that any of his subjects should show spontaneous courtesy to the stranger. A man who spoke to me while I was on the road to Kabul was seized and thrown into prison. A man who offered me a pomegranate as I rode into Kandahar was severely beaten and imprisoned and deprived of his property.

Nevertheless, this monarch, at once a patriot and a monster, a great man and almost a fiend, laboured hard and unceasingly for the good of his country.

Sir Francis Younghusband

(1863–1942)

English soldier, diplomat and explorer, and player in the Great Game in which Britain and Russia sought for control of the North-West Frontier. Younghusband explored Manchuria, travelled 1250 miles from Peking to India and discovered the route to India via the Mustagh Pass. He pioneered a route to Tibet, and became British resident in Kashmir, 1906–9. Younghusband wrote several books on Asia. This traveller of extraordinary toughness, who travelled to Tibet in 1903 with sixty-seven shirts, became increasingly absorbed by mystical religion after an experience in Lhasa, 'a curious sense of being literally in love with the world'.

Winter quarters at Kashgar

We were to make Kashgar our winter quarters, and we found a native house prepared for us on the north side of the old city. It was pleasantly situated on some rising ground, and looked out to the north over the cultivated and tree-covered plain round Kashgar to the snowy peaks of the Tian-shan. From far away on the east, round to the north, and then away again on the east, these snowy mountains extended; and from the roof of our house we could see that magnificent peak, the mustagh-ata, rising twenty-one thousand feet above the plain. About the house was a garden, which gave us seclusion, and in this garden I had pitched a Kirghiz yurt, which I had bought on the Pamirs. One night up there we had found an unusually large and very tastefully furnished yurt provided for us. It was quite new, was twenty feet in diameter, and about fourteen feet high in the centre, with walls six feet high all round. But what surprised us most was to find it most elegantly decorated. The walls were made of a very handsome screenwork, and round the inside of the dome-like roof were dados of fine carpeting and embroidery. I was so taken with this tent, that I persuaded the owner to sell it to me, and carried it off to Kashgar on a couple of camels, and lived in it the whole winter. With good carpets on the ground, and a stove to warm it, it made a very comfortable place to live in, and, personally, I preferred it to a house.

This tent I found ready pitched on my arrival in Kashgar, and it was very delightful to feel myself comfortably settled down again after our rough and constant travelling.

Rudyard Kipling

(1865–1936)

English writer, poet and traveller. Born in Bombay, his father was the artist and teacher John Lockwood Kipling. After education in England, described in his novel *Stalky and Co.*, Kipling became a journalist in India, and then a celebrated writer, author of the two *Jungle Books*, *Just So Stories*, *Kim* and many other books and poems.

The valley of Boondi

The *munshies* and the vakils and the runners had departed after seeing that the Englishman was safe for the night, so the freedom of the little gathering on the bund was unrestrained. The *chowkidar* came out of his cave into the firelight. He took a fish and incontinently choked, for he was a feeble old man. Set right again, he launched into a very long and quite unintelligible story, while the sepoys said reverently: 'He is an old man and remembers many things.' As he babbled, the night shut in upon the lake and the valley of Boondi. The last cows were driven into the water for their evening drink, the waterfowl and the monkeys went to bed, and the stars came out and made a new firmament in the untroubled bosom of the lake. The light of the fire showed the ruled lines of the bund springing out of the soft darkness of the wooded hill on the left and disappearing into the solid darkness of a bare hill on the right. Below the bund a man cried aloud to keep wandering pigs from the gardens whose tree-tops rose to a level with the bund-edge. Beyond the trees all was swaddled in gloom. When the gentle buzz of the unseen city died out, it seemed as though the bund were the very Swordwide Bridge that runs, as every one knows, between this world and the next. The water lapped and muttered, and now and again a fish jumped, with the shatter of broken glass, blurring the peace of the reflected heavens.

Sven Hedin

(1865–1952)

Swedish geographer and explorer. Having crossed Central Asia and the Elburz Mountains by the age of twenty-two, Hedin planned to 'conquer all Asia ... content with nothing less than to tread paths where no European had ever set foot'. On his second expedition he travelled through the Siberian winter to Tashkent. In nineteen days he had 'traversed eleven and a half degrees of latitude, passed thirty thousand telegraph poles, employed one hundred and eleven drivers, used three hundred and seventeen horses and twenty-one camels'. From Tashkent he made his way across the Pamirs in mid-winter, with temperatures sinking to −37°. The next stage was through the Takla Makan desert east of Kashgar, with sand ridges 150 feet high, a terrible sea of sand that nearly took the party's lives and drove them to drink camels' urine mixed with vinegar, sheep's blood, and in Hedin's case, methylated spirit. Not all survived. His next journey covered 10,500 kilometres. Hedin also went to Tibet three times and made the first detailed map – for the Chinese government.

Bokhara

This city, too, was sacked by Jenghiz Khan and taken by Tamerlane. In 1842, Colonel Soddart and Captain Connolly visited Bokhara. The cruel Nasr-ullah was then Emir. He arrested the two Englishmen, tortured them, threw them into the famous vermin-pit and beheaded them. Vambéry, disguised as dervish, managed to get to the city in 1863, and described its remarkable features.

The population is composed of several diverse elements. The most important are the Tajiks, or Iranian stock, to which the educated classes and the priests belong; the Uzbegs and Jaggatai Turks of the Mongolian race; and the Sarts, a mixed race, to which the populace and the permanent population in general belong. Many other Oriental peoples are represented, among them being Persians, Afghans, Kirghiz, Turks, Tatars, Caucasians and Jews.

In the archways of the bazaars, where twilight always reigns, the bustling life of the Orient has a motley of its own. There one may admire the marvels of the Bokharan textile art; and in the antique shops one runs across Greek and Sassanian silver and gold coins and other rarities. Cotton, sheep-wool, lambskins and raw silk are exported in great quantities; and in the caravanserai courts connected with the bazaars, bales are piled mountain high. There are nice restaurants and coffee-houses; and from a distance one detects the odour of pastry made with onions and spices, and of coffee and tea. A small tart cost one *pool* (64 pool = 20 copecks = 1 tenge; 20 tenge = 1 tillah = 4 roubles).

I never tired of walking in the beautiful narrow streets, between funny two-storey houses, with camel-caravans jostling their way among carts, horsemen and pedestrians. I stopped frequently to sketch a mosque or a tempting street scene. A noisy crowd would gather round me, and Saïd Murad, one of the servants of the Russian legation, would keep bold urchins at a distance by using his braided knout. Once I went for a stroll without him, and then the lads took their revenge, bombarding me systematically, which rendered drawing out of the question. They rushed at me from all sides, their missiles being rotten apples, lumps of earth and all sorts of refuse. After vainly trying to defend myself I hastily retreated to the legation and fetched Saïd Murad.

Sir Edwin Lutyens

(1869–1944)

Architect noted initially for romantic country houses. With Sir Herbert Baker, Lutyens was the designer of New Delhi, 1913–20. He served on the Imperial War Graves Commission and designed the Cenotaph in Whitehall and many public buildings. His delightfully illustrated, if

sometimes xenophobic letters to his wife, Lady Emily, have
been co-edited by his great granddaughter.

Simla

They say Simla has grown very much. The hills and depths below one
are heroic, the buildings and conception of the place by the P[ublic]
W[orks] D[epartment] mind is beyond the beyond and if one was told
the monkeys had built it all one would have said what wonderful
monkeys, they must be shot in case they do it again. It is inconceivable
– and consequently very English! – to have a capital as Simla is entirely
of tin roofs, and then the tin roofs monkeying better materials and
reducing the whole show to absurdity.

The Taj by moonlight

The Taj by moonlight becomes so bald and indefinite, the patterns
disappear and the arch-forms merge into a fog of white reflection,
leaving the great turnip of a dome as a bubble poised in space. It is
wonderful but it is not architecture and its beauty begins where architecture ceases to be. And so it is with all these Indian builders. Anything
really admirable has been done by an Italian or a Chinaman. For the
rest it is all pattern – just the same as on any carpet hung up, on ceilings,
walls, inside or outside. The buildings are tents in stone and little more.
Elaborated to howdahs. Stone buildings which when put up are carved
and carved and carved without any relation to the stone, its purpose or
location. The Indians of today have no sense of construction decorated.

Sir Charles Bell

(1870–1945)

As an Indian administrator, Bell advised on Tibetan affairs
and was a close friend of the 13th Dalai Lama. He visited
Lhasa in 1920–1. Bell wrote an English-Tibetan colloquial

dictionary and travelled in Mongolia, Manchuria and Siberia, and well as in the Himalayan kingdoms. His book *The People of Tibet* is a first-hand account of life in the country.

Tibetan picnics

Most households in Lhasa have two or three picnics every month, for all love this kind of entertainment. Often they go at midday, men and women, after finishing necessary tasks. Clad in bathing drawers known as 'Water Cotton' (*chu-re*), from the waist to the knees, they enjoy a bathe in the river that flows so near their city. Mixed bathing is not encouraged. After the bathe to sit by the little Tibetan tables and enjoy tea and fruit will not come amiss.

The monks have their own separate parties. They have foot-races, jumping contests, &c. In all these picnics a spirit of kindliness prevails, and it has a softening influence even on the hotheads.

Rose Macaulay

(1889–1958)

English traveller. A prolific writer, of novels more than travel books; but one who inspired her readers to get up and travel. *The Pleasure of Ruins*, is a wonderful meditation on the appeal of ruins.

Old Goa

From its zenith, Goa's wealth and high fortune had begun by the end of the sixteenth century to decline. It had formidable and harassing trade rivals in the Dutch; cholera and hostile neighbours occurred; the population, interbred with the natives, weakened physically and mentally in stamina; luxury and a tropical climate softened their energy, their military fortifications and defences were outgrown by the city's spread.

The accounts of visitors through the seventeenth century trace its gradual decadence; they speak at first of markets continually busy, of slaves and Arab horses sold, of the Portuguese who all claim to be fidalgos, shun work, go through the streets on horses or in palanquins, followed by servants on foot, of the excessive number of churches, convents, priests and religious orders, of rich food, dances and masques, of women in covered palanquins; later they write of the rich become poor, of many houses ruinous, of unhealthiness, of the removal of the viceroy to a palace in the faubourgs. In 1759 the seat of government was moved to Panjum; the houses and public buildings of Goa were abandoned and allowed to slip into decay; the population had fallen to a few hundred. Old Goa was presently deserted and used as a quarry for the new town. It lingered on in decay, a dwindling, dying city, full of churches and convents ringing their bells across empty streets. As early as 1710 a Jesuit wrote that it was so ruined and deserted that its ancient grandeur could only be guessed from the magnificence of the convents and churches, which were still preserved with great veneration and splendour. A century later, people spoke of the shapes of streets and squares just distinguishable among ruins covered with coconut trees; the houses were a few wretched buildings in a vast solitude. In 1835 the religious Orders were dispersed, and their convents abandoned or destroyed; the last spark of life in the city was extinct; Goa was, wrote Fonseca in 1878, a wilderness infested with snakes, in which it was hard to trace the overgrown buildings. Sir William Russell, who went there with the Prince of Wales in their tour of 1877, wrote of it with melancholy interest. "The river washes the remains of a great city; an arsenal in ruins; palaces in ruins; quay walls in ruins; churches in ruins; all in ruins. We saw the site of the Inquisition, the Bishop's palace, a grand Cathedral, great churches, chapels, convents, religious houses, on knolls surrounded by jungle . . . We saw the crumbling masonry which once marked the lines of streets and enclosures of palaces, dockyards with weeds and desolate cranes." The quays lay deserted. "Instead of the bustle which once prevailed there, a complete silence now reigns, broken only by the wind whistling through the branches of the palm trees which grow luxuriantly on the spot."

Jogendra Nath Bhattacharya

(fl. 1890s)

Indian writer. His book is a guide to the intricacies of life among Hindus in India.

Punka-pullers and others

With regard to the caste of the other classes of domestics in Anglo-Indian households, it may be observed, generally, that the Mahomedans have the monopoly of such as appertain to the stable. Even in Hindu households, the coachmen and the footmen are always followers of Islam. The cooks, scullions and butlers are either Mahomedans (or Aracanese) or Madrasis of the low castes called Paria and Tiyan. The punka-pullers are either Goalas of Orissa or Kahars of Behar. Oriyas and Kahars are employed also as *farashes* for wiping off the dust from the furniture, and for cleansing and lighting the lamps. The washerman is the Hindu Dhobi, Vannan or Agasia; while the scavengers and the nightsoil men are all usually of such aboriginal tribes as are called Hari, Methar, Churha, &c.

Ella Maillart

(1903–97)

Swiss explorer, actress, stuntwoman, writer and world-class athlete. Maillart travelled on her own, living among nomads in Russian Turkestan in 1932, and later, with Peter Fleming, made a 3500-mile journey from Peking to India. She was still travelling energetically in Nepal, Tibet and other parts of Asia in her eighties. Here she visits Bamiyan in 1939, described in her book, *The Cruel Way*.

Bamian

The early morning filled me with delight. The colours were bright but mellow, as if edged with mother-of-pearl – the emerald of the short-napped grass, the violet and orange of the cliffs, the yellows of the fields, the sparkling of poplar leaves; and above it all the incredible blueness of the sky, a deep rich blue as we have it over the snowfields in Switzerland.

The Koh-i-Baba floated grey and vaporous, as if very far. To the north, beyond the pink cliffs and their sculptured figures, rose high hills with velvety blue furrows dotted here and there with little blots of snow . . .

Having crossed the hamlet of Bamian, we reached the great Buddha who dominates lucerne and melon-fields from his height of a hundred and seventy-five feet. The legs have been almost entirely destroyed and part of the head (the ear alone is twice my size). From the top of the head the world looked splendid in the clear mountain air – the chequer-board of fields, the smiling vale of Kakrak and beyond, the gentle Koh-i-Baba. The nearby frescoes showed darkly draped Bodhis-attvas in the traditional seated posture; they are dated back to the third century.

With its spirit of smiling restfulness, the landscape was the best part of Bamian. That is probably why Buddhists came here to build monasteries at the beginning of our era. Hsuan Tsang, my guide in so many places, was here in 632, twenty years before the Islamic conquest added to the damage begun by the White Huns. He counted ten monas-teries with several thousand monks. Of the people he wrote that, "they are hard and fierce by nature, but they are superior to their neighbours in the candour of their faith".

Cecil Beaton

(1904–80)

British photographer, stage designer and traveller. He kept
the most piquant of diaries.

In the Street of Moonlight, Old Delhi

In the Chadni Chowk (the Street of Moonlight), at one time considered the richest street in the world, now an alleyway full of bar-
gains and trash, a begging Sadhu, naked and daubed with dung, an
'exponent of destitution', extends a withered arm. Other holy men have
whitened faces; and there are boys with heavily kohl-painted eyes, their
teeth, tongue and lips scarlet with betel nut. In the thoroughfares,
pedestrians, bicycles, carts and sacred animals are wedged together in
an almost inextricable confusion. Women resemble human beehives,
entirely covered with whitish cloth except for the small letter-box
slot through which their painted eyes peer. The shops, no more than
window-recesses, offer spangled tassels, glittering phials of perfume,
filigree jewels and vivid foodstuffs. A stall of vile-coloured drinks, in
bottles stopped with fans of magenta paper, has been built around a
sprawling peepul tree; its bark, painted emerald green, adds to the
general gaudiness.

At the Tomb of Humayan, Delhi

From the parapet of the Tomb of Humayan, in the precious moments
of twilight, one sees India at her best. Beyond the domes of mosques lies
the lilac-coloured jungle. A crescent moon appears, in silvery contrast to
the few wisps of golden cloud that are hurrying to be away before the
sky becomes completely dark: cranes and other large birds are flying
home and their wings make a breathless flapping noise; while parrots,
very small, but tightly clustered, give the impression, as they pass, of
a flying carpet. Jackals come out and slink off again, horrible hangtail

scavengers. A shepherd, rather sadly, is playing on his flute; and from the distance comes the echoing call to evening prayer.

Robert Byron

(1905–41)

English historian, art critic and traveller. His *Road to Oxiana*, a search for the origins of Islamic architecture in Persia and Afghanistan in 1932, is a classic of travel writing. Byron travelled as far as China and Tibet and wrote four other books. He was killed when his ship was torpedoed in the Mediterranean in 1941.

Afghanistan with a Rolls

I arrived here in great state, *driving* a Rolls. I must say I never thought the first time I should drive a Rolls would be in Afghanistan – or, for that matter, that I should arrive in Herat, which has been the goal of my plans for the last year, driving a Rolls with 2 Englishwomen beside me, Noel asleep in the back, and another woman crying because of the bumps. I drove very well – much better than Noel, with fewer crashes and greater speed. The road was indescribable. We were out half the night the other side of the frontier. The other Rolls, a huge dowager's limousine, got impaled on a culvert and had to be dug out with *grandpa's knife*. That knife, which I popped in at the last moment to sharpen my pencils with, has proved the mainstay of my journey – I eat with it. It is also the only thing about me which provokes any respect or admiration.

A Hungarian arrived here today from Kabul, having been unable to eat for a fortnight. I gave him Ovaltine and soup and a charcoal pill – he seemed really on the point of collapse. So I hope he will post this in Persia, as he is going on to Meshed.

Peter Fleming

(1907–71)

English writer, soldier and traveller, the brother of Ian Fleming. As a journalist, Fleming interviewed Chiang Kai-Shek for *The Times*. In 1935 he and Ella Maillart travelled 3500 miles through China on foot and pony. They travelled through the forbidden provinces of Sinkiang. He made many other journeys including, in 1932, a 3000-mile amateur expedition to find the lost explorer, Colonel H.P. Fawcett who had disappeared in the Matto Grosso region of the Amazon in 1925. 'Our ignorance of Portugese, like our lack of a fish-hook, was a constant source of irritation,' he commented.

Meeting another explorer

Night had fallen. Electric lights, wan and uncertain, lit the interior of the dining-car. A fat general, who looked like a Moslem from the Northwest, was supping very audibly with two of his staff. A young Pekingese, with YMCA stamped all over his European clothes, was eating foreign food unhappily; his unsuccessfully overweening manner had earned the contempt of the waiter. An English couple were deploring the length and discomforts of the journey to Hankow. 'Well, there's only another twenty-four hours.' 'Darling, I don't *think* I should eat that fish if I were you. It's much safer to stick to boiled food on these trains. You know what happened to Elsie . . .' 'Very well, dear. Boy!'

The door behind me opened and Kini came in.

'I've slept for eighteen hours,' she said. 'Let's eat.'

I had first met Kini during the previous summer in London. The guests of a distinguished Orientalist, we found ourselves drinking beer together in a night club, 'How do I get into the Soviet Republic in South China?' asked Kini. 'You don't,' I said, and told her why; at that time I used to pose as an authority on the Chinese Communists. We parted with the migrant's casual formula, which men forget but fate sometimes remembers. 'See you in China, probably?' 'Yes. See you in China.' Kini went off with a strong dislike for me. I thought her nice, and suspected her of being effective.

James Cameron

(1911–85)

British journalist. He travelled widely as a foreign correspondent reporting on events such as the Chinese invasion
of Tibet, the atomic bomb tests on the Bikini Atoll in
1946 and the Vietnam War. Despite these experiences, his
memoirs remain vivid and amusing.

The Himalaya Hotel, Kalimpong

Vaguely in the centre of this pageant of fantastics was the Himalaya Hotel. This is a commonplace name for a most exceptional place. If I keep so persistently harping on hotels it is only that, having spent quite a disproportionate part of my life in them, I have come to classify and record them much as I believe, accomplished winelovers define clarets, less for their appearance and cost as for their associations and bouquet. The Himalaya was, by those standards, a collector's piece. It was (and I hope still is) the nearest thing to what I imagine the seventeenth-century English inn must have been, in its broadminded and casual attitude to the one factor absent from almost all other hotels, hospitality. People came in, and drifted about, and occupied themselves with erratic pur-suits, and told incredible stories in several languages, and made abrupt appearances in extravagant clothes, and no one was there an hour before he would find himself involved and embraced in the inescapable com-munity life of the place. Which was all the odder since the place was full of those most exclusive and (as we always imagined) unclubbable of all peoples, Tibetans.

That night I bathed in a large tin tub and went into what in any other hotel would have been called a lounge, for what anywhere else would have been called a quick drink, before what in most other places would have been dinner. In no single particular was this purpose accomplished; rather, in every aspect did it materialize some ten times life-size. To call this room a lounge would have been ridiculous; it was a salon, a caravanserai, a large room crowded, as we saw with surprise, with a multitude of striking and picturesque people in richly-coloured costume and exceptional hairdressings; they were occupied not, as one might have thought, in being photographed for the *National Geographic Magazine*, but in a variety of pleasantly domestic occupations such as pouring tots of rum and knitting socks, and discussing questions of mutual interest in an animated and formal way. Most of them were Tibetans; there were also several people who might have been economics lecturers on vacation, refugees from Cheltenham Ladies' College, and at least one who was quite evidently a Benedictine monk in disguise. Before our entry we had considered dubiously whether our appearance — unshaven, khaki-shirted, carpet-slippered — might have been thought indecorous. We need not have worried.

J.E. Power

(c. 1912)

A Lieutenant in the 19th Lancers of the Indian Army, Power wrote this manual for the benefit of other officers going out to serve in India.

Luggage for India

... you should find room in or near the cabin for a suit-case and a helmet-box, and a moderate-sized Gladstone or kit-bag. In the way of mufti you will find flannels and a good supply of soft shirts and collars most useful. In any case, be prepared for extremes of climate, as in the Mediterranean Sea you may experience severely cold weather, and in the Indian Ocean quite the reverse. The amount of baggage you are allowed and other restrictions may vary according to the boat you go in, whether hired transport or private line's vessel, but within reasonable limits the restrictions will not be harshly enforced. When sorting your property to pack it, remember that your boxes will require various labels, which are:

1. For baggage room (not wanted on voyage) – white.
2. Change of clothing (accessible once or twice a week) – blue.
3. Packages for cabin – yellow.

An important point to remember when packing will be not to forget due precautions against moths and the ravages of air and water. Have your uniform and any other damageable kit in air-tight boxes, and note that gold or silver lace is not only injured by camphor, but also if not folded in tissue paper, lace will tarnish if the clothes are simply folded without this precaution, by mere contact with the cloth. The best prevention against moths is to scatter amongst your clothes plenty of naphthaline balls. When your boxes are all packed, take care that each of them has your rank, name, and Regiment plainly painted upon the front, and in addition it is most useful to have on each a coloured distinguishing mark or sign, such as circle, or cross, or bands of colour all the way round them. If this is done, it will help you considerably to distinguish your own luggage when among a pile of other boxes, and servants will certainly identify it more quickly.

Now, as regards size and quantity of luggage authorised: When proceeding by transport, you will be provided with official instructions which should not leave you in doubt, and full particulars will be found in a useful pamphlet, issued gratis by Messrs. Grindlay & Co., of 54, Parliament St., SW. In the same way as shown in Chapter 1., your agents at home will be most serviceable in many ways . . .

Dress and undress in India

Full dress and frock dress are tabulated as follows:–

      I. Dragoon Guards and Dragoons.
     II. Hussars.
    III. Lancers.
    IV. RA, RE, ASC, RAMC.
     V. Infantry of the Line and fusiliers.

UNIFORM AND EQUIPMENT

I. – Dragoon Guards and Dragoons.

FULL DRESS

Tunic.

Overalls.

Pantaloons.

Helmet and plume.

Sword.

Sword belt and slings.

Sword knot.

Girdle.

Shoulder belt and pouch.

Gauntlets.

Spurs.

Jack boots.

Wellingtons.

Horse plume.

Lambskin.

FROCK DRESS –

Frock coat.

Overalls.

Parade spurs.

Forage caps.

Accoutrements as in full dress.

White buck gloves.

II. – Hussars.

FULL DRESS –
Tunic.
Overalls.
Pantaloons.
Busby and plume.
Busby lines.
Shoulder belt and pouch.
Sword belt and slings.
Sword.
Sword knot.
Gloves.
Spurs.
Wellington boots.
Jack boots and spurs.
Leopardskin and lambskin.
Horse plume.

LEVEE DRESS –
Hessian boots.
Spurs.
Pantaloons.

FROCK DRESS –
Frock coat.
Girdle.
Forage cap.
Overalls and accoutrements as in full dress.

Fosco Maraini

(1912–)

Italian mountaineer, traveller and writer. In 1958 he went
to the Hindu Kush to climb Mount Saraghrar, described in
his book *Where Four Worlds Meet*. Before this he travelled
extensively in Tibet.

Butter, bones and silence in Tibet

Butter (like bones and silence) constitutes one of the most characteristic
features of Tibet. It seems impossible that the thin females of the yak,
grazing among stones and sand, should produce such an enormous flow
of butter. But Tibet is full of it. It is on sale in the most remote villages;
it is used for offering to the gods in every temple and private chapel; it
is carved in masterly fashion into statues and complicated ornamental
patterns, and then coloured with extraordinary delicacy; it is burned
in lamps, and taxes are paid with it; women spread it on their hair, and
often on their faces; it is always an acceptable gift; it is mixed with
tsampa for food and with tea for drink. In Tibet there is butter, butter
everywhere. It is used all the time, for every conceivable purpose, and
you can never get away from it.

Bones are as universal in Tibet as butter. Many more animals die
or are killed in other countries than in Tibet; but nowhere else in the
world, so far as I know, do you see so many carcasses, skulls, thigh-bones,
vertebrae and ribs scattered along the roads, outside the houses, along
the mountain passes. There is no reason whatever in the nature of things
why it should be so; it is just a curious cultural trait. The bones of
animals are not buried, or hidden from sight, or destroyed; they are
just left, like stones on the road outside the doorstep. Children play
with them, or throw them at one another. I suggest that there must be
an active side to this apparent passivity; the Tibetans must positively
like having bones lying about. They must regard them as a kind of
flower, a decoration, a comfort, a pleasure. Are they perhaps a reminder

of the illusory nature of the temporal world, from which man must escape if he desires salvation? Who knows?

The third characteristic feature of Tibet, after the butter and the bones, is the tremendous silence. Modern physics talks of a four-dimensional space-time continuum. Tibet consists of a four-dimensional space-silence continuum. There is the yellow, ochre silence of the rocks; the blue-green silence of the ice-peaks; the silence of the valleys over which hawks wheel high in the sun; and there is the silence that purifies everything, dries the butter, pulverizes the bones and leaves in the mind an inexpressible, dreamy sweetness, as if one had attained some ancient fatherland lost since the very beginning of history.

Eric Newby

(1919–)

English traveller and writer, formerly an apprentice on a four-masted barque, a soldier and a buyer in the fashion trade.

Down the Ganges

We set off down the Ganges at two o'clock in the afternoon. It was 6 December, my forty-fourth birthday. Our immediate destination was the Balawali Bridge, twenty-five miles as the crow flies from Hardwar, a journey which we believed would take two days. The boat was deep-loaded, so deeply and with such a quantity of gear that only three of the five oarsmen's benches could be occupied. Besides the six occupants (we had recruited two more boatmen and the Irrigation Engineer had sent one of his own men to ensure that his own boat was not misused) there was now the augmented luggage, plus further purchases we had made in the bazaar at Hardwar; sacks of chilli powder and vegetables, namdars – blankets made from a sort of coarse felt; teapots, kettles, hurricane lamps and reed mats. I had even bought an immense bamboo pole from a specialist shop in the bazaar as a defence against dacoits (robbers) whose supposed whereabouts were indicated on some rather depressing maps which G. had annotated with this and similar information, in the same way as medieval cartographers had inscribed "Here be dragons" on the blank expanses of their productions. G. himself had made an even more eccentric purchase from the same establishment – two officer's swagger-canes about a foot and a half long which now, as he stood in the middle of the boat directing its final trimming with them, made him look like an old-fashioned sailor semaphoring. Our bills were paid. We had left a hundred rupees for a lorry-man to come and collect the boat down-stream. Prudently we had put this into the hands of the men from Shell who by this time, together with the one who had told me that I had liked roses, were the only people we trusted. We had paid the thirty-two men who had come tottering barefooted across a mile of hot shingle with the boat upside down over their heads all the way from the Canal to the Ganges; we had shaken hands with everybody – some, whom we had never seen before, had wept, and for the second time in two days we had advanced money to boatmen for them to buy provisions for the journey (we never saw the first two boatmen again). We were ready to go.

As we crouched low in the boat while the current took us under the bridge, an old bridge-builder who was wearing spectacles as large as the headlamps of a Rolls Royce, dropped sacred sweets on us as a provision for the journey. His tears wetted our heads. The boatmen put their oars in the rowlocks and rowed off smartly. We were off.

Two hundred yards below the bridge and some twelve hundred miles from the Bay of Bengal the boat grounded in sixteen inches of water. This was no shoal. There was no question of being in the wrong channel. At this point the uniform depth of the river was sixteen inches. I looked upstream to the bridge but all those who had been waving and weeping had studiously turned their backs. The boatmen uttered despairing cries for assistance but the men at the bridge bent to their tasks with unwonted diligence. As far as they were concerned we had passed out of their lives. We might never have existed.

Peter Levi

(1931–2000)

English poet, author, translator and Jesuit priest from 1964–77. His grandfather was a Jewish indigo merchant who came to England from Germany in the 1880s and established himself as a carpet dealer. Levi was Oxford Professor of Poetry from 1984–9; he wrote many books and volumes of poetry. In the 1960s he travelled in Afghanistan with Bruce and Elizabeth Chatwin looking for vestiges of the country's Classical past.

In Kabul

Kabul is high up, lost among mountains; it is an untidy town surrounded by wheatfields like rough mats and by grey and black mountains still fretted with snow at the end of June. As you come down out of the air you see the tents and flocks of nomads around it. When you reach the ground the mountains take on their height, and the snow on them is a long pattern of streaks and smears; it looks like Kufic writing stamped on the intense background of the air. The heat is Indian. You enter a curling, sprawling settlement around the edges of four or five hills; it has almost no bourgeois suburbs, in fact it still has some of the character-istics of a mountain village or a fur traders' post; you see pelts and furs hanging up for sale in the streets. There is a comic Wagnerian royal palace which used to have sentries in Nazi helmets and swastikas, because the Afghans believe they were the ancestors of the Aryan race, but no buildings of any architectural merit, although there are trees and private gardens on a generous scale. The town is 6900 feet above sea-level, but at mid-summer this height is expressed in nothing but a little breeze. The characteristic smell is a mixture of balsam poplars and crudely refined petrol. In all Afghanistan only Kabul has most of its main roads asphalted.

The life of the wider streets is less appalling. You see a wide variety of dress, some of it in deep, pure colours faded with age and sun. Shopwindows and stall displays are obsessively decorated in exactly the same spirit as the designs of Islamic textiles or a sixteenth-century minaret; it is the same instinctive feeling for strong motifs and repeated contrasts, self-conscious in the one case and quite instinctive in the other, that makes everyday life in Kabul so invigorating to the eyesight. There are cold drinks you can buy in the street coloured like those imaginative liquids that used to advertise chemists' shops before the war. The bottles are stopped with marbles and shriek like mandrakes as they open; they are iced with muddy-looking snow. There are street traders selling small pebbles of lapis lazuli from Badakshan. The pelts of snow-leopards hang outside fur shops. The first day I was in Kabul I saw three men riding on one bicycle, one in a fur hat, one in a Persian skullcap, and one in a turban.

Geoffrey Moorhouse

(1931–)

English author and traveller, who has written many books of history and travel. In 1972 Moorhouse attempted to cross the African continent from Mauretania to the Nile via Timbuktu. The desert defeated him; he described the ghastly experience in *The Fearful Void*. His book on Calcutta is something of a tour de force, making sense out of the apparent chaos of that city.

Calcutta from the air

As the Boeing flexes its wings in descent, the traveller begins to observe the details of a landscape which has changed somewhat since his taste of Bombay or Delhi. There the ground seemed barren and burnt from the sky but here it looks wonderfully fertile. The predominant colour is green, sometimes vivid and deep, sometimes nearly yellow, but always the promise of growth. And there is water: water in craters, water in canals, water in lakes and, just over there, a great gleaming swamp of saturated fields with what looks like chickweed floating on the top between the dykes. A city appears, enormous and sprawling around a wide brown river which has shaped itself in a dog-leg and which has ships hanging at anchor. Silver oil tanks sparkle in the piercing light but there is a haze of smoke over the city which renders a range of high dockside cranes as an indistinct thicket of industry and a vast row of factory roofs as a rusty sheet of corrugated iron. It could almost be Liverpool on a sensational summer's day. But as the Boeing cants over and skims even lower above the gleaming swamp and past the lunar grey of some gigantic reclamation from the waters, the traveller knows it is no such thing. For there are palm trees here and a brown man coaxing a black bullock along a straggling road and, gracious me, a dazzlingly white Early English church tower poking up from jungle. Then the plane is down, and as it bounds and sways along the runway, the traveller notices that he is about to disembark at a spanking inter-national airport, as new as Prague's, as inviting as Rome's. He blinks yet again, and wonders whether rumour has lied once more. For he has come to Calcutta. And everything he has heard about it sounds quite remarkably unpleasant.

Sir Mark Tully

(1935–)

Journalist, broadcaster and writer who has spent most of his career observing and writing about India.

Babas and pandas at the Kumbh Mela

While the devotees were thronging around the saint's platform, I found two of his disciples. I asked them to tell me about the baba's routine. One who was a printer – not, apparently, the printer of that commentary – said, 'The baba lives and is everywhere. He has no fixed place, but always stays by riverbanks. He is an ageless man who has travelled all over India on foot. Everyone claims that the baba comes from his area. Some say that he was born of water. He takes bath in the river four or five times every day.'

'Why does he live on a platform?'

'Because he says that the public are infected with worms which he will get if he stays on their level. The baba's memory is like a computer – people will tell you that he remembers what they told him thirty years ago.'

'Some people say he's three hundred years old. How old is he really?'

'No one knows exactly what exercises he does, but he has mastered age and will die only when he wants to. He is a sidh yogi [an ascetic whose mastery of the yogic arts is so great that he has attained supernatural powers and transcended them] – all the time he is practising the yoga position of Udyan Band, which means his stomach touches his back.'

'What does he eat?'

'Air. He doesn't even eat fruit. You see, any great yogi can extend his tongue from inside until it touches the top of his head. That's where the nectar is situated, and one drop of nectar is all you need to live for a very long time.'

I couldn't help wondering what happened to all the baskets of fruit which were being given to the baba as offerings.

'Is it true', I asked, 'that Indira Gandhi used to come to see the baba?'

'Yes, she came several times.'

'What about Rajiv?'

'No. He will come when his heart is cleaner.'

A group of pilgrims with shaven heads were sitting in a circle on the sand in front of the panda's stall. Two scruffy young men dressed in trousers and sweaters were moving round the pilgrims asking them how much they were going to pay for the ceremony for their dead. An old man was proving particularly recalcitrant. 'Come on, make your commitment,' said one of the pandas irascibly. 'Don't waste my time.' Another pilgrim wanted to offer only twenty-five rupees. The panda told him, 'That's not enough. Other people have given 101.' Eventually the pilgrim handed over fifty-one rupees. The panda pocketed the cash and was turning away when his client asked anxiously, 'Aren't you going to bless me?' The panda bent down, patted his head and said a brief mantra. The pilgrim touched his feet. The priest laughed and said, 'Now you've had your blessing on the cheap.' The pandas were very skilled operators – they knew exactly when to upbraid, when to cajole and when to give up to get the most out of their clients without losing any of them.

Alexander Frater

(1937–)

English journalist and author, Frater was born on the hurricane-prone South Pacific island of Vanuatu, where his father was a missionary. *Chasing the Monsoon* follows the path of the monsoon from Trivandrum in South India, to Cherrapunji in Assam, the wettest place on earth.

Into the monsoon with Ravi

On the tiny flight desk the young co-pilot sat peering around the valley. 'Hurry, hurry, hurry,' he murmured. Ravi drove the Fokker out to the threshold like a fire engine. 'Strap yourself in tight,' he said. He pushed the throttles forward before he was even aligned, accelerating into the turn, then bounding forward as the usual Umroi fog came rolling down behind and, in front, another black wall began closing on the runway. But this one rippled with tongues of flame and gave off small, eddying puffs of smoke. Above the racket of the engines Ravi shouted, 'They're shooting at us!' I stared wordlessly ahead. The base of the smoking, burning rampart scraped along the valley floor but its dome soared upwards to form part of the substructure of heaven itself. And it came from the south. I wondered whether this was a full-blown Cherrapunji *son et lumière* production, diverting through Umroi to show me something I would never forget.

We crashed into it ten feet off the ground. Huge internal vortices tossed us up another fifty. The rain drummed like buckshot and lightning fitfully illuminated the flight deck. Bottles were breaking in the galley and the stewardess, strapped in behind, cried out. For almost a quarter of an hour the Fokker, creaking and groaning, wings flexing like a planing gull's, went lurching and porpoising through the maelstrom.

Then, as if the monsoon had finally wearied of my presence and decided to spit me out, we burst into calm air and sunshine so blinding it made us blink. Before us the sapphire plains of Bangladesh were stippled with the shadows of benign clouds drifting through the huge, pale Indian sky. In a month the rains would withdraw, travelling down India the way they had come, the final showers passing across Trivandrum and then vanishing over the horizon in, perhaps, a valedictory puff of smoke.

I looked back for a last glimpse of Cherrapunji. But it lay beneath a lavender-coloured canopy that reached past the Himalayas and on, drawing the eye much further than it would actually go. It seemed to cover half the world, and I imagined that at long last the summer monsoon was flowing free, unimpeded by those mountain ramparts.

Ravi, steering carefully round the clouds, began talking to someone on the radio.

William Dalrymple

(1965–)

British writer and historian, born in Scotland. Dalrymple lived in Delhi for six years researching *City of Djinns*; he now writes mostly about India.

The Falaknuma Palace, Hyderabad

Look a little further, and you discover that small pools of the old world do still survive, often out of bounds to the casual visitor. The Falaknuma Palace is one such place. A huge and magnificent complex of white classical villas and mansions raised above the town on its own acropolis, the Falaknuma was the principal residence of the sixth Nizam, the father of Osman Ali Khan. But today it is the subject of a bitter legal dispute

333

between the Taj group, who wish to turn it into a hotel, and the last Nizam's grandson, now mainly resident on a sheep farm in Australia, who claims never to have sold it. While the buildings await the decision of the courts, they lie empty and semi-ruinous, locked by court order, with every window and doorway sealed with red wax.

Wipe the dust from the windows and peer inside, and you see cobwebs the size of bedsheets hanging in the corners of the rooms. The skeletons of outsized Victorian sofas and armchairs lie dotted around the parquet floors, their chintz entirely eaten away by white ants, so that all that remain are the wooden frames, the springs and a little of the stuffing. Vast imperial desks, big enough to play billiards on, stand on rotting red carpets peppered with huge holes, as if they have been savaged by some terrible outsized supermoth. On one wall hangs a giant portrait of Queen Mary, on another a strange, faded Victorian fantasy of Richard the Lionheart on the battlements at Acre. Beyond are long, gloomy corridors, leading to unseen inner courtyards and *zenana* wings: mile upon mile of empty classical arcades and melancholy bow fronts, now quite empty but for a pair of lonely *chowkidars* shuffling around with their *lathis* and whistles. Outside stretch acres of scrub flats, once presumably soft green lawns, dotted here and there with kitsch statues of naked cupids, waterless fountains, giant silver oil lamps and paint-flaking flagpoles leaning at crazy angles.

Stanley Stewart

(1952–)

Formerly a farmer, fisherman, film cameraman and erector of circus tents, Stewart is now a writer and journalist.

A Mongolian wedding battle

New reserves of *airag* were now arriving. An elder sister of the bride arose at this point with a rather sarcastic vote of thanks followed by the announcement that the family were now taking their leave. Apparently the feeling was that the groom's family were being rather too generous with the drink, and trying to belittle the bride's family by outdoing their hospitality of the morning. On cue Wyatt Earp and the singer rose to depart followed by the massed ranks of the bride's family. The groom's family, alarmed by this sudden turn of events, sprang to their feet. 'You must stay,' they cried. 'Food is coming. There is more *airag*. You must enjoy yourselves.' Beneath their protestations lay the idea that the bride's family were insulting them by not accepting their hospitality with good grace.

Much pulling now ensued. The groom's family pulled at the bride's family to keep them from departing while the bride's family pulled strenuously towards the door. In no time the pulling, common to the friendliest of Mongolian drinking circles, had degenerated into a brawl. Someone had pulled too hard and toppled forward, flattening a granny. Someone else accidentally upset a bowl of *airag*.

Suddenly the *ger* was in uproar, and blows were being exchanged. Wyatt Earp laid into a row of young men, felling three of them with a roundhouse right. The man who lived in the railway carriage, smiling more widely than ever, floored the singer, sending the stove and an elderly aunt flying. Lenin tried to rescue the situation with one of his speeches. 'We will drink! We will feast! We will sing!' he shouted above the mayhem. But no one was listening. He chopped two of the bride's sisters to the ground and tried to push his way towards the door to block their escape route. One of the sharp-kneed aunts at my back had taken up a horsewhip and was merrily flaying in the direction of her new in-laws. Eight bowls of *airag* had not done much for her aim and the blows were raining down on my own shoulders. The bridal couple, wisely taking no part in the fisticuffs, sat side by side, eyes politely downcast, as if the warfare that now raged about them was just another embarrassing speech. The only other non-participant was the lama, who viewed the fray with the beady eyes of a fight promoter while taking the opportunity of the general distraction to help himself to another bowl of *arkhi*.

The brawl came to an abrupt end with a strange good grace. It appeared fierce enough – there were at least a couple of bloody noses – but afterwards, with victory going to the groom's family for preventing what they saw as premature departure, everyone settled down to another round of drinking and songs. No one seemed to consider a wedding punch-up odd. With my own judgement slightly deranged by *airag* I was happy to fall in with this consensus, and decided that this mixture of camaraderie and violence, with a few songs thrown in, was a rather healthy business. It cleared the air nicely. A wedding reception where you got to give your new in-laws a good thumping was the kind of thing that people in the West could only dream about.

Far Asia

MONGOLIA

CHINA

Peking ●

JAPAN

Sea of Japan

Nagoya ●

Yellow Sea

Nagasaki ●

TIBET

Shanghai ●

East China Sea

Shaoshan ●

North

ropic of Cancer

BURMA

Macao ●

Pacific

Hong Kong ●

Ocean

THAILAND

Andaman Islands

Angkor ●

VIETNAM

PHILIPPINES

South China Sea

Nicobar Islands

Saigon ●

MALAYA

Malacca ●

Malay Archipelago

SUMATRA

BORNEO

Indian Ocean

I N D O N E S I A

Ma Huan

(*fl.* 1416–35)

Chinese naval secretary and interpeter. Ma Huan travelled
with several of the voyages sent by the Emperor of China
to explore the 'Western Oceans', under the command of
the brilliant Cheng Ho, who had been superintendent of
the office of eunuchs at the Imperial court. Fleets of ships
laden with treasures visited more than thirty countries in
seven expeditions, recorded by Ma Huan and others. The
expeditions were considered to be one of the great achieve-
ments of the Ming Dynasty.

Names of the foreign countries

The country of Chan city [Champa, Central Vietnam]
The country of Chao-wa [Java]
The country of Old Haven [Palembang]
The country of Hsien Lo [Siam, Thailand]
The country of Man-la-chia [Malacca]
The country of Ya-lu [Aru, Deli]
The country of Su-men-ta-la [Semudera, Lho Seumawel]
The country of Na-ku-erhs [Nagur, Peudada]
The country of Li-tai [Lide, Meureudu]
The country of Nan-p'o-li [Lambri, Atjeh]
The country of Hsi-lan [Ceylon]
The country of Little Ko-lan [Quilon]
The country of Ko-chih [Cochin]
The country of Ku-li [Calicut]

The country of Liu Mountains [Maldive and Laccadive islands]
The country of Tsu-fa-erh [Dhufar]
The country of A-tan [Aden]
The country of Pang-ko-la [Bengal]
The country of Hu-lu-mo-ssu [Hormuz]
The country of The Heavenly Square [Mecca]

In the country of Chan-city

Oxen, pigs and goats – all these they have. Geese and ducks are scarce. The fowls are small; the largest ones do not exceed two *chin* [in weight]; [and] their legs are one and a half *ts'un* and at the most two *ts'un*, in height. The cock birds have red crowns and white ears, with small waists and high tails; they crow, too, when people take them up in their hands; [they are] very likeable.

For fruits, they have such kinds as the plum, orange, water-melon, sugarcane, coconut, jack-fruit and banana. The jack-fruit resembles the gourd-melon; the outside skin is like that of the litchi from Ch'uan; inside the skin there are lumps of yellow flesh as big as a hen's egg, which taste like honey; inside [these lumps] there is a seed resembling a chicken's kidney; [and] when roasted and eaten, it tastes like a chestnut.

For vegetables, they have the gourd-melon, cucumber, bottle-gourd, mustard plant, onion and ginger, and that is all; other fruits and vegetables are entirely lacking.

Most of the men take up fishing for a livelihood; they seldom go in for agriculture, and therefore rice and cereals are not abundant. In the local varieties of rice the kernel is small, long, and reddish. Barley and wheat are both wanting. The people ceaselessly chew areca-nut and betel-leaf.

When men and women marry, the only requirement is that the man should first go to the woman's house, and consummate the marriage. Ten days or half a moon later, the man's father and mother, with their relatives and friends, to the accompaniment of drums and music escort husband and wife back to [the paternal] home; then they prepare wine and play music.

As to their wine: they take some rice and mix it with medicinal herbs, seal [the mixture] in a jar, and sit around; [then they] put in some water according to the number of persons, and take it in turns to suck up [the wine] and drink it; when [the jar] is sucked dry, they again add water and drink; [this they do] until there is no [more] taste [of wine]; [and] then they stop.

As to their writing: they have no paper or pen; they use [either] goat-skin beaten thin or tree-bark smoked black; and they fold it into the form of a classical book [in which] with white chalk, they write characters which serve for records.

As to the punishable offences [in this] country: for light [offences], they employ thrashing on the back with a rattan stick; for serious [offences], they cut off the nose; for robbery, they sever a hand; for the offence of adultery, the man and the woman are branded on the face so as to make a scar; for the most heinous offences, they take a hard wood [stick], cut a sharp point to it, and set it up on a [log of] wood which resembles a small boat; [this] they put in the water; [and] they make the offender sit on the wood spike; the wood [stick] protrudes from his mouth and he dies; [and] then [the corpse] is left on the water as a warning to the public.

Tomé Pires

(*c.* 1468–1540)

Portugese apothecary who travelled to India and Malacca, where his profession made him a wealthy man. His book, *Suma Oriental*, was written there. In 1517 Pires went to China as an Ambassador but the mission was not a success. Among other crimes, the Portugese were accused of buying Chinese children and roasting them. Twenty-three Portugese were hideously executed. Pires had a daughter by a Chinese woman at Sampitay on the Grand Canal. He died in China.

The Chinese people

According to what the nations here in the East say, things of China are made out to be great, riches, pomp and state in both the land and people, and other tales which it would be easier to believe as true of our Portugal than of China. China is a large country with beautiful horses and mules, they say, and in large numbers.

The king of China is a heathen with much land and many people. The people of China are white, as white as we are. Most of them wear black cotton cloth, and they wear sayons of this in five pieces with gores, as we do, only they are very wide. In the winter they wear felt on their legs by way of socks, and on top well-made boots which do not reach above the knee, and they wear their clothes lined with lambskin and other furs. Some of them wear pelisses. They wear round silk net caps like the black sieves we have in Portugal. They are rather like Germans. They have thirty or forty hairs in their beards. They wear very well-made French shoes with square toes.

All the Chinese eat pigs, cows and all other animals. They drink a fair amount of all sorts of beverages. They praise our wine greatly. They get pretty drunk. They are weak people, of small account. Those who are to be seen in Malacca are not very truthful, and steal – that is the common people. They eat with two sticks, and the earthenware or china bowl in their left hand close to their mouth, with the two sticks to suck in. This is the Chinese way . . .

The women look like Spanish women. They wear pleated skirts with waistbands, and little loose coats longer than in our country. Their long hair is rolled in a graceful way on the top of their heads, and they put many gold pins in it to hold it, and those who have them put precious stones around, and golden jewelry on the crown of their heads and in their ears and on their (necks). They put a great deal of ceruse on their faces and paint on the top of it, and they are so made up that Seville has no advantage over them; and they drink like women from a cold country. They wear pointed slippers of silk and brocade. They all carry fans in their hands. They are as white as we are, and some of them have small eyes and others large, and noses as they must be.

Vasco da Gama

(c. 1469–1524)

Portuguese navigator who discovered the sea route to the India via the Cape of Good Hope, discovered by Diaz ten years earlier. His second journey, as admiral of a fleet of twenty-one armed ships, punitively enforced the Portuguese presence in the East Indies. After doing nothing for twenty years, in 1524 da Gama was made sixth viceroy of India, but died when he reached Cochin.

Black-toothed inhabitants of Malacca

Eight hundred miles from Coloen is a large town called Melatk, whence come the beft cloves and nutmegs, valuable goods, and precious ftones.

The people of this country have black teeth, becaufe they eat the leaves of the trees and a white thing like chalk actually with the leaves, and it comes from it that the teeth become black, and that is called tombour, and they carry it always with them wherever they go or are travelling. The pepper grows as the vine does in our country.

There are in the country cats as big as our foxes, and it is from them that the mufk comes, and it is very dear, for a cat is worth 100 ducats, and the mufk grows between his legs, under his tail.

Ginger grows as a reed, and cinnamon as a willow; and every year they ftrip the cinnamon from its bark, however thin it is, and the youngeft is the better. The true fummer is in December and January.

Joao Rodrigues

(c. 1562–?)

Portuguese traveller who sailed to Japan with Portuguese
Jesuits in 1577. Japan was then in a period of extended
civil war when local barons or *daimyo* were fighting to
extend their powers. Rodrigues learned fluent Japanese. In
1610, Rodrigues had to leave Japan, as victim of a political
incident involving a Portuguese ship; he spent the remaining twenty-three years of his life in Macao and China
where he travelled extensively and learned Chinese.

Some strange fauna

In these islands there are some wonderful things outside the ordinary
course of nature, for some animals and beasts change into another
species without dying or being corrupted, as happens in other natural
changes. For as the Philosopher says, 'The generation of one thing is
the corruption of another.' But while they are thus still living, they
gradually change into another species of animal until they are as perfectly
formed in this new species as they had been in their former one. This
would seem quite impossible if there were not quite clear experience of
this here, for such animals have been seen here before they began to
change, others half-changed, while others completely changed. But it is
done in such a way that the natives of this land know quite clearly by
certain and evident signs which of that species was born quite naturally
from its seed just like other animals, and which of them have become
members of the species through this change.

Philosophers now seek the cause of all this for they declare that
is impossible, especially for animals, to change from one species into
another without corrupting and dying, because the corruption and
expulsion of the form of one is the generation of another. It seems here
that we are bound to admit that the first form corrupted to make way
for the second without the actual subject corrupting. This is like the

form of the embryo that is animated by the vegetative and sensitive forms, but these give way when the rational soul is infused. It also seems that these animals have a certain disposition and were, so to speak, all ready for the form that was ultimately introduced, although the natural cause that goes with this was not lacking. Nor do these animals finish by chance before they are changed, because all of them are born in the seed of this first species and do not change. Nor is this so only of those that change, for some are born into one species from seed while others are changed into it.

What is certain is that God Our Lord is wonderful in His works of nature and that our weak wit cannot unlock the secrets hidden therein, and this is one of those secrets.

For in these islands there are three sorts of changes from one thing into another.

1. Some land and water animals with feet and paws change into fishes.
2. Other sea things, such as shellfish, change into birds.
3. Animals of one species change into another, and those of another species change into wood or stone . . .

There is a kind of shellfish with two large shells that are very long at the tips and at the bottom, where they are joined because they open narrow. The people call them *torigai* and they breed in the deep mud of the sea. Some of them change into certain seabirds like ducks; the fish within the shell changes into this bird that they call *chidori*. It has beautiful and elegant feathers of various colours. They are also born from eggs of the same seed just like other birds.

Jean de Lacombe de Quercy Lacombe

(c. 1640–?)

A French soldier in Louis XIV's army, and a traveller. Lacombe went to England, to Quebec and along the coast of the Americas as far as Brazil. He travelled via the Cape of Good Hope to Batavia in Java, probably with the Dutch East India Company. He spent three years in Ceylon where he claims to have seen the tombs of Adam and Eve, which he describes in great detail. He went to Medina and Mecca, and was arrested at the twenty-ninth gate in Peking, while attempting to catch sight of the Imperial Throne.

The Bird of Paradise

From Nambonne we took again our way, toward the kingdom of Banda which is composed of several islands. The first that we came to was that of Poupou, which is very singular in one thing, and that is a certain sort of birds, surnamed *of Paradise*, and very properly, inasmuch as they are a marvel of Nature. They are as thickly plumaged in their bodies as a Turtle-dove, and are fleshed like one of the tiniest of birds, and a full arm of half an ell long, ordinarily: that is to say, with their tail, which is of great extent and well feathered & is so hardly distinguishable from their body and wings (which are of the same plumage) that the whole bird resembles nothing but a tail: for where its body is is no enlargement and from head to tail it is all of one size, and even when it spreads what it has of wings, they may not be distinguished from the rest. Their beaks are black and turned downward from above, and they have neither legs nor thighs, of which Nature has deprived them as a thing superfluous, by reason that they never alight nor perch like other birds; but are always in a perpetual flight. Their nourishment is quite different from that of other birds, and is not of what the earth produces, for, staying always by their flight in the middle regions of the air, they gather the delicious vapours before they change into the manna that falls each morning in this island: and this is the only thing on which they subsist . . .

These birds are no more immortal than anything else in the world, and when death robs them of life and, in consequence, of movement, the weight of their bodies pulls at them and they fall to the earth. And for this reason no one has ever seen any living ones: for they hover up to the last moment of their powers, or, if they lose them entirely before succumbing, their region is so high that they expire before arriving at the end of their descent. They never die while they are fat: for all that are found, when they have but just fallen, are as dry as if they had been broiled and deprived of all their juices. They fall in this island or in the seas about it, and are collected and transported all over the East, where they are used for parade and pomp by the princes and seigneurs, who wear them in their turbans and caps, as we do a feather in our hats in Europe ... But that which crowns with wonder this marvel of Nature is their incorruptibility in any way, and thus their feathers remain always the same without falling of themselves. There is also no small question to ask oneself, as to why fall only in this island, and in no other place: not even in any other island of this Kingdom. And if one wishes to answer this simply, it is because of its singular nature, which may be recognized chiefly in that manna which falls there each morning, which is not ordinary elsewhere.

Englebert Kaempfer

(1651–1716)

German physician. After working in Persia, Indonesia, and Thailand, Kaempfer joined the Dutch East India Company and was in Nagasaki from 1690–2. The Company paid an annual visit to the *shogun* at Edo (Tokyo); this was the only opportunity for foreigners to see the interior of Japan. Kaempfer was also able to go beyond the Dutch compound at Deshima in Nagasaki harbour, in his capacity as a doctor. He collected a great deal of unique information on Japan and made detailed notes and drawings, edited for publication after his death.

An audience with the Emperor

The Ambassador was ask'd concerning his children, how many he had, what their names were, and also how far distant Holland was from Nagasaki. In the mean while some shutters were open'd on the left hand, by order of the Emperor, probably to cool the room. We were then further commanded to put on our hats, to walk about the room discoursing with one another, to take off our perukes. I had several opportunities of seeing the Empress, and heard the Emperor say in Japanese, how sharp we look'd at the room, where he was and that sure we could not but know, or at least suspect him to be there, upon which he remov'd and went to the ladies, which sate just before us. Then I was desired once more to come nearer the skreen, and to take off my peruke. Then they made us jump, dance, play gambols and walk together, and upon that they ask'd the ambassador and me how old we guess'd Bingo to be, he answer'd 50, and I 45 which made them laugh. Then they made us kiss one another, like man and wife, which the ladies particularly shew'd by their laughter to be well pleas'd with. They desir'd us further to shew them what sorts of compliments it was customary in Europe to make to inferiors, to ladies, to superiors, to princes, to kings. After this they begg'd another song of me, and were satisfy'd with two, which the company seem'd to like very well. After this farce was over, we were order'd to take off our cloaks, to come near the skreen one by one, and to take our leave in the very same manner we would take it of a Prince, or King in Europe, which being done, seemingly to their satisfaction, we went away. It was already four in the afternoon, when we left the hall of audience, after having been exercis'd after this manner for two hours and a half . . .

William Dampier

(1652–1715)

English navigator and buccaneer. Dampier was orphaned as a child and apprenticed to a ship's master at Weymouth. He fought in the Dutch War with the Royal Navy, became under-manager of an estate in Jamaica, sailed in the West India trade and the timber trade to Yucatan. He joined pirates off the American coasts and accompanied Captain Cook on his last voyage to the south Seas. After Cook died, Dampier and other members of the crew deserted on the Nicobar Islands. Dampier later achieved some respectability, being sent by the Admiralty to lead two expeditions to the South Seas and Australia, where he was the first Englishman to explore the coast. He proved less of a commander than an adventurer, but is an observant and most engaging writer.

The Chinese

The Chinese in general are tall, straight-bodied, raw-boned men. They are long-visaged, and their foreheads are high; but they have little eyes. Their noses are pretty large, with a rising in the middle. Their mouths are of a mean size, pretty thin lips. They are of an ashy complexion; their hair is black, and their beards thin and long, for they pluck the hair out by the roots, suffering only some few very long straggling hairs to grow about their chin, in which they take great pride, often combing them, and sometimes tying them up in a knot, and they have such hairs too growing down from each side of their upper lip like whiskers. The ancient Chinese were very proud of the hair of their heads, letting it grow very long, and stroking it back with their hands curiously, and then winding the plaits all together round a bodkin, thrust through it at the hinderpart of the head; and both men and women did thus. But when the Tatars conquered them, they broke them of this custom they were so fond of by main force; insomuch that they resented this imposition worse than their subjection, and rebelled upon it; but being still worsted, were forced to acquiesce; and to this day they follow the fashion of their masters the Tatars, and shave all their heads, only reserving one lock, which some tie up, others let it hang down to a great or small length as they please. The Chinese in other countries still keep their old custom, but if any of the Chinese is found wearing long hair in China, he forfeits his head; and many of them have abandoned their country to preserve their liberty of wearing their hair, as I have been told by themselves.

The Chinese have no hats, caps, or turbans; but when they walk abroad, they carry a small umbrella in their hands, wherewith they fence their head from the sun or the rain, by holding it over their heads. If they walk but a little way, they carry only a large fan made of paper, or silk, of the same fashion as those our ladies have, and many of them are brought over hither; one of these every man carries in his hand if he do but cross the street, screening his head with it, if he has not an umbrella with him.

The common apparel of the men is a loose frock and breeches. They seldom wear stockings, but they have shoes, or a sort of slipper rather. The men's shoes are made diversly. The women have very small feet, and consequently but little shoes; for from their infancy their feet are kept swathed up with bands, as hard as they can possibly endure them; and from the time they can go till they have done growing they bind them up every night. This they do purposely to hinder them from growing, esteeming little feet to be a great beauty. But by this unreasonable custom they do in a manner lose the use of their feet, and instead of going they only stumble about their houses, and presently squat down on their breeches again, being as it were confined to sitting all days of their lives. They seldom stir abroad, and one would be apt to think, that as some have conjectured, their keeping up their fondness for this fashion were a stratagem of the men's, to keep them from gadding and gossiping about, and confine them at home.

Evariste Regis Huc

(1813–60)

French Catholic missionary. Disguised as Tibetan lamas, he and a colleague, Father Gabet, set off from their Lazarist mission in China to convert Tibet. After an extraordinary and hazardous two-year journey, they reached Lhasa but two months later were expelled on the initiative of a Chinese resident. He eventually returned to France, his health broken by his ordeals.

Chinese tea porters

Notwithstanding the difficulties and dangers of the road across this mountain, it is much frequented by travellers, for there is no other way to Ta-tsien-lou, a great place of trade between China and the tribes of Thibet. You meet every moment on these narrow paths long files of porters carrying brick tea, which is prepared at Khioung-Tcheou, and forwarded from Ta-tsien-lou to the different provinces of Thibet. This tea, after having been subjected to strong pressure, is made up into bales in coarse matting, and fastened by leathern thongs to the backs of Chinese porters, who carry enormous loads of it. You even see among them old men, women, and children, who go climbing, one after another, up the steep sides of the mountain. They advance in silence, with slow steps, leaning on great iron-pointed sticks, and with their eyes fixed on the ground; and beasts of burden would certainly not endure so well, the constant and excessive fatigue to which these slaves of poverty are subjected. From time to time, he who is at the head of the file gives the signal for a short halt, by striking the mountain with his iron-pointed stick; those who follow him imitate this signal in succession, and soon the whole line has stopped, and each individual placing his stick behind him, so as to relieve himself a little of the weight, lifts up his head, and utters a long whistling sound like a sign of pain. In this way they endeavour to recover their strength, and get a little air into their exhausted lungs; but after a minute or two's rest, the heavy weight again falls on the back and head, the body is again bent towards the ground, and the caravan is once more in motion.

Alfred Russel Wallace

(1823–1913)

British naturalist. In 1848 he went to Brazil, where he spent four years exploring and collecting in the Amazon basin, initially with the naturalist Henry Walter Bates (**q.v.**). They then travelled separately in order to save time. On the return journey to England, Wallace's ship caught fire and the huge collections and notes were lost, but he was able to publish the *Narrative* of his expedition. He then spent eight years in the Malay Archipelago, where, suffering from malaria, he wrote a letter in a single night on the theory of natural selection that provoked Darwin (**q.v.**) to complete and publish his *Origin of Species*. Besides Wallace's scientific contribution to the theory of evolution, and aside from his curious obsession with killing and stuffing animals, his books are marvellous accounts of the flora and fauna of the primordial environments in which he lived. He was saved from ultimate destitution by a Crown pension arranged by Darwin and his friends.

Chasing butterflies in the Malay archipelago

During my very first walk into the forest at Batchian, I had seen sitting on a leaf out of reach, an immense butterfly of a dark colour marked with white and yellow spots. I could not capture it as it flew away high up into the forest, but I at once saw that it was a female of a new species of *Ornithoptera* or "bird-winged butterfly", the pride of the Eastern tropics. I was very anxious to get it and to find the male, which in this genus is always of extreme beauty. During the two succeeding months I only saw it once again, and shortly afterwards I saw the male flying high in the air at the mining village. I had begun to despair of ever getting a specimen, as it seemed so rare and wild; till one day, about the beginning of January, I found a beautiful shrub with large white leafy bracts and yellow flowers, a species of Mussænda, and saw one of these noble insects hovering over it, but it was too quick for me, and flew away. The next day I went again to the same shrub and succeeded in catching a female, and the day after a fine male. I found it to be as I had expected, a perfectly new and most magnificent species, and one of the most gorgeously coloured butterflies in the world. Fine specimens of the male are more than seven inches across the wings, which are velvety black and fiery orange, the latter colour replacing the green of the allied species. The beauty and brilliancy of this insect are indescribable, and none but a naturalist can understand the intense excitement I experienced when I at length captured it. On taking it out of my net and opening the glorious wings, my heart began to beat violently, the blood rushed to my head, and I felt much more like fainting than I have done when in apprehension of immediate death. I had a headache the rest of the day, so great was the excitement produced by what will appear to most people a very inadequate cause.

Isabella Bird

(1831–1904)

English traveller and writer. Despite a lifelong spinal complaint and the fact that she did not start travelling until she was in her forties, there are few parts of the world that Isabella Bird (Mrs Isabella Bishop) did not visit, and visit in earnest, often living in the most primitive conditions. She wrote three books about the United States, including one about her travels in the Rocky Mountains, one about the Sandwich Islands, which she visited on a journey to Australia and Hawaii, one on Japan, and another on Malaya. After the death of her husband in 1886, Bird travelled in the Himalayas, Persia, Kurdistan, Korea and then eight thousand miles in the interior of China, writing books about each of them. As well as all this she founded five hospitals in Asia, and rode one thousand miles across Morocco at the age of sixty-nine, on a black stallion given to her by the Sultan.

Dinner parties with apes in Malaya

I was received by a magnificent Oriental butler, and after I had had a delicious bath, dinner, or what Assam was pleased to call breakfast, was "served". The word "served" was strictly applicable, for linen, china, crystal, flowers, cooking, were all alike exquisite. Assam, the Madrassee, is handsomer and statelier than Babu at Malacca; a smart Malay lad helps him, and a Chinaman sits on the steps and pulls the punkah. All things were harmonious, the glorious coco-palms, the bright green slopes, the sunset gold on the lake-like river, the ranges of forest-covered mountains etherealising in the purple light, the swarthy faces and scarlet uniforms of the Sikh guard, and rich and luscious odours, floated in on balmy airs, glories of the burning tropics, untellable and incommunicable!

My valise had not arrived, and I had been obliged to re-dress myself in my mud-splashed tweed dress, therefore I was much annoyed to find the table set for three, and I hung about unwillingly in the verandah, fully expecting two Government clerks in faultless evening dress to appear, and I was vexed to think that my dream of solitude was not to be realised, when Assam more emphatically assured me that the meal was "served", and I sat down, much mystified, at the well-appointed table, when he led in a large ape, and the Malay servant brought in a small one, and a Sikh brought in a large retriever and tied him to my chair! This was all done with the most profound solemnity. The circle being then complete, dinner proceeded with great stateliness. The apes had their curry, chutney, pine-apple, eggs, and bananas on porcelain plates, and so had I. The chief difference was that, whereas I waited to be helped, the big ape was impolite enough occasionally to snatch something from a dish as the butler passed round the table, and that the small one before very long migrated from his chair to the table and, sitting by my plate, helped himself daintily from it. What a grotesque dinner party! What a delightful one! My "next of kin" were so reasonably silent; they required no conversational efforts; they were most interesting companions. "Silence is golden," I felt; shall I ever enjoy a dinner party so much again?

Sodden in Ikarigaseki, Japan

We entered Ikarigaseki from the last bridge, a village of 800 people, on a narrow ledge between an abrupt hill and the Hirakawa, a most forlorn and tumble-down place, given up to felling timber and making shingles; and timber in all its forms – logs, planks, faggots, and shingles – is heaped and stalked about. It looks more like a lumberer's encampment than a permanent village, but it is beautifully situated, and unlike any of the innumerable villages that I have ever seen.

The street is long and narrow, with streams in stone channels on either side; but these had overflowed, and men, women, and children were constructing square dams to keep the water, which had already reached the *doma*, from rising over the *tatami*. Hardly any house has paper windows, and in the few which have, they are so black with smoke as to look worse than none. The roofs are nearly flat, and are covered with shingles held on by laths weighted with large stones. Nearly all the houses look like temporary sheds, and more are as black inside as a Barra hut. The walls of many are nothing but rough boards tied to the uprights by straw ropes.

In the drowning torrent, sitting in puddles of water, and drenched to the skin hours before, we reached this very primitive *yadoya*, the lower part of which is occupied by the *daidokoro*, a party of storm-bound students, horses, fowls, and dogs. My room is a wretched loft, reached by a ladder, with such a quagmire at its foot that I have to descend into it in Wellington boots. It was dismally grotesque at first. The torrent on the unceiled roof prevented Ito from hearing what I said, the bed was soaked, and the water, having got into my box, had dissolved the remains of the condensed milk, and had reduced clothes, books, and paper into a condition of universal stickiness. My *kimono* was less wet than anything else, and, borrowing a sheet of oiled paper, I lay down in it, till roused up in half an hour by Ito shrieking above the din on the roof that the people thought that the bridge by which we had just entered would give way; and, running to the river bank, we joined a large crowd, far too intensely occupied by the coming disaster to take any notice of the first foreign lady they had ever seen.

Lord Redesdale

(1837–1916)

A.B. Freeman-Mitford, British author and diplomat; attaché in Peking and Japan. On inheriting his cousin's title in 1886, he went to live at Batsford Park in Gloucestershire where he created an exotic arboretum. He became an authority on bamboos and contributed to the design of Hyde Park, St James's Park and the gardens of Buckingham Palace in London.

Boatwomen of Hong Kong

These Chinese boatwomen are real wonders. Hardy, strong, and burnt by the sun, they look and probably are as sturdy as any of the men. At any rate I saw one woman fight and thrash a couple of stalwart young boatmen; and a good stand-up fight it was, give and take. They did not spare her, and she belaboured them most lustily, screaming and chattering all the while in a way that would have frightened Billingsgate itself into silence. The boats seem to hold whole families, even the nursery, the small boys wearing corks or bottles to keep them afloat when they tumble overboard. The girls, being reckoned of no value, take their chance, and wear nothing to protect them. As soon as we came to an anchor the boats of the great commercial firms came alongside, each probably steered by a partner eager to hear the latest news or to welcome a friend. One by one the passengers disappear, and he who has letters for one of the merchant princes of China may look forward to luxurious quarters and a warm welcome, for nowhere else is hospitality carried to such an extent as it is here.

Nikolai Mikailovich Prejevalsky

(1839–88)

Russian soldier and explorer. After travelling in the Far East, Prejevalsky (also Przhevalsky) was sent by the Imperial Geographical Society of St Petersburg to explore southern Mongolia. The small expedition took three years and covered seven thousand miles; it took them to China, Tibet and across the Gobi desert. In all, Prejevalsky travelled some twenty thousand miles in Central Asia, systematically collecting specimens. One of his most remarkable discoveries was 'Prejevalsky's Horse', possibly the last truly wild horse, which has recently been reintroduced into its native habitat.

At Bautu

About midday the Mandarin sent a messenger to ask us to go and see him again. We accordingly started for his house, taking the watch with us. While awaiting our interview, we were shown into the soldiers' barracks, where we remained half-an-hour, and had an opportunity of inspecting the domestic arrangements of the Chinese soldiers. Five thousand military are quartered at Bautu, most of whom are from the south of China, the so-called 'Khotens,' besides Manchus and a few Solones. All these men are armed with matchlocks, a few European muskets, swords, and long bamboo spears, with great red flags attached to the end of the shafts.

The demoralised and degraded state of the soldiery defies all description. They are the terror of the peaceable inhabitants, and are almost all opium smokers. Lighted lamps are kept constantly burning in all the barracks, the smokers sit round in a circle, while others who have finished their pipes lie about the floor buried in lethargic sleep. The general, unable to cure his men of this vile practice, entreated us on the occasion of our first interview, to tell him if there were not some antidote for opium, and offered a handsome reward if such could be found.

Rudyard Kipling

(1865–1936)

English writer, poet and traveller. Born in Bombay, his father was artist and teacher John Lockwood Kipling. After education in England, described in his novel *Stalky and Co.*, Kipling became a journalist in India, and then a celebrated writer, author of the two *Jungle Books*, *Just So Stories*, *Kim* and many other books and poems. In the 1880s Kipling visited Japan.

"You must take off your boots"

'You must take off your boots,' said Y-Tokai.

I assure you there is no dignity in sitting down on the steps of a tea-house and struggling with muddy boots. And it is impossible to be polite in your stockinged feet when the floor under you is as smooth as glass and a pretty girl wants to know where you would like tiffin. Take at least one pair of beautiful socks with you when you come this way. Get them made of embroidered *sambhur* skin, of silk if you like, but do not stand as I did in cheap striped brown things with a darn at the heel, and try to talk to a tea-girl.

Luigi Barzini

(1874–1947)

Italian writer, journalist, and editor of the *Corriere Della Sera*. He reported on an expedition to China against the Boxers in 1900, the beginning of the Russo-Japanese War in 1904 and the 1906 San Francisco earthquake. He wrote a classic account of Prince Borghese's Great Horseless Race, a journey by car from Peking to Paris in 1907. They achieved then unheard-of speed of 60 m.p.h. across the Gobi desert.

City of men

The people of Maimachen were greatly impressed by our arrival. They had seen us come down the sandy hills, and now they ran out upon the roads to meet us. There soon stood before us a crowd of Chinese people with their blue garments and their waving fans. There was not a single woman among them. For this is a peculiarity of Maimachen – the strangest you can think of in a city of thousands of inhabitants: there are no women. I do not know whether this is due to any clause in the treaties with Russia – for Russia fears the numbers of the yellow population on the whole line of its Oriental frontier – or whether it is due to a resolution of the Chinese themselves, who have a great repugnance against settling far from their country, afraid, as they are, through traditional religious beliefs, of having to suffer after death a most grievous exile of the soul. Be that as it may, the fact remains that Maimachen is a city entirely composed of men. Exactly the opposite extreme is met in a village at three li from Maimachen, which is inhabited by women only.

A Chinese youth made a sign to us to stop, and addressed us in English. He begged the honour of giving us hospitality, even if only for a few minutes, as all his colleagues had done from Kalgan to Urga. He was the director of the telegraph office.

"I have sent word of your arrival to the Chief of the Police of Kiakhta," he said to us, welcoming us into his own private house, "and in the meantime, you can rest awhile, wash, take some refreshment . . ."

We had been reduced by our journey to an almost indescribable condition. Our faces were literally black with dust, and over our clothes was a thick crust of all the different kinds of mud with which we had come into intimate contact along our way – the black mud of the bogs, the yellow mud of the Chara-gol, the white mud of the Iro. We were given hot water, cold water, soap, combs, towels, brushes; and then cigarettes, wine, milk, biscuits, and jam. We used or tasted everything, and were transformed within and without. Then we went off, grateful and comforted, to the Chief of the Police, who, we were told, was waiting to see us.

A moment later we were out of the Celestial Empire.

Near the frontier-marking pillar, on the green, stood at attention the first *gorodovoi* we met, in his white tunic, wearing the flat uniform-cap, his sword slung across his shoulder, his breast adored with red braiding. He raised his hand, commanding:

"*Stoi!* (Stop!)."

He gave us a stiff military salute, at the same time clapping his heels together. Then he got on to the car. Standing upon the step he pointed in the direction we were to follow, and commanded, "Forward, to the right."

The car moved, as obediently as a recruit.

We were entering the Russian Empire.

John Foster Fraser

(fl. 1896–99)

Fraser was an Englishman who with two companions, rode 19,237 miles around the world on bicycles. *Round the World on a Wheel*, is an inimitable and very good read.

More rain in Japan

We had rain in the afternoon, and pulled up for shelter at a tiny town. The little streets ran torrents. We left our bicycles at an inn, and, borrowing umbrellas, went out for a walk. They were immense bamboo sort of umbrellas; with three tremendous Chinese inscriptions on each, and as we sauntered down the lane, jumping the puddles, and with those outlandish marquees over our heads, we presented to each other an amusing spectacle. The little *mousmees* came out on their verandahs to see the three foreigners, and they shrieked with laughter. We had to buy sweetmeats for all the girls in the place.

That night we lay at Nagoya, an inoffensive old town with a fourteenth-century citadel. There were soldiers running about in French uniforms, and Maxim guns being dragged down the streets, and bicycles, belonging evidently to the early Iron Age, careering along madly, irrespective of the wishes of their riders. The rage for cycling in London is a bagatelle compared to the rage in Nagoya. We saw hundreds of them, thousands of them. I issued a proclamation that I would race the whole town backwards, but the challenge was unaccepted.

Graham Greene

(1904–91)

English novelist, playwright and critic. Greene's extensive travels are reflected in his novels and his other writings. He was in Africa, Mexico, Haiti, Cuba, South America and Indo-China, as well as places nearer to home: wartime Vienna, Stalinist Poland, Monte Carlo and the seedy resort of *Brighton Rock*, collectively known as Greeneland.

Diary of an opium smoker

My experience of opium began in October 1951 when I was in Haiphong on the way to the Baie d'Along. A French official took me after dinner to a small apartment in a back street – I could smell the opium as I came up the stairs. It was like the first sight of a beautiful woman with whom one realizes that a relationship is possible: somebody whose memory will not be dimmed by a night's sleep.

The madame decided that as I was a *débutant* I must have only four pipes, and so I am grateful to her that my first experience was delightful and not spoiled by the nausea of over-smoking. The *ambiance* won my heart at once – the hard couch, the leather pillow like a brick – these stand for a certain austerity, the athleticism of pleasure, while the small lamp glowing on the face of the pipe-maker, as he kneads his little ball of brown gum over the flame until it bubbles and alters shape like a dream, the dimmed lights, the little chaste cups of unsweetened green tea, these stand for the '*luxe et volupté*'.

Each pipe from the moment the needle plunges the little ball home and the bowl is reversed over the flame lasts no more than a quarter of a minute – the true inhaler can draw a whole pipeful into his lungs in one long inhalation. After two pipes I felt a certain drowsiness, after four my mind felt alert and calm – unhappiness and fear of the future became like something dimly remembered which I had thought important once. I, who feel shy at exhibiting the grossness of my French,

363

found myself reciting a poem of Baudelaire to my companion, that beautiful poem of escape, *Invitation au Voyage*. When I got home that night I experienced for the first time the white night of opium. One lies relaxed and wakeful, not wanting sleep. We dread wakefulness when our thoughts are disturbed, but in this state one is calm – it would be wrong even to say that one is happy – happiness disturbs the pulse. And then suddenly without warning one sleeps. Never has one slept so deeply a whole night-long sleep, and then the waking and the luminous dial of the clock showing that twenty minutes of so-called real time have gone by. Again the calm lying awake, again the deep brief all-night sleep. Once in Saigon after smoking I went to bed at 1.30 and had to rise again at 4.00 to catch a bomber to Hanoi, but in those less-than-three hours I slept all tiredness away.

Vientiane, 1954

Up early to catch a military plane to Vientiane, the administrative capital of Laos. The plane was a freighter with no seats. I sat on a packing case and was glad to arrive.

After lunch I made a rapid tour of Vientiane. Apart from one pagoda and the long sands of the Mekong river, it is an uninteresting town consisting only of two real streets, one European restaurant, a club, the usual grubby market where apart from food there is only the debris of civilization – withered tubes of toothpaste, shop-soiled soaps, pots and pans from the Bon Marché. Fishes were small and expensive and covered with flies. There were little packets of dyed sweets and sickly cakes made out of rice coloured mauve and pink. The fortune-maker of Vientiane was a man with a small site let out as a bicycle park – hundreds of bicycles at 2 piastres a time (say 20 centimes). When he had paid for his concession he was likely to make 600 piastres a day profit (say 6000 francs). But in Eastern countries there are always wheel within wheels, and it was probably that the concessionaire was only the ghost for one of the princes.

Sometimes one wonders why one bothers to travel, to come eight thousand miles to find only Vientiane at the end of the road, and yet there is a curious satisfaction later, when one reads in England the war communiqués and the familiar names start from the page – Nam Dinh,

Vientiane, Luang Prabang – looking so important temporarily on a newspaper page as though part of history, to remember them in terms of mauve rice cakes, the rat crossing the restaurant floor as it did tonight until it was chased away behind the bar. Places in history, one learns, are not so important.

Norman Lewis

(1908–2003)

English writer and traveller who has covered most of the globe, and written many very fine travel books. *A Dragon Apparent* is about Indo-China before its devastation by decades of war. *Naples '44* is considered one of the best books about the Second World War.

Saigon

It was clear from the first moment of picking my way through these crowded, torrid streets that the lives of the people of the Far East are lived in public. In this they are different from people in almost any other part of the world. The street is the extension of the house and there is no sharp dividing line between the two. At dawn, or, in the case of Saigon, at the hour when the curfew is lifted, people roll out of bed and make for the pavement, where there is more space, to perform most of their toilet. Thereafter they eat, play cards, doze, wash themselves, have their teeth seen to, are cupped and massed by physicians, visit fortune-tellers; all in the street. There is none of the desire for privacy that is so strong in Europe and stronger still in the Islamic countries. Even the better houses seemed to consist on the ground floor of one large room in which the family lived communally while visitors drifted in and out through the open doors.

People took small snacks at frequent intervals, seating themselves at wayside booths decorated with painted glass screens that had perhaps been imported from Japan, as the subjects were Japanese: scowling

Samurai and winged tigers. Great store was set by the decorative presentation of food. Diaphanous baby octopuses were suspended before acetylene lamps. There were tasteful groupings of sliced coxcomb about cured pigs' snouts on excellent china plates. Roast chickens and ducks lacquered bright red, were displayed in heraldic attitudes, with gracefully arched necks, or completely flattened-out, like kippers. There were segments of pigs, sundered with geometrical precision which, after the denaturalizing art to which they had been submitted, seemed with their brilliant, glossy surfaces as unreal as the furnishings of a toy butcher's shop. Here the appetites were solicited under frivolous rather than brutal forms.

One wondered about the origin of some of the delicacies; the ducks' heads fried in batter and the webbed feet of some wading bird or other. Were they the fruit of a laborious empirical process, appealing to palates of extraordinary refinement, since in either case fleshy sustenance was practically non-existent? Or were they, as a Vietnamese suggested, along with such traditional Chinese dishes as edible birds' nests and sharks' fins, the last resort of famine-stricken populations who gradually developed a taste for what, in the original emergency, they probably ate with the greatest repugnance?

Angkor Vat

My last daylight hours at Angkor were spent by the lake of Sram Srang. The Khmers were always digging out huge artificial lakes, which, if the preliminary surveying had been correctly carried out, and temples and statues were erected according to accepted precedents round their margins or on a centre island, could always be declared to possess purificatory qualities. For this reason Sram Srang was supposed to have been a favourite royal bathing place, with its grand approach, its majestic flight of steps, flanked with mythical animals, and its golden barges.

Now the lions were faceless, and the nagas had lost most of their heads. The severe rectangularity of old had been softened by subsidences of the banks, which had solidified into little peninsulas on which trees were growing. Buffaloes stood motionless in the virtuous water with only their heads showing. Sometimes even their heads were withdrawn for a few moments below the surface. Giant kingfishers flashed past, linked to their reflections; twin shooting stars in a grey-green firmament. Until forty years ago the Cambodians exported these birds' skins to China where they were made into mandarins' jackets, taking in exchange pottery and silk. And then the vogue for European goods grew up, and the industry languished.

Gavin Young

(1928–2001)

English writer and traveller. Young has lived with and written about the Marsh Arabs of southern Iraq and south-western Arabia. He has sailed from Greece to China and back again.

Shanghai

Shanghai! Past the dim outlines of islands to seaward, we turned up the Huangpu. Rows of ships moored on either side, chimneys, gantries, derricks, smoke mingling with a light drizzle: the smoke and soot of industrial China.

The first sight of the Shanghai Bund – the former European business section on the riverfront – thrilled me as I was thrilled by Paris and New York years ago. 'The living heart of China,' Malraux called it, and the waterfront I gazed at now was something I had seen in my dreams and imagination for a very long time. Imagination had not lied. I had taken a step into the past. With its old-fashioned skyscrapers, its neo-Babylonian towers and pinnacles, the Shanghai exposed by the river was exactly the metropolis I had expected; a city of the 1920s, architecturally paralysed by circumstance. To approach it by sea was as unreal as approaching it in my dream. I thought: I have been here before. Thomas Dor stood by me, saying, 'British people coming back here after many years say, "Oh, everything is the same. Nothing's changed. No new buildings." A city with no change for thirty years, that's very rare in the world today.' A petrified city like this was not merely rare, but unique. Here, two eras impinged – Yesterday and Today swirled together as the muddy waters of the Yangtze and Huangpu commingled at the entrance to the East China Sea . . .

The piped musak was interrupted by a girl's voice telling us that the captain and crew wished us a happy stay in Shanghai. We glided alongside a quay, close to a long warehouse. Sailors threw ropes to each other. The gangway went down.

'I'll come and see you at the Peace Hotel,' said Thomas Dor. 'Some time this afternoon. Say, 12.30 or 1 p.m. You're sure to be in that hotel. If not, I shall find you in another. There aren't too many.'

'I don't want you to waste your holiday time looking for me.' I hoped he would come.

'Oh, I will come.'

A jostling began around the tables in the lounge where immigration and customs men were examining passports and asking about currency. But there was no delay. I was soon free to go. Wei Kuen and Ah Po were in the queue. When I went to say goodbye Wei Kuen said, 'We will come to your hotel. Tomorrow.' Ah Po nodded his head until I thought he would shake loose the kangaroo on his cap.

I said, 'I hope so,' but I doubted that I would see them again; not here. They had given me their Hong Kong addresses, but I was sure they'd be too busy with their families in Shanghai to bother about me. In any case, I suspected that their in-laws, waiting for official sanction to leave China, would advise them against contact with a foreigner. Might they not be pointlessly drawing suspicion on themselves? Or was I now the victim of paranoia?

'We will come,' said Wei Kuen.

We shall see, I thought.

Nicolas Bouvier

(1929–)

Swiss travel writer and photographer who spent more than
thirty years travelling in Japan. His book is a marvellously
detailed account of life in Japan experienced at first-hand.

In an onsen

At Noboribetsu, the largest *onsen* in Japan, I spotted a 'Massages' sign,
and I asked to have one, to try it. It took four phone calls to the
concierge, a half-hour wait ... and in comes an old woman who could
have been a nun, her legs covered with black veins. She has a handsome
face, worn and luminous, like the face of a blind person. But she can
see, and she leads me up the dizzying stairs to a closet that is her room.
There is a cast-iron stove, a mattress covered with a clean sheet, a
reproduction of a Dufy, and an old man she's just finished, who is lying
there sighing, a towel knotted around his head. I take off my clothes;
she has me lie down on my side and starts with my neck. She closes
her eyes while she works so that her fingers, which are hard as boxwood,
can communicate clearly. From time to time, her hands fall on a knot,
on a pain I didn't know I had, in a part of my body that is not very
lived in. So she searches it out, roughs it up, dislodges it, and it is as
painful as a visit to the dentist. She works down to my toes, then she
attacks the other side. I look at the waxy face behind the closed eyes,
peaceful, working, and ask myself if, forty years ago, she too was one
of the "sweet young things" that people tut-tut about. Maybe, like the
toads in fairy tales, she would turn into a lascivious young princess.
Maybe there is an open sesame, a magic word I could say, but it is not
in my Japanese vocabulary. And besides I would have lost the naturalness
her ugliness gives me, and here that is a much rarer commodity than
sex appeal. When she is finished, my whole body tingles, loosened all
the way to my fingertips. I feel as if I have rediscovered the innumerable
ins and outs of my body, like a hundred-room hotel under my skin.

Colin Thubron

(1939–)

English traveller and writer. Thubron first travelled in Asia and North Africa, then wrote five books about the Middle East, and books about Russia and China, where he spent some months investigating a country in the aftermath of Maoism. 'The opening-up of China had stirred me unbearably. It was like discovering a new room in a house in which you'd lived all your life.'

The Chairman's boudoir

Several miles beyond the station, the old hamlet of Shaoshan spread pretty in its cup of hills. The wealth which it attracted during the Cultural Revolution had left its public buildings clean-faced, its houses tall and white among their trees. Now it had fallen quiet. The village square was so empty that a farmer had spread rice over its tarmac to dry, and somebody had set up a billiard-table under the willows.

I booked in to a near-empty guesthouse. It had been built in 1959, said the desk clerk – to accommodate Mao, his wife, and Liu Shaoqi when they visited the village. Her voice held the hurt pride with which the Shaoshan people speak of their dethroned hero.

Might I see his rooms, I asked?

She took me up a path to a separate building, where two suites had accommodated Mao and his wife. In his big, single bedroom stood a scarred desk and a four-poster bed clouded in mosquito netting. Tenderly the woman pulled back its quilt to show the bare boards beneath. 'He didn't like bedclothes. He slept on that.'

'Do people still use this room?'

'It's given to visitors sometimes,' she said. 'Do you want to take it?'

'Mao Zedong's bed?' My voice sounded thin, alarmed. I was touched by a schizophrenic pang of unworthiness and revulsion. I stared around. Were the mosquitoes which whined about the walls, I wondered, the offspring of those which had bitten the Great Helmsman? Then I said that perhaps, if no important officials were spending the night here, then yes . . .

A minute later I was left alone in His room.

I padded noiselessly across the heavy blue carpet, as if Mao were in residence and I a ghost. When I looked at myself in the wardrobe mirror, I half expected to see Him instead. I felt a tremor of the pilgrim's excitement: He touched this, he sat on that. The room was heady with mana. Had He, I wondered, sat in that great creased armchair pondering the crash of the Great Leap Forward? Did He compose his poem on Shaoshan at the desk where I was scribbling my notes?

I crossed the sitting-room to Jiang Qing's suite. It was almost identical. I returned and peered into Mao's (and my) bathroom. It contained a bidet and the biggest bath I had seen in China – a huge, Mao-shaped oblong set in a white-tiled surround and reached by tiled steps. Above it hung a bar by which the Chairman could haul up his ageing body, and near the tap was a red button for emergencies.

For two days I wandered the Maoist shrines of Shaoshan. The troops of votaries who had thronged here in the 1960s and 70s under their streaming banners in reverent silence had left an echoing void. Several sites were all but abandoned. Here was the duck-pond where the Great Teacher swam, the field which he ploughed, the school where he studied (with an apocryphal picture of Mao astounding his teachers). And at the far end of the village I came to the house where he was born.

It had been built by Mao's father, a tight-fisted peasant who prospered as a grain dealer and money-lender. Nestled beside a valley-mouth where rice-fields surged from the hills, it was at once mellow and mean – a long bungalow of golden brick, its windows barred with wood. Inside, I tramped over stone floors through claustrophobic rooms. They had been pampered and scrubbed into a clinical version of themselves. Yet even in this holy of holies I was almost alone. Only once, a party of young men hurried through as if searching for something else.

But the doors still swung in their wooden pivots, and the outhouses were full of pestles and grinding-stones. In the washroom the carrying-poles and iron-basined furnace were still in place, with stone storage jars in the kitchen and a hook for smoking pig above the clay oven. Photographs of Mao's parents hung beside the narrow bed which had thrust them together at night: the hard-faced man and oppressed-looking woman. They reminded me uncannily of portraits somewhere else, but for a minute I could not recall where or whose. Then I remembered: photographs of Stalin's parents, hanging in his cottage-museum at Gori.

Redmond O'Hanlon

(1947–)

English scholar, naturalist, and author of very funny but erudite books about his intrepid travels. In 1983, he travelled into the heart of Borneo, with the poet James Fenton. O'Hanlon's account of this adventure has become a classic.

Off to Borneo

As a former academic and a natural history book reviewer I was astonished to discover, on being threatened with a two-month exile to the primary jungles of Borneo, just how fast a man can read.

Powerful as your scholarly instincts may be, there is no matching the strength of that irrational desire to find a means of keeping your head upon your shoulders; of retaining your frontal appendage in its accustomed place; of barring 1700 different species of parasitic worm from your bloodstream and Wagler's pit viper from just about anywhere; of removing small, black, wild-boar ticks from your crutch with minimum discomfort (you do it with Sellotape); of declining to wear a globulating necklace of leeches all day long; of sidestepping amoebic and bacillary dysentery, yellow and blackwater and dengue fevers, malaria, cholera, typhoid, rabies, hepatitis, tuberculosis and the crocodile (thumbs in its eyes, if you have time, they say).

North America

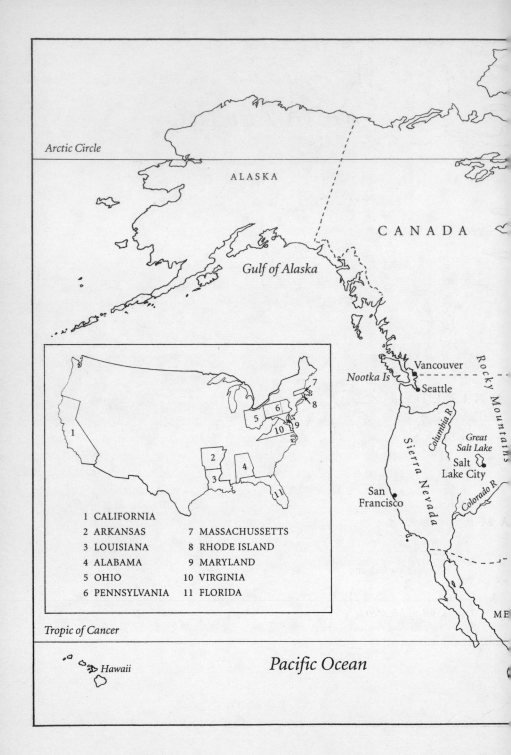

Arctic Circle

ALASKA

CANADA

Gulf of Alaska

Vancouver
Nootka Is
Seattle

Rocky Mountains

1 CALIFORNIA
2 ARKANSAS   7 MASSACHUSSETTS
3 LOUISIANA   8 RHODE ISLAND
4 ALABAMA   9 MARYLAND
5 OHIO   10 VIRGINIA
6 PENNSYLVANIA   11 FLORIDA

Columbia R

Great
Salt Lake

Salt
Lake City

Sierra Nevada

San
Francisco

Colorado R

ME

Tropic of Cancer

Hawaii

Pacific Ocean

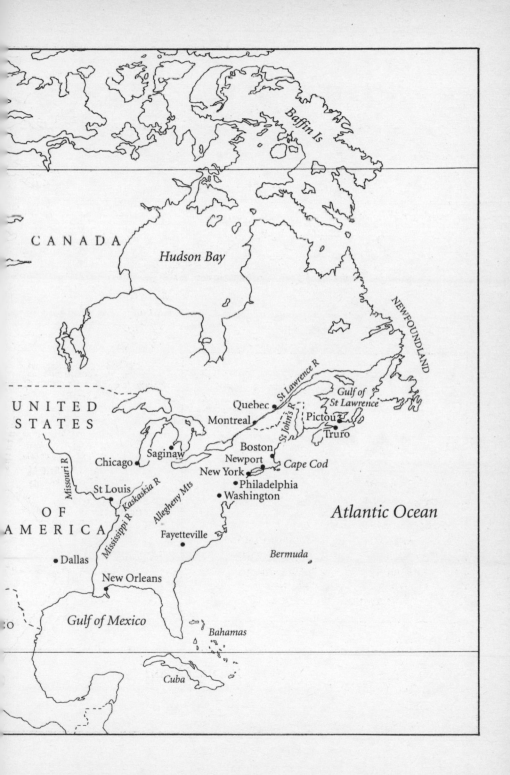

Jacques Cartier

(1491 1557)

French navigator, sent by Francis I of France to find a passage through the northern seas. He sailed to Newfoundland in 1534, discovered the St Lawrence river, and returned to sail upriver piloted by two Huron natives, to villages that became the cities of Quebec and Montreal. The local people believed him to be the son of Heaven and capable of performing miracles. On the return journey, Cartier's ships were frozen into the ice, and both crew and natives suffered from cold and scurvy, which was cured with the juice of an indigenous plant, annedda or *Thuja occidentalis*. Dazzled by tales of gold and precious stones, Cartier kidnapped a Chief and other Indians. His last expedition, intended to settle a motley assortment of French Emigrants, was not a success.

Beluga: a fish as large as a porpoise

The next morning, we made sail and got under way in order to push forward, and discovered a species of fish, which none of us had ever seen or heard of. This fish is as large as a porpoise but has no fin. It is very similar to a greyhound about the body and head and is as white as snow, without a spot upon it. Of these there are a very large number in this river, living between the salt and the fresh water. The people of the country call them *Adhothuys* and told us they are very good to eat. They also informed us that these fish are found nowhere else in all this river and country except at this spot.

As hot as powdered pepper

Furthermore they have a plant, of which a large supply is collected in summer for the winter's consumption. They hold it in high esteem, though the men alone make use of it in the following manner. After drying it in the sun, they carry it about their necks in a small skin pouch in lieu of a bag, together with a hollow bit of stone or wood. Then at frequent intervals they crumble this plant into powder, which they place in one of the openings of the hollow instrument, and laying a live coal on top, suck at the other end to such an extent, that they fill their bodies so full of smoke, that it streams out of their mouths and nostrils as from a chimney. They say it keeps them warm and in good health, and never go about without these things. We made a trial of this smoke. When it is in one's mouth, one would think one had taken powdered pepper, it is so hot.

Pierre Llemoyne d'Iberville

(1661–1706)

French Canadian soldier of fortune who became the first Canadian hero after successfully fighting against British fur and fisheries interests. He was then sent to protect Louis XIV's colony in the Gulf of Mexico. Iberville found a way through to the Mississippi river from the Gulf among innumerable and nameless tributaries blocked with vegetation. He made three expeditions in the area and eventually died of malaria at Havana. His Journals were intended as official reports to the French government.

Guideless on a tributary of the Mississippi

The Mougoulascha, whom I had in my canoe and who got out 3 leagues from here, leading us to believe that he would catch up with us at these forks, failed to make his way here and apparently returned to his village, which cannot be more than 6 to 7 leagues from here in a straight line. There is a well-trodden road leading to within a league of his village. The place where I am is one of the prettiest spots I have seen, fine level ground, beautiful woods, clear and bare of canes; but the whole country becomes inundated to a depth of 5 or 6 feet during high water. We are hearing many turkeys gobble but have been unable to kill any. In these streams are many fish and crocodiles. It would be easy to clear out this stream during low water and make it navigable all the way to the Myssysypy. Those portages have worn us out today, me in particular, as I had to carry the front end of my canoe and guide it for fear of having it split, because Deschyers, one of my Canadians, was sick. Three leagues from here I took the elevation of the sun and found 31°3'.

The 26th. Although I am without a guide, I have gone on nevertheless, even though it is a rather venturesome undertaking with four men; but if I turn back and go by way of the Myssysypy I shall not catch up with my longboats, and I prefer to follow this stream and show the Indians that, without a guide, I go wherever I want to go. In any event, I shall still come out at the ships, even though I have to go overland, abandon my canoes, and make some more wherever I shall find at the seashore tree bark that peels easily at this season.

Conrad Weiser

(1696–?)

A German born American who was 'adopted' as a child into a nearby Mohawk tribe, and became fluent in their language. Weiser became an interpreter and skilled nego-tiator with native American tribes. He kept vivid journals of his travels. These are typical entries.

On the road in the Alleghanies

22d. Crossed Alleghany Hill & came to the Clear Fields, 16 Miles.
23d. Came to the Shawonese Cabbins, 34 Miles.

24th. Found a dead Man on the Road who had killed himself by Drinking too much Whisky; the Place being very stony we cou'd not dig a Grave; He smelling very strong we covered him with Stones & Wood & went on our Journey; came to the 10 Mile Lick, 32 Miles.

25th. Crossed Kiskeminetoes Creek & came to Ohio that Day, 26 Miles.

26th. Hired a Cannoe; paid 1000 Black Wampum for the loan of it to Logs Town. Our Horses being all tyred, we went by Water & came that Night to a Delaware Town; the Indians used us very kindly.

John Bartram

(1699–1777)

American naturalist, with a particular interest in botany. A man of huge energy, curiosity and determination, Bartram travelled extensively in the southwest of North America at a time when it was still an unmapped wilderness, funds were limited and there were dangers of every kind. In 1738 he travelled some eleven hundred miles through Maryland and Virginia; in 1765 he explored the St John's river by canoe. He established the first botanical garden in America, which still exists in Philadelphia, and freed his most valuable male slave as a gesture towards abolition. His son William (**q.v.**) made several journeys with him.

The Great Water Turtles

The great Water Turtle of New England, I take to be our great Mud Turtle [snapping turtle. Ed.] which is much hunted for, to feast our gentry withal; and is reckoned to be as delicious a morsel as those brought from Summer Islands.

. . . They are very large – of a dark muddy color – large round tail, and feet with claws – the old ones mossy on the back, and often several horse leeches sucking the superfluous blood; a large head, sharp nose, and mouth large enough to cram one's fist in – very sharp gums, or lips, which you will, with which they will catch hold of a stick, offered to them – or, if you had rather, your finger – which they will hold so fast that you may lift the turtle by it as high as your head, if you strength or courage enough to lift them up so high by it. But as for their barking, I believe thy relator *barked*, instead of the turtle. They creep all over, in the mud, where they lie *perdu*; and when a duck, or fish, swims near them, they dart out their head as quick as light, and snap him up. Their eggs are round as a bullet, and choice eating.

Jean Bernard Bossu

(*b*. 1720–?)

French naval officer who spent twelve years exploring Louisiana, then a French colony, up the Mississippi and into Alabama. Bossu was fascinated by everything he saw: native life, magic, medicine, fauna and flora. Surviving various sea battles, he narrowly escaped death when a twenty-foot alligator dragged him from his tent one night, and was also saved from drowning in the Mississippi by an Arkansas Indian.

A fingular event

I muft not clofe my letter without informing you of a fingular event, which, though of very little importance, may however be very ufeful to me, during my ftay in *America*. The *Akanzas* have adopted me; they have acknowledged me as a warrior and a chief, and have given me the mark of it, which is the figure of a roe-buck imprinted on my thigh. I have willingly undergone this painful operation, which was performed in the following manner: I was feated on a tyger's fkin; an Indian burnt fome ftraw, the afhes of which he diluted with water: he made ufe of this fimple mixture to draw the roe-buck; he then followed the drawing with great needles, pricking them deep into the flefh, till the blood comes out; this blood mixing with the afhes of the ftraw, forms a figure which can never be effaced. I fmoked the calumet after that; they fpread white fkins under my feet, on which I walked; they danced before me crying out for joy, they told me afterwards, that I could go to all the people who were their allies, prefent the calumet, and fhew my mark, and I would be well received; that I was their brother, and that if any one killed me, they would kill him; now I am a noble *Akanza*.

Captain James Cook

(1728–79)

English explorer and navigator. The son of a farm labourer, Cook taught himself mathematics, astronomy and navigation and joined the Royal Navy. His first voyage was to survey the coasts of Newfoundland and Labrador. Cook subsequently circumnavigated the world three times. The first expedition, in 1768–71, was a journey to observe the transit of Venus across the sun at Tahiti. Besides observing Venus, Cook charted the coast of New Zealand, sailed to eastern Australia, through the Torres Straits to Batavia, returning via the Cape of Good Hope. On his second voyage, Cook mapped the Pacific and disproved the idea of a Southern Continent. He reached Easter Island and was greeted with great celebrations, including fire-works, on his return to Tahiti. His third voyage was intended to find the elusive northerly passage from the Pacific side. Cook corrected previously inaccurate maps of the northwest coast of America, reaching Nootka Sound at 49° 33' and the edge of the continent at the Bering Strait, turning back only when they reached solid ice. Cook was killed by natives in Hawaii, after an unfortunate series of incidents.

The inhabitants of Nootka Sound

Our friends the natives attended us till we were almost out of the Sound, some on board the ships, and others in their canoes. One of the chiefs, who had some time before attached himself to me, was among the last who left us; and, having received from him a handsome beaver-skin cloak which he then wore, in return for some presents, I gave him a new broadsword with a brass hilt, the possession of which made him completely happy.

The common dress of the inhabitants of Nootka is a flaxen garment, or mantle, ornamented on the upper edge by a narrow strip of fur, and at the lower edge by fringes or tassels. It passes under the left arm, and is tied over the right shoulder by a string before and one behind near its middle, by which means both arms are left free; and it hangs evenly, covering the left side, but leaving the right open, unless when the mantle is fastened by a girdle of coarse matting or wool round the waist, which is often done. Over this, which reaches below the knees, is worn a small cloak of the same substance, likewise fringed at the lower part. In shape this resembles a round dish-cover, being quite close, except in the middle, where there is a hole just large enough to admit the head; and then, resting upon the shoulders, it covers the arms to the elbows, and the body as far as the waist. Their head is covered with a cap, of the figure of a truncated cone, or like a flower-pot, made of fine matting, having the top frequently ornamented with a round or pointed knob, or bunch of leathern tassels; and there is a string that passes under the chin, to prevent its blowing off. Besides the above dress, which is common to both sexes, the men frequently throw over their other garments the skin of a bear, wolf, or sea-otter, with the hair outward, and tie it as a cloak near the upper part, wearing it sometimes before and sometimes behind. In rainy weather they throw a coarse mat about their shoulders. They have also woollen garments, which, however, are little in use. The hair is commonly worn hanging down loose; but some, when they have no cap, tie it in a bunch on the crown of the head. Their dress, upon the whole, is convenient, and would not be inelegant were it kept clean. But as they rub their bodies constantly over with a red paint, mixed with oil, their garments by this means contract a rancid, offensive smell and a greasy nastiness, so that they make a very wretched, dirty appearance.

383

The ears of many of them are perforated in the lobe, where they make a pretty large hole, and two others higher up on the outer edge. In these holes they hang bits of bone, quills fixed upon a leathern thong, small shells, bunches of woollen tassels, or pieces of thin copper, which our beads could never supplant. The septum of the nose on many is also perforated, through which they draw a piece of soft cord; and some wear at the same place small thin pieces of iron, brass, or copper, shaped almost like a horse-shoe, the narrow opening of which receives the septum, so that the two points may gently pinch it and the ornament that hangs over the upper lip. The rings of our brass buttons, which they eagerly purchased, were appropriated to this use.

William Bartram

(1739–1823)

American naturalist and traveller. The son of John Bartram, whom Linnaeus described as 'the greatest natural botanist in the world'. The Bartrams explored the St John's river in Florida by canoe in 1765–6, and worked often together. William became a worthy heir to his father, and his writings about previously unseen parts of America reached a wide public. Here he is in arcadian Florida.

Through groves of Zanthoxilon

The enchanting little Isle of Palms. This delightful spot, planted by nature, is almost an entire grove of Palms, with a few pyramidal Magnolias, Live Oaks, golden Orange, and the animating Zanthoxilon; what a beautiful retreat is here! blessed unviolated spot of earth! rising from the limpid waters of the lake; its fragrant groves and blooming lawns invested and protected by encircling ranks of the Yucca gloriosa; a fascinating atmosphere surrounds this blissful garden; the balmy Lantana, ambrosial Citra, perfumed Crinum, perspiring their mingled odours, wafted through Zanthoxilon groves.

What a most beautiful creature is this fish before me! gliding too and fro, and figuring in the still clear waters, with his orient attendants and associates: the yellow bream or sunfish ... the whole fish is of a pale gold (or burnished brass) colour, darker on the back and sides; the scales are of a proportionate size, regularly placed, and everywhere variably powdered with red, russet, silver, blue and green specks, so laid on the scales as to appear like real dust or opaque bodies, each apparent particle being so projected by light and shade, and the various attitudes of the fish, as to deceive the sight; ... the fins are of an Orange colour; and like all the species of the bream, the ultimate angle of the branchios-tega terminate by a little spatula, the extreme end of which represents a crescent of the finest ultramarine blue, encircled with silver, and velvet black, like the eye in the feathers of a peacock's train.

André Michaux

(1746–1802)

French botanist and agriculturalist. Michaux spent eleven years travelling in North America and the Bahamas with his son, making investigations on forest trees for the French government. In 1796 he returned to France as he had not been paid; then went on an expedition to New Holland and died of fever in Madagascar.

An Illinois traveller's diary

Sunday first of November I was obliged to defer my departure, my Horse not having been found.

Friday the 6th my Horse was brought back to the Fort and I at once made ready to start for the Illinois. Started the same day and journeyed about 18 Miles.

The 7th the Rain began early in the morning and continued all day. Remained camped under a Rock where I had stopped the previous day with my Guide.

Sunday the 8th traveled through woods and Hills.

The 9th, the same.

The 10th arrived toward evening at the Prairies.

The 11th crossed the Prairies.

The 12th toward evening Re-entered the Woods once more and slept 7 Miles from Kaskaskia river.

The 13th arrived before breakfast at Kaskaskia about 130 Miles from Fort Massac.

The 13th of November I rested.

Sunday the 14th went out to hunt Canada Geese.

The 15th put my Collections of seeds in order.

The 16th same occupation.

The 17th I went Hunting.

Thursday 18th started for Prairie du Rocher.

The 19th Duck Hunting.

The 20th Goose Hunting.

Sunday 22nd paid visits.

The 23rd, 24th, 25th, 26th, 27th and 28th visited the Mountains of Rock bordering on the inhabited Country; Opossums, Raccoons, aquatic Birds etc.

Sunday 29th of November went to the Village of St Philippe called the Little Village.

The 30th visited Fort de Chartres.

Tuesday the 1st of December started for Kaskaskias and remained there.

The 2nd and 3rd of the same Made arrangements with Richard to go by water to Cumberland.

The 4th returned to Prairie du Rocher.

The 5th prepared to start. Stuffed a white-headed wild Goose.

The 6th started once more for Kaskaskias.

Thaddeus Mason Harris

(1768–1842)

American scholar and pastor. Harris's career was determined by his health; he had to give up an appointment as private secretary to President Washington because he caught smallpox. He later contracted yellow fever, and travelled in the Alleghenies to convalesce.

An infallible specific

The *Seneca Indian Oil* in so much repute here is *Petroleum*; a liquid bitumen, which oozes through fissures or the rocks and coal in the mountains, and is found floating on the surface of the waters of several springs in this part of the country, whence it is skimmed off, and kept for use. From a strong vapour which arises from it when first collected, it appears to combine with it sulphureous particles. It is very inflammable. In these parts it is used as a medicine; and, probably, in external applications with considerable success. For chilblains and rheumatism it is considered as an infallible specific. I suppose it to be the bitumen which Pliny describes under the name of Naptha, Lib. II. ch. 105.

Frances Trollope

(1780–1863)

English writer, and mother of the writer Thomas, and of his more famous brother, Anthony Trollope. Her husband's career was not a success, and she attempted to set up an English goods store in Cincinnati, but business was not her forte. Frances took up writing, particularly travel books and after her husband's death, settled in Florence. Volume appeared to be a family characteristic; she wrote 115 books.

In the forests of New Orleans

By far the most agreeable hours I passed at New Orleans were those in which I explored with my children the forest near the town. It was our first walk in "the eternal forests of the western world", and we felt rather sublime and poetical. The trees, generally speaking, are much too close to be either large or well grown; and, moreover, their growth is often stunted by a parasitical plant, for which I could learn no other name than "Spanish moss"; it hangs gracefully from the boughs, converting the outline of all the trees it hangs upon into that of weeping willows. The chief beauty of the forest in this region is from the luxuriant under-growth of palmetos, which is decidedly the loveliest coloured and most graceful plant I know. The pawpaw, too, is a splendid shrub, and in great abundance. We here, for the first time, saw the wild vine, which we afterwards found growing so profusely in every part of America, as naturally to suggest the idea that the natives ought to add wine to the numerous productions of their plenty-teeming soil. The strong pendant festoons made safe and commodious swings, which some of our party enjoyed, despite the sublime temperament above-mentioned.

John James Audubon

(1785–1851)

Born in Santo Domingo, the illegitimate son of a Creole woman and French sailor who took him back to France. There he studied painting under the artist David. Returning to America, he married and tried, unsuccessfully, to become a merchant. He painted portraits while making illustrations of birds as he travelled in America, charming society with his somewhat wild appearance. After successful exhibitions in Britain, he published *Birds of America* at vast expense in 1827–8; it consisted of 87 portfolios with 1065 coloured, life-sized depictions of birds. A more manageable edition in seven volumes was successfully published. This was followed by a work on quadrupeds, completed by his sons.

Hidden crevasses of the Mississippi

Following the river in your canoe, you reach those parts of the shores that are protected against the overflowing of the waters, and are called *Levees*. There you find the whole population of the district at work repairing and augmenting those artificial barriers, which are several feet above the level of the fields. Every person appears to dread the opening of a *crevasse*, by which the waters may rush into his fields. In spite of all exertions, however, the crevasse opens, the water bursts impetuously over the plantations, and lays waste the crops which so lately were blooming in all the luxuriance of spring. It opens up a new channel, which, for aught I know to the contrary, may carry its waters even to the Mexican Gulf.

I have floated on the Mississippi and Ohio when thus swollen, and have in different places visited the submersed lands of the interior, propelling a light canoe by the aid of a paddle. In this manner I have traversed immense portions of the country overflowed by the waters of these rivers, and, particularly whilst floating over the Mississippi bottomlands, I have been struck with awe at the sight. Little or no current is met with, unless when the canoe passes over the bed of a bayou. All is silent and melancholy, unless when the mournful bleating of the hemmed in deer reaches your ear, or the dismal scream of an eagle or a raven is heard, as the foul bird rises, disturbed by your approach, from the carcass on which it was allaying its craving appetite. Bears, cougars, lynxes, and all other quadrupeds that can ascend the trees, are observed crouched among their top branches.

Charles Lyell

(1797–1875)

Distinguished English geologist, who trained as a lawyer, but gave up the profession on account of weak eyesight. Lyell took to long-distance walking in Britain and Europe, and first-hand observation was the basis of his work as the founder of modern geology. His *Principles of Modern Geology* had run to twelve editions by 1875, and has been reprinted in the late twentieth century. He visited the United States twice on geological tours.

A great bore on the Shubenacadie

After leaving Pictou, I made an expedition with Mr Dawson to the Shubenacadie and at Truro we were joined by Mr Duncan, by whose advice we started at an early hour each morning in a boat, after the great tidal wave or bore had swept up the estuary, and were then carried ten, fifteen, or twenty miles with great rapidity up the river, after which as the tide ebbed, we came down at our leisure, landing quietly wherever we pleased, at various points where the perpendicular cliffs offered sections on the right or left bank.

On one occasion, when I was seated on the trunk of a fallen tree, on a steep sloping beach about ten feet above the level of the river, I was warned by my companion that, before I had finished my sketch, the tide might float off me and the tree, and carry both down to the Basin of Mines. Being incredulous, I looked at my watch, and observed that the water remained nearly stationary for the first three minutes, and then, in the next ten, rose about three feet, after which it gained very steadily but more slowly, till I was obliged to decamp. A stranger, when he is looking for shells on the beach at low tide, after the hot sun has nearly dried up the sandy mud, may well be surprised if told that in six hours there will be a perpendicular column of salt water sixty feet high over the spot on which he stands.

Nathaniel Hawthorne

(1804–64)

American writer. In Concord, Massachussetts, Hawthorne was a neighbour of Emerson and Thoreau, and he was later a friend and supporter of Herman Melville. His book, *The Scarlet Letter* was the first major American novel, but he had to work for the Customs Department in times of financial difficulty.

A country dentist

Scenes and characters – A young country fellow, twenty or thereabouts, decently dressed, pained with the toothache. A country doctor – passing on horseback, with his black leather saddle-bags behind him, a thin, frosty-haired man. Being asked to operate, he looks at the tooth, lances the gum; and the fellow being content to be operated upon on the spot, he seats himself in a chair on the stoop, with great heroism. The doctor produces a rusty pair of iron forceps; a man holds the patient's head; the doctor perceives, that it being a difficult tooth, wedged between the two largest in the head, he shall pull very moderate; and the forceps are introduced. A turn of the doctor's hand; the patient begins to utter a cry; but the tooth comes out first, all bloody, with four prongs. The patient gets up, half amazed, spits out a mouthfull of blood, pays the doctor ninepence, pockets the tooth; and the spectators are in glee and admiration.

A little Irish hamlet in the woods

In a small and secluded dell, that opens upon the most beautiful cove of the whole lake, there is a little hamlet of huts or shanties, inhabited by the Irish people who are at work upon the rail-road. There are three or four of these habitations, the very rudest, I should imagine, that civilized men ever made for themselves, constructed of rough boards, with protruding ends. Against some of them the earth is heaped up to the roof, or nearly so; and when the grass has had time to sprout upon them, they will look like small natural hillocks, or a species of ant-hill, or something in which nature has a larger share than man. These huts are placed beneath the trees, (oaks, walnuts, and white pines) wherever the trunks give them space to stand; and by thus adapting themselves to natural interstices instead of making new ones, they do not break or disturb the solitude and seclusion of the place. Voices are heard, and the shouts and laughter of children, who play about like the sunbeams that come down through the branches. Women are washing beneath the trees, and long lines of whitened clothes are extended from tree to tree, fluttering and gambolling in the breeze. A pig, in a style even more extemporary than the shanties, is grunting, and poking his snout through the clefts of his habitation. The household pots and kettles are seen at the doors, and a glance within shows the rough benches that serve for chairs, and the bed upon the floor. The visiter's nose takes note of the fragrance of a pipe. And yet, with all these homely items, the repose and sanctity of the old wood do not seem to be destroyed or prophaned; she overshadows these poor people, and assimilates them, somehow or other, to the character of her natural inhabitants. Their presence did not shock me, any more than if I had merely discovered a squirrel's nest in a tree.

Alexis de Tocqueville

(1805–59)

French historian and political scientist who went to America to study the prison system. *Democracy in America* was written as a result of his observations. A more personal account of his often intrepid travels has been collected in *Journey to America*.

Saginaw: last outpost of Europeans

Then for the first time we saw in daylight the village of Saginaw which we had come so far to seek.

A small cultivated plain bounded on the south by a lovely, tranquil stream, on the east, west and north by the forest, is up to now the whole territory of the city to be . . .

The village of Saginaw is the last point inhabited by Europeans to the northwest of the huge peninsula of Michigan. One may regard it as an advanced station, a sort of observation post, which the whites have established in the midst of the Indian tribes.

The revolutions of Europe and all the noisy bustle forever ringing in the well-policed part of the world, hardly reach here at long intervals, and ring like the echoes of a sound whose nature and origin the ear cannot identify.

Fanny Kemble

(1809–93)

English actress and writer. Frances Anne Kemble was born into a theatrical family, her aunt was Sarah Siddons, and was herself a brilliant success on the stage, from her debut as Juliet at Covent Garden in 1829. In 1832, she travelled to America with her actor father Charles Kemble, and met and married Pierce Butler, owner of a plantation in Georgia. Fanny retired from the stage until her marriage ended in 1848, but wrote a most interesting account of life on a southern plantation in her eight-volume auto-biography; she disliked being a slave owner.

Shocked by the Shakers

I do not know whether you have ever heard of a religious sect called the Shakers; I never did till I came into their neighbourhood: and all that was told me before seeing them fell short of the extraordinary effect of the reality. Seven hundred men and women, whose profession of religion has for one of its principal objects the extinguishing of the human race and the end of the world, by devoting themselves and persuading others to celibacy and the strictest chastity. They live all together in one community and own a village and considerable tract of land in the beautiful hill country of Berkshire. They are perfectly moral and exemplary in their lives and conduct, wonderfully industrious, miraculously clean and neat, and incredibly shrewd, thrifty and money-making.

Their dress is hideous, and their worship, to which they admit spectators, consists of a fearful species of dancing, in which the whole number of them engage going round and round their vast hall or temple of prayer, shaking their hands like the paws of a dog sitting up to beg, and singing a deplorable psalm-tune in brisk jig time. The men without their coats, in their shirt-sleeves, with their lank hair hanging on their shoulders, and a sort of loose knee-breeches – knicker-bockers – have a grotesque air of stage Swiss peasantry. The women without a single hair escaping from beneath their hideous caps, mounted upon very high-heeled shoes, and every one of them with a white handkerchief folded napkin-fashion and hanging over her arm. In summer they all dress in white, and what with their pale immovable countenances, their ghost-like figures, and ghastly mad spiritual dance, they looked like the nuns in "Robert the Devil", condemned, for their sins in the flesh, to post-mortem decency and asceticism, to look ugly, and to dance like ill-taught bears.

The whole exhibition was at once so frightful and so ludicrous, that I very nearly went off into hysterics, when I first saw them.

Charles Dickens

(1812–70)

One of the most celebrated writers of the nineteenth century, whose career began as a shorthand reporter of Commons debates (see *Sketches by Boz*). Dickens visited

America in 1842, 1857 and 1868, and spoke about international copyright and the abolition of slavery, among other issues.

Specimens of advertisements for runaway slaves

Ran away, a negro boy about twelve years old. Had round his neck a chain dog-collar with 'De Lampert' engraved on it.

Ran away, the negro Hown. Has a ring of iron on his left foot. Also, Grise, *his wife*, having a ring and chain on the left leg.

Ran away, a negro woman and two children. A few days before she went off, I burnt her with a hot iron, on the left side of her face. I tried to make the letter M.

Ran away, a negro woman named Rachel. Has lost all her toes except the large one.

Ran away, a negro named Arthur. Has a considerable scar across his breast and each arm, made by a knife; loves to talk much of the goodness of God.

John Charles Fremont

(1813–90)

American explorer, mathematician, surveyor and explorer. Fremont's ambition was the scientific exploration of the North American continent. He outfitted a wagon as a travelling map workshop for his first expedition to the Alleghanies and the Mississippi and Missouri rivers. In 1842, accompanied by Kit Carson, he crossed the Rocky Mountains, mapping the routes for others to follow, including the Transcontinental Railroad. Fremont also explored the Great Salt Lake, the mouth of the Columbia river, the Rio Grande and crossed the Sierra Nevada to California. He then became a politician and a soldier.

A strange cavalcade on its way to the Rocky Mountains

Our cavalcade made a strange and grotesque appearance; and it was impossible to avoid reflecting upon our position and composition in this remote solitude. Within two degrees of the Pacific Ocean; already far south of the latitude of Monterey; and still forced on south by a desert on one hand and a mountain range on the other; guided by a civilized Indian; attended by two wild ones from the Sierra; a Chinook from the Columbia; and our own mixture of American, French, German – all armed; four or five languages heard at once; above a hundred horses and mules, half wild; American, Spanish, and Indian dresses and equipments intermingled – such was our composition. Our march was a sort of procession. Scouts ahead and on the flanks; a front and rear division; the pack animals, baggage, and horned cattle, in the centre; and the whole stretching a quarter of a mile along our dreary path. In this form we journeyed; looking more as if we belonged to Asia than to the United States of America.

Anthony Trollope

(1815–82)

English writer, and son of the writer Frances Trollope (**q.v.**). Trollope pursued a career with the Post Office for much of his life, perhaps in response to his family misfortunes. This apparently sedentary position took him to Ireland, the West of England, Scotland, Egypt, the West Indies and the United States in the course of duty. He also visited other parts of the world including Australia and New Zealand, Ceylon, South Africa and Iceland. Trollope was also a prolific novelist, best known for his series of 'Barsetshire' novels.

At the Ocean Hotel, Newport

In England we know nothing of hotels prepared for six hundred visitors, all of whom are expected to live in common. Domestic architects would be frightened at the dimensions which are needed, and at the number of apartments which are required to be clustered under one roof. We went to the Ocean Hotel at Newport, and fancied, as we first entered the hall under a verandah as high as the house, and made our way into the passage, that we had been taken to a well-arranged barrack. "Have you rooms?" I asked, as a man always does ask on first reaching his inn. "Rooms enough," the clerk said. "We have only fifty here . . ."

We were a melancholy set, the ladies appearing to be afflicted in this way worse than the gentlemen, on account of their enforced abstinence from tobacco. What can twelve ladies do scattered about a drawing-room, so-called, intended for the accommodation of two hundred? The drawing-room at the Ocean Hotel, Newport, is not as big as Westminster Hall, but would, I should think, make a very good House of Commons for the British nation. Fancy the feelings of a lady when she walks into such a room intending to spend her evening there, and finds six or seven other ladies located on various sofas at terrible distances, all strangers to her. She has come to Newport probably to enjoy herself; and as, in accordance with the customs of the place, she has dined at two, she has nothing before her for the evening but the society of that huge furnished cavern. Her husband, if she have one, or her father, or her lover, has probably entered the room with her. But a man has never the courage to endure such a position long. He sidles out with some muttered excuse, and seeks solace with a cigar. The lady, after half an hour of contemplation, creeps silently near some companion in the desert, and suggests in a whisper that Newport does not seem to be very full at present.

Henry David Thoreau

(1817–62)

American poet, naturalist and writer. Thoreau abandoned teaching to help his father make pencils, then began his long walks and travels, mostly in his native Massachusetts. In 1854 he achieved his dream of living close to nature, by building a cabin in the woods beside Walden Pond, supporting himself by writing and doing odd jobs. *Walden*, his description of this life in the wild, became an American classic.

The Highland Light-house, Cape Cod

The Highland Light-house, where we were staying, is a substantial-looking building of brick, painted white, and surmounted by an iron cap. Attached to it is the dwelling of the keeper, one story high, also of brick, and built by government. As we were going to spend the night in a light-house, we wished to make the most of so novel an experience, and therefore told our host that we would like to accompany him when he went to light up. At rather early candle-light he lighted a small Japan lamp, allowing it to smoke rather more than we like on ordinary occasions, and told us to follow him. He led the way first through his bedroom, which was placed nearest to the light-house, and then through a long, narrow, covered passage-way, between whitewashed walls like a prison entry, into the lower part of the light-house, where many great butts of oil were arranged around; thence we ascended by a winding and open iron stairway, with a steadily increasing scent of oil and lamp-smoke, to a trapdoor in an iron floor, and through this into the lantern. It was a neat building, with everything in apple-pie order, and no danger of anything rusting there for want of oil. The light consisted of fifteen argand lamps, placed within smooth concave reflectors twenty-one inches in diameter, and arranged in two horizontal circles one above the other, facing every way excepting directly down the Cape. These were surrounded, at a distance of two or three feet, by large plate-glass windows, which defied the storms, with iron sashes, on which rested the iron cap. All the iron work, except the floor, was painted white. And thus the light-house was completed. We walked slowly round in that narrow space as the keeper lighted each lamp in succession, conversing with him at the same moment that many a sailor on the deep witnessed the lighting of the Highland Light.

Overwhelmed by cod at the Cape

A great many of the houses here were surrounded by fish-flakes close up to the sills on all sides, with only a narrow passage two or three feet wide, to the front door; so that instead of looking out into a flower or grass plot, you looked on to so many square rods of cod turned wrong side outwards. These parterres were said to be least like a flower-garden in a good drying day in midsummer. There were flakes of every age and pattern, and some so rusty and overgrown with lichens that they looked as if they might have served the founders of the fishery here. Some had broken down under the weight of successive harvests. The principal employment of the inhabitants at this time seemed to be to trundle out their fish and spread them in the morning, and bring them in at night.

Henry Bradshaw Fearon

(fl. 1818)

Englishman who travelled in America in 1817–18, to find useful information for prospective emigrants. His book is a detailed account of everything from climate to the cost of a feather bed.

In the church of Ebenezer

I went at 8 o'clock in the evening. The door was locked; but the windows being open, I placed myself at one of them, and saw that the church within was crowded almost to suffocation. The preacher indulged in long pauses, and occasional loud elevations of voice, which were always answered by the audience with deep groan. When the prayer which followed the sermon had ended, the minister descended from the pulpit, the doors were thrown open, and a considerable number of the audience departed. Understanding however that something was yet to follow, with considerable difficulty I obtained admission. The minister had departed, the doors were again closed, but about four hundred persons remained. One (apparently) of the leading members gave out a hymn, then a brother was called upon to pray: he roared and ranted like a maniac; the male part of the audience groaned, the female shrieked; a man sitting next to me shouted; a youth standing before me continued for half an hour bawling, "Oh Jesus! come down, come down, Jesus! my dear Jesus! I see you! bless me, Jesus! Oh! oh! oh! Come down, Jesus!" The madness now became threefold increased and such a scene presented itself as I could never have pictured to my imagination . . . Had the inhabitants of Bedlam been let loose, they could not have exceeded it. From forty to fifty were praying aloud and extemporaneously at the same moment of time: some were kicking, many jumping, all clapping their hands and crying out in chorus, "Glory! glory! glory! Jesus Christ is a very good friend! Jesus Christ is a very good friend!"

Sir William Howard Russell

(1821–1907)

English lawyer and newspaper correspondent. His reports from the Crimea awakened the British public to the condition of the British soldiers there. Russell also reported on the Indian Mutiny, the American Civil War and the

Franco-Prussian War. He later travelled with the Prince
of Wales as his private secretary.

Robins on toast at Willard's Hotel, Washington

Close to these rises the great pile of Willard's Hotel, now occupied
by applicants for office, and by the members of the newly-assembled
Congress. It is a quadrangular mass of rooms, six stories high, and some
hundred yards square; and it probably contains at this moment more
scheming, plotting, planning heads, more aching and joyful hearts, that
any building of the same size ever held in the world . . .

It was a remarkable sight, and difficult to understand unless seen.
From California, Texas, from the Indian Reserves, and the Mormon
territory, from Nebraska, as from the remotest borders of Minniesota,
from every portion of the vast territories of the Union, except from the
Seceded States, the triumphant republicans had winged their way to the
prey.

There were crowds in the hall through which one could scarce make
his way – the writing-room was crowded, and the rustle of pens rose
to a little breeze – the smoking-room, the bar, the barbers, the reception-
room, the ladies' drawing-room – all were crowded. At present not less
than 2500 people dine in the public room every day. On the kitchen
floor there is a vast apartment, a hall without carpets or any furniture
but plain chairs and tables, which are ranged in close rows, at which
flocks of people are feeding, or discoursing, or from which they are
flying away. The servants never cease shoving the chairs to and fro with
a harsh screeching noise over the floor, so that one can scarce hear his
neighbour speak. If he did, he would probably hear as I did, at this very
hotel, a man order breakfast, "Black tea and toast, scrambled eggs, fresh
spring shad, wild pigeon, pigs' feet, two robins on toast, oysters," and
a quantity of breads and cakes of various denominations.

Meeting the President

Soon afterwards there entered, with a shambling, loose, irregular, almost
unsteady gait, a tall, lank, lean man, considerably over six feet in height,
with stooping shoulders, long pendulous arms, terminating in hands of

extraordinary dimensions, which, however, were far exceeded in proportion by his feet. He was dressed in an ill-fitting, wrinkled suit of
black, which put one in mind of an undertaker's uniform at a funeral;
round his neck a rope of black silk was knotted in a large bulb, with
flying ends projecting beyond the collar of his coat; his turned-down
shirt-collar disclosed a sinewy muscular yellow neck, and above that,
nestling in a great black mass of hair, bristling and compact like a ruff
of mourning pins, rose the strange quaint face and head, covered with
its thatch of wild republican hair, of President Lincoln.

Frederick Law Olmsted

(1822–1903)

American landscape architect and travel writer. He
reported on his travels in the southern slaveholding states
for the *New York Times*, and went on a six-month walking
tour of the British Isles. Olmsted is also remembered for
the design of New York's Central Park (with W. Calvert
Vaux) and public spaces in many other cities. He was put
in charge of the Yosemite Valley and Mariposa Big Tree
Grove in California.

Black dandies of Virginia

Some were dressed with laughably foppish extravagance, and a great
many in clothing of the most expensive materials, and in the latest style
of fashion. In what I suppose to be the fashionable streets, there were
many more well-dressed and highly-dressed colored people than white,
and among this dark gentry the finest French cloths, embroidered waistcoats, patent-leather shoes, resplendent brooches, silk hats, kid gloves,
and *eau de mille fleurs*, were quite as common as among the New York
"dry-goods clerks", in their Sunday promenades, in Broadway. Nor was
the fairer, or rather the softer sex, at all left in the shade of this splendor.
Many of the colored ladies were dressed not only expensively, but with

good taste and effect, after the latest Parisian mode. Many of them were quite attractive in appearance, and some would have produced a decided sensation in any European drawing-room. Their walk and carriage was more often stylish and graceful than that of the white ladies who were out. About one quarter seemed to me to have lost all distinguishingly African peculiarity of feature, and to have acquired, in place of it, a good deal of that voluptuousness of expression which characterizes many of the women of the south of Europe. I was especially surprised to notice the frequency of thin, aquiline noses.

Wagoners at Fayetteville, North Carolina

Having observed, from my room in the hotel at Fayetteville, a number of remarkable, bright lights, I walked out, about eleven o'clock, in the direction in which they had appeared, and found, upon the edge of an old-field, near the town, a camp of wagoners, with half-a-dozen fires, around some of which were clustered groups of white men and women and negroes cooking and eating their suppers (black and white from the same kettle, in many cases), some singing Methodist songs, and some listening to a banjo or fiddle-player. A still larger number appeared to be asleep, generally lying under low tents, about as large as those used by the French soldier. There were thirty or forty great wagons, with mules, cattle, or horses, feeding from troughs set upon their poles. The grouping of all among some old sycamore trees, with the fantastic shadows and wavering lights, the free flames and black brooding smoke of the pitch-pine fires, produced a most interesting and attractive spectacle, and detained me long in admiration. I could easily imagine myself to be on the Oregon or California trail, a thousand miles from the realm of civilization – not readily realize that I was within the limits of one of the oldest towns on the American continent.

Francis Parkman

(1823–93)

American traveller, horticulturalist and historian of the French and English struggle for power in North America. As a young man, Parkman spent his vacations walking and canoeing through New England. In 1846 he travelled with his cousin from Boston to Independence, Missouri, and along the Oregon Trail, living among the Sioux, and various kinds of frontiersmen. This was in spite of perpetual ill-health; Parkman found writing so difficult that he had a special frame constructed with wires to guide his hand.

How the West was tamed

For Indian teepees, with their trophies of bow, lance, shield, and dangling scalplocks, we have towns and cities, resorts of health and pleasure seekers, with an agreeable society, Paris fashions, the magazines, the latest poem, and the last new novel. The sons of civilization, drawn by the fascinations of a fresher and bolder life, thronged to the western wilds in multitudes which blighted the charm that had lured them.

The buffalo is gone, and of all his millions nothing is left but bones. Tame cattle and fences of barbed wire have supplanted his vast herds and boundless grazing grounds. Those discordant serenaders, the wolves that howled at evening about the traveller's camp-fire have succumbed to arsenic and hushed their savage music. The wild Indian is turned into an ugly caricature of his conqueror; and that which made him romantic, terrible, and hateful, is in large measure scourged out of him. The slow cavalcade of horsemen armed to the teeth has disappeared before parlor cars and the effeminate comforts of modern travel.

The rattlesnakes have grown bashful and retiring. The mountain lion shrinks from the face of man, and even grim "Old Ephraim", the grizzly bear, seeks the seclusion of his dens and caverns. It is said that he is no longer his former self, having found by an intelligence not hitherto set to his credit, that his ferocious strength is no match for a repeating rifle; with which discovery he is reported to have grown diffident, and abated the truculence of his more prosperous days. One may be permitted to doubt if the blood-thirsty old savage has really experienced a change of heart; and before inviting him to single combat, the ambitious tenderfoot, though the proud possessor of a Winchester with sixteen cartridges in the magazine, would do well to consider not only the quality of his weapon, but also that of his own nerves.

He who feared neither bear, Indian, nor devil, the all-daring and all-enduring trapper, belongs to the past, or lives only in a few gray-bearded survivals. In his stead we have the cowboy, and even his star begins to wane.

The Wild West is tamed, and its savage charms have withered.

George Augustus Sala

(1828–96)

English journalist and writer. Sala was first apprenticed to a miniature painter and then became a clerk, a scene painter, and learned etching and engraving before turning to journalism. He was sent by Dickens to report on the Crimean War for his magazine *Household Words*, and in 1863 went to witness the American Civil War. He also wrote two articles a day for twenty-five years for the *Daily Telegraph*. Sala is sometimes verbose, sometimes opinionated, but nearly always fresh and fascinating to read.

A surfeit of pie

Talk not to me of an inflated currency, of Seranton coals at fourteen dollars a ton, and tea at twenty-five cents an ounce; of the scarcity of nickel or copper cents, of measuring-worms and Fourth of July fireworks, of municipal jobs and railway monopolies; the real social curse of the Atlantic States is Pie. In the West it is pronounced "poy", and the backwoodsmen are fond of it; but a man who lives in a log-hut and is felling trees or toiling in the prairies all day long can eat Pie with impunity. It is in the North and in the East, in cities and townships and manufacturing districts, where dense populations congregate, and where the occupations of men, women, and children are sedentary, that an unholy appetite for Pie works untold woes. There the Pie fiend reigns supreme; there he sits heavy on the diaphragms and on the souls of his votaries. The sallow faces, the shrunken forms, the sunken eyes, the morose looks, the tetchy temperament of the Northerners are attributable not half so much to iced water, candies, tough beefsteaks, tight lacing, and tobacco-chewing, as to unbridled indulgence in Pie.

Isabella Bird

(1831–1904)

English traveller and writer. Despite a lifelong spinal complaint and the fact that she did not start travelling until she was in her forties, there are few parts of the world that Isabella Bird (Mrs Isabella Bishop) did not visit, and visit in earnest, often living in the most primitive conditions. She wrote three books about the United States, including one about her travels in the Rocky Mountains, one about the Sandwich Islands, which she visited on a journey to Australia and Hawaii, one on Japan, and another on Malaya. After the death of her husband in 1886, Bird travelled in the Himalayas, Persia, Kurdistan, Korea and then eight thousand miles in the interior of China, writing books about each of them. As well as all this she founded five hospitals in Asia, and rode one thousand miles across Morocco at the age of sixty-nine, on a black stallion given to her by the Sultan.

A true temple of Morpheus

Precisely at 11 p.m. the huge Pacific train, with its heavy bell tolling, thundered up to the door of the Truckee House, and on presenting my ticket at the stable door of a "Silver Palace" car, the slippered steward, whispering low, conducted me to my berth – a luxurious bed three and a half feet wide, with a hair mattress on springs, fine linen sheets, and costly California blankets. The twenty-four inmates of the car were all invisible, asleep behind rich curtains. It was a true Temple of Morpheus. Profound sleep was the object to which everything was dedicated. Four silver lamps hanging from the roof, and burning low, gave a dreamy light. On each side of the centre passage, rich rep curtains, green and crimson, striped with gold, hung from silver bars running near the roof, and trailed on the soft Axminster carpet. The temperature was carefully kept at 70°. It was 29° outside. Silence and freedom from jolting were secured by double doors and windows, costly and ingenious arrangements of springs and cushions, and a speed limited to eighteen miles an hour.

R.M. Ballantyne

(1835–94)

Scottish writer, mainly of exciting books for boys, such as *Coral Island*. Ballantyne spent six years trading in Rupert Land for the Hudson's Bay Company. His experiences were described in his book *Hudson's Bay*, and became the basis for *Snowflakes and Sunbeam – or The Young Fur Traders*, his first book for young people.

The Cree Indians

As the Crees were the Indians with whom I had the most intercourse, I shall endeavour to describe my old friends more at length.

The personal appearance of the men of this tribe is not bad. Although they have not the bold daring carriage of the wilder tribes, yet they have active-looking figures, fine intelligent countenances, and a peculiar brightness in their dark eyes, which, from a constant habit of looking around them while travelling through the woods, are seldom for a moment at rest. Their jet black hair generally hangs in straight matted locks over their shoulders, sometimes ornamented with beads and pieces of metal, and occasionally with a few partridge feathers; but they seldom wear a hat or cap of any kind, except in winter, when they make clumsy imitations of foraging caps with furs, preferring, if the weather be warm, to go about without any head-dress at all, or, if it be cold, using the large hood of their capotes as a covering. They are thin, wiry men, not generally very muscular in their proportions, but yet capable of enduring great fatigue. Their average height is about five feet five inches; and one rarely meets with individuals varying much from this average, nor with deformed people, among them. The step of a Cree Indian is much longer than that of a European, owing, probably, to his being so much accustomed to walking through swamps and forests, where it is necessary to take long strides. This peculiarity becomes apparent when an Indian arrives at a fort and walks along the hard ground inside the walls with trader, whose short, bustling, active step, contrasts oddly with the long, solemn, ostrich-like stride of the savage; which, however appropriate in the woods, is certainly strange and ungraceful on a good road.

John Muir

(1838–1914)

American naturalist, explorer and conservationist. Muir was born in Scotland and went to North America in 1849. After being nearly blinded in a factory accident at Indianapolis, Muir set off for the Gulf of Mexico, a journey of one thousand miles, which he did mostly on foot. He became particularly interested in forests and glaciers and spent years studying them in Yosemite, in California, and other parts of America and in Alaska. Muir pioneered the establishment of conservation laws in America. He also visited Russia, India and Australia.

Tree music

There is always something deeply exciting, not only in the sounds of winds in the woods, which exert more or less influence over every mind, but in their varied waterlike flow as manifested by the movements of the trees, especially those of the conifers. By no other trees are they rendered so extensively and impressively visible, not even by the lordly tropic palms or tree-ferns responsive to the gentlest breeze. The waving of a forest of the giant Sequoias is indescribably impressive and sublime, but the pines seem to me the best interpreters of winds. They are mighty waving goldenrods, ever in tune, singing and writing wind-music all their long century lives. Little, however, of this noble tree-waving and tree-music will you see or hear in the strictly alpine portion of the forests. The burly Juniper, whose girth sometimes more than equals its height, is about as rigid as the rocks on which it grows. The slender lash-like sprays of the Dwarf Pine stream out in wavering ripples, but the tallest and slenderest are far too unyielding to wave even in the heaviest gales. They only shake in quick, short vibrations. The Hemlock Spruce, however, and the Mountain Pine, and some of the tallest thickets of the Two-leaved species bow in storms with considerable scope and gracefulness. But it is only in the lower and middle zones that the meeting of winds and woods is to be seen in all its grandeur.

Edward Whymper

(1840–1911)

English wood-engraver and mountaineer. He made the first ascent of Pointe des Ecrins, in Dauphiné, and of several peaks in the Mont Blanc chain. In 1865 Whymper made the first successful ascent of the Matterhorn, with

Michel Croz, a Chamonix guide, but four men were killed
on the descent; he described this awful event in his modestly entitled *Scrambles in the Alps*. He also studied the
effect of altitude in Andean Ecuador, 1888, devised the
'Whymper tent' for mountaineering expeditions; wrote
mountaineering handbooks and worked as an engraver
and illustrator.

Moving house in San Francisco

As the streets improve, the older board-and-shingle "frame buildings"
are moved to the outskirts on rollers, and often on large, wide, low
carts, with small wheels, drawn by fifteen or twenty horses. Sometimes
the family continues to occupy it as usual, and you see the smoke issuing
from the "stove pipe", or chimney, as it travels through the streets. The
furniture and carpets remain "as they were", and are carried bodily
with the house. A travelling hawker's caravan creates more notice here
in England than this "house moving" does in San Francisco; it is a
common occurrence in all Western and Pacific towns. A house is often
deposited at the corner, or in the middle of a street, for the night.

Frank S. Dellenbaugh

(c. 1852–?)

Dellenbaugh explored the Colorado river in 1871–3 with
the indefatigable Colonel Wesley Powell, veteran of the
American Civil War, whose 'right arm had remained on
the battlefield of Shiloh'. Dellenbaugh was nineteen at the
time.

Climbing with a one-armed major

The next day Powell took me with him on a climb to the top. We had
little trouble in getting out. On the way back the Major's cut-off arm

was on the rock side of a gulch we had followed up, and I found it necessary, two or three times, to place myself where he could step on my knee, as his stump had a tendency to throw him off his balance. Had he fallen at these points the drop would have been four hundred or five hundred feet. I mention this to show how he never permitted his one-armed condition to interfere with his doing things. The walls here were eighteen hundred feet, a gain of three hundred feet over the Junction.

Captain R.B. Marcy

(fl. 1860)

Marcy's book *The Prairie and Overland Traveller* book is subtitled 'A Companion for Emigrants, Traders, Travellers, Hunters and Soldiers' and tells the reader how to travel overland by wagon to the Pacific. Marcy evidently did the journey himself, at least in a military capacity.

Smoke signals

The transparency of the atmosphere upon the Plains is such that objects can be seen at great distances: a mountain, for example, presents a distinct and bold outline at fifty or sixty miles, and may occasionally be seen as far as a hundred miles.

The Indians, availing themselves of this fact, have been in the habit of practising a system of telegraphing by means of smokes during the day and fires by night, and, I daresay, there are but few travellers who have crossed the mountains to California that have not seen these signals made and responded to from peak to peak in rapid succession.

The Indians thus make known to their friends many items of information highly important to them. If enemies or strangers make their appearance in the country, the fact is telegraphed at once, giving them time to secure their animals and to prepare for attack, defence, or flight.

War or hunting parties, after having been absent a long time from their erratic friends at home, and not knowing where to find them, make use of the same preconcerted signals to indicate their presence.

Very dense smokes may be raised by kindling a large fire with dry wood, and piling upon it the green boughs of pine, balsam, or hemlock. This throws off a heavy cloud of black smoke which can be seen very far.

This simple method of telegraphing, so useful to the savages both in war and in peace, may, in my judgment, be used to advantage in the movements of troops co-operating in separate columns in the Indian country . . .

. . . During the day an intelligent man should be detailed to keep a vigilant look-out in all directions for smokes, and he should be furnished with a watch, pencil, and paper, to make a record of the signals, with their number, and the time of the intervals between them.

Hariot, Marchioness of Dufferin and Ava

(d. 1936)

In 1862 Hariot married the Marquis of Dufferin and Ava (q.v.). She thus became consort to the Governor-General of Canada, ambassador at Rome and in France, and then Viceroy of India. She wrote entertainingly and without pomposity about their life in these places. The Marchioness had three daughters and outlived her husband by thirty-four years; she was made a DBE.

Journey to the centre of the earth

We arrived at last at the house of a farmer, the owner of a cave, which cave was the end and object of our expedition. Here we lunched, and then, guided by the farmer, we proceeded on our way two miles along a lumber snow road, very narrow and bumpy. We left the carriages on a lake, and climbed up a hill to the mouth of the cave, where we took off our fur cloaks, and, each taking a lighted candle, entered the cave.

After examining a part of it, which I may call the hall and ante-room of this subterranean mansion, we proceeded on hands and knees through a very low passage to the drawing-room. We ladies had great difficulty with our petticoats, especially when in this doubled-up position we had to cross a pool of water on a narrow plank, and were greatly relieved when we were able to stretch ourselves upright again. New perils were, however, before us, and the gentlemen were astonished to find that Lady Harriet and I really did intend to descend the ladders which, in the darkness, appeared to lead down to the middle of the earth. But, as we very naturally observed to them, we had not driven twenty miles, and crawled on hands and knees to the spot, to be deterred by a small difficulty; so down we went, and saw two more large rooms in the basement of said mansion. Of course the place requires a geologist's eye to appreciate it thoroughly. It is made of – no; I won't even attempt to describe its origin.

We came out from our crawling very dirty indeed, and, returning to our carriages, drove homewards.

W.H. Davies

(1871–1940)

Welsh poet, writer and wanderer. At twenty-two, he emigrated to the United States and became a hobo, peddler and casual labourer. He returned to England after losing a leg while jumping a train. Davies carried on tramping, until his *Autobiography of a Super-Tramp*, and his poems and other writing brought him success.

A lynching in the Deep South

For it was now I remembered reading of this man's offence, and it was of the most brutal kind, being much like the work of a wild beast. They now marched him from the jail, their strong arms supporting his terror stricken limbs, but no man reviled him with his tongue, and I saw no cowardly hand strike him. Soon they came to a group of trees on the outskirts of the town, and, choosing the largest of these, they threw the rope's end over its strongest branch, the prisoner at the same time crying for mercy, and trying to throw his body full on the ground. When this was done a dozen hands caught the rope's end, made one quick jerk, and the prisoner's body was struggling in the air. Then all these men shouldered their guns, fired one volley, and in a second the body was hanging lifeless with a hundred shots. In five minutes after this, nothing but the corpse remained to tell of what had occurred, the men having quietly scattered towards their homes.

Rupert Brooke

(1887–1915)

English poet. Studied at Cambridge and became a Fellow of King's College. In 1913 he travelled in the USA, Canada, New Zealand and the South Seas before joining the Navy in 1914. Brooke died of septicaemia from an infected mosquito bite on Skyros, Greece, in 1915 on his way to serve in the Dardanelles. Brooke was a romantic, heroic figure. The *Daily News* wrote that, 'To look at he was part of the youth of the world.'

Twentieth century peasants in Canada

Our train was boarded by a crowd of Ruthenians or Galicians, brown-eyed and beautiful people, not yet wholly civilised out of their own costume. The girls chatted together in a swift, lovely language, and the children danced about, tossing their queer brown mops of hair. They clattered out at a little village that seemed to belong to them, and stood waving and laughing us out of sight.

I pondered on their feeling, and looked for the name of the little Utopia these aliens had found in a new world. It was called (for the railway companies name towns in this country) 'Milner'.

Henry Miller

(1891–1980)

American writer and perpetual wanderer. *The Air-Conditioned Nightmare* is his epistle to the America he found in the late 1940s, written both in love and hate. His earlier books, *Tropic of Cancer* and *Tropic of Capricorn*, were banned in Britain and America.

Dream places of the Old South

There are beautiful regions, such as in the vicinity of Charlottesville, for example, where there seem to be nothing but millionaires. There are mill towns in the Carolinas, for instance, which, like the mining towns of Pennsylvania or West Virginia, fill one with terror and disgust. There are farming regions, in what was once the Old Dominion, where the land assumes a beauty and serenity unrivalled anywhere in the Old World. There are vistas, such as at Chattanooga, Harpers Ferry, Asheville, or along the crest of the Blue Ridge, or in the heart of the Great Smokies, to mention but a few, which instill in the human heart a deep, abiding peace. There are swamps, such as Okefinokee and the Great Dismal Swamp of Virginia, which inspire an unspeakable dread and longing. There are trees, plants, shrubs, flowers such as are seen nowhere else, and which are not only extraordinarily beautiful but haunting and almost overwhelmingly nostalgic. At Biloxi, Mississippi, there is a row of live oaks planted a century ago by a Greek which are of such staggering loveliness and magnificence as to make one breathless. From the steps of Black Mountain College in North Carolina one has a view of mountains and forests which makes one dream of Asia. In Louisiana there are stretches of bayou country whose beauty is of a nature such as only the Chinese poets have captured. In New Iberia, La., to signal only one example, there is a house and garden belonging to Weeks Hall which constitute in essence and in fact the dream made real . . .

There are thousands of dream places in the old South. You can sit on a bench in a tiny Confederate Park or fling yourself on the banks of a levee or stand on a bluff overlooking an Indian settlement, the air soft, still, fragrant, the world asleep seemingly, but the atmosphere is charged with magical names, epoch-making events, inventions, explorations, discoveries. Rice, tobacco, cotton – out of these three elements alone the South created a great symphonic pageant of human activity.

It is all over now. A new South is being born. The old south was ploughed under. But the ashes are still warm.

Steven Runciman

(1903–2000)

British historian, notably of the Roman and Byzantine Empires. *A Traveller's Alphabet* is a peripatetic autobiography.

A night on a waterbed

There was no one to meet me at the airport. A telephone call revealed that my hosts were away till the morrow; but after further calls I found a kind friend who was willing to house me for the night. He took me to his apartment, high in a tower block, and showed me into a room furnished with a water-bed. As I lay there sleepless – for the waves would not allow me to lie on my side but kept pushing me on to my back – I kept wondering what would happen were there to be an earthquake. The heavy contraption would quite certainly bring the building down and would itself burst open. So, if I were not crushed to death I would undoubtedly be drowned.

Tom Wolfe

(1931–)

American author. *The Right Stuff* is the classic account of
early American adventures in space.

"You're on your way, José!"

Time seemed to speed up tremendously in the final thirty seconds of
the countdown. In thirty seconds the rocket would ignite right underneath his back. In those last moments his entire life did not pass before
his eyes. He did not have a poignant vision of his mother or his wife
or his children. No, he thought about abort procedures and the checklist
and about not fucking up. He only half paid attention to Deke Slayton's
voice over his headset as he read out the final "ten . . . nine . . . eight
. . . seven . . . six . . ." and the rest of it. The only word that counted,
here in this little blind stuffed pod, was the last word. Then he heard
Deke Slayton say it: "Fire! . . . You're on your way, José!"

Jonathan Raban

(1942–)

English writer and traveller. Raban has written extensively
about North America, about Arabia and about the sea.

A tomb for eternity

Every excursion that I made from the boat took me through the grave-
yard. The more I saw of it, the more I liked the place, its quiet streets
of little whitewashed houses, its birds and lizards, its odd epitaphs. It
would be a good spot to be buried in, and I could think of no better

site for an American ending. After the continuous motion of life in the United States, the striving and becoming, you'd land up here to rot in sunny indolence in a whitewashed building within the sound of the sea.

I wasn't ambitious. I didn't want a grand place. I would settle for a modest, Alice-sized apartment, a one-bed affair in a multi-storey block.

From a payphone on the dock, I called the public works department at City Hall, and asked for Cemeteries. I had been thinking, I said, of ordering a tomb.

"For a relative?"

"No."

"Is this for a deceased party?"

"No, not yet. Actually, it's for me."

"I get you. What exactly do you have in mind?"

"You know those kind of condo blocks at the south end?"

"The multiple occupancy units. And this would be just one unit, right?"

"Yes. What's the cost on those?"

"Well, the price has just been raised. Like everything else, cost's going up all the time. Two years back, you could have had one for $600. Right now, it'll cost you $825 clear."

"Is that leasehold or freehold?"

"I don't follow you."

"Is it for eternity?"

After an uneasy pause, the man laughed.

"Yeah, it's yours for keeps."

"It sounds like a good buy."

"It's the only property not taxed in the city."

"Could I buy one this afternoon?"

"Well – no. There's been a lot of demand for those units lately. We're doing what we can to stay ahead of the game; we used to build 16 of 'em at a time, but last time we were up to 64 . . . Next time, we may be going up as high as 96 . . ."

"How long would I have to wait?"

"That's difficult. You think you can hold out for two years?"

High clouds were moving in the sky. The wind was from the south-west, the water was flecked with small waves. There were many things

I wanted to do. For a start, I wanted to sail up the Atlantic side of the Keys, go under the Seven Mile Bridge and strike north for the Everglades. After that . . .

"Well, I can try," I said.

Central and South America
and The Caribbean

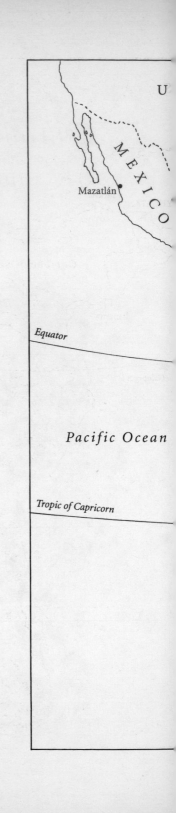

U

MEXICO

Mazatlán

Equator

Pacific Ocean

Tropic of Capricorn

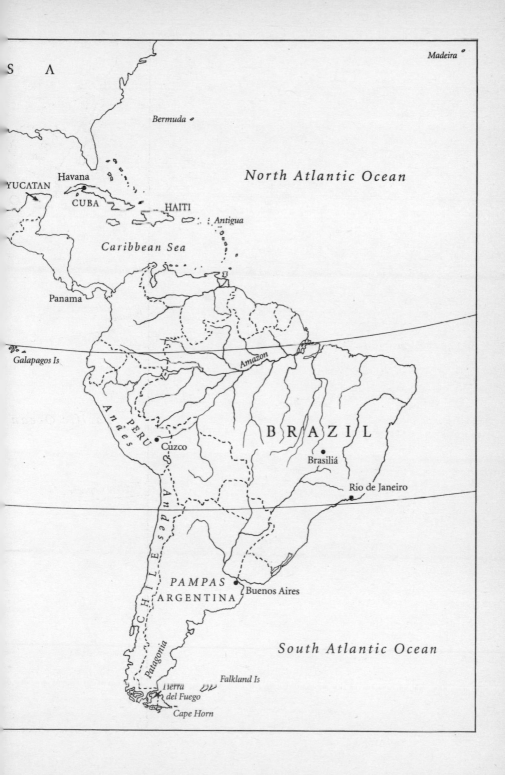

S A

Madeira

Bermuda

North Atlantic Ocean

YUCATAN Havana

CUBA

HAITI

Antigua

Caribbean Sea

Panama

Galapagos Is

Amazon

PERU

B R A Z I L

Cuzco

Brasiliá

Rio de Janeiro

Andes

CHILE

PAMPAS

ARGENTINA Buenos Aires

South Atlantic Ocean

Patagonia

Falkland Is

Tierra
del Fuego

Cape Horn

Christopher Columbus

(1451–1506)

Italian navigator, and, as discoverer of the New World, one of the most famous explorers in human history. By the time he sailed on his epic voyage in 1492, Columbus had already fought in sea battles, been shipwrecked, been to Iceland and back as well as to the Cape Verde Islands and Sierra Leone. After years of effort (opposed by the ideas of men who thought the world was square), he persuaded King Ferdinand and Queen Isabella of Spain to sponsor his expedition across the Atlantic, where he expected to find India. He made four journeys. His first landfalls, which he believed to be in Asia, were at San Salvador in the Bahamas, and the Islands of Cuba and Hispaniola (now Haiti and the Dominican Republic), where he founded a European settlement. On his second voyage he reached the West Indies and on his third discovered the South American mainland. Columbus was sent home in chains for his poor administration of the 'colony' (Venezuela), and without the anticipated treasure. His final voyage, made in tired vessels and with much opposition, was to the Gulf of Mexico and Panama, where he tried but failed to find a strait – to India. This time he caught sight of Incas wearing gold, that long-sought metal but he never found the source. Columbus died within two years of returning to Spain, but his mortal remains continued to travel, being buried at Seville, transferred to Hispaniola, then to the Cathedral at Havana, and finally back to Seville.

Cannibal of the Caribbees

These women also say that the Caribbees use them with such cruelty as would scarcely be believed; and that they eat the children which they bear to them, and only bring up those which they have by their natural wives. Such of their male enemies as they can take alive, they bring to their houses to make a feast of them, and those who are dead they devour at once. They say that man's flesh is so good, that there is nothing like it in the world; and this is pretty evident, for of the bones which we found in their houses, they had gnawed everything that could be gnawed, so that nothing remained of them, but what from its great hardness, could not be eaten: in one of the houses we found the neck of a man, undergoing the process of cooking. When they take any boys prisoners, they dismember them, and make use of them until they grow up to manhood, and then when they wish to make a feast they kill and eat them; for they say that the flesh of boys and women is not good to eat. Three of these boys came fleeing to us thus mutilated.

Requests supplies from Spain

I think it would be well that all ships that come here should be ordered to bring, besides the ordinary stores and medicines, shoes, and leather for making shoes, shirts, both of common and superior quality, doublets, laces, some peasants' clothing, breeches, and cloth for making clothes, all at moderate prices; they might also bring other articles, such as sweetmeats, which do not enter into the daily ration, nor are absolutely necessary to health. The Spaniards that are here would always be happy to receive such articles as these in lieu of part of their pay; and if they were purchased by men who were selected for their known loyalty, and who take an interest in the service of their Highnesses, great economy would result from this arrangement. If their Highnesses find that this plan is expedient for the service, it is desirable that it should be adopted immediately . . .

I think it would be desirable that two hundred cuirasses, a hundred arquebuses, a hundred arbalists, and many other articles of defensive armour, should be sent over to us; for we have great need of them to arm those who are present without them.

Amerigo Vespucci

(1454–1512)

Florentine explorer whose name was given to both American continents. At the age of thirty-nine, Vespucci went
to Spain, where he was in charge of fitting out the ships
for Columbus' Third Voyage, which sailed in 1498. He
was fifty years old when he too set off in Columbus'
wake, under Hojéda. They explored the coast of Venezuela.
Vespucci claimed to have made four journeys to the
New World, and possibly reached South America before
Columbus. His accounts have been strongly disputed, but
his sometimes fantastic encounters such as dragons with
bound feet and two-tailed lizards make good reading. Vespucci made some remarkable navigational discoveries; he
devised a way of calculating longitude with some precision,
got close to an accurate estimate of the earth's circumference, and recognised that South America was not part of
Asia, as believed by his countryman, Columbus.

The natives of Brazil

As regards the people: we have found such a multitude in those countries
that no one could enumerate them, as we read in the Apocalypse. They
are people gentle and tractable, and all of both sexes go naked, not
covering any part of their bodies, just as they came from their mothers'
wombs, and so they go until their deaths. They have large, square-built
bodies, and well proportioned. Their colour reddish, which I think
is caused by their going naked and exposed to the sun. Their hair is
plentiful and black. They are agile in walking, and of quick sight. They
are of a free and good-looking expression of countenance, which they
themselves destroy by boring the nostrils and lips, the nose and ears:
nor must you believe that the borings are small, nor that they only have
one, for I have seen those who had no less than seven borings in the
face, each one the size of a plum. They stop up these perforations with

427

blue stones, bits of marble, of crystal, or very fine alabaster, also with very white bones and other things artificially prepared according to their customs; which, if you could see, it would appear a strange and monstrous thing. One had in the nostrils and lips alone seven stones, of which some were half a palm in length. It will astonish you to hear that I considered that the weight of seven such stones was as much as sixteen ounces. In each ear they had three perforations bored, whence they had other stones and rings suspended. This custom is only for the men, as the women do not perforate their faces, but only their ears. Another custom among them is sufficiently shameful, and beyond all human credibility. Their women, being very libidinous, make the penis of their husbands swell to such a size as to appear deformed; and this is accomplished by a certain artifice, being the bite of some poisonous animal, and by reason of this many lose their virile organ and remain eunuchs.

They have no cloth, either of wool, flax, or cotton, because they have no need of it; nor have they any private property, everything being in common. They live amongst themselves without a king or ruler, each man being his own master, and having as many wives as they please. The children cohabit with the mothers, the brothers with the sisters, the male cousins with the female, and each one with the first he meets. They have no temples and no laws, nor are they idolaters. What more can I say!

Francis de Orellana

(c. 1490–1549)

Spanish soldier and explorer. In 1541 Orellana joined the Pizarro expedition which crossed the Andes in mid-winter, in search of gold and cinnamon trees. Once across the Cordillera, he was sent ahead of the main party and ended up travelling the entire length of the Amazon to the sea in primitive boats. He named the river after the fierce native women he encountered on the journey. Orellana lost an eye while fighting natives.

Orellana among the Amazon Indians

They remained at this village for three days, eating plentifully. The captain calculated that they had sailed down the river for three hundred leagues from Aparia, two hundred of which were through uninhabited regions. Having embarked a good supply of the biscuit which the Indians make from maize, yucas, and fruit, they set sail on the Sunday after Ascension; and a league further on, Orellana found that another great stream entered the river, with three islands at its mouth, for which reason he called it the river of the Trinity. The land appeared to be well peopled and fertile, and many canoes came out into the river.

On another day they discovered a small village in a very beautiful spot, and, though the Indians resisted, they entered it and found plenty of provisions. There was a country house containing very good jars of earthenware, vases, and goblets of glass enamelled with many bright colours, resembling drawings and paintings. The Indians at this place said that these things came from the interior, together with much gold and silver. They also found idols worked from palm wood in a very curious fashion, of gigantic stature, with wheels in the fleshy part of the arms. The Spaniards found in this village, gold and silver; but as they only thought of discovery and of saving their lives, they did not care for anything else.

The multitude of people, and the number of villages, which were not half a league distant from each other, as well on the south side of the river, as in the interior, showed Captain Orellana the dangers which he must encounter, and induced him to keep his people well together, and advance cautiously. Hence they took particular care to notice the qualities of the country, which appeared genial and fertile. The forest consisted of ever-green oaks, and cork trees, and contained plenty of game of all kinds. Orellana named this country "the Province of St John", extending more than one hundred and fifty leagues. From the time that they entered it, they sailed in the middle of the river, until they came to a number of islands which they believed to be uninhabited; but the natives, on seeing the vessels, came in two hundred piraguas, each one containing thirty or forty persons, decked out in warlike dresses, with many drums, trumpets, an instrument played with the mouth, and another with three strings. They attacked the brigantine with loud shouts; but the arquebusses and cross-bows stopped their onslaught; and on shore there were a vast number of people with the same instruments. The islands appeared, high, fertile, and very beautiful, the largest being fifty leagues long. The brigantines went on, always followed by the piraguas, and they were unable to get any provisions.

Having left this province of St John, and the piraguas having desisted from following them, they determined to rest in a forest. Captain Orellana, by means of a vocabulary which he had made, asked many questions of a captured Indian, from whom he learned that that land was subject to women, who lived in the same way as Amazons, and were very rich, possessing much gold and silver. They had five houses of the sun plated with gold, their own houses were of stone, and their cities defended by walls; and he related other details, which I can neither believe nor affirm, owing to the difficulty in discovering the truth. The tales of Indians are always doubtful, and Orellana confessed that he did not understand those Indians, so that it seems that he could scarcely have made, in such a few days, so correct and copious a vocabulary as to be able to understand the minute details given by this Indian: but each reader may believe just as much as he likes.

Bernal Diaz del Castillo

(c. 1492–1581)

Spanish historian of the conquest of Mexico. He joined Cortes on his expedition to conquer Mexico in 1519 and wrote it all up at the age of eighty-four. Here Diaz describes the watery approach to one of the Aztec cities in the great lagoon surrounding the capital, Tenochtitlan.

The Cuitlahuac causeway

The next day, in the morning, we arrived at a broad causeway, and continued our march towards Iztapalapa, and when we saw so many cities and villages built in the water and other great towns on dry land

and that straight and level causeway going towards Mexico, we were amazed and said that it was like the enchantments they tell of in the legend of Amadis, on account of the great towers and cues and buildings rising from the water, and all built of masonry. And some of our soldiers even asked whether the things that we saw were not a dream? It is not to be wondered at that I here write it down in this manner, for there is so much to think over that I do not know how to describe it, seeing things as we did that had never been heard of or seen before, not even dreamed about.

Thus, we arrived near Iztapalapa, to behold the splendour of the other Caciques who came out to meet us, who were the Lord of the town named Cuitlahuac, and the Lord of Culuacan, both of them near relations of Montezuma. And then when we entered that city of Iztapalapa, the appearance of the palaces in which they lodged us! How spacious and well built they were, of beautiful stone work and cedar wood, and the wood of other sweet scented trees, with great rooms and courts, wonderful to behold, covered with awnings of cotton cloth.

When we had looked well at all of this, we went to the orchard and garden, which was such a wonderful thing to see and walk in, that I was never tired of looking at the diversity of the trees, and noting the scent which each one had, and the paths full of roses and flowers, and the many fruit trees and native roses, and the pond of fresh water. There was another thing to observe, that great canoes were able to pass into the garden from the lake through an opening that had been made so that there was no need for their occupants to land. And all was cemented and very splendid with many kinds of stone [monuments] with pictures on them, which gave much to think about. Then the birds of many kinds and breeds which came into the pond. I say again that I stood looking at it and thought that never in the world would there be discovered other lands such as these, for at that time there was no Peru, nor any thought of it. [Of all these wonders that I then beheld] to-day all is overthrown and lost, nothing left standing.

Sir John Hawkyns

(1532–95)

English navigator, pirate and slave trafficker. He accompanied Drake on his third voyage in 1567, fought the Spanish Armada and died at Puerto Rico.

The Potatoe

Neere about this place, inhabited certaine Indians, who the next day after we came thither, came down to us, presenting mill and cakes of breade, which they had made of a kinde of corne called Maiz, in bignesse of a pease, the eare whereof is much like to a teasell, but a spanne in length, having thereon a number of granes. Also they brought down to us Hennes, potatoes and Pines, which we bought for beades, pewter whistles, glasses, knives, and other trifles.

These Potatoes be the most delicate rootes that may be eaten, and doe farre exceed our passeneps or carets. Their pines be of the bignes of two fists, the outside whereof is of the making of a pine-apple, but it is soft like the rinde of a Cucomber, and the inside eateth like an apple, but it is more delicious then any sweet apple sugred.

Father Cristoval de Acuna

(1597–c. 1676)

Jesuit priest and 'Censor of the Supreme General Inquisition'. He went down the Amazon as far as Pará with the Portuguese traveller Pedro Teixeira. He died at Lima.

Natives of the Amazon

These savages all go naked, both men and women, their wealth only supplying them with small ornaments, with which they adorn their ears and noses, by piercing holes through them. They affect these holes in the ears so much, that many have them to cover the whole of the lower part whence the earrings are hung. These holes are ordinarily filled with a bundle of leaves.

Opposite all these settlements, the land is flat, and so shut in by other rivers, branches of the Caqueta, that great lakes are formed many leagues long, extending until, mingling with the Rio Negro, they unite with the main stream. Islands are thus formed, which are peopled by many tribes, but that which is the largest and most populous, is the island of Zuanas.

Sir Joseph Banks

(1743–1820)

Botanist, natural historian and President of the Royal Society from 1778–1820. Banks travelled in Newfoundland and Labrador and then accompanied Captain Cook on his voyage round the world on the *Endeavour* in 1768–71. He made a substantial financial contribution to the expedition and supplied many of its scientific instruments. On the journey, Banks made botanical collections and was responsible for the transplanting of fruits such as the mango and breadfruit around the world.

Inhabitants of Tierra del Fuego

Their clothes are nothing more than a kind of cloak of guanaco or seal skin, thrown loosely over their shoulders, and reaching nearly to their knees; under this they have nothing at all, nor anything to cover their feet, except a few who had shoes of raw seal hide drawn loosely round their instep like a purse. In this dress there is no distinction between men and women, except that the latter have their cloak tied round their waist with a kind of belt or thong.

Their ornaments, of which they are extremely fond, consist of neck-laces, or rather solitaires, of shells, and bracelets, which the women wear both on their wrists and legs, the men only on their wrists; but to compensate for this the men have a kind of brown worsted which they wear over their foreheads, so that in reality they are more ornamented than the women.

They paint their faces generally in horizontal lines, just under their eyes, and sometimes make the whole region round their eyes white, but these marks are so much varied that no two we saw were alike. Whether they were marks of distinction or mere ornaments I could not at all make out. They seem also to paint themselves with something like a mixture of grease and soot on particular occasions, for when we went to their town there came out to meet us two who were daubed with black lines in every direction, so as to form the most diabolical countenance imaginable. These two seemed to exorcise us, or at least make a loud and long harangue, which did not seem to be addressed to us or any of their countrymen.

Janet Schaw

(fl. 1776)

Under the nom-de-plume of 'A Scottish lady of Quality', Janet Schaw wrote an animated account of her journey across the Atlantic to the West Indies, North America and Portugal on a small ship called the *Jamaica Packet*. She travelled with her husband, and miscellaneous children. At one point their supplies and livestock were swept over-board, and they were fortunate to avoid starvation or other disasters under their disreputable captain. Schaw's tales are of particular interest as she stayed in Cape Fear, North Carolina, just before the American War of Independence.

The palmetto tree, Antigua

Here I had an opportunity of seeing and admiring the Palmetto tree, with which this Lady's house is surrounded, and entirely guarded by them from the intense heat. They are in general from forty to sixty feet high before they put out a branch, and as straight as a line. If I may compare great things with small, the branches resemble a fern leaf, but are at least twelve or fifteen feet long. They go round the boll of the tree and hang down in the form of an Umbrela; the great stem is white, and the skin like Satin. Above the branches rises another stem, for about twelve or fourteen feet in height, coming to a point at the top, from which the cabbage springs, tho' the pith or heart of the whole is soft and eats well. This stem is the most beautiful green that you can conceive, and is a fine contrast to the white one below. The beauty and figure of this tree, however, rather surprised than pleased me. It had a stiffness in its appearance far from being so agreeable as the waving branches of our native trees, and I could not help declaiming that they did not look as if they were of God's making.

Plenty of puddings in the Caribbean

I will finish the table in this letter, for tho' I like to see it, yet I hope to find twenty things more agreeable for the Subject of my future letters; yet this will amuse some of our eating friends. The pastry is remarkably fine, their tarts are of various fruits, but the best I ever tasted is a sorrel, which when baked becomes the most beautiful Scarlet, and the sirup round it quite transparent. The cheese-cakes are made from the nut of the Cocoa. The puddings are so various, that it is impossible to name them: they are all rich, but what a little surprised me was to be told, that the ground of them all is composed of Oat meal, of which they gave me the receipt. They have many dishes that with us are made of milk, but as they have not that article in plenty, they must have something with which they supply its place, for they have sillabubs, floating Islands, etc. as frequently as with you. They wash and change napkins between the Courses. The desert now comes under our observation, which is indeed something beyond you. At Mr Halliday's we had thirty two different fruits, which tho' we had many other things, certainly was the grand part, yet in the midst of this variety the Pine apple and Orange still keep their ground and are preferred. The pine is large, its colour deep, and its flavour incomparably fine, yet after all I do not think it is superior to what we raise in our hot houses, which tho' smaller are not much behind in taste even with the best I have seen here, tho' in size and beauty there is no comparison. As to the Orange it is quite another fruit than ever I tasted before, the perfume is exquisite, the taste delicious, it has a juice which would produce Sugar.

Charles Kingsley

(1819–75)

English author, academic and cleric; an exponent of muscular Christianity. He was the author of *Westward Ho!* and *The Water Babies*. Son of a clergyman; he started writing sermons at the age of four; was fond of plants and geology; learned boxing under black prizefighter at Oxford. In 1869 he visited the West Indies at invitation of his friend, the Governor of Trinidad. Kingsley had a bad stammer; and according to Leslie Stephen in the *Dictionary of National Biography* 'The excessive fervour of his emotions caused early exhaustion.'

The devil's woodyard

We had some difficulty in finding our quest, the Salse, or mud-volcano. But at last, out of a hut half buried in verdure on the edge of a little clearing, there tumbled the quaintest little old black man, cutlass in hand, and, without being asked, went on ahead as our guide. Crook-backed, round-shouldered, his only dress a ragged shirt and ragged pair of drawers, he had evidently thriven upon the forest life for many a year. He did not walk nor run, but tumbled along in front of us, his bare feet splashing from log to log and mud-heap to mud-heap, his grey woolly head wagging right and left, and his cutlass brushing almost instinctively at every bough he passed, while he turned round every moment to jabber something, usually in Creole French, which, of course, I could not understand.

He led us well, up and down, and at last over a flat of rich muddy ground, full of huge trees, and of their roots likewise, where there was no path at all. The solitude was awful; so was the darkness of the shade; so was the stifling heat; and right glad we were when we saw an opening in the trees, and the little man quickened his pace, and stopped with an air of triumph not unmixed with awe on the edge of a circular pool of mud and water some two or three acres in extent.

'Dere de debbil's woodyard,' said he, with somewhat bated breath. And no wonder; for a more doleful, uncanny, half-made spot I never saw. The sad forest ringed it round with a greed wall, feathered down to the ugly mud, on which, partly perhaps from its saltness, partly from the changeableness of the surface, no plant would grow, save a few herbs and creepers which love the brackish water. Only here and there an Echites had crawled out of the wood and lay along the ground, its long shoots gay with large cream-coloured flowers and pairs of glossy leaves; and on it, and on some dead brushwood, grew a lovely little parasitic Orchis, an Oncidium, with tiny fans of leaves, and flowers like swarms of yellow butterflies.

There was no track of man, not even a hunter's footprint; but instead, tracks of beasts in plenty.

Henry Walter Bates

(1825–92)

English naturalist and explorer. Bates started out in the hosiery and brewing trades, but taught himself entomology and in 1848 went to explore the Amazon with Alfred Russel Wallace (q.v.). He remained there for eleven years, collecting over 14,000 zoological specimens, more than half of them previously unknown to science. He and Wallace were guests at an extraordinary dinner party given at

Santarem in 1849 by the wealthy Captain Hislop; all of the most distinguished naturalists of the Amazon were present. Bates suffered from yellow fever and other tropical ailments. He returned home to engage in the discussion of natural selection with a scientific paper on mimicry. He wrote his scientific but extremely readable and dramatically illustrated *A Naturalist on the River Amazons* and became a secretary of the Royal Geographical Society.

Amazonian ants

I will pass over the many other orders and families of insects, and proceed at once to the ants. These were in great numbers everywhere, but I will mention here only two kinds. We were amazed at seeing ants an inch and a quarter in length, and stout in proportion, marching in single file through the thickets.

In our first walks we were puzzled to account for large mounds of earth, of a different colour from the surrounding soil, where were thrown up in the plantations and woods. Some of them were very extensive, being forty yards in circumference, but not more than two feet in height. We soon ascertained that these were the work of the Saübas, being the outworks, or domes, which overlie and protect the entrances to their vast subterranean galleries. On close examination, I found the earth of which they are composed to consist of very minute granules, agglomerated without cement, and forming many rows of little ridges and turrets. The difference in colour from the superficial soil of the vicinity is owing to their being formed of the undersoil, brought up from a considerable depth. It is very rarely that the ants are seen at work on these mounds; the entrances seem to be generally closed; only now and then, when some particular work is going on, are the galleries opened. The entrances are small and numerous; in the larger hillocks it would require a great amount of excavation to get at the main galleries; but I succeeded in removing portions of the dome, in smaller hillocks, and then I found that the minor entrances converged, at the depth of about two feet, to one broad elaborately-worked gallery or mine, which was four or five inches in diameter.

The underground abodes of this wonderful ant are known to be very extensive. The Rev. Hamlet Clark has related that the Saüba of Rio de Janeiro, a species closely allied to ours, has excavated a tunnel under the bed of the river Parahyba, at a place where it is as broad as the Thames at London Bridge. At the Magoary rice mills, near Pará, these ants once pierced the embankment of a large reservoir: the great body of water which it contained escaped before the damage could be repaired. In the Botanic Gardens, at Pará, an enterprising French gardener tried all he could think of to extirpate the Saüba. With this object he made fires over some of the main entrances to their colonies, and blew the fumes of sulphur down the galleries by means of bellows. I saw the smoke issue from a great number of outlets, one of which was seventy yards distant from the place where the bellows were used. This shows how extensively the underground galleries are ramified.

F.B. Head

(fl. 1826)

Scottish engineer who went to Argentina as manager of a gold and silver mining company on the Rio de la Plata, which employed Cornish miners. He travelled over 12,000 miles, mostly on horseback, inspecting mines, a journey made particularly difficult by the extreme variations of the climate.

Journey across the Pampas

I was on duty at Edinburgh, in the corps of Engineers, when it was proposed to me to take charge of an Association, the object of which was to work the Gold and Silver Mines of the Provinces of Rio de la Plata; and, accordingly, at a very few days' notice, I sailed from Falmouth, and landed at Buenos Aires about a week after the Cornish Miners had arrived there.

Accompanied by two highly respectable Captains of the Cornish Mines, a French Assayer, who had been brought up by the celebrated

Vauquelin, a Surveyor, and three miners, I proceeded across the great plains of the Pampas to the Gold Mines of San Luis, and from thence to the Silver Mines of Uspallata which are beyond Mendoza, about a thousand miles from Buenos Aires.

The Pampas Indians

From being constantly on horseback, the Indians can scarcely walk. This may seem singular, but from their infancy they are unaccustomed to it. Living in a boundless plain, it may easily be conceived, that all their occupations and amusements must necessarily be on horseback, and from riding so many hours the legs become weak, which naturally gives a disinclination to an exertion which every day becomes more fatiguing; besides, the pace at which they can skim over the plains on horseback is so swift, in comparison to the rate they could crawl on foot, that the latter must seem a cheerless exertion.

As a military nation they are much to be admired, and their system of warfare is more noble and perfect in its nature than that of any nation in the world. When they assemble, either to attack their enemies, or to invade the country of the Christians, with whom they are now at war, they collect large troops of horses and mares, and then uttering the wild shriek of war, they start at a gallop. As soon as the horses they ride are tired, they vault upon the bare backs of fresh ones, keeping their best until they positively see their enemies. The whole country affords pasture to their horses, and whenever they choose to stop, they have only to kill some mares. The ground is the bed on which from their infancy they have always slept, and they therefore meet their enemies with light hearts and full stomachs, the only advantages which they think men ought to desire.

W.H. Hudson

(1841–1922)

Author and naturalist, born in Buenos Aires; he grew up on ranches on Rio de la Plata. Hudson returned to England in 1869 on account of a weak heart; and lived in dreary boarding houses. Things improved when he moved to Hampshire, a life recounted in *Hampshire Days*, 1903. He wrote beautifully about the natural history of South America and England.

The Magellanic owl

The black horns stood erect, while in the centre of the wheel-shaped head the beak snapped incessantly, producing a sound resembling the clicking of a sewing-machine. This was a suitable setting for a pair of magnificent furious eyes, on which I gazed with a kind of fascination, not unmixed with fear when I remembered the agony of pain suffered on former occasions from sharp, crooked talons driven into me to the bone. The irides were of a bright orange colour, but every time I attempted to approach the bird they kindled into great globes of quivering yellow flame, the black pupils being surrounded by a scintillating crimson light which threw out minute yellow sparks into the air. When I retired from the bird this preternatural fiery aspect would instantly vanish.

The dragon eyes of that Magellanic owl haunt me still, and when I remember them, the bird's death still weighs on my conscience, albeit by killing it I bestowed on it that dusty immortality which is the portion of stuffed specimens in a museum.

Robert Baird

(*fl.* 1849)

Scotsman who set off on a tour of the West Indies and
North America for the sake of his health. He travelled on
Brunel's *Great Western*, the first steamship to cross the
Atlantic, but found the accommodation 'Cabined, cribbed
and confined'. From the West Indies, where he stayed for
some of the time at Government House, Antigua, Baird
continued to Cuba, from the Gulf of Mexico to Mobile
and New Orleans, on up the Mississippi and Ohio rivers
to Cincinnati, then via the Great Lakes to Canada and
back along the Hudson river to New York. Presumably
he had recovered his stamina by this time.

Houses of Havanna

And admirably are the Havanna houses adapted for receiving that free
circulation. The ceilings are in general extremely lofty. The windows
are also wide, and so high that they extend from the ceiling to the floor;
and, being unglazed, and only closed by blinds which do not exclude
the air, there is at all times a free circulation, without which the climate
would be absolutely insupportable. These blinds are but seldom drawn,
even in the evening; and it has a singular effect to a European or
American eye, to observe that, as you walk along the narrow *trottoirs* of
the narrow streets, you occasionally brush clothes with the handsomely
dressed signoras and signores, as they lounge at their evening parties,
or family reunions, leaning against the iron bars which run from the
top to the bottom of their lofty windows, diving them from the street.
The same circumstance – the openness of the windows, and the unfre-
quency of drawn blinds – enables, nay almost compels the passenger,
as he walks along the street, to see the domestic operations and attitudes
of the persons (generally the smaller class of shop and storekeepers)
who occupy the houses fronting the narrower streets. But it is only fair

to add that the privilege is one which is seldom abused, and one an abuse of which would meet with an immediate and indignant check, by the offender being at once given into charge for punishment.

Cecil Gosling

(1870–1944)

British diplomat, latterly Envoy Extraordinary and Minister Plenipotentiary to the Republic of Bolivia. His book, as promised by its title, tells of *Travels and Adventures in Many Lands*.

My mule sucked dry by vampire bats

These vast tropical forests, such as the one we were traversing, are the home of that strange and malignant beast the vampire bat, and we unfortunately did not escape its attentions. We camped one night in a clearing in the forest, so small as to give us only just sufficient space for ourselves and animals, which we tethered to the trees. I slept under my mosquito-net, which I attached to the bough of a tree overhead, and was awakened some hours later by a faint tingling in the toe of my right foot, which had got outside the net. Inspection showed a small round hole and a dark spot of blood or two on my blanket, so probably the vampire, for such it was, had been disturbed at his work by my awakening. But others of his kind were abroad, and not sleeping very well after this, I rose at the first streak of dawn and looked out of my mosquito-net with the intention of calling Carapé to get me a cup of coffee. A strange sight arrested me. The yellow mule, one of the cargo animals, was standing in a most dejected attitude, its withers a mass of dried, coagulated blood, while blood was also streaming down its side on to the ground. "Carapé," I cried, "the *baya* has been mauled by a tiger." My servant's tousled head looked out of the blankets and, gazing at the mule for a moment, he said: "*Por Dios, Patron, si.*" We went up to examine the animal, but found that we were both wrong in our conjecture. The mule was the unfortunate victim of two, or possibly more, vampire bats, and she was literally sucked dry.

Henry Major Tomlinson

(1873–1958)

Tomlinson worked in a shipping office from age of thirteen, and then became a journalist. In 1909, tired of his London life, he caught a tramp steamer at Swansea that sailed to Brazil and then two thousand miles along the Amazon and Madeira rivers, returning via Jamaica and Florida. He was a war correspondent in the 1914–18 war.

In Amazonia

On the Madeira, as elsewhere in the world of the Amazons, some of the forest is on "*terra firme*", as that land is called which is not flooded when the waters rise. There the trees reach their greatest altitude and diameter; it is the region of the *caá-apoam*, the "great woods" of the Indians. A stretch of it shows as a low, vertical bank of clay, a narrow ribbon of yellow earth dividing the water from the jungle. More rarely the river cuts a section through some undulating heights of red conglomerate – heights I call these cliffs, as heights they are in this flat country, though at home they would attract no more attention than would the side of a gravel-pit – and again the bank may be of that cherry and saffron clay which gives a name to Ita-coatiara. On such land the forest of the Madeira is immense, three or four species among the greater trees lording it in the green tumult expansively, always conspicuous where they stand, their huge boles showing in the verdant façade of the jungle as grey and brown pilasters, their crowns rising above the level roof of the forest in definite cupolas. There is one, having a neat and compact dome and a grey, smooth, and rounded trunk, and dense foliage as dark as that of the holm oak; and another, resembling it, but with a flattened and somewhat looser crown. I guessed these two giants to be silk-cottons. Another, which I supposed to be of the leguminous order, had a silvery bole, and a texture of pale green leafage open and light, which at a distance resembled that of the birch. These three trees when assembled and well grown made most stately riverside groups. The trunks were smooth and bare till somewhere near ninety feet from the ground. Palms were intermediate, filling the spaces between them, but the palms stood under the exogens, growing in alcoves of the mass, rising no higher than the beginning of the branches and foliage of their lords. The whole overhanging superstructure of the forest – not a window, an inlet, anywhere there – was rolling clouds of leaves from the lower rims of which vines were catenary, looping from one green cloud to another, or pendent, like the sundered cordage of a ship's rigging. Two other trees were frequent, the *pao mulatto*, with limbs so dark as to look black, and the *castanha*, the Brazil nut tree.

Hiram Bingham

(1876–1956)

American historian, explorer and mountaineer. He retraced Simon Bolivar's march of 1819 across the north coast of South America. With the assistance of a local youth, he became the modern discoverer of Machu Picchu, the ruined Inca city in the Peruvian Andes.

A royal mausoleum

Suddenly I found myself confronted with the walls of ruined houses built of the finest quality of Inca stone work. It was hard to see them for they were partly covered with trees and moss, the growth of centuries, but in the dense shadow, hiding in bamboo thickets and tangled vines, appeared here and there walls of white granite ashlars carefully cut and exquisitely fitted together. We scrambled along through the dense undergrowth, climbing over terrace walls and in bamboo thickets, where our guide found it easier going than I did. Suddenly, without any warning, under a huge overhanging ledge the boy showed me a cave beautifully lined with the finest cut stone. It had evidently been a royal mausoleum. On top of this particular ledge was a semicircular building whose outer wall, gently sloping and slightly curved, bore a striking resemblance to the famous Temple of the Sun in Cuzco. This might also be a temple of the sun. It followed the natural curvature of the rock and was keyed to it by one of the finest examples of masonry I had ever seen. Furthermore it was tied into another beautiful wall, made of very carefully matched ashlars of pure white granite, especially selected for its fine grain. Clearly, it was the work of a master artist. The interior surface of the wall was broken by niches and square stone-pegs. The exterior surface was perfectly simple and unadorned. The lower courses, of particularly large ashlars, gave it a look of solidity. The upper courses, diminishing in size towards the top, lent grace and delicacy to the structure. The flowing lines, the symmetrical arrangement of the ashlars, and the gradual gradation of the courses, combined to produce a wonderful effect, softer and more pleasing than that of the marble temples of the Old World. Owing to the absence of mortar, there were no ugly spaces between the rocks. They might have grown together. On account of the beauty of the white granite this structure surpassed in attractiveness the best Inca walls in Cuzco, which had caused visitors to marvel for four centuries. It seemed like an unbelievable dream. Dimly, I began to realize that this wall and its adjoining semicircular temple over the cave were as fine as the finest stonework in the world.

D.H. Lawrence

(1885–1930)

English poet and novelist. Lawrence was the son of a Nottinghamshire miner and suffered from tuberculosis for most of his life. He travelled in Europe before the First World War, and in 1914 married Frieda von Richtofen, cousin of the German flying baron. This made living in England difficult, and they subsequently led a nomadic life mainly in Italy, America and Mexico; finally returning to Italy.

Mornings in Mexico

One says Mexico: one means, after all, one little town away South in the Republic: and in this little town, one rather crumbly adobe house built round two sides of a garden *patio*: and of this house, one spot on the deep, shady verandah facing inwards to the trees, where there are an onyx table and three rocking-chairs and one little wooden chair, a pot with carnations, and a person with a pen. We talk so grandly, in capital letters, about Morning in Mexico. All it amounts to is one little individual looking at a bit of sky and trees, then looking down at the page of his exercise book.

It is a pity we don't always remember this. When books come out with grand titles, like *The Future of America* or *The European Situation*, it's a pity we don't immediately visualize a thin or a fat person, in a chair or in bed, dictating to a bob-haired stenographer or making little marks on paper with a fountain pen.

Still, it is morning, and it is Mexico. The sun shines. But then, during the winter, it always shines. It is pleasant to sit out of doors and write, just fresh enough, and just warm enough. But then it is Christmas next week, so it ought to be just right.

Market day in Mexico

They are mostly small people, of the Zapotec race: small men with lifted chests and quick, lifted knees, advancing with heavy energy in the midst of dust. And quiet, small, round-headed women running barefoot, tightening their blue *rebozos* round their shoulders, so often with a baby in the fold. The white cotton clothes of the men so white that their faces are invisible places of darkness under their big hats. Clothed darkness, faces of night, quickly, silently, with inexhaustible energy advancing to the town.

And many of the serranos, the Indians from the hills, wearing their little conical black felt hats, seem capped with night, above the straight white shoulders. Some have come far, walking all yesterday in their little black hats and black-sheathed sandals. Tomorrow they will walk back. And their eyes will be just the same, black and bright and wild, in the dark faces. They have no goal, any more than the hawks in the air, and no course to run, any more than the clouds.

Aimé Felix Tschiffley

(1895–1954)

Swiss school teacher turned writer and traveller. He travelled 10,000 miles through three Americas from Buenos Aires to Washington with two horses, Mancha and Gato.

On horseback through South America

Let me start this foreword with an apology. I am well aware that critics may, and probably will, find fault with the style of writing. For that I apologise, but it is unavoidable. I have no pretensions to being a writer, and have only done my best to give an accurate description of the countries through which I passed and the many and varied types of people whom I met.

I rode some 10,000 miles in two and a half years. From Argentina I came north, over cold, barren 16,000-foot ranges; then down into steamy jungles, across the Isthmus of Panama, up through Central America and Mexico, and so to the United States.

I reached Washington with the same two horses with which I started – ponies that were 15 and 16 years old when my ride began.

Remote from cities and seaports – far from white men's haunts – ran much of my lonely trail. One night camp might be pitched far from any human habitation; again, I ate and slept with ancient Indian tribes in stone villages older than the Incas.

Of high adventures, hair-breadth escapes, and deeds of daring, there were few; yet in all the annals of exploration I doubt if any traveller, not excepting Marco Polo himself, had more leisure than I to see and understand the people, the animals and plant life of the countries traversed.

Peter Fleming

(1907–71)

English writer, soldier and traveller, the brother of Ian Fleming. As a journalist, Fleming interviewed Chiang Kai-Shek for *The Times*. In 1935 he and Ella Maillart travelled 3500 miles through China on foot and pony. They travelled through the forbidden provinces of Sinkiang. He made many other journeys including, in 1932, a 3000-mile amateur expedition to find the lost explorer, Colonel H.P. Fawcett who had disappeared in the Matto Grosso region of the Amazon in 1925. 'Our ignorance of Portuguese, like our lack of a fish-hook, was a constant source of irritation,' he commented.

Amazonian cross-roads

We reached the mouth of the Tapirapé in the third week in August and camped opposite it, at the foot of a little conical hill on the shores of the island of Bananal, the largest effluvial island in the world.

I remember that little hill with affection. It was not more than 300 feet high, but it was the first eminence of any sort that we had seen since we dropped down into the river valley at Leopoldina three weeks before. Somehow it made a great difference. The wide impersonal river had become a prison. The wider it got, the more marked, the more oppressive, grew the sense of captivity. The emptiness of our horizons had created in me a need which was not acknowledged until the little hill satisfied it. It added, almost, another dimension to our world. It belonged to the order of eternal, reassuring things from which we were indefinitely parted but of which we did not consciously feel the lack: things like Saturdays, and bacon, and bare branches against a grey sky. I was grateful for the little hill.

Roger and I climbed one of the trees which crowned it. Below us, half a mile away, was the mouth of the Tapirapé; a sufficiently romantic-looking mouth, with a little island set in the middle of it. Beyond the mouth the silver coils of the river writhed mysteriously westward through dense jungle. We were encouraged by the sight of what looked like big stretches of open country breaking the green opacity of the forest. Far away to the north-west – how far, in that hazy light, we could not even guess – we could see high ground which was not marked on our map and which, indeed, since our course thereafter lay south-west, we never identified.

Martha Gellhorn

(1908–98)

American journalist and writer who met and married Ernest Hemingway while reporting on the Spanish Civil War. In a distinguished career, Gellhorn reported on wars in Java, Vietnam, the Middle East and Central America.

Voodoo in Haiti

The waiter invited me to the Voodoo ceremony. I was flattered and interested: exotic mysteries in the Haitian jungle. In those days Voodoo was a secret religion; now it figures in a popular TV serial. Slaves, in the seventeenth century in Haiti, invented Voodoo from confused West African tribal memories. Voodoo remains the true religion of the peasants, the majority of Haitians. That night, in a crumbling shack lit by kerosene lamps, I wondered whether these barefoot ragged people looked much different from their slave ancestors. The priest, a bony fiery-eyed man in a cloak and trousers, crouched and cavorted, tracing magical signs on the dirt floor, but kept a calculating eye on the believers. He seemed a dubious manipulator. A woman, another woman, a man, became possessed by a Voodoo god and thrashed about violently, ran, staggered, shouting in unintelligible unnatural voices. If enough people ended up foaming and fainting, presumably the priest was a success. The result of all the chanting and drumming and hysteria was fear. I could see it on the faces around me. When the priest grabbed a squawking chicken, preparatory to biting off its head in sacrifice, I moved silently out the door.

Sybille Bedford

(1911–)

English writer, born in Charlottenberg, Germany. As a young girl, Bedford was taken to Italy and then the South of France, where she spent an idyllic life, mixing with artists and writers, including Aldous Huxley whose biography, *A Legacy*, she wrote. She became a legal reporter, and covered the Auschwitz trials. Her book, *A Visit to Don Ottavio*, is the engaging account of a journey to Mexico.

Train to Mazatlán

That night I lay in my bunk across from where Madame Crapaude's daughters had squeezed themselves into one upper, dozing wakefully, lucid and lonely. The train jerked, pitched, halted, in our slow advance over one of the world's most uninhabited mountain passes. *Que diable allais-je chercher dans cette galère?*

We were due at Mazatlán at 5 am; in itself a prospect not conducive to a quiet night's rest. The stops became longer. At last I decided we were going to be late, and fell asleep. I was woken by voices. Cannot get through, I heard. Line's washed away; we'll have to go back. And indeed after another wait the train began to reverse. It had become impossibly stuffy inside the bunks, so by six o'clock everybody was up and dressed, sticky and dirty with only a tepid trickle to wash under in the stinking lavatory, and ready to face the situation. No one knew what that was. Engine trouble, said some. A bridge was down. There had been floods though the rains *ought* to be over, and the line was under water. A local tribe, inimical to railways, had tampered with the ties. Meanwhile we had gone back a stretch and come to a halt in what the breaking light of day revealed to be a swamp; a further light, a supposed station.

The name RUIZ was peeling off a board nailed to a degraded hut, housing no doubt some signals and the stationmaster's family. This hut was the extent of the station buildings. There were no further huts, no platform, no facilities; no village in sight. There was no shelter of any kind. We were now across the Sierra Madre, and Ruiz would be in Nayarít, the territory of the Nayarítos, the only aborigines who managed to dawdle over their conversion to the Catholic faith from the Conquest well into the eighteenth century, and Nayarít lay in the coastal plains and therefore in the hot zone. Even at that early hour there was no need of such geography to make it clear that this was going to be as hot a day as any of us had ever feared to live through. Mosquitoes, too, were already up and about. A number of pigs now assembled round the train, and presently boarded it, looking and begging for food. They were dripping with liquid yellow mud. Information as to the length of our sojourn at Ruiz was not unanimous. Some said six hours, some ten; some said we would leave at midday, some at nightfall. Some said next morning, others in three days. The last train from the North had been four days late. There was also the hypothesis that we would be returned to Guadalajara. None of this was improbable.

Lawrence Durrell

(1912–90)

Writer and poet; he also worked as a press attaché in Greece, Cairo, Alexandria and Cyprus.

One eats endless beef and is so bored one could scream

You envy us? Argentina is a large flat melancholy and rather superb-looking country full of stale air, blue featureless sierras, and businessmen drinking Coca-Cola. One eats endless beef and is so bored one could scream. It is the most lazy-making climate I have struck: not as bad as

Egypt, of course: but I'd give a lifetime of Argentina for three weeks of Greece, fascist or no fascist. Here one is submerged in dull *laisser faire* and furious boredom. People quite nice in a very superficial and childish way. I think the States would be better. However I'm contracted for a year so I can't think of escape until next March. The only fun is horse-back riding which we do plenty of – across the blue sierras, *à la* Zane Grey. But it's all very dreary really. As for the meat it's rapidly driving me vegetarian.

Hydrographic Department of the Admiralty

The British Admiralty established its Hydrographic Department in 1795, and two years later produced its first navigational chart. It eventually published complete guides to the watery surfaces of the globe, in the public interest. These covered navigational tables, tidal currents and streams, deep sea soundings, indexes of stars and 'methods of clearing lunar distance', lists of lights, local climate, general dangers, the whereabouts of supplies, buoys, pilots and tugboats, quarantine regulations, fog patches and the perils of driftwood in the Amazon Basin. This list gives but a slight indication of their usefulness.

South Patagonia, Tierra del Fuego and Cape Horn

South Patagonia and the Islands includes the region embracing the Strait of Magellan and the Patagonian channels westward of it, with the mainland and islands bordering on them.

Mountainous and rocky, intersected by deep and tortuous fiords of a complexity unsurpassed elsewhere, and with a climate more continu-ously tempestuous and rainy than any other part of the world, the greater part of the Magellanic area is inhabited by savages of the lowest civilisation, and offers but few inducements to the European beyond the facilities the channels afford for smooth water passage from the Atlantic to the Pacific.

Natives – The natives of Tierra del Fuego are known as Onas; they appear to be an intermediate race between the large-sized Patagonians and the stunted Fuegians; they have no canoes, and live largely on the produce of hunting; they are rapidly decreasing in number, and in 1910 there were estimated to be only about 225 remaining. A report made in 1912 states that there are no Indians in Tierra del Fuego.

The natives of the Beagle channel and the islands to the southward are known as Yahgans; they pass most of their time in their canoes; like the Onas they are a dwindling race, and in 1911 numbered only 180.

Tierra del Fuego and Cape Horn – Fogs are rare on the coast of Tierra del Fuego and in the vicinity of Cape Horn, but thick rainy weather prevails, with strong winds, the sky even in moderate weather being generally overcast and cloudy; a clear day is a rare occurrence.

Gales of wind often succeed each other at short intervals, and last several days. The weather may be fine and settled for perhaps a fortnight occasionally, but this is rare. Westerly winds prevail during the greater part of the year. Easterly winds occur chiefly in the winter months, and are then strong; they seldom occur in summer.

Winds from the eastward invariably begin gently, and are accompanied at first with fine weather; as they gradually increase the weather changes, and a determined heavy gale is often the result. More frequently, however, they rise to a strong breeze, then die away gradually, or shift to another quarter, showing that the disturbance causing them has passed to the northward.

Gales from the southward, and squalls from the south-west, are preceded, and may be foretold, by heavy banks of large white clouds rising in those quarters, having hard edges, and appearing rounded and solid.

Gales from the southward are heaviest and most lasting, but they do not shift.

Sailing vessels – Sailing vessels bound from the Atlantic to the Pacific should keep within 100 miles of the eastern coast of Patagonia . . .

Mr J.M. Gray, commanding the British barque *Shun Lee*, from long experience recommends that sailing vessels from the northward should not attempt to enter the strait until one hour after high water. He states that it is his practice on arriving near the strait to wait 5 or 6 miles to the northward, until a little after high water. Also, that in March, 1881, he entered the strait at that time of tide, and although it was blowing a gale from the south-west the ship drove through rapidly.

Northerly and north-easterly winds are often accompanied by thick, misty weather; vessels approaching the strait are thus often compelled to lie-to for a time.

Rounding Cape Horn – The days being short, and the weather cold, make June and July unpleasant, though they are, perhaps, the best months for making a passage to the westward, as the wind is then often in the eastern quarter. During the summer months good passages have been made into the Pacific by going as far south as the parallel of 60°. April, May, and June, are preferable, and fair passages have been made in these months by keeping nearer to the land and sighting the Islas Diego Ramirez. August and September are bad months, heavy gales with snow and hail occurring about the equinox; good passages are said to have been made at this season by going as far south as 60°.

After passing Staten island, if the wind be westerly, the vessel should be kept upon the starboard tack, unless it veers to the southward of SSW, until in latitude 60° S, then on the tack upon which most westing may be made. On this parallel the wind is thought by some persons to prevail more from the eastward than any other quarter.

CAUTION – Off Cape St John, the eastern point of Staten island, a heavy tide-rip extends for a distance of 5 or 6 miles, or even more, to seaward. When the wind is strong and opposed to the tidal stream, the overfalls are overwhelming, and very dangerous, even to a large and well-found vessel. Seamen must use every precaution to avoid this perilous area.

Ben Box

(1952–)

Ben Box is the author of many travel guidebooks. Footprint's *Handbook to South America* has been published
annually since 1924 and is regarded as essential luggage
for travellers to the region.

Darién and how to get to Colombia in 1990

By Land – The Pan-American Highway runs E 60 km from Panama
City to the sizeable town of *Chepo*, full of friendly blacks. From Chepo
the Highway has been completed to Yaviza, 240 km from Panama City;
it is gravel from Chepo until the last 30 km which are of earth (sometimes
impassable in rainy season). 35 km E of Chepo it crosses the new Lago
Bayano dam by the bridge (the land to the N of the Highway as far as
Cañazas is the Reserve Indigena del Bayano). The road will eventually
link Panama with Colombia. (Bus to Chepo from Panama City leaves
from Plaza 5 de Mayo.)

Darién – East of Chepo is Darién, almost half the area of Panama and
almost undeveloped. Most villages are accessible only by air or river
and on foot. At Bahia Piñas is the *Tropic Star Lodge*, where a luxury
fishing holiday may be enjoyed on the sea and in the jungle for over
$1000 a week. (Information from *Hotel el Panamá*.)

The Darién Gap road will not be open for some years, so the usual
way of getting to Colombia is by sea or air. It is possible to go overland:
the journey is in fact more expensive than going by air, and while still
challenging, the number of travellers going overland is increasing . . .
The main villages . . . have electricity, radios and cassette decks, canned
food is available in Yaviza, Pucuro and Paya (but no gasoline), only the
Chocó Indians and the Cuna women retain traditional dress. Prices are
rising steeply and friendliness is declining; the route is also used for
drug trafficking, with its attendant tensions.

There are 5 buses from Panama to Yaviza between 0600 and 1200, US$15, 10 hrs. This service has its problems, the road is bad and may be washed out after rains. Find out before you leave how far you can get. Alternatively there is an irregular boat, about three times a week. The only sleeping accommodation is the deck and there is one primitive toilet for about 120 people. The advertised travel time is 16 hours, but it can take as much as 28.

Hugh Thomson

(1960–)

English documentary film maker. In 1982 Thomson went to South America to rediscover Inca ruins in the footsteps of Hiram Bingham (**q.v.**) and other explorers. *The White Rock* is Chuquipalta, deep in Vilcabamba. He has also made a film about Cortes' invasion of Mexico for the BBC.

Return to Cuzco

Landing again at Cuzco in 1999 was a shock. The population of the city had tripled since 1982. The old airport had been in an isolated field: the new improved one was already surrounded by fast growing suburbs.

My young taxi-driver Carlos was intrigued that I'd been away for so long (he couldn't have been born long much before I left). 'The city used to be *chiquissimo*,' he said, using the affectionate diminutive, 'now it's *grandote*.' But the heart of the city, the area around the Plaza de Armas, was much the same as ever, a mixture of stately colonial architecture and tourist opportunism. It was with some embarrassment that Carlos gave me his card, emblazoned with the slogan 'Magical Mystery Tours'. 'It's just the name of the travel agency I work for,' he explained, 'nothing to do with the Beatles.'

The hotels had changed out of all recognition, as had my need to stay in the cheapest. I checked out a few. The El Dorado looked like something out of Las Vegas: in the entrance hall, the lift-shaft was completely free-standing and had been plastered to look like a tree rising up into a cavernous space – the corridors ran like branches off the 'tree' to bedrooms that were lit with startling neon pinks and reds. Soft new-age muzak was piped into every room. '*Algo un poco diferente?* A little different, isn't it?' murmured the porter who showed me around.

Thomson, Ian

(1961–)

Writer, Italian translator and biographer.

"*I am going to the fingers*"

We left the Carré d'As at half past eleven; not one star showed in the curtain of cloud, it was a night without light. Aliès carried a lamp fashioned from a condensed-milk can.

'Pick up some of these,' he advised, bending to gather a handful of stones. 'There are bad dogs round here.'

Presently we gained the Avenue Privert where a pack of tawny pariahs came out of the shadows by the Mormon church, snapping and barking at our approach. Aliès flung a missile in their midst and it struck with a dullish thud.

'Dogs should be considered a natural hazard,' he said stiffly. 'Like werewolves.'

The road took us into a clearing of forest.

'How far now to Monsieur Mortelle?'

'His people are coming,' Aliès replied with apparent irrelevance, and then: 'Stand still!'

There was a smell in the air of rubber smouldering and I could hear a low chanting of voices which grew louder as a group of men and women, twelve or so, materialised from deep within the forest. They moved at the pace of a funeral cortège, bearing torches made of palm branches that burned with a fierce flame. These were the diabolical noctambulists of Bizango and they wore black trousers or skirts with a large black cross stitched to their red shirts.

'Order and respect for the night!' Aliès said in a loud firm voice.

A man bearing a banner of black and red (the colours, incidentally, of the Haitian flag under Papa Doc) came forward and repeated: 'Order and respect for the night!'

There followed a complicated procedure of handshakes and *mots de passage*, passwords.

'Who are you?'

'*Bêtes Sereines*. Animals of the Evening Dew,' Aliès answered.

'Who is your God?'

'Baron Cimetière.'

'Where are you coming from?'

'I come from the fist.'

'Where are you going?'

'I am going to the fingers.'

One may laugh in retrospect; at the time I was frankly terrified.

Australasia

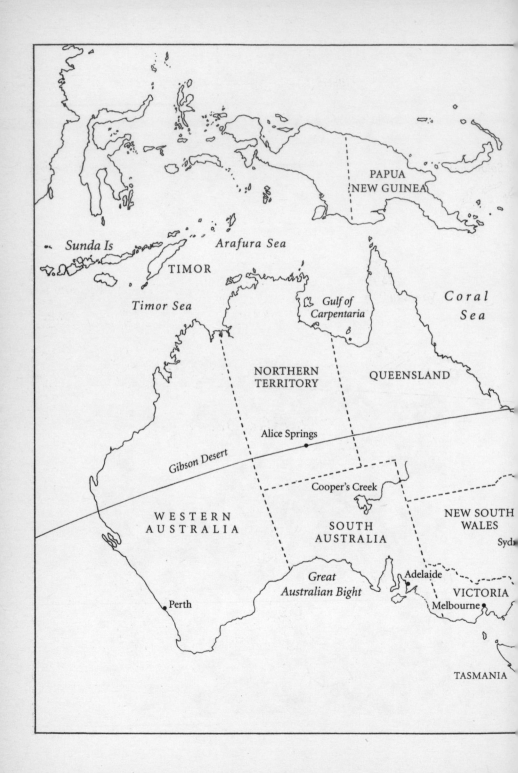

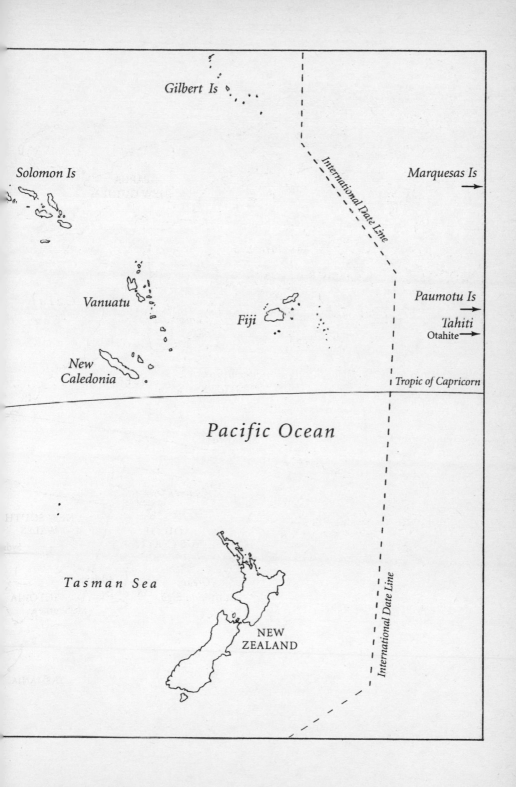

Gilbert Is

Solomon Is

Marquesas Is →

International Date Line

Vanuatu

Fiji

Paumotu Is →

Tahiti →
Otahite

New
Caledonia

Tropic of Capricorn

Pacific Ocean

Tasman Sea

NEW
ZEALAND

International Date Line

Captain James Cook

(1728–79)

English explorer and navigator. The son of a farm labourer, Cook taught himself mathematics, astronomy and navigation and joined the Royal Navy. His first voyage was to survey the coasts of Labrador, Newfoundland and Labrador. Cook subsequently circumnavigated the world three times. The first expedition, in 1768–71, was a journey to observe the transit of Venus across the sun at Tahiti. Besides observing Venus, Cook charted the coast of New Zealand, sailed to eastern Australia, through the Torres Straits to Batavia, returning via the Cape of Good Hope. On his second voyage, Cook mapped the Pacific and disproved the idea of a Southern Continent. He reached Easter Island and was greeted with great celebrations, including fireworks, on his return to Tahiti. His third voyage was intended to find the elusive northerly passage from the Pacific side. Cook corrected previously inaccurate maps of the northwest coast of America, reaching Nootka Sound at 49° 33' and the edge of the continent at the Bering Strait, turning back only when they reached solid ice. After an unfortunate series of incidents, Cook was killed by natives in Hawaii.

A second discovery of New Zealand

On 10 February, at four in the afternoon, we discovered the land of New Zealand; and soon after came to an anchor in Queen Charlotte's Sound. Here several canoes filled with natives came alongside of the ships; but very few of them would venture on board, which appeared the more extraordinary as I was well known by them all. There was one man in particular among them whom I had treated with remarkable kindness during the whole of my stay when I was last there. Yet now, neither professions of friendship nor presents would prevail upon him to come into the ship. This shyness was to be accounted for only on the supposition that they were apprehensive we had revisited their country in order to revenge the death of Captain Furneaux's people.

Sir Joseph Banks

(1743–1820)

Botanist, natural historian and President of the Royal Society from 1778–1820. Banks travelled in Newfoundland and Labrador and then accompanied Captain Cook on his voyage round the world on the *Endeavour* in 1768–71. Made a substantial financial contribution to the expedition and supplied many of its scientific instruments. On the journey, Banks made botanical collections and was responsible for the transplanting of fruits such as the mango and breadfruit around the world.

Surfing at Otahite (May 1769)

29th. We saw the Indians amuse or exercise themselves in a manner truly surprising. It was in a place where the shore was not guarded by a reef, as is usually the case, consequently a high surf fell upon the shore, and a more dreadful one I have not often seen; no European boat could have landed in it, and I think no European who had by any means got into it could possibly have saved his life, as the shore was covered with pebbles and large stones. In the midst of these breakers ten or twelve Indians were swimming. Whenever a surf broke near them they dived under it with infinite ease, rising upon the other side; but their chief amusement was being carried on by an old canoe; with this before them they swam out as far as the outermost beach, then one or two would get into it, and opposing the blunt end to the breaking wave, were hurried in with incredible swiftness. Sometimes they were carried almost ashore, but generally the wave broke over them before they were half-way, in which case they dived and quickly rose on the other side with the canoe in their hands. It was then towed out again, and the same method repeated. We stood admiring this very wonderful scene for fully half an hour, in which time no one of the actors attempted to come ashore, but all seemed most highly entertained with their strange diversion.

A building made of coral

We afterwards took a walk towards a point on which we had from afar observed trees of *etoa (Casuarina equisetifolia)*, from whence we judged that there would be some *marai* in the neighbourhood; nor were we disappointed, for we had no sooner arrived there than we were struck with the sight of a most enormous pile, certainly the masterpiece of Indian architecture in this island, and so all the inhabitants allowed. Its size and workmanship almost exceed belief. Its form was similar to that of *marais* in general, resembling the roof of a house, not smooth at the sides, but formed into eleven steps, each of these four feet in height, making in all 44 feet; its length was 267 feet, its breadth 71 feet. Every one of these steps was formed of white coral stones, most of them neatly squared and polished; the rest were round pebbles, but these, from their uniformity of size and roundness, seemed to have been worked. Some of the coral stones were very large, one I measured was 3½ by 2½ feet. The foundation was of rock stone, likewise squared; the corner-stone measured 4 feet 7 inches by 2 feet 4 inches. The building made part of one side of a spacious area walled in with stone; the size of this, which seemed to be intended for a square, was 118 by 110 paces, and it was entirely paved with flat paving-stones. It is almost beyond belief that Indians could raise so large a structure without the assistance of iron tools to shape their stones or mortar to join them; which last appears almost essential, as most of them are round: but it is done, and almost as firmly as an European workman would have done it, though in some things they seem to have failed. The steps for instance, which range along its greatest length, are not straight; they bend downward in the middle, forming a small segment of a circle. Possibly the ground may have sunk a little under the immense weight of such a great pile; such a sinking, if it took place regularly, would have this effect. The labour of the work is prodigious, the quarried stones are but few . . .

George Robertson

(fl. 1760s)

English sailor and from 1766–78, Master of the *Dolphin*, a sixth-rate man-of-war which had previously carried Commodore John Byron who took possession of the Falkland Islands. The ship landed on Pacific atolls, where the crew recovered their health with scurvy grass and coconuts. Looking for the Southern Continent, the expedition discovered Tahiti. 'This made us all rejoice and fild us with the greatest hopes imaginable.' During their stay, they witnessed an eclipse of the sun and Robertson was able to help the Queen of Tahiti observe it through his dark Glass.

The girls of Tahiti

But our Young men seeing several very handsome Young girls, they could not help feasting their eyes with so agreeable a sight and this was observed by some of the Elderly men, and several of the Young Girls was drawn out, some a light coper colour oythers a mullato, and some almost White. The old men made them stand in Rank, and made signs for our people to take which they lyked best, and as many as they lyked and for fear our men hade been Ignorant and not known how to use the poor young Girls, the old men made signs how we should behave to the Young women, this all the boats crew seemd to understand perfectly well, and begd the Officer would receive a few of the Young Women onboard, at same time they made signs to the young Girls, that they were no so Ignorant as the old men supposed them, this seemd to please the Old men Greatly when they saw our people merry, but the poor young Girls seemd a little afraid, but soon after turnd better aquanted.

The Officer in the boat having no orders to bring off any of the natives, would not receive the Young Girls but made signs that he would see them afterwards, and Orderd all our men on bd the Boats, and returnd onbd the Ship, when our boats returned to the ship all the sailors swore they neaver saw handsomer made women in their lives, and declard they would all to a man, live on two thirds allowance, rather nor lose so fine an opportunity of geting a Girl apiece – this piece of news made all our men madly fond of the shore, even the sick which hade been on the Doctors list for some weeks before, now declard they would be happy if they were permited to go ashore, at same time said a Young Girl would make an Excelent Nurse, and they were Certain of recovering faster under a Young Girls care nor all the Doctor would do for them, we past this Night very merry supposing all hostilitys was now over and to our great joy it so happend.

Allan Cunningham

(1791–1839)

English botanist and explorer who arrived in Sydney via Brazil, where he was botanist on the *Beagle* expedition. Cunningham joined the surveying expedition of the Australian coast under Philip Parker King (**q.v.**), and later led his own expeditions to investigate the interior of eastern Australia. In 1827, he discovered the Darling Downs, the best grazing country in Queensland, and the Cunningham Gap – the way to it through the Great Dividing Range. He continued to make important botanical collections on this and other expeditions; in 1817 alone he discovered 450 new plant species.

Through the Gap

At about 2¾ miles the ridge bends to the northward of west, and immediately the summit of the pass appeared broad before us, bounded on each side by most stupendous heads. These heads were towering at least 2000 feet above the Gap.

Here the difficulties of the passage commenced. We had arrived at the actual foot of the pass without the smallest difficulty; it remained to ascend, by a steep slope, to the level of its entrance. This slope is occupied by a very close wood, in which red cedar, sassafras, palms and other ornamental trees are frequent. Through this shaded wood we climbed up a steep bank of very rich, loose earth where a very compact rock (of white stone) is embedded. At length we gained the foot of a wall of bare rock which we found stretching from the southward into the Pass.

This face of naked rock we perceived (by tracing its base northerly) gradually to fall to the common level; so, that, without the smallest difficulty, and to my utmost surprise, we found ourselves in the highest part of the Pass, having fully ascertained the extent of the difficult part, from the entrance into the wood, to this point, not to exceed 400 yards. We now pushed our way westerly through this extraordinary defile, and, in less than half a mile of level surface, clothed with a thick brush of plants common to the Brisbane River, reached the opposite side of the main range, where I observed the waters fell westerly to Millar's Valley beneath us.

Sir Thomas Livingstone Mitchell

(1792–1855)

Australian explorer, born in Scotland. After serving in the Peninsula War, Mitchell became Surveyor-General to the government of New South Wales, surveying the route to the western plains and Bathurst. Mitchell made four expeditions to the interior of eastern Australia; on the third he found the junction of the Darling and Murray rivers and followed the Glenelg river to the sea. He also tried to find an overland route to the Gulf of Carpentaria and discovered the sources of the Barcoo river in Queensland.

A cold night in the desert

At this camp, where we lay shivering for want of fire, the different habits of the aborigines and us, strangers from the north, were strongly contrasted. On that freezing night, the natives, according to their usual custom, stript off all their clothes, previous to lying down to sleep in the open air, their bodies being doubled up around a few burning reeds. We could not understand how they could lay thus naked, when the earth was white with hoar frost; and they were equally at a loss to know, how we could sleep in our tents without a bit of fire to keep our bodies warm. For the support of animal heat, fire and smoke are almost as necessary to them, as clothes are to us. The naked savage, however, is not without some reason on his side, for fire is the only means he possesses to warm his body when cold, and it is, therefore, the only comfort he ever knows; whereas we require both fire and clothing, and have no conception of the intensity of enjoyment imparted to the naked body of a savage by the glowing embrace of a cloud of smoke in winter. In summer also, he may enjoy, unrestrained by dress, the luxury of a bath in any pool, when not content with the refreshing breeze that fans his sensitive body during the intense heat. Amidst all this exposure, the skin of the Australian native remains as smooth and soft as velvet, and it is not improbably, that the obstructions of drapery would constitute the greatest of his objections, in such a climate, to the permanent adoption of a civilized life.

Philip Parker King

(1793–1856)

King was born on Norfolk Island, where his father was governor. He joined the navy, and in 1817–22 conducted survey of Coast of Australia and Tasmania, mainly in an inadequate boat. He then surveyed the southern coast of South America.

Memorandum

The following will be among the most important subjects, on which it will be more immediately your providence, assisted by your officers, to endeavour to obtain information on any occasion which may offer.

The general nature of the climate, as to heat, cold moisture, winds, rains, periodical seasons; the temperature regularly registered from Fahrenheit's thermometer, as observed at two or three periods of the day.

The direction of the mountains, their names, general appearance as to shape; whether detached or continuous in ranges.

The animals, whether birds, beasts, or fishes; insects, reptiles, &c., distinguishing those that are wild from those which are domesticated.

The vegetables, and particularly those that are applicable to any useful purposes, whether in medicine, dyeing, carpentry, &c.; any scented or ornamental woods, adapted for cabinet work and household furniture, and more particularly such woods as may appear to be useful in shipbuilding; hard woods for tree-nails, block-sheaves, &c., of all which it would be desirable to procure small specimens labelled and numbered, so that an easy reference may be made to them in the journal, to ascertain the quantities in which they are found; the facility or otherwise of floating them down to a convenient place for shipment, &c.

Minerals, any of the precious metals, or stones; how used, or valued by the natives.

The description and characteristic difference of the several tribes or people on the coast.

The occupation and means of subsistence, whether chiefly, or to what extent by fishing, hunting, feeding sheep or other animals, by agriculture or by commerce.

The principal objects of their pursuits, as mentioned in the preceding paragraphs.

A circumstantial account of such articles growing on the sun-coast, if any, as might be advantageously imported into Great Britain, and those that would be required by the natives in exchange for them.

The state of the arts, or manufactures, and their comparative perfection in different tribes.

A vocabulary of the language spoken by every tribe with which you may meet, using in the compilation of much the same English words.

Charles Sturt

(1795–1869)

British soldier, born in India, and regarded by many as the 'father of Australian exploration'. After serving in the Napoleonic wars, Sturt was sent to Australia in charge of a group of convicts. He went on to lead three major expeditions from Sydney, and became the first person to explore the Darling and lower Murray Rivers. In 1844 he attempted to reach the centre of the continent, with fifteen men including Stuart (q.v.). The exceptional temperatures reached 57° Centigrade; the animals needed a thousand gallons of water a day, the men's hair and the wool on the sheep ceased to grow, the lead dropped out of their pencils, the ink in their pens dried as they wrote. Like other explorers of Australia, they suffered terribly from scurvy. Eventually, the attempt was abandoned; Sturt's eyesight was irretrievably damaged, and he eventually retired to Cheltenham.

Journey to the Centre

I regret to add, that the effects of the sun on the plain over which we passed on the 23d produced a return of inflammation in the eyes of the men, I have named in my journals, and caused the same in the eyes of several others of my party. I halted, therefore, to expedite their recovery. They are doing well now, and we can proceed in the cool of the morning without any fear of their receiving injury by it. One of the men, who were to return to Wellington Valley, was attacked slightly with dysentery, but the medicines I gave him carried it off in the course of a day or two. I have taken every precaution with regard to the health of the men, in preparing them for the country into which they are going; and I have to request that you will inform the governor that the conduct of the whole party merits my approbation, and that I have no fault to find. The men from Sydney are not so sharp as those from Wellington Valley, but are equally well disposed. The animals, both horses and bullocks, are in good order, and I find the two soldiers of infinite service to me. The boat has received some damage from exposure to intense heat, but is otherwise uninjured. We still retain the carriage, and have every prospect of dragging it on with us.

Peter Egerton Warburton

(1813–1939)

Australian explorer, Indian army officer and commissioner of police. At the age of sixty, Warburton travelled a thousand miles from Adelaide to Alice Springs, then set off for the Indian ocean during a drought, with his son, a surveyor, two Afghan camel drivers, a cook, an aboriginal boy and seventeen camels. The camels all died or ran away; those that collapsed were eaten; every bit was boiled up 'until it became like the inside of a carpenter's glue pot'. The party just about survived to become the first to cross to the West Coast.

"We have tried to do our duty"

We are at our last drop of water, and the smallest bit of dried meat choked me. I fear my son must share my fate, as he will not leave me. God have mercy upon us, for we are brought very low, and by the time death reaches us we shall not regret exchanging our present misery for that state in which the weary are at rest.

We have tried to do our duty, and have been disappointed in all our expectations. I have been in excellent health during the whole journey, and am so still, being merely worn out from want of food and water. Let no self-reproaches afflict any one respecting me. I undertook the journey for the benefit of my family, and I was quite equal to it under all the circumstances that could be reasonably anticipated, but difficulties and losses have come upon us so thickly for the last few months that we have not been able to move; thus our provision are gone, but this would not have stopped us could we have found water without such laborious search. The country is terrible. I do not believe men ever traversed so vast an extent of continuous desert . . .

13th – My rear party could only advance eight miles, when the camels gave in. Our food is scanty enough, but our great want is water. We have a little, but dare not take more than a spoonful at a time, while the heat is so great that the slightest exposure and exertion bring on a parching thirst. We are as low and weak as living men well can be, and our only hope of prolonging our lives is in the advance-party finding some native camp; we have seen smokes, but are in too crippled a state to go to them.

14th – Early this morning my son took our man White, and started in the direction of the smoke we had last seen. At midday, whilst I was sipping in solitude a drop of water out of a spoon, Lewis came up with a bag of water. Never shall I forget the draught of water I then got, but I was so weak that I almost fainted shortly after drinking it.

Augustus Earle

(fl. 1815–31)

English artist and traveller, known as 'the wandering painter'. Earle spent nine years wandering the world from Europe to South America and was stranded for six weeks on the desolate island of Tristan da Cunha. His experience of New Zealand was apparently not much more cheerful. Earle went on to India and south Asia; some of the paintings he did there were turned into panoramas. He survived these adventures to become draughtsman alongside Darwin on the historic voyage of HMS *Beagle*.

A night to remember in New Zealand

It proved a rainy, miserable night; and we were a large party, crowded into a small smoky hut, with a fire lighted in the middle; as, after our supper, the natives, in order to have as much of our company as possible, crowded in till it was literally crammed. However annoying this might be, still I was recompensed by the novelty and picturesque appearance of the scene. Salvator Rosa could not have conceived a finer study of the horrible. A dozen men, of the largest and most athletic forms, their cakahoos (or mat-dresses) laid aside, and their huge limbs exposed to the red glare of the fire; their faces rendered hideous by being tattooed all over, showing by the fire-light quite a bright blue; their eyes, which are remarkable for their fierce expression, all fixed upon us, but with a look of good temper, commingled with intense curiosity. All my fears had by this time subsided, and being master of myself, I had leisure to study and enjoy the scene; we smoked a social pipe with them (for they are all immoderately fond of tobacco), and then I stretched myself down to sleep amidst all their chattering and smoke.

But all my attempts at slumber were fruitless. I underwent simultaneous attack of vermin of all descriptions; fleas, musketoes and sandflies, which, beside their depredations on my person, made such a buzzing noise, that even the chattering of the natives could not drown it, or the smoke from the fire or pipes drive them away.

John McDouall Stuart

(1815–66)

Scottish-born explorer of Australia. Stuart trained as an engineer, and became a survey draughtsman when he reached Australia. He joined Sturt's expedition of 1844, then led six expeditions into the interior of Australia, becoming the first man to reach the geographical centre of the continent, on 23 April 1860, with only two men and thirteen horses. Stuart was also the first to return alive from crossing it from south to north in 1860, although for part of the journey he had to be carried on a horse-stretcher, until the horse collapsed. His health never recovered, and he died in extremely modest circumstances, having mapped a route later followed by the telegraph, railway and highways.

Explorations in Australia

Saturday, 7 April, Rain Water under Sandstone Hills. Started on the same course 330°, over low sand rises and spinifex, for six miles. It then became a plain of red soil, with mulga bushes, and for several miles was as fine a grassed country as any one would wish to look at; it could be cut with a scythe. Dip of the country to the east, sand hills to the west afterwards it became alternate sand hills and grassy plains, mulga, mallee, and black oak. From the top of one of the sand hills, I can see a range which our line will cut; I shall make to the foot of that to-night, and I expect I shall find a creek with water there. Proceeded through another long plain sloping towards the creek, and covered with grass. At about one miles from the creek we again met with sand hills and spinifex, which continued to it. Arrived and camped; found water. It is very broad, with a sandy bottom, which will not retain water long; beautiful grass on both banks. Wind east, and cool.

Robert O'Hara Burke

(1821–61)

Irish adventurer who joined first the Austrian Army, then the Irish Mounted Constabulary, and finally the police force in Australia. In 1860 he led an expedition across the Continent from north to south, from Cooper's Creek to the Gulf of Carpentaria, in competition with McDouall Stuart. The expedition was the most expensive ever organised in Australia, and the first to use camels. Choosing to travel light, Burke recklessly discarded equipment, and, after 1500 miles, missed the backup parties by hours. Four men died of scurvy because he abandoned the supplies of lime juice provided. Eventually only one member of his party survived, and not a great deal was discovered.

William John Wills

(1834–61)

English explorer of Australia, born in Totnes, Devon. Trained as a doctor, he worked at the new meteorological observatory in Melbourne. He joined Burke's doomed expedition as a surveyor, and was made second-in-command when Burke quarrelled with his predecessor, Landells, who had brought the camels over from India. Burke's mismanagement made it impossible for the scientists to do their work satisfactorily; the expedition was split and communications between the parties failed. Burke and Wills died of exhaustion and starvation, some ten months after starting out from Melbourne.

Wills' last words

Friday, June 28. Clear, cold night; slight breeze from the E.; day beautifully warm and pleasant. Mr Burke suffers greatly from the cold, and is getting extremely weak. He and King start to-morrow up the creek to look for the blacks; it is the only chance we have of being saved from starvation. I am weaker than ever, although I have a good appetite and relish the nardoo much; but it seems to give us no nutriment, and the birds here are so shy as not to be got at. Even if we got a good supply of fish, I doubt whether we could do much work on them and the nardoo alone. Nothing now but the greatest good luck can save any of us; and as for myself, I may live four or five days if the weather continues warm. My pulse is at forty-eight, and very weak, and my legs and arms are nearly skin and bone. I can only look out, like Mr Micawber, "for something to turn up". Starvation on nardoo is by no means very unpleasant, but for the weakness one feels, and the utter inability to move oneself; for as far as appetite is concerned, it gives me the greatest satisfaction. Certainly, fat and sugar would be more to one's taste; in fact, those seem to me to be the great stand-by for one in this extraordinary continent; not that I mean to depreciate the farinaceous food, but the want of sugar and fat in all substances obtainable here is so great that they become almost valueless to us as articles of food, without the addition of something else.

(Signed) W.J. WILLS

And thus, fitly closing with his own great name, the diary of the brave man ended.

Ernest Giles

(1835–97)

English explorer of Australia. His family emigrated to Australia when he was young, and he started his career in the Melbourne Post Office. Inspired by the 'romance' and 'chivalry' of exploration, Giles set off. He joined a search party for the remains of Ludwig Leichhardt, but it never got going. After this Giles made six serious expeditions through Central and Western Australia, which took him across the continent twice; he survived conditions of the most desperate, waterless, hardship. His 1873 expedition took him through the desert named for one of his companions, Alfred Gibson, the 'first white victim to its horrors'. He was alone when he lost Gibson, with only a gallon of water to support him for the next sixty miles. He returned in 1875 to cross this terrible desert, and the continent, twice, this time with camels.

Christmas in the outback

Our last discharge drove away the enemy, and soon after, Jimmy came with all the horses. Gibson shot a wallaby, and we had fried chops for our Christmas dinner. We drew from the medical department a bottle of rum to celebrate Christmas and victory. We had an excellent dinner (for explorers), although we had eaten our Christmas pudding two days before. We perhaps had no occasion to envy any one their Christmas dinner, although perhaps we did. Thermometer 106° in the shade. On this occasion Mr Tietkens, who was almost a professional, sang us some songs in a fine, deep, clear voice, and Gibson sang two or three love songs, not altogether badly; then it was Jimmy's turn. He said he didn't know no love songs, but he would give us Tommy or Paddy Brennan.

Forsaken by God

Although the region now was all a plain, no views of any extent could be obtained, as the country still rolled on in endless undulations at various distances apart, just as in the scrubs. It was evident that the regions we were traversing were utterly waterless, and in all the distance we had come in ten days, no spot had been found where water could lodge. It was totally uninhabited by either man or animal, not a track of a single marsupial, emu, or wild dog was to be seen, and we seemed to have penetrated into a region utterly unknown to man, and as utterly forsaken by God. We had now come 190 miles from water, and our prospects of obtaining any appeared more and more hopeless ... And now, when days had many of them passed away, and no places had been met where water was, the party presented a sad and solemn procession, as though each and all of us was stalking slowly onward to his tomb. Some murmurs of regret reached my ears; but I was prepared for more than that. Whenever we camped, Saleh would stand before me, gaze fixedly into my face and generally say: "Mister Gile, when you get water?" I pretended to laugh at the idea, and say: "Water? pooh! there's no water in this country, Saleh. I didn't come here to find water, I came here to die, and you said you'd come and die too." Then he would ponder awhile, and say: "I think some camel he die to-morrow, Mr Gile." I would say: "No, Saleh, they can't possibly live till to-morrow, I think they will all die to-night." Then he: "Oh, Mr Gile, I think we all die soon now." Then I: "Oh yes, Saleh, we'll all be dead, in a day or two." When he found he couldn't get any satisfaction out of me he would begin to pray, and ask me which was the east. I would point south: down he would go on his knees, and abase himself in the sand, keeping his head in it for some time. Afterwards he would have a smoke, and I would ask: "What's the matter, Saleh? what have you been doing?" "Ah, Mr Gile," was his answer, "I been pray to my God to give you a rock-hole to-morrow." I said, "Why, Saleh, if the rock-hole isn't there already there won't be time for your God to make it; besides, if you can get what you want by praying for it, let me have a fresh-water lake, or a running river, that will take us right away to Perth. What's the use of a paltry rock-hole?" Then he said solemnly, "Ah, Mr Gile, you not religious."

Samuel Butler

(1835–1902)

English writer, painter and musician. Butler's *A First Year in Canterbury Settlement* was compiled by his father, a clergyman, from letters and journals sent from New Zealand. Butler emigrated there to escape from a life in the clergy, and became a sheep farmer at 'Mesopotamia' in the Rangitata Valley of Canterbury. He only lasted five years there; the following extract may explain why. Some of his experiences reappeared in his satirical, Utopian novel, *Erewhon*.

Cold mutton and Moa bones

Next morning, I rode some miles into the country, and visited a farm. Found the inmates (two brothers) at dinner. Cold boiled mutton and bread, and cold tea without milk, poured straight from a huge kettle in which it is made every morning, seem the staple commodities. No potatoes – nothing hot. They had no servant, and no cow. The bread, which was very white, was made by the younger. They showed me, with some little pleasure, some of the improvements they were making, and told me what they meant to do; and I looked at them with great respect. These men were as good gentlemen, in the conventional sense of the word, as any with whom we associate in England – I daresay, *de facto*, much better than many of them. They showed me some moa bones which they had ploughed up (the moa, as you doubtless know, was an enormous bird, which must have stood some fifteen feet high), also some stone Maori battle-axes. They bought this land two years ago, and assured me that, even though they had not touched it, they could get for it cent per cent upon the price which they then gave.

John Forrest

(1847–1918)

Australian explorer who led a search party for the German explorer Ludwig Leichardt, in Western Australia in 1869. He was then sent to find a livestock route along the Great Australian Bight to Adelaide. This was not successful, because of the lack of water, but Forrest made useful maps. His subsequent expedition to explore Western Australia was a success. Baron Forrest of Bunbury received great public recognition and a public career as a surveyor and politician.

Signs of civilisation

About noon I could descry the land turning to the southward, and saw, with great pleasure, we were fast approaching the Head of the Great Australian Bight. Reached the sand-patches at the extreme Head of the Bight just as the sun was setting, and found abundance of water by digging two feet deep in the sand. Gave the horses as much as I considered it safe for them to have at one time. I have never seen horses in such a state before and hope never to do so again. The horses, which four days ago were strong and in good condition, now appeared only skeletons, eyes sunk, nostrils dilated, and thoroughly exhausted. Since leaving Eucla to getting water at this spot, a period of nearly ninety hours, they had only been allowed one gallon of water each, which was given them from our water-drums. It is wonderful how well they performed this journey; had they not started in good condition, they never could have done it. We all felt very tired. During the last sixty hours I have only had about five hours' sleep, and have been continually in a great state of anxiety – besides which, all have had to walk a great deal.

18th – This is a great day in my journal and journey. After collecting the horses we followed along the beach half a mile, when I struck N. for Peelunabie well, and at half a mile struck a cart track from Fowler's Bay to Peelunabie. After following it one mile and a quarter, came to the well and old sheep-yards and camped. Found better water in the sand-hills than in the well. There is a board nailed on a pole directing to the best water, with the following engraved on it: "G. Mackie, April 5th, 1865, Water α 120 yards."

Robert Louis Stevenson

(1850–94)

Scottish writer, from a family of lighthouse builders. His first book, *An Inland Voyage*, was the story of a canoe journey through France and Belgium. The same year, he did his *Travels with a Donkey in the Cévennes*. Hampered throughout his life by tuberculosis, Stevenson, his wife and stepson eventually settled in Samoa, where the writer is buried at the foot of Mount Vaea. *In the South Seas* is an account of two cruises in the Marquesas, Paumotus and Gilbert Islands in 1889.

Dusk in the South Seas

Towards dusk the passers-by became more gorgeous. The men broke out in all the colours of the rainbow – or at least of the trade-room, – and both men and women began to be adorned and scented with new flowers. A small white blossom is the favourite, sometimes sown singly in a woman's hair like little stars, now composed in a thick wreath. With the night, the crowd sometimes thickened in the road, and the padding and brushing of bare feet became continuous; the promenades mostly grave, the silence only interrupted by some giggling and scampering of girls; even the children quiet. At nine-bed-time struck on a bell from the cathedral, and the life of the town ceased. At four the next morning the signal is repeated in the darkness, and the innocent prisoners set free; but for seven hours all must lie – I was about to say within doors, of a place where doors, and even walls, are an exception – housed, at least, under their airy roofs and clustered in the tents of the mosquito-nets. Suppose a necessary errand to occur, suppose it imperative to send abroad, the messenger must then go openly, advertising himself to the police with a huge brand of cocoa-nut, which flares from house to house like a moving bonfire.

484

A palace of women

The palace court at noon is a spot to be remembered with awe, the visitor scrambling there, on the loose stones, through a splendid nightmare of light and heat; but the sweep of the wind delivers it from flies and mosquitoes; and with the set of sun it became heavenly. I remember it best on moonless nights. The air was like a bath of milk. Countless shining stars were overhead, the lagoon paved with them. Herds of wives squatted by companies on the gravel, softly chatting. Tembinok' would doff his jacket, and sit bare and silent, perhaps meditating songs; the favourite usually by him, silent also. Meanwhile in the midst of the court, the palace lanterns were being lit and marshalled in rank upon the ground – six or eight square yards of them; a sight that gave one strange ideas of the number of 'my pamily': such a sight as may be seen about dusk in a corner of some great terminus at home. Presently these fared off into all corners of the precinct, lighting the last labours of the day, lighting one after another to their rest that prodigious company of women. A few lingered in the middle of the court for the card-party, and saw the honours shuffled and dealt, and Tembinok' deliberating between his two hands, and the queens losing their tobacco. Then these also were scattered and extinguished; and their place was taken by a great bonfire, the night-light of the palace. When this was no more, smaller fires burned likewise at the gates. These were tended by the crones, unseen, unsleeping – not always unheard. Should any approach in the dark hours, a guarded alert made the circuit of the palisade; each sentry signalled her neighbour with a stone; the rattle of falling pebbles passed and died away; and the wardens of Tembinok' crouched in their places silent as before.

Daisy Bates

(1863–1951)

Anthropologist and aboriginal welfare worker, born in Tipperary, Ireland. Devoted her life to Aboriginal people, living in isolated camps on the edge of the Nullarbor Plain, at Ooldea, a water-hole on the Trans-Australian railway, and in a tent on the Murray River.

A Trappist mission in the Outback

Perhaps the first woman in history to sleep in a Trappist bed, I was allotted the abbot's bag bed and seaweed pillow, and the sawn-off log for my chair or table. I woke to hear the natives singing a Gregorian chant in the little chapel near by. Half clothed and, for all the untiring work of the missioners, still but half-civilized, they comprised the Nyool-nyool tribe, of the totem of a local species of snake. Most of the women and men had their two front teeth knocked out, and some still wore bones through their noses. Infant cannibalism was practised, where it could not be prevented – as it still is among all circumcised groups. One of the old men, Bully-bulluma, having been an epic meat-hunter in his day, had eight wives. Another, Goodowel, was dressed in trousers and shirt, one stocking, his face painted red with white stripes from each corner of his mouth in broad lines. A red band was round his head, the hair drawn back to form a tight knob, and stuck in the knob was a tuft of white cockatoo feathers and a small wooden emblem. I know now that he was in the sixth degree of initiation.

The Hon. David Wynford Carnegie

(1871–1900)

Mathematician, surveyor and explorer. After working on a tea plantation in Ceylon, Carnegie, Ninth Earl of Southesk, emigrated to Australia, where he worked as a miner, engine driver and gold prospector. He contracted typhoid while crossing the desert with camels laden with gold he had been entrusted to bank at Coolgardie. He then financed a thirteen-month expedition to cross the continent from south to north, surviving an almost complete lack of water with the help of Aboriginal people. One man and several

animals died. Carnegie returned to England in 1898, learnt
Arabic and then went to Nigeria as a popular Assistant
Resident and magistrate. He died from a poisoned arrow
while trying to catch a robber.

The horrors of spinifex

There are two varieties of spinifex known to bushmen – "spinifex" and
"buck" (or "old man") spinifex. The latter is stronger in the prickle
and practically impossible to get through, though it may be avoided by
twists and turns. There are a few uses for this horrible plant; for example,
it forms a shelter and its roots made food for the kangaroo, or spinifex
rat, from its spikes the natives (in the northern districts) make a very
serviceable gum, it burns freely, serves in a measure to bind the sand
and protect it from being moved by the wind, and makes a good mattress
when dug up and turned over. I should advise no one to try and sleep
on the plant as it grows, for "He who sitteth on a thistle riseth up
quickly." But the thistle has one advantage, viz., that it does not leave
its points in its victim's flesh. In Northern Australia spinifex is in seed
for three weeks, and when in this state, forms most excellent feed for
horses, and flattens almost as quickly as oats; for the rest of the year it
is useless.

I can imagine any one, on being suddenly placed on rising ground
with a vast plain of waving spinifex spreading before him – a plain
relieved occasionally by the stately desert oak, solemn, white, and mysterious – saying, "Ah! what a charming view – how beautiful that rolling
plain of grass! its level surface broken by that bold sandhill, fiery-red
in the blaze of the sun!" But when day after day, week after week, and
month after month must be passed always surrounded by the hateful
plant, one's sense of the picturesque becomes sadly blunted.

A desert dinner; largely reptilian

Dressed in the fashionable desert costume of nothing at all, excepting
a band of string round his forehead, and a similar belt round his waist,
from which hung all round him the spoils of the chase, with a spear in
one hand and throwing-sticks in the other he looked a queer figure in

the setting sun – iguanas and lizards dangling head down from his hair and his waist-string – indeed a novel way of carrying game. His lady followed him with a cooliman under her arm, with a further supply of reptiles and rats.

The whole family established themselves close to us. Their camp had been near the crest of the ridge, but, apparently liking our company, they shifted their household goods, and, starting a fire within twenty yards of us, were soon engaged in cooking and eating their supper.

Esther Managku

(c. 1928–)

In 2001 Esther Managku was the oldest living member of the Nalangbali clan of the Kunwinjku people of West Arnhem Land in Australia's Northern Territory, living a mainly traditional way of life.

Bush medicine

Gabo (green ant) is good bush medicine too. They build nests in trees. If we have bad cold and coughing or ache a little bit, we can use that ant. First put that nest in cold, fresh water. Smash them like that (rubbing hands together) or squeeze him tight. I been watching my grandmother, my mother – they been drinking those ants. Eggs and new green ants coming in November. And then we eat those eggs and those new ants too. That's the strongest medicine. Gabo too strong for me now. Gabo also good for headache, or we tie mandjol (bush string) around our head.

We go look around for sugarbag (native bee's nest), just watching to see if those little bees go into a cave or maybe a tree. They cut that nest when it fat (has lots of wax), clean it and put that fat one in billycan. Drink the sugarbag eggs for tummyache. All the old people they been taste 'em and drink. Oh good! When we used to live in bush – I seen them, all those old people drinking that sugarbag.

The Arctic
and The Antarctic

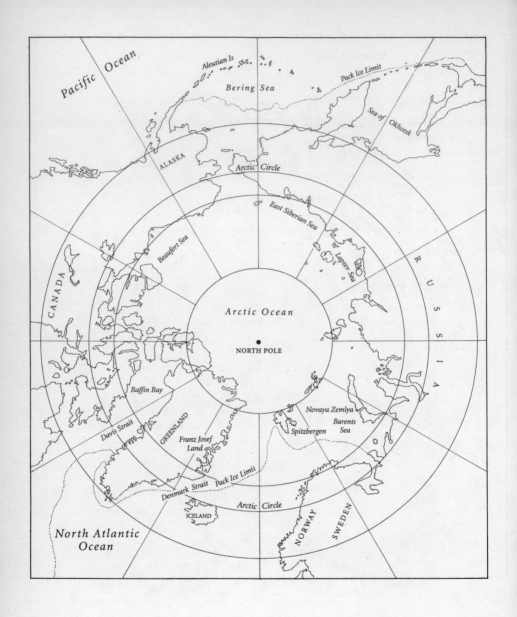

Pacific Ocean

Aleutian Is

Bering Sea

Pack Ice Limit

Sea of Okhotsk

ALASKA

Arctic Circle

East Siberian Sea

Beaufort Sea

Laptev Sea

R U S S I A

CANADA

Arctic Ocean

•
NORTH POLE

Baffin Bay

Novaya Zemlya

Barents
Sea

Davis Strait

Spitzbergen

GREENLAND

Franz Josef
Land

Denmark Strait   Pack Ice Limit

Arctic Circle

NORWAY

SWEDEN

ICELAND

North Atlantic
Ocean

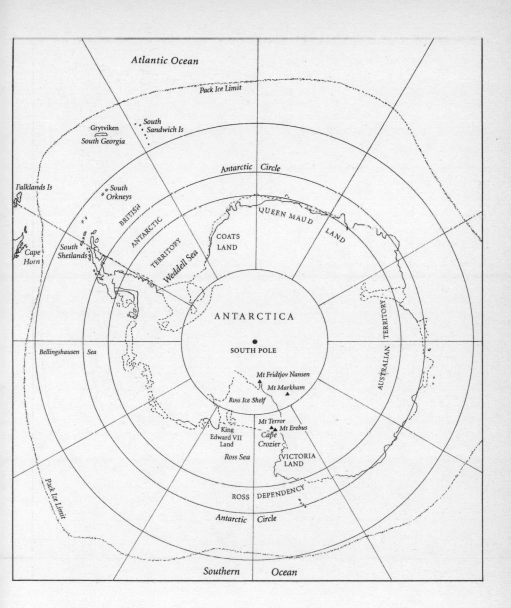

Atlantic Ocean

Pack Ice Limit

Grytviken
South Georgia

South
Sandwich Is

Antarctic   Circle

Falklands Is

South
Orkneys

QUEEN MAUD
LAND

BRITISH

ANTARCTIC

COATS
LAND

Cape
Horn

South
Shetlands

TERRITORY

Weddell Sea

ANTARCTICA

SOUTH POLE

Bellingshausen   Sea

Mt Fridtjov Nansen

Mt Markham

Ross Ice Shelf

AUSTRALIAN   TERRITORY

Pack Ice Limit

King
Edward VII
Land

Ross Sea

Mt Terror

Mt Erebus

Cape
Crozier

VICTORIA
LAND

ROSS   DEPENDENCY

Antarctic   Circle

Southern   Ocean

The Arctic

Sir Martin Frobisher

(c. 1535–94)

English navigator. Frobisher sailed to Guinea in 1554 and made the first voyage in search of the North West Passage. He became Admiral of the Cathay Company, explored territory south of Meta Incognita and brought back 200 tons of gold from the Countess of Warwick's Island. He discovered a new strait in Southern Greenland and reached Labrador. In 1586 Frobisher joined Drake's West Indian expedition. After this he commanded the *Triumph* against the Spanish Armada; became a Vice-Admiral and was fatally wounded on the expedition to relieve Brest.

The people of Meta Incognita

They are men very active and nimble. They are a strong people, and very warlike, for in our sighte, uppon the toppes of the hilles, they would often muster themselves, and after the maner of a skirmish, trace their ground very nimbly, and mannage their bowes and dartes with great dexteritie. They goe clad in coates made of the skinnes of beastes, as of ceales, dere, beares, foxes, and hares. They have also some garments of feathers, being made of the cases of foules, finely sowed and compact togither. Of all which sortes, we broughte home some with us into England, which we founde in their tents. In sommer, they use to weare the hearie side of their coates outwarde, and sometime go naked for too much heate. And in winter (as by signes they have declared) they weare foure or five folde uppon their bodies with ye heare (for warmth) turned inward.

These people are in nature verye subtil, and sharpe witted, readye to conceive our meaning by signes, and to make answere, well to be understoode againe. As if they have not seene the thing whereof you aske them, they wyll winck, or cover their eyes with their hands, as who would say, it hath bene hyd from their sighte. If they understande you not, whereof you aske them, they will stoppe their eares. They will teach us the names of each thing in their language, which we desire to learne, and are apt to learne any thing of us. They delight in musicke above measure, and will keep time and stroke to any tune which you shal sing, both wyth their voyce, heade, hande and feete, and wyll sing the same tune aptlye after you. They will rowe with our oares in our boates, and kepe a true stroke with oure mariners, and seeme to take great delight therein. They live in caves of the earth and hunte for their dinners or praye, even as the beare or other wilde beastes do. They eate rawe fleshe and fishe, and refuse no meate, howsoever it be stinking. They are desperate in their fight, sullen of nature, and ravenous in their manner of feedinge.

Their sullen and desperate nature doth herein manifestly appeare, that a companie of them being environed of our men, on the toppe of a high cliffe, so that they coulde by no meanes escape our handes, finding themselves in this case distressed, chose rather to cast themselves headlong downe the rockes into the sea, and so to be brused and drowned, rather than to yeeld themselves to our men's mercies.

For their weapons, to offended their enimies, or kill their pray withall, they have dartes, slings, bowes, and arrows headed with sharp stones, bones, and some with yron. They are exceedingly friendly and kinde harted, one to the other, and mourne greatly at the losse or harme of their fellowes, and expresse their griefe of minde.

William Baffin

(c. 1584–1622)

English explorer and navigator. Baffin went to Greenland in 1612, joined the Muscovy Company, became chief pilot to the Spitsbergen fisheries and pilot on the North West Passage expedition of 1615. The next year he explored the Davis Strait. He found the entrance to the North West Passage, but the way through it was not found until 1905 by Roald Amundsen (q.v.). Baffin then joined the East India Company; sailed in the Persian Gulf and was eventually killed on a Persian expedition to expel the Portuguese from Ormuz.

Scuruie grass and salmon in Greenland

The next day, going on shoare on a little iland, we found great abundance of the herbe called scuruie grasse, which we boyled in beere, and so dranke thereof, vsing it also in sallets, with sorrell and orpen, which here groweth in abundance; by meanes hereof, and the blessing of God, all our men within eight or nine dayes space were in perfect health, and so continued till our arriuall in England.

Wee rode in this place three dayes before any of the people came to vs; then, on the first of August, six of the inhabitants in their canoas brought us salmon peele, and such like, which was a great refreshment to our men; the next day following, the same six came againe, but after that we saw them no more vntill the sixt day, when we had wayed anchor, and were almost cleere of the harbour; then the same six and one more brought vs of the like commodities, for which we gaue them glasse beads, counters, and small peeces of iron, which they doe as much esteeme as we Christians do gold and siluer.

In this Sound we saw such great scoles of salmon swimming to and fro that it is much to be admired; here it floweth about eighteene foote water, and is at the highest on the change day at seuen a clocke: it is a uery good harbour, and easie to be knowne, hauing three round high hils like piramides close adioyning to the mouth of it, and that in the middest is lowest, and along all this coast are many good harbours to be found, by reason that so many ilands lye off from the maine.

The sixt of August, by three a clocke in the afternoone, wee were cleere of this place, hauing a north north west winde, and faire weather, and the Lord sent vs a speedy and good passage homeward as could be wished; for, in nineteene dayes after, wee saw land on the coast of Ireland, it being on the fiue and twentieth day; the seuen and twentieth at noone we were two leagues from Silly, and the thirtieth day, in the morning, wee anchored at Douer in the roade, for the which and all other His blessings the Lord make vs thankfull.

Gerrit de Veer

(fl. 1596–97)

Dutch seaman and explorer. De Veer recorded the expeditions led by William Barents (d. 1597) in search of the North East Passage. On the third voyage, they reached the ice pack north of Spitzbergen in June 1596; by August, their ship was frozen into the ice off Novaya Zemlya. The sight and sound of the ice pressure so terrified the explorers that it 'made all the hair of our heads to rise upright with fear'. In September, they built a house from driftwood and had to spend the winter there, suffering from severe scurvy. They eventually travelled to safety in two small boats the following June. The hut was found intact by a Norwegian fisherman in 1871.

Frozen in

The 28 of Nouember it was foule stormie weather, and the wind blew hard out of the north, and it snew hard, whereby we were shut vp againe in our house, the snow lay so closed before the doores.

The 29 of Nouember it was faire cleare wether and a good aire, ye wind northerly; and we found meanes to open our doore by shoueling away the snowe, whereby we got one of our dores open; and going out we found al our traps and springes cleane couered ouer with snow, which we made cleane, and set them vp again to taxe foxes; and that day we tooke one, which as then serued vs not onely for meat, but of the skins we made caps to were vpon our heads, therewith to keep them warm from the extreame cold.

The 30 of Nouember it was faire cleare weather, the wind west and [when the watchers were about south-west, which according to our calculations was about midday,] sixe of vs went to the ship, all wel prouided of arms, to see how it lay; and when we went vnder the fore decke, we tooke a foxe aliue in the ship.

The 1 of December it was foule weather, with a southwest wind and great stoare of snow, whereby we were once againe stopt vp in the house, and by that meanes there was so great a smoke in the house that we could hardly make fire, and so were forced to lye all day in our cabens, but the cooke was forced to make fire to dresse our meat.

The 2 of December it was still foule weather, whereby we were forced to keep stil in the house, and yet we could hardly sit by the fire because of the smoake, and therefore stayed still [for the most part] in our cabens; and then we heated stones, when we put into our cabens to warm our feet, for that both the cold and the smoke were vnsupportable.

The 3 of December we had the like weather, at which times as we lay in cabans we might heare the ice crack in the sea, and yet it was at the least halfe a mile [two miles] from vs, which made a hugh noyse [of bursting and cracking], and we were of oppinion that as then the great hils of ice which wee had seene in the sea in summer time [lying so many fathoms thick] brake one from the other. And for that during those 2 or 3 days, because of the extream smoake, we made not so much fire as we commonly vsed to doe, it froze so sore within the house that the wals and roofe thereof were frozen two fingers thicke with ice, and also in our cabans where we lay. All those three daies, while we could not go out by reason of the foule weather, we set vp the [sand-]glas of 12 houres, and when it was run out we set it vp againe, stil watching it lest we should misse our time. For the cold was so great that our clock was frozen, and might not goe although we hung more waight on it then before.

Sir John Franklin

(1786–1847)

English Arctic explorer, who fought at the Battle of Trafalgar under Nelson and was Governor of Van Dieman's Land (Tasmania), 1834–45. In 1819 Franklin was sent to explore the Coppermine river and coasts of Arctic Canada. His party travelled 5000 miles, under appalling conditions. Returning from an overland journey they survived the winter by eating leather and edible lichen called *tripe de roche*, and thanks to the kindness of the native Inuit. Franklin died on a voyage to find the North West Passage when both ships on the expedition disappeared on their way to Lancaster Sound.

Nursed by Indians

November 8 – The Indians this morning requested us to remove to an encampment on the banks of the river, as they were unwilling to remain in the house in which the bodies of our deceased companies were lying exposed to view. We agreed to remove, but the day proved too stormy, and Dr Richardson and Hepburn having dragged the bodies to a short distance, and covered them with snow, the objections of the Indians to remain in the house were removed, and they began to clear our room of the accumulation of dirt and fragments of pounded bones. The improved state of our apartment, and the large and cheerful fires they kept up, produced in us a sensation of comfort to which we had long been strangers. In the evening they brought in a pile of dried wood, which was lying on the river-side, and on which we had often cast a wishful eye, being unable to drag it up the bank. The Indians set about every thing with an activity that amazed us. Indeed, contrasted with our emaciated figures and extreme debility, their frames appeared to us gigantic, and their strength supernatural. These kind creatures next turned their attention to our personal appearance, and prevailed upon us to shave and wash ourselves. The beards of the Doctor and Hepburn had been untouched since they left the sea-coast, and were become of a hideous length, and peculiarly offensive to the Indians. The Doctor and I suffered extremely from distention, and therefore ate sparingly. Hepburn was getting better, and Adam recovered his strength with amazing rapidity*.

Elisha Kent Kane

(1820–57)

American naval surgeon, naturalist and Arctic explorer. Kane travelled in Asia, Arabia and Europe before joining the expeditions of Henry Grinnell in 1853, to search for the body of Sir John Franklin (q.v.). In view of the dreadful overland journey the party endured, it is remarkable that the observations in his book, *Arctic Explorations*, have such a light touch. It was published in 1856 to great acclaim.

Eskimo appetites

The Esquimaux, however gluttonously they may eat, evidently bear hunger with as little difficulty as excess. None of the morning party had breakfasted; yet it was after ten o'clock at night before they sat down to dinner. "Sat down to dinner!" This is the only expression of our own gastrology which is applicable to an Esquimaux feast. They truly sit down, man, woman, and child, knife in hand, squatting cross-legged around a formidable joint – say forty pounds – and, without waiting for the tardy coction of the lamp, falling to like college commoners after grace. I have seen many such feeds. Hans's account, however, of the glutton-festival at Etah is too characteristic to be omitted:

---

* The first alvine discharges after we received food, were, as Hearne remarks on a similar occasion, attended with excessive pain. Previous to the arrival of the Indians the urinary secretion was extremely abundant, and we were obliged to rise from bed in consequence upwards of ten times in a night. This was an extreme annoyance in our reduced state. It may, perhaps, be attributed to the quantity of the country tea that we drank.

"Why, Cappen Ken, sir, even the children ate all night; you know the little two-year-old that Awiu carried in her hood – the one that bit you when you tickled it? Yes. Well, Cappen Ken, sir, that baby cut for herself, with a knife made out of an iron hoop, and so heavy that it could barely lift it, and cut and ate, and ate and cut, as long as I looked at it."

"Well, Hans, try now and think; for I want an accurate answer: how much as to weight or quantity would you say that child ate?" Hans is an exact and truthful man: he pondered a little and said that he could not answer my question. "But I know this, sir, that it ate a *sipak*" – the Esquimaux name for the lump which is cut off close to the lips – "as large as its own head; and three hours afterward, when I went to bed, it was cutting off another lump and eating still." A sipak, like the Dutch governor's foot, is, however, a varying unit of weight.

Black with Arctic blubber

6 January, 1855, Saturday – If this journal ever gets to be inspected by other eyes, the colour of its pages will tell of the atmosphere it is written in. We have been emulating the Esquimaux for some time in everything else; and now, last of all, this intolerable temperature and our want of fuel have driven us to rely on our lamps for heat. Counting those which I have added since the wanderers came back, we have twelve constantly going, with the grease and soot everywhere in proportion.

I can hardly keep my charts and registers in anything like decent trim. Our beds and bedding are absolutely black, and our faces begrimmed with fatty carbon like the Esquimaux of South Greenland. Nearer to us, our Smith's Straits Esquimaux are much more cleanly in this branch of domestic arrangements. They attend their lamps with assiduous care, using the long radicles of a spongy moss for wick, and preparing the blubber for its office by breaking up the cells between their teeth. The condense blubber, or, more properly, fat, of the walrus, is said to give the best flame.

Earl of Dufferin

(1826–1902)

English traveller, diplomat and statesman, born Frederick Temple Hamilton Blackwood, Dufferin became ambassador to St Petersburg, Constantinople, Rome and France, governor general of Canada and Viceroy of India His book, *Letters from High Latitudes*, published in 1859, recounts an intrepid cruise in his yacht, *Foam*, to Iceland and Spitzbergen; lordly standards appear to have been maintained throughout. His wife, Hariot (**q.v.**), also wrote engagingly about their experiences in diplomatic climates.

"Four points, my Lord"

Still, I own, the style of his service was slightly depressing. He laid out my clean shirt of a morning as if it had been a shroud; and cleaned my boots as though for a man *on his last legs*. The fact is, he was imaginative and atrabilious, contemplating life through a medium of the colour of his own complexion.

This was the cheerful kind of report he used invariably to bring me of a morning. Coming to the side of my cot with the air of a man announcing the stroke of doomsday, he used to say, or rather *toll* –

"Seven o'clock, my Lord!"

"Very well; how's the wind?"

"Dead ahead, my Lord – *dead*!"

"How many points is she off her course?"

"Four points, my Lord – full four points!" (Four points being as much as she could be.)

"Is it pretty clear? eh! Wilson?"

"Can't see your hand, my Lord! – can't see your hand!"

"Much ice in sight?"

"Ice all round, my Lord – ice a-all ro-ound!" – and so exit, sighing deeply over my trousers.

On the edge of the ice

It was now eleven o'clock at night; Fitz and Sigurdr went to bed, while I remained on deck to see what the night might bring forth. It blew great guns, and the cold was perfectly intolerable; billow upon billow of black fog came sweeping down between the sea and the sky, as if it were going to swallow up the whole universe; while the midnight sun, now completely blotted out, now faintly struggling through the ragged breaches of the mist, threw down from time to time an unearthly red-brown glare on the waste of roaring waters.

For the whole of that night did we continue beating up along the edge of the ice, in the teeth of a whole gale of wind; at last, about nine o'clock in the morning, but two short hours before the moment at which it had been agreed we should bear up, and abandon the attempt, we came up with a long low point of ice, that had stretched further to the Westward than any we had yet doubled, and there, beyond, lay an open sea! – open not only to the Northward and Westward, but also to the Eastward! You can imagine my excitement. "Turn the hands up, Mr Wyse!" "'Bout ship!" "Down with the helm!" "Helm a-lee!" Up comes the schooner's head to the wind, the sails flapping with the noise of thunder, blocks rattling against the deck, as if they wanted to knock their brains out, ropes dancing about in galvanised coils, like mad serpents, and everything to an inexperienced eye in inextricable confusion; till gradually she pays off on the other tack, the sails stiffen into dealboards, the staysail sheet is let go, and, heeling over on the opposite side, again she darts forward over the sea like an arrow from the bow. "Stand by to make sail!" "Out all reefs!" (I could have carried sail to sink a man-of-war!), and away the little ship went, playing leapfrog over the heavy seas, and staggering under her canvas, as if giddy with the same joyful excitement which made my own heart thump so loudly.

Nils Adolf Erik Nordenskjöld

(1832–1901)

Swedish Arctic explorer and navigator. Having failed to achieve the ambition of reaching the North Pole, in 1878–9, Nordenskjöld became the first man to navigate the North East Passage from the Atlantic to the Pacific, in a 300-ton ship, the *Vega*.

Lemming tunnels

The lemming is not found on Spitzbergen, but must certain seasons occur in incredible numbers on Novaya Zemlya. For at the commencement of summer, when the snow has recently melted away, there are to be seen, everywhere in level fertile places in the very close grass of the meadows, footpaths about an inch and a half deep, which have been formed during winter by the tramplings of these small animals, under the snow, in the bed of grass of lichens which lies immediately above the frozen ground. They have in this way united with each other the dwellings they had excavated in the ground, and constructed for themselves convenient ways, well protected in the severe cold of winter, to their fodder-places. Thousands and thousands of animals must be required in order to carry out this work even over a small area, and wonderfully keen must their sense of locality be, if, as seems probable, they can find their way with certainty in the endless labyrinth they have thus formed. During the snow-melting season these passages form channels for running off the water, small indeed, but everywhere to be met with, and contributing in a considerable degree to the drying of the ground. The ground besides is in certain places so thickly strewed with lemming dung, they must have a considerable influence on the condition of the soil.

William Morris

(1834–96)

Poet, designer, craftsman and socialist. Morris made two
journeys to Iceland, in 1871 and 1873, inspired by the Icelandic sagas, which he translated with one of his travelling
companions, the Icelandic theologian, Eríkr Magnússon.

The geysir

27 July 1871

'Now he's coming up,' and there was a roar in the crater as we all
scuttled away at our fastest, and up shot a huge column of mud, water,
and steam, amongst which we could see the intrusive turfs: then it fell
and rose again several times as we turned and walked back to camp,
playing for about twenty minutes in a fitful way: nay a full hour afterwards as we sat at dinner it made a last excursion into the air.

So back to camp, and the night being fine made a fire easily, fried
our fish, and dined, talking prodigiously, and so to bed after a very
merry evening.

Friday, 28 July 1871

IN CAMP AT THE SAME PLACE

I had been sleeping rather restlessly, when about six a.m. I was awoke
by the Gusher growling in a much more obstinate way than we had
heard him yet; then the noise seemed to get nearer till it swelled into
a great roar in the crater, and we were all out in the open air in a
moment, and presently saw the water lifted some six feet above the
crater's lip, and then fall again heavily, then rise again a good bit higher
and again fall, and then at last shoot up as though a spring had been
touched into a huge column of water and steam some eighty feet high,
as Faulkner and Evans guessed it; it fell and rose again many times, till
at last it subsided much as it began with rumblings and thumpings of
the earth, the whole affair lasting something less than twenty minutes:

afterwards about nine thirty a.m. as we were busy washing our clothes in the Blesi stream there was a lesser eruption: this one being over we put on our shoes and went off to the crater and walked over the hot surface of the outer one to look at the inner one where the water was sunk a long way down. People thought us lucky to have seen this, as Geysir had gushed the morning of Evans's and my arrival, and he doesn't often go off within six days of his last work: nay sometimes people will stay for a fortnight at the Geysirs without seeing it . . .

We spent this afternoon in repitching Faulkner's and Magnússon's tent, and in wringing and hanging out to dry our wash, stretching a line between the two tents, and hanging the things thereon, Faulkner having made some ingenious clothes pegs out of firewood; I was quite pleased with the cosy homelike look of the camp when I came back to it after a walk and found everything in apple-pie order: you see wet weather in camp plays the deuce with order, one is so huddled up, there is nowhere to put things. We bought a lamb of Sigurd today, and parboiled a quarter of him in Blesi, and then fried a shoulder or so for our dinner and ate him with peas (preserved) and in fact had quite a feast. Then the moon rose big and red, the second time we had seen him so in Iceland, for last night though calm and unrainy was hazy: he scarcely cast a shadow yet though the nights were got much darker, so much so that when we sat down for our first game of whist in Iceland we had to light up to see the cards. We were all in high spirits, I in special I think, for I had fretted at the delay in this place sacred principally to Mangnall, and there had seemed a probability of the expedition being spoiled or half spoiled. So to bed and sound sleep.

Fritdjof Nansen

(1861–1930)

Norwegian explorer. In 1895, after many years of physical and practical preparation, Nansen reached the highest latitude ever achieved, 86° 13' N. He had the original idea of building a ship, the *Fram*, that would be able to drift with the pack ice without being crushed by it. It would also prove the existence of Arctic currents. The ship left Oslo in June 1893 and after sixteen months' drifting, the ship was four hundred miles south of the Pole. Nansen and Hjalmar Johansen set off across the ice with dogs, sledges and kayaks. At 'farthest North' they had to spend the winter in a hut, living on bear meat, not realising that Frederick Jackson's Polar expedition was less than a hundred miles off.

Menu on board the Fram, 29 September 1893

Soupe à la julienne avec des macaroni-dumplings.
Potage de poison (sic) avec des pommes de terre.
Pudding de Nordahl.
Glacé du Greenland.
De la table bière de la Ringnæes.
Marmalade intacte.

Farthest north

Sunday, 7 April (−24.2°C.). The ice grew worse and worse. Yesterday it brought me to the verge of despair, and when we stopped this morning I had almost decided to turn back. I will go on one day longer, however, to see if the ice is really as bad farther northwards as it appears to be from the ridge, 30 feet in height, where we are encamped. We hardly made 4 miles yesterday. Lanes, ridges, and endless rough ice, it looks like an endless moraine of ice-blocks; and this continual lifting of the sledges over every irregularity is enough to tire out giants. Curious this rubble-ice.

Monday, 8 April. No, the ice grew worse and worse, and we got no way. Ridge after ridge, and nothing but rubble to travel over. We made a start at two o'clock or so this morning, and kept at it as long as we could, lifting the sledges all the time; but it grew too bad at last. I went on a good way ahead on snowshoes, but saw no reasonable prospect of advance, and from the highest hummocks only the same kind of ice was to be seen. It was a veritable chaos of ice-blocks, stretching as far as the horizon. There is not much sense in keeping on longer; we are sacrificing valuable time and doing little. If there be much more such ice between here and Franz Josef Land, we shall, indeed, want all the time we have.

I therefore determined to stop, and shape our course for Cape Fligely.

On this northernmost camping-ground we indulged in a banquet, consisting of lobscouse, bread-and-butter, dry chocolate, stewed 'tytle-bær', or red whortleberries, and our hot whey drink, and then, with a delightful and unfamiliar feeling of repletion, crept into the dear bag, our best friend. I took a meridian observation yesterday, by which I see that we should be in latitude 86° 10' N., or thereabouts. This morning I took an observation for longitude. At 8.30 a.m. – 25.6°Fahr. (–32°C.).

The return

Saturday, 13 April. We have traversed nothing but good ice for three days. If this goes on, the return journey will be quicker than I thought. I do not understand this sudden change in the nature of the ice. Can it be that we are travelling in the same direction with the trend of the ridges and irregularities, so that now we go along between them instead of having to make our way over them? The lanes we have come across seem all to point to this; they follow our course pretty closely. We had the misfortune yesterday to let our watches run down; the time between our getting into the bag on the previous night and encamping yesterday was too long. Of course we wound them up again, but the only thing I can now do to find Greenwich mean time is to take a time-observation and an observation for latitude, and then estimate the approximate distance from our turning-point on 8 April, when I took the last observation for longitude. By this means the error will hardly be great.

I conclude that we have not gone less than 14 miles a day on average the last three days, and have consequently advanced 40 or more miles in a direction S. 22° W. (magnetic). When we stopped here yesterday Barbara [one of the dogs] was killed. These slaughterings are not very pleasant episodes. Clear weather; at 6.30 this morning –22° Fahr. (–30°C.); wind south (6 to 9 feet).

Roald Amundsen

(1872–1928)

Norwegian explorer. At the age of seventeen, Amundsen witnessed Nansen's homecoming in Oslo, and decided to become a Polar explorer. In 1905, he became the first man to sail through the North West Passage in his second-hand boat, the *Gjöa*. On 14 December 1911 he went on to become the first man to reach the South Pole, narrowly beating Scott. In 1925, he attempted to fly over the North Pole with two seaplanes, but they had to make a forced landing and were frozen into the ice. It took twenty-four days to cut the planes out. The next year a successful attempt was made by airship. Amundsen died on a mission to rescue the crew of a second dirigible attempt which ended in disaster.

Sighting an American flag; meeting Capt. McKenna

"I wonder what he'll think when he sees it?"

"He'll think it is a venerable old flag."

"Perhaps he's an American."

"I shouldn't be surprised if he were an Englishman."

"Yes, he will see by the flag what we are!"

"Oh, yes – he will see we are boys from good old Norway!"

The vessels were approaching each other very rapidly.

"There! up goes the American flag," sang out the watchman. He had the long telescope which had been placed on deck. This proved to be correct, and we could now all see the Stars and Stripes under the vessel's gaff. They had seen and recognised our flag by now, that was certain. Dense steam was issuing from the vessel's side; evidently they had a motor, the same as we had, and were advancing rapidly.

It was time now to tidy ourselves a little in preparation for the first meeting. Four of us were to go on board the ship, the other three had to remain on the *Gjöa* and look after our vessel. Our best clothes were hurriedly got out. We dressed ourselves according to our individual taste. Some preferred Eskimo costumes, and others our Norwegian russet. One found that sealskin boots looked best for the occasion, others preferred ordinary sea-boots. We also cleared up on deck as well as we could. The American could certainly scan our deck in every detail, from his crow's nest, through his telescope, and we wanted to make as decent an impression as possible. We were now so near each other that the whole ship was visible from our deck. It was a small, two masted schooner, painted black; she had a powerful motor, and the foam at her bows was spurting high. She also carried sail. We got the boats clear, hove to, and lowered the dory, the most seaworthy of them. It was certainly not much to look at, and the commander had no easy stern-sheets, with a flag, to sit on. But the boat was in the style of the vessel to which it belonged, and we were not on a pleasure trip. The American had stopped his engine, and was waiting for us. With two men at the oars we were soon alongside of him. A line was thrown down to us; I caught it, and was again linked with civilisation. It did not, however, make its appearance in any great glory.

The *Charles Hanson*, of San Francisco, did not seem to be rigged out in a very luxurious manner. A ladder, by-the-bye, was superfluous, as the ship was deep in the water. We took hold of the chain-wales and crawled on board. Our first impression was most peculiar. Every available space on deck was occupied to such an extent that it was nearly impossible to get along. Eskimo women in red dresses, and negroes in the most variegated costumes were mingling together, just as in a land of fable.

An elderly man with a white beard advanced towards me on the quarter-deck. He was newly shaven, and nicely dressed, evidently the master of the ship. "Are you Captain Amundsen?" was his first remark. I was quite surprised to hear that we were known so far away and answered in the affirmative, owning that I was the man. "Is this the first vessel you have met?" the old man asked. And when I admitted it was so, his countenance brightened up. We shook hands long and heartily. "I am exceedingly pleased to be the first one to welcome you on getting through the North West Passage." We were then most courteously invited down below to his cabin.

Ejnaar Mikkelsen

(fl. 1910)

Danish explorer of the Arctic. In 1910, Mikkelsen was marooned for 865 days on the coast of Greenland with Iver Iversen, while looking for material including maps believed to have been left by Mylius Erichsen a few years earlier. At last, having closely faced death and the prospect of cannibalism, they were rescued.

A ship! A ship!

Half-an-hour later we are lying in our sleeping bags, and have said good-night to each other, repeating once more the old refrain, "Who knows – there may be a ship to-morrow!" And as I lie there, my eyes wander over the wall of the cabin – there is the picture of the four generations, there the street scenes from Copenhagen, and then a little empty space, always the first and last I see. There was a picture there once, a little card with the woods of Frederiksdal, so green and splendid – but I had to take it down, it was too painful. I burnt the card, but I could not burn the place where it had hung, and the empty space grins at me now, as if to say, "Do you remember?" And I remember all too well, it was a foolish thing to burn the card, for the empty space is worse. "Coward," it seems to say, "you dare not think of the future, you dare not hope to ever reach home again!"

Soon all is still in the house, and we sleep. Suddenly I am wakened by the noise of a case upset outside, and as I open my eyes, there is Iversen dashing across the room, bare-legged, with nothing on but a striped jersey, and with a wild look in his eyes. A bear! is my first thought, and in a moment I am out of my bunk, seize my gun, and am about to follow, but before I have got halfway, I stop, petrified with astonishment – Iversen has got the door open, and is crying "Morning – good-morning!"

God – a ship at last! In a moment I am standing beside my faithful comrade, staring at a host of men – an endless army of men – the whole shore is full of men.

What happened next I do not know. We put some clothes on, I suppose, but there is a blank spot in my memory, and the next thing I remember is that Iversen has disappeared, and going out to look for him, I find him standing on a rock, waving his cap and shouting, "A ship! a ship! a ship!"

With a bound I am at his side. True enough, out there where we have never seen anything but water and ice, a little steamer is lying. We look at each other with bright eyes, and do not know what to say. It is eight-and-twenty months since we last saw a human face. Then we go up behind the house, where nobody can see us, and shake hands – hard. We have been through a rough time together, and now it is over. A moment we stand holding each other's hands, then Iversen bursts out suddenly – "I say – I'm glad we didn't shoot those guillemots yesterday – jolly little things!"

Then we go down to the others, who had been so startled at our first appearance that they had actually run away. It seems as if we had never seen so many people all at once; it looks like an army – and there are only eight of them. They are quite pleased to see us now, but at the first meeting, Lillenæs, who was standing with his back to the door, sprang into the air with astonishment when Iversen opened it. We must have given him a shock, I dare not say a fright, for we learned later that this bold seaman had captured a musk ox once, off his own bat.

Another of them, the steward, dashed back down the shore as fast as his legs could carry him. He thought we were dangerous lunatics, and, indeed, we must have made a queer figure, with our bushy hair and beards, striped jerseys, and nothing more.

They tell us the news of the world. First we learn of the death of the King – the men spied his picture on the wall, and one said laconically – "Well, he's dead and gone now!" They tell us of the *Titanic*, and the many souls that drowned, of Italy, now at war with Turkey, or Egypt, or the Hottentots – they are not quite sure.

Barry Lopez

(1945–)

American writer. Born in New York State; he grew up
in rural Southern California. *Arctic Dreams* is the result
of four years travelling in and investigating the Arctic,
between the Bering Strait and Davis Strait, and is a precise
but poetic account of nature at below zero.

An Arctic evening

Lying there in the tent, I knew, as does everyone I think who spends some
time hunting with Eskimos, that they are not idyllic people, errorless in
the eyes of God. But they are a people, some of them, still close to the
earth, maintaining the rudiments of an ancient philosophy of accommodation with it that we have abandoned. Our first wisdom as a species,
that unique metaphorical knowledge that distinguishes us, grew out of
such an intimacy with the earth; and, however far we may have come
since that time, it did not seem impossible to me that night to go back
and find it. I wanted to enquire among these people, for what we now
decide to do in the North has a certain frightening irrevocability about it.

I wanted to enquire, as well, among thoughtful visitors, people who
were taken with the land. Each culture, it seemed to me, is a repository
of some good thought about the universe; we are valuable to each other
for that. Lying there, I thought of my own culture, of the assembly of
books in the library at Alexandria; of the deliberations of Darwin and
Mendel in their respective gardens; of the architectural conception
of the cathedral at Chartres; of Bach's cello suites, the philosophy of
Schweitzer, the insights of Planck and Dirac. Have we come all this way,
I wondered, only to be dismantled by our own technologies, to be
betrayed by political connivance or the impersonal avarice of a cor-
poration?

I had no idea as I lay on those caribou skins that evening precisely
where wisdom might lie. I knew enough of quantum mechanics to

understand that the world is ever so slightly but uncorrectably out of focus, there are no absolutely precise answers. Whatever wisdom I would find, I knew, would grow out of the land. I trusted that, and that it would reveal itself in the presence of well-chosen companions.

I looked out of the tent. It was after one in the morning. A south wind blew, but so slightly. The kind of wind nineteenth-century sailors called "inclinable to calm". Nakitavak lay stretched out on caribou skins and a cotton sleeping bag on his bag sled, his qamutik, watching the still black water between two massive ice flocs, the open lead into which narwhals would come, sooner or later. His brother David, both hands wrapped around a mug of tea, was looking to the west, the direction from which he thought they would come. His lips stretched to the steaming, hot surface of the tea, and in the chill air I heard the susurrations of his sipping.

The Tununiarusirmiut men, relatives of the Tununirmiut to the east who had met the whalers 160 years ago, knew beyond a shadow of a doubt, beyond any hesitation, what made them happy, what gave them a sense of satisfaction, of wealth. An abundance of animals.

And so, we waited.

The Antarctic

Fabian Gottlieb von Bellinghausen

(1779–1852)

Russian naval officer and one of the greatest Antarctic
explorers. In 1803, he was fifth officer on the first Russian
circumnavigation of the globe. The sketches made on
Bellinghausen's survey of the southern side of South
Georgia were still used by the British Admiralty in 1930.
In 1820, he made the first crossing of the Antarctic circle
since his hero Captain Cook, reaching the most southerly
point ever and almost attaining the mainland of Antarctica. The following is a list of gifts taken on the expedition
for distributing to natives encountered during the voyage.

Presents for the natives

We were ordered to distribute medals at any islands or shores which
we might discover, and also during our stay in other places during the
long voyage – silver medals for important personages, and bronze ones
for those of lesser importance. These medals were specially struck at
the St Petersburg Mint, bearing on the obverse the image of His Imperial
Majesty Alexander I, and on the reverse the inscription, "The sloops
Vostok and *Mirnyi*, 1819", i.e., the year of our departure.

In order to induce the natives to friendly behaviour towards us,
and also as a means of barter for fresh provisions and specimens of
native work, various articles were issued to us at St Petersburg which
might prove attractive to such natives as were in a primitive stage of
culture.

Here follows a list of the articles:

Knives, assorted	400	Fringes of different	60 arsheen
Cobbler's knives	100	colours	(47 yd)
Pruning knives	20	Ticking and tent cloth,	100 arsheen
Knives ¾ arsheen in	2	striped	(78 yd)
length (21 in.)		Unbleached linen	250 arsheen
Vices	10		(195 yd)
Gimlets	125	Tinder	10 lb
Rasps and files	100	Dyed thread	10 lb
Graters	50	Flints	1000
Axes	100	Hussar jackets	10
Choppers	50	Glasses	120
Shipbuilder's augers	50	Decanters	12
Scissors, assorted	50	Copper wire	100 lb
Lamps	300	Iron wire	80 lb
Small bells and trumpets	185	Drums	1
Red and blue linen,	500 arsheen	Tambourines	2
striped	(389 yd)	Huntsmen's horns	5
Old buttons	12 dozen	Threading needles	40 packets
Handsaws	10	Cotton wick	80 lb
Cross-cut saws	10	Wax candles	1000
Planes	15	Fishing lines	12 pood
Pincers, large and small	10		(430 lb)
Chisels	30	Various wrought-iron	27½ pood
Night lamps	24	vessels	(1000 lb)
Combs, horn	250	Various kinds of mirrors	1000
Combs, wooden	50	Flower and vegetable seeds	100 lb
Knitting needles, assorted	5000	Kaleidoscopes	24
Studs	100	Burning glasses	18
Lead in 2½ pood portions,	10 pood	Large iron fish hooks	6
4 pieces	(360 lb)	Wire fish hooks, coarse and fine	
Rings	250		1800
Earrings	125 pairs	Red baize	218 arsheen
Beads	20 bunches		(169 yd)
Garnets	5 bunches	Blue and green flannel	62 arsheen
Glass beads (large and			(48 yd)
small)	20 bunches	Frieze blankets	70
Linen printed handkerchiefs	100	Tobacco twist	26 pood
			900 lb)

Robert Falcon Scott

(1868–1912)

English sailor and explorer of the Antarctic. In 1900–4, Scott commanded the National Antarctic Expedition in the *Discovery*, explored the Ross Sea and found King Edward VII Land. In 1910, he made for the South Pole, in the *Terra Nova*. After a terrible journey, pulling sledges across the ice, and with misadventures including the potentially fatal loss of a tent, Scott and four others reached the Pole on 17 January 1912, only to find a message from Amundsen, wishing them a safe return. 'Great God!' Scott wrote in his Journal, 'this is an awful place and terrible enough for us to have laboured to it without the reward of priority . . . Now for the run home . . . I wonder if we can do it.' They did not. They were defeated by weather of exceptional severity. Evans died after a head injury; Oates, suffering from extreme frostbite, disappeared into the wilderness; Bowers, Wilson and Scott lay down to await death in their tent, only eleven miles from a supply of provisions laid down months beforehand.

Loss and recovery of the tent

As it was still dark when we had finished we lay in our bags again for a bit. Daylight appeared, and we at once turned out, and it was by no means reassuring to find that the weather in the south still looked as bad and thick as it possibly could. We therefore lost no time at all in getting away down wind to look for the tent. Everywhere we found shreds of green canvas about the size of a pocket-handkerchief, but not a sign of the tent, until a loud shout from Bowers, who had gone more east to the top of a ridge than Cherry and I, told us he had seen it. He hurried down, and slid about a hundred yards down a hard snow slope, sitting in his haste, and there we joined him where he had found the whole tent hardly damaged at all, a quarter of a mile from where we had pitched it. One of the poles had been twisted right out of the cap, and the lower stops of the tent lining had all carried away more or less, but the tent itself was intact and untorn.

We brought it back, pitched it in the old spot in the snow hollow below our hut, and then brought down our bags and cooker and all essential gear, momentarily expecting the weather to break on us again. It looked as thick as could be and close at hand in the south.

We discussed the position, and came to the conclusion that as our oil had now run down to one can only, and as we couldn't afford to spend time trying to fix up an improvised blubber stove in a roofless hut, we ought to return to Cape Evans. It was disappointing to have seen so very little of the Emperor penguins, but it seemed to me unavoidable, and that we had attempted too difficult an undertaking without light in the winter.

I had also some doubt as to whether our bags were not already in such a state as might make them quite unusable should we meet with really low temperatures again in our journey home.

I therefore decided to start for Hut Point the next day. To this end we sorted out all our gear, and made a depot in a corner of the stone hut of all that we could usefully leave there for use on a future occasion. This depot I fixed up finally with Cherry the next morning while Bowers packed up the sledge at our tent. We put rocks on our depot and the nine-foot sledge, and the pick, with a matchbox containing a note tied to the handle, where it could not be missed. We also fixed up bamboos round the walls to attract attention to the spot.

Apsley Cherry-Garrard

(1886–1959)

English explorer. As assistant zoologist with Captain Scott's second Antarctic expedition, he made a harrowing and ultimately pointless winter journey to the Emperor Penguin rookery at Cape Crozier to collect penguin eggs. In 1912 Cherry-Garrard went alone to One Ton Depot in an attempt to meet Scott's returning party. He was a member of the search party that found their frozen bodies.

A baddish time

"We shall have to go a bit slower," said Bill, and "we shall get more used to working in the dark." At this time, I remember, I was still trying to wear spectacles.

We spent that night on the sea-ice, finding that we were too far in towards Castle Rock; and it was not until the following afternoon that we reached and lunched at Hut Point. I speak of day and night, though they were much the same, and later on when we found that we could not get the work into a twenty-four hour day, we decided to carry on as though such a convention did not exist; as in actual fact it did not. We had already realized that cooking under these conditions would be a bad job, and that the usual arrangement by which one man was cook for the week would be intolerable. We settled to be cook alternately day by day. For food we brought only pemmican and biscuit and butter; for drink we had tea, and we drank hot water to turn in on.

Pulling out from Hut Point that evening we brought along our heavy loads on the two nine-foot sledges with comparative ease; it was the first, and though we did not know it then, the only bit of good pulling we were to have. Good pulling to the sledge traveller means easy pulling. Away we went round Cape Armitage and eastwards. We knew that the Barrier edge was in front of us and also that the break-up of the sea-ice had left the face of it as a low perpendicular cliff. We had therefore to find a place where the snow had formed a drift. This we came right up against and met quite suddenly a very keen wind flowing, as it always does, from the cold Barrier down to the comparatively warm sea-ice. The temperature was −47° F., and I was a fool to take my hands out of my mitts to haul on the ropes to bring the sledges up. I started away from the Barrier edge with all ten fingers frost-bitten. They did not really come back until we were in the tent for our night meal, and within a few hours there were two or three large blisters, up to an inch long, on all of them. For many days those blisters hurt frightfully.

We were camped that night about half a mile in from the Barrier edge. The temperature was −56°. We had a baddish time, being very glad to get out of our shivering bags next morning (29 June). We began to suspect, as we knew only too well later, that the only good time of the twenty-four hours was breakfast, for then with reasonable luck we need not get into our sleeping-bags again for another seventeen hours.

The horror of the nineteen days it took us to travel from Cape Evans to Cape Crozier would have to be re-experienced to be appreciated; and any one would be a fool who went again: it is not possible to describe it. The weeks which followed them were comparative bliss, not because later our conditions were better – they were far worse – but because we were callous. I for one had come to that point of suffering at which I did not really care if only I could die without much pain. They talk of the heroism of the dying – they little know – it would be so easy to die, a dose of morphia, a friendly crevasse, and blissful sleep. The trouble is to go on.

It was the darkness that did it. I don't believe minus seventy temperatures would be bad in daylight, not comparatively bad, when you could see where you were going, where you were stepping, where the sledge straps were, the cooker, the primus, the food; could see your footsteps lately trodden deep into the soft snow that you might find your way back to the rest of your load; could see the lashings of the food bags; could read a compass without striking three or four different boxes to find one dry match; could read your watch to see if the blissful moment of getting out of your bag was come without groping in the snow all about; when it would not take you five minutes to lash up the door of the tent, and five hours to get started in the morning.

Sir Vivian Fuchs

(1908–)

British geologist and Antarctic explorer. In 1955 he led the British Commonwealth Expedition to Antarctica – a ten-man, 2200-mile journey of detailed scientific observation, completed in ninety-nine days.

The journey begins

On 22 December I sent the following message to Hillary summarizing the situation:

> Personal for Hillary. We arrived South Ice 21 December after severe crevasse trouble and three major recoveries of Sno-cats. Distance travelled in 29 days 349 miles but consider this worst stage of journey and expect rapid travel from here on. Thanks for your information and proposed crevasse recce. Hope you will be able to mark route through or limit of area with snow cairns or stakes. We leave here with four Sno-cats three Weasels one Muskeg will probably reach you with four Cats and one Weasel. Two dog teams will travel ahead. We expect leave South Ice 25th then Otter and four RAF fly there to await suitable day for flight to Scott. Hope for radio contact with you are arranged 26th onwards. Happy Christmas to you all.
>
> Bunny.

With the dog teams away, we turned our attention to unlashing and reloading the sledges. It was certainly a busy scene, for there were eight vehicles, counting the two that were already up at South Ice, together with twelve large sledges and a number of smaller ones. Everywhere stood piles of material, scores of fuel barrels, dozens of jerricans, stacks of boxes, ropes in profusion, a hundred other items sorted or to be sorted, stowed and lashed down before we could leave on the next leg of our journey to the Pole.

Meanwhile, David Pratt and Roy Homard were working hard on the vehicles, preparing them for the long journey ahead. One major task which they had expected would be necessary at South Ice was the replacement of the damaged pontoon on 'Rock 'n Roll'. We had been putting this off time after time, on the grounds that the more mileage we could get from the old one, the further we should be able to go after fitting the new. This situation still obtained, for there was very little additional wear, and we decided to go on carrying the spare as long as the old parts remained serviceable.

When we went to our sleeping bags on 24 December, 320 gallons of petrol had been used to fill the tanks of all eight vehicles, the sledges bore another 109 barrels, totalling 5200 gallons and weighing approximately 21 tons. In addition, we were carrying ½ ton of lubricants, and 1½ tons of tools and spare parts. The remaining nine tons of pay-load included ½ ton of explosive for the seismic work, 1½ tons of food and ½ ton of paraffin – major items these – the rest being made up of scientific equipment, tents, camping gear, ropes, skis, ice axes and all the other minor needs of a party that is to be entirely self-contained for three or four months.

The journey ends

Just after midday, on 4 January, we drove through the last few miles of soft snow into the American South Pole Station. It was very pleasant to be greeted by friendly faces and welcoming voices and to feel we could relax again. Our tractors had performed quite remarkably when one considered their limitations, but we weren't sorry to clamber out of their cold seats for the last time and to know that our 1250-mile trip was over.

Jenny Diski

(1947–)

English writer. *Skating to Antarctica* is an autobiographical account of a journey to Antarctica on a cruise ship, in search of whiteness both literal and metaphorical.

The abandoned whaling station at Grytviken

The abandoned whaling station at Grytviken is either lovingly preserved in its natural state or derelict, depending on how you choose to look at it. If derelict landscapes, like the murkier parts of King's Cross and the old unreconstructed docklands appeal, then Grytviken is a pearl of desolation. A rust-bucket ghost town, left to rot in its own beautiful way. Approached from the bay in the Zodiac, it was a small hamlet of white-walled, red-roofed one- and two-storey buildings nestling on the handkerchief-sized edge of the island, surrounded on all sides by rising black volcanic mountains, topped with white and smeared with snow and ice in the dips and crevasses. It looked idyllic, if a little vulnerable, as if a brave attempt at human assertion were being pushed ineluctably into the sea by the encroaching island itself. Once we were close up we could see that a different aspect of nature had taken command, as the neat white houses turned out mostly to be decaying sheds and ware-houses, stained by weather, with rotting doors hanging off rusting hinges, dotted inside with broken and corroded implements and hefty languishing chains. It was a lovely place, as I stepped on to the decaying planking of the flensing plan, where the whales were hefted up and tiny men with hockey stick-shaped knives at the end of a long pole took their positions around the bulk of the dead mammal and carved away the inches-thick layer of blubber from the flesh. It was a town memorializing the efficiency of commerce. We wandered around and discovered this place for the rendering of the blubber, that for the butchering of the flesh, another for the processing of the bones. A purposeful place made beautiful by its dereliction and the delicate carvings and ornately cut patterns of rust on iron. A couple of dead hulks of half-sunk whaling ships to either side of the inlet finished off the symmetry of decline.

Sara Wheeler

(1961–)

English traveller, journalist and broadcaster. She has also written about Chile and a life of the Antarctic explorer Apsley Cherry-Garrard.

To the South Pole

The only other passenger on the fuel flight to the South Pole was a physicist in his late twenties from Boston. On the way to the ice runway he told me that he had been south before, and was about to spend a year at the Pole, a prospect which filled him with great joy. He reminded me of an overgrown puppy.

The sun was shining, and the ice runway was pitted with waterholes. The following day, 17 December, air operations were shifted to the former skiway at Willy Field. We picked our way over to a metal hut on stilts containing a drum of drinking water, a quantity of blue plastic padded chairs, the usual bewildering array of rubbish bins and a box of yellow plastic earplugs. The walls were bare except for two brightly coloured waste management posters, and the blue lino floor was smudged with dirty snow. When we had settled down, the physicist handed me a photograph of his telescope at the Pole. He was carrying a stash of them in his pocket.

We could see our plane squatting on the ice, attached to umbilical tubes of fuel and tended by diminutive khaki figures. After an hour, the pilot arrived and announced that we were 'all set'. We made our way over to the steps of the Hercules. On the Flight Information board in the hold it said, 'Only eight shopping days till Christmas'. As we belted up in the red webbing seats, the pair of us alone in the cavernous fuselage, a crewman appeared and said, 'As far as emergency exits go, if you have to, get out any way you can.'

Mountains

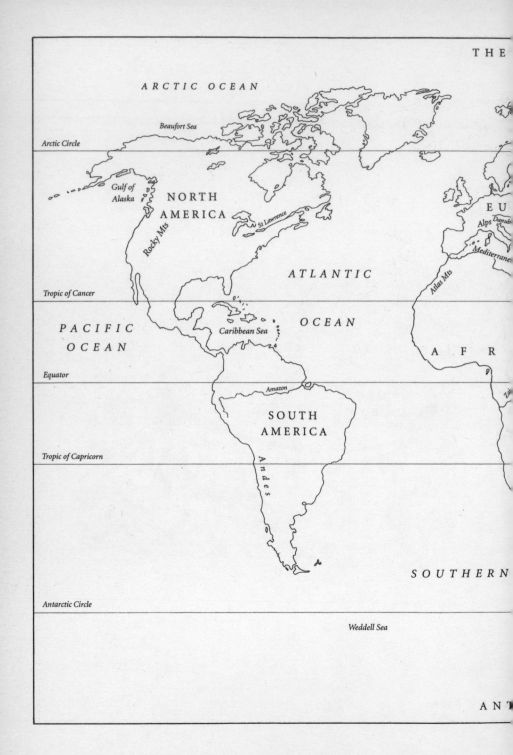

THE

ARCTIC OCEAN

Beaufort Sea

Arctic Circle

EU

Gulf of
Alaska

NORTH
AMERICA

Alps Danub

St Lawrence

Mediterranea

Rocky Mts

ATLANTIC

Atlas Mts

Tropic of Cancer

PACIFIC
OCEAN

OCEAN

A F R

Caribbean Sea

Equator

Amazon

Zã

SOUTH
AMERICA

Tropic of Capricorn

A
n
d
e
s

SOUTHERN

Antarctic Circle

Weddell Sea

AN

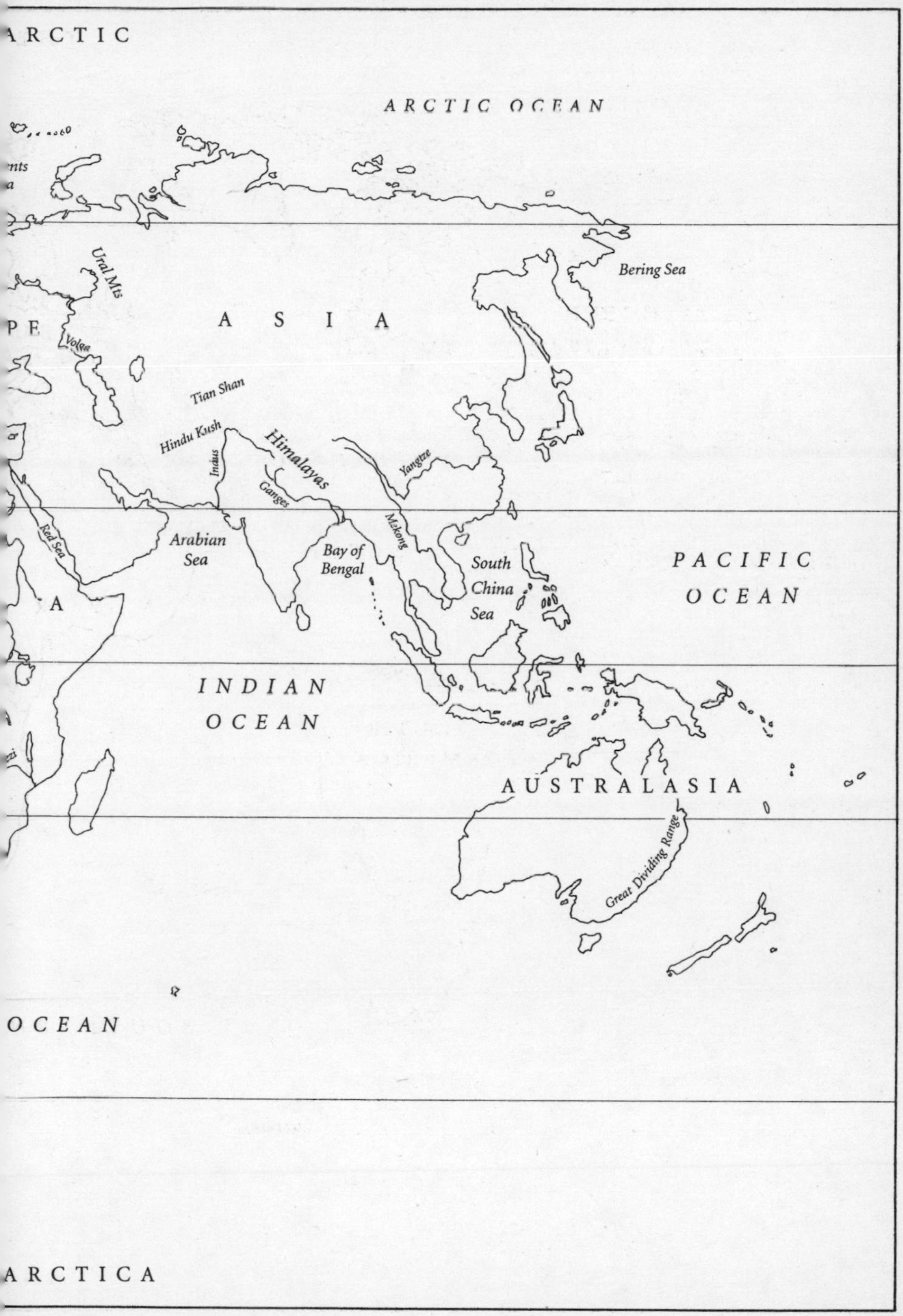

ARCTIC

ARCTIC OCEAN

Bering Sea

Ural Mts

ASIA

PE

Volga

Tian Shan

Hindu Kush

Indus

Himalayas

Yangtze

Ganges

Red Sea

Arabian
Sea

Bay of
Bengal

Mekong

South
China
Sea

PACIFIC
OCEAN

A

INDIAN
OCEAN

AUSTRALASIA

Great Dividing Range

OCEAN

ARCTICA

Hernando Cortés

(1485–1547)

Spanish conquistador. In 1518 he set sail for Mexico; landed in Yucatan, burnt his ships at Vera Cruz, went on to invade the Aztec capital Tenochtitlán and imprison the Aztec ruler, Montezuma, who had originally received him hospitably. After a terrible siege, much fighting and huge losses on both sides, including the death of Montezuma, Cortés was appointed governor and captain-general of the New Spain. Despite the ruthlessness of Cortés and the Spanish conquerors, he was an intrepid leader of his men, as his account of crossing the mountains of Honduras reveals; this was part of his *Fifth Letter to the Emperor Charles V*.

Cortes and his men cross the mountains

After traversing six leagues of level country we began to ascend the mountain pass, which is one of the most wonderful things in the world to behold; for were I to attempt its description, and picture to your Majesty its roughness, as well as the difficulties of every kind we had to surmount, I should utterly fail in the undertaking. I can, however, assure your Majesty that neither I nor those who are more eloquent could find words to give a proper idea of it; even if we did, we could never be understood except by those who saw it with their own eyes, and experienced the fatigues and perils of the ascent. It will be sufficient to inform your Majesty that we were twelve days in making the eight leagues across the pass, and that we lost on this occasion no less than sixty-eight of our horses, that either fell down precipices or were hamstrung and disabled by their fall. The rest arrived so fatigued and hurt that scarcely one was of service to us, and three months passed before any of them were fit for riding. All the time we were ascending this awful pass it never ceased raining day and night, and yet the mountains we had to cross were so shaped, having no crevices wherein the rain might stop, that we had no water to drink, and were greatly tormented by thirst, most of our horses perishing through it. Indeed, had it not been for some which we were able to collect in copper kettles and other vessels, whilst encamping at night in huts made for that purpose, no man or horse could have escaped alive.

Whilst crossing this mountain pass, a nephew of mine fell down and broke his leg in two or three places; and after this misfortune – while all of us deplored – we had the greatest difficulty to carry him over to the other side in the state in which he was.

Alexander von Humboldt

(1769–1859)

German naturalist and traveller, a son of the chamberlain to the King of Prussia. He spent five years privately exploring in Central and South America (1799–1804), with the French naturalist Bonpland. They followed the course of the Orinoco and tributaries of the Amazon, collecting specimens of plants and butterflies, and produced wonderful illustrated volumes about their discoveries. The Spanish authorities made the journey difficult as they feared rivals to their power. In their attempt on Chimborazo, now in Ecuador, they reached 19,286 feet, they were not far from the summit. After a period in Europe, von Humboldt then travelled nearly 10,000 miles in Central Asia, with the assistance of Tsar Nicholas II and 12,244 horses.

Attempt on Chimborazo, 1802

Suddenly the stratum of mist which had hidden every distant object began to clear. Once more we recognized the dome-shaped summit of

Chimborazo, now very close. What a grand and awe-inspiring spectacle! The hope of conquering it renewed our strength. The rocky ridge, which only had a thin sprinkling of snow here and there, became somewhat wider. With this surer surface underfoot we hurried on – only to be stopped dead in our tracks by a ravine some 400 feet deep and 60 feet wide. This was an insurmountable barrier. The softness of the snow and the steepness of the slopes made it impossible to scale the sides.

It was now 1 pm. We fixed up the barometer with great care and found it stood at 13 inches 11 2/10 lines. The air temperature was only 3°C below freezing but after our long stay in the tropics even this amount of cold was quite benumbing. Our boots were wet through with snow water. According to the barometric formula given by Laplace we had now reached an altitude of 19,286 feet.

We stayed only a short time in this dreary waste, for we were soon enveloped in mist again, which hung about us motionless. We saw no more of the summit of Chimborazo, nor of the neighbouring Sierra Nevada, still less the high plain of Quito. We felt as isolated as in a balloon.

As the weather was becoming increasingly threatening, we hurried down along the ridge of rock and found that even greater caution was necessary than during the ascent. We delayed no longer than sufficed to collect fragments of rocks as specimens of the mountain structure, as we foresaw that in Europe we should frequently be asked for a fragment from Chimborazo.

When we were at a height of about 17,400 feet we ran into a violent hailstorm and twenty minutes later into a snowstorm so heavy that the ridge was soon several inches deep. We saw a few rock lichens above the snow line, at a height of 16,920 feet. The last green moss we noticed was growing about 2600 feet lower down. M. Bonpland captured a butterfly at a height of 15,000 feet and a fly was seen 1600 feet higher. We did not see any condors, however, which had been so numerous on Pichincha. At a few minutes past two we reached the spot where we had left the mules.

Henriette d'Angeville

(c. 1793–1871)

D'Angeville came from a noble French family; her grand-father was guillotined during the French Revolution. She developed a romantic desire to climb Mont Blanc, and planned her ascent meticulously. She did not climb it until she was forty-four and made her twenty-first and final Alpine ascent at the age of sixty-nine.

Packing for the ascent

My clothing consisted of:
  Combinations of English flannel, to be worn next to the skin
  A man's shirt, to be worn on top
  A foulard cravat
  Two pairs of silk stockings
  Two pairs of very thick woollen stockings
  Two pairs of nailed boots, waterproof and of different sizes
  A pair of trousers, cut full, corded at the top, with gaiters at the bottom to tuck into the boots. These trousers were made of Scottish wool plaid with a warm, soft, fleece lining
  A blouse of the same material and lining, cut full, with tucks front and back to protect chest and back with six layers of wool
  A leather belt, arranged so as to sit rather low on the waist
  One pair of knitted gloves with a fur lining
  One pair of gloves with the fur outside, large enough to fit over the others, with deep fur cuffs to keep out the air
  A boa
  A close bonnet of the same material as the blouse, lined as well, trimmed with black fur, and with a green veil attached to the brim
  A large straw hat from Chamonix, with a green lining and four strings to hold it firmly in place
  A black velvet mask

A long stick with a ferrule

A plaid

A pelisse, fur-lined throughout, for the night and the coldest part of the day

This costume, as I wore it from the Grands Mulets onwards, weighed fourteen full pounds (counting just one pair of boots), and the pelisse and plaid that I put on at some points weighed another seven pounds (making twenty-one pounds in all).

To the summit

There was one moment when I did believe victory would elude me. I have explained that I needed about two minutes rest at each halt. Once, we tried cutting this time, but to no avail, since I had not been three steps before I collapsed in a state of such prostration that it was feared I might be too weak to stand.

'If I die before reaching the summit, promise me that you will carry my body to the top and leave it there,' I said, my eyes already half-closed.

'Have no fear, you will reach it dead or alive.'

Consoled by this promise, I fell into a deep sleep; I heard Couttet calling my name but I could not move or reply. I was so comfortable there that I felt better able to lift the mountain from the ground than to get to my feet once more.

'Should we carry her?' asked Mugnier. 'I am ready to do so, I am still strong enough. Mademoiselle, do you want to be carried? . . .'

In view of my debilitated condition, the guides had to exert great skill to manipulate the sticks round corners without mishap, for the least instability made me stagger. The same was true of the rope; I was well content to know that I was supported, but it was fatal to try to pull me up, as the only result of any attempts to hasten my progress was that I fell flat on my face in the snow. I had to go gently, conscious that I was sustained by rope and sticks; any other form of active impulsion would only have contributed to my exhaustion by obliging me to adopt a speed that I could no longer maintain.

In this way I gradually drew near my goal. I had fallen into one of my relentless sleeps, when I heard Couttet's voice saying: '*Courage! there is the summit! This time we shall reach it!'* I immediately looked up, and indeed, I could see the summit about thirty or thirty-five paces away from me, in electrifying proximity. Leaping to my feet, I ran rather than walked towards the object of my dreams! . . . I could not have been three paces off, but I could go no further, and sank down, crushed yet again by the inexplicable desire for sleep! . . .

This time, they allowed me five minutes' rest; when I awoke, I untied the rope, now useless, and even rejected the stick, so that it was alone and unaided that I took the three steps that lay between me and victory. At twenty-five past one, I finally set foot on the summit of Mont Blanc and drove the ferrule of my stick into its flank, as a soldier plants his standard on a captured citadel.

Charles Darwin

(1809–82)

English natural scientist. From 1836, Darwin was naturalist on HMS *Beagle*, on a surveying expedition to South America; this included the Galapagos Islands, Tahiti, New Zealand, Tasmania and the Keeling Islands, as well as much of South America. In South America, Darwin had the opportunity to make long inland journeys, including 600 miles across the Pampas with *gauchos*, and across the Cordillera of the Andes via the dangerous Portillo Pass. Here he discovered fossilised shells over 13,000 feet above sea level. The voyage was to have greater significance than anyone imagined, since the observations made by Darwin were to form the basis of his great work on natural selection. After years of development and thought, the publication of *The Origin of Species* in 1859 was hastened by the similar ideas sent by his contemporary Alfred Russell Wallace (**q.v.**) in a letter from the Malay Archipelago.

Passage of the Cordillera

About noon we began the tedious ascent of the Peuquenes ridge, and then for the first time experienced some little difficulty in our respiration. The mules would halt every fifty yards, and after resting for a few seconds the poor willing animals started of their own accord again. The short breathing from the rarefied atmosphere is called by the Chilenos "puna"; and they have most ridiculous notions concerning its origin. Some say "all the waters here have puna;" others that "where there is snow there is puna" – and this no doubt is true. The only sensation I experienced was a slight tightness across the head and chest, like that felt on leaving a warm room and running quickly in frosty weather. There was some imagination even in this; for upon finding fossil shells on the highest ridge, I entirely forgot the puna in my delight. Certainly the exertion of walking was extremely great, and the respiration became deep and laborious: I am told that in Potosi (about 13,000 feet above the sea) strangers do not become thoroughly accustomed to the atmosphere for an entire year. The inhabitants all recommend onions for the puna; as this vegetable has sometimes been given in Europe for pectoral complaints, it may possibly be of real service: for my part I found nothing so good as the fossil shells!

When about halfway up we met a large party with seventy loaded mules. It was interesting to hear the wild cries of the muleteers, and to watch the long descending string of the animals; they appeared so diminutive, there being nothing but the bleak mountains with which they could be compared. When near the summit, the wind, as generally happens, was impetuous and extremely cold. On each side of the ridge we had to pass over broad bands of perpetual snow, which were now soon to be covered by a fresh layer. When we reached the crest and looked backwards, a glorious view was presented. The atmosphere resplendently clear; the sky an intense blue; the profound valleys; the wild broken forms; the heaps of ruins, piled up during the lapse of ages; the bright-coloured rocks, contrasted with the quiet mountains of snow; all these together produced a scene no one could have imagined. Neither plant nor bird, excepting a few condors wheeling around the higher pinnacles, distracted my attention from the inanimate mass. I felt glad that I was alone: it was like watching a thunderstorm, or hearing in full orchestra a chorus of the Messiah.

Edward Arthur Fitzgerald

(1846–1927)

British mountaineer and professional soldier. Fitzgerald made several first ascents in New Zealand: Mounts Tasman, Sefton, Haidinger, Silberhorn and Sealy. While climbing Mount Sefton, a boulder knocked him off a 300-foot perpendicular face; he was saved by his climbing companion Matthias Zurbriggen of Macugnaga. In 1897 the pair led the first successful expedition to climb Mount Aconcagua in the Central Andes, at 22,835 feet the highest mountain in the Western Hemisphere. Besides the frightful conditions and severe frostbite, Fitzgerald was defeated by altitude sickness, and only Zurbriggen reached the summit.

A wild night in the Andes

We turned into our sleeping-bags after the sun went down. The sunset had been remarkable, almost menacing in its grandeur: great banks of clouds lay spread beneath us far out to sea, dyed scarlet by the sinking sun. They changed rapidly, assuming curious and fantastic shapes, till finally they shot up all at once like tongues of flame to the sky, while the heavens turned a brilliant purple from their reflected light. As I looked on this sea of fire stretched out beneath me for over one hundred and sixty miles, it seemed at moments like looking down into some infernal region.

Soon after we had turned in we heard the wind moaning fitfully about the tent. The men became restless, and tossed about as they slept, while a strange uneasiness seemed to move them, as when a herd of cattle on the pampas scents an approaching storm. The wind gradually increased, and soon the men's breathing was silenced by the roar of the hurricane, as it shrieked and howled round our little tent, threatening every moment to rend in shreds the canvas which strained and tugged at the guy-ropes. We tightly fastened up the double door, and lay panting and struggling for breath. Thus, hour after hour, the night passed slowly – how slowly I am afraid to say; it was unspeakably long.

William Spotswood Green

(1847–1919)

Irish clergyman, civil servant and mountaineer. Green made a valiant attempt on Mount Cook, the highest mountain in New Zealand, in 1882 with Emil Boss and Ulrich Kaufmann of Grindelwald. The weather conditions forced them back only 200 feet from the summit. If the ascent had been bad, the descent was worse; the party was forced to spend a night standing on a two-foot wide ledge, at over 10,000 feet, sucking meat lozenges, singing songs and telling stories to stay awake. The summit was eventually reached twelve years later by three New Zealand climbers.

An attempt on Mount Cook

At 5.30 we reached the highest rocks, from which an easy slope led up to an icicled bergschrund, which, starting from the cornice of the arête, ran round the cap of the summit from left to right, and Boss remarked, "If we had taken to the Mount Tasman arête that would have cut us off." The wind now for the first time struck us with full fury; we had to shout in order to make each other hear. And though we had ocular demonstration that it was not actually freezing, the blast seemed bitterly cold.

We bore away to the left to avoid the highest part of the bergschrund above us, and surmounting the cornice without any difficulty, at 6 p.m. stepped on to the topmost crest of Ao-Rangi.

Our first glance was, of course, down the great precipice beneath us towards the Tasman Glacier – the precipice up which we had gazed so often – but the dark grey masses of vapour swirling round the ice-crags shut out all distant view.

A look backwards, down into the dark, cloud-filled abyss out of which we had climbed, was enough to make us shudder, it looked fathomless; and this white icy ridge on which we stood, with torn mists driving over it before the fierce nor'-wester, seemed the only solid thing in the midst of chaos.

Mount Cook was now practically conquered. We advanced rapidly along the cornice; which rose at an angle of about 20° towards what was mathematically the highest point, now and then cutting a step for greater security, but in most cases trusting to the grip gained by the nails in our boots.

Sometimes a blast would come upon us with such force as to compel us to crouch low and drive in our axes firmly, to guard against our being blown off into space. Fierce squalls would shatter the icicles of the cornice and send them down the slopes up which we had climbed. Descending with a swishing sound, they soon pounded themselves to pieces, and so accounted for the showers of coarse hail which had proved so disagreeable on the final ice-slope. Now the mists would vanish, giving us a clear view of the summit. Again the inky black clouds would come on, almost obliterating Kaufmann from my sight, though he was only eight yards distant. From the moment we had gained the arête, anxiety about beginning the descent had filled our minds – as should darkness overtake us on the summit of the mountains, our chances of ever returning to the haunts of men would be but slight. The weather was settling in for a thoroughly bad night. The storm at present blowing was sufficiently unpleasant; if it came on to blow any harder we would not be able to hold our grip. There was no chance of a view. We were hundreds of feet above any rocks, so that we could build no cairn, or leave any record of our ascent. We were all agreed that we were fairly on the summit of the peak, and that we ought to commence the descent. Ten minutes more and the last bit of snow would be under the sole of my boot, when there came a sudden gap in the cornice. A bergschrund broke through it. There was no open crevasse, but a step down off the cornice of five or six feet, a flat, and then a step up of eight feet.

William Martin Conway

(1856–1937)

English art historian, collector and mountaineer. Baron Conway of Allington led the first properly organised expedition to the Himalayas in 1892, which made large-scale maps of glaciers invaluable to later expeditions. He was knighted for his expedition to the Karakorum three years later. Conway also made the first crossing of Spitz-bergen and a great traverse of the Alps from Monte Viso to the Gross Glockner, with Edward FitzGerald (**q.v.**) and two Gurkhas.

Early morning on the Karakorum-Himalaya

25 August – The night was bitterly cold, and sleep by no means easily wooed. The minimum was 16° Fahr. Poor McCormick was again troubled with a combination of headache and toothache, which only slumber could remove. About half-past two, when all were finally settled down, the clink of axes was heard on the hard snow without, and Bruce, with three Gurkhas, appeared upon the scene. It was far too early for a start, and far too cold for us to let them remain outside; so all seven of us crowded into the tent, and sleep was no longer possible for any.

By five o'clock Zurbriggen was stirring. His was the laborious duty of preparing a warm drink of chocolate, with indifferent spirit to burn, and no space to manœuvre the apparatus in. The Russian lamp began to roar like a falling avalanche; and, while the chocolate was cooking, we struggled out of our bags and into our boots, and wound the *pattis* round our legs, first greasing our feet with marmot fat, for protection against the cold. The needful preparations occupied a long time, for every movement was a toil. After lacing a boot, one had to lie down and take breath before one could lace the next. At five minutes to six all were ready, and, with a farewell to McCormick, we left the tents and started upwards.

Tom Longstaff

(1875–1964)

Doctor and mountaineer who climbed in the Caucasus, Himalayas, Karakorum and Canadian Rockies. Longstaff spent long periods at high altitudes, once surviving fifty four days at between 16,000 and 21,000 feet in the Himalayas. He spent one night on a snow crest at 23,000 feet without a tent. He also served in India, 1914–18, went on expeditions to Spitsbergen, Greenland and joined the 1935 attempt on Everest. He became Honorary Secretary and then Vice President of the Royal Geographical Society and President of the Alpine Club.

A descent by avalanche, Tibet

Just as I was turning to gather in the slack of Henri's rope I heard his warning cry and a hissing sound – *shshshshsh* – like the surge of a spent wave up a smooth shore, but menacing. The surface layer of the snow, melted by the day's sun, had parted from the harder frozen layer beneath and was avalanching under Henri. He shot down lying flat on the moving snow and swept me from my feet as the snow on which I stood started to move too. As I shot down past Alexis, I felt his hand close on the back of my coat and his struggles to stop me. But we went together. We were lying on a bed of moving snow, heavy and wettish, not so bad as powder-snow would have been, and this was pushing the surface layers into motion *ahead* of us. We all tried hard to stop ourselves with the picks of our axes, but could get no hold. My mind seemed quite clear, but curious about the end rather than terrified. Thoughts passed at incredible speed, while bodily sensation was blotted out. The glacier two or three thousand feet below seemed to rush towards us, its crevasses widening and widening just as the engine of a passing express train seems to grow higher and higher as it rushes towards the platform. I had no sensation of physical pain, nor even of discomfort, though my hand was deeply cut. I had got turned head downwards, and seeing rocks ahead clawed off my snow spectacles to save my eyes when the smash came!

We had fallen some 3000 feet in a minute or two. The damage was a few cuts. Each of the men had broken a crampon. We had lost our three hats and worst of all our ice-axes. Now that it was all over I found that I was trembling – from shock, for I had experienced no feeling of fear, anxiety or pain. The two Piedmontese showed no concern at all. Leaving me to select and wall in a sleeping-place in the rocks below, they started at once straight up the track of the avalanche after the ice-axes. The accident happened about five o'clock and they did not return for three hours, having climbed over 1000 feet to well above the last little cliff. They retrieved all three axes. Theirs was a grand performance.

Belmore Browne

(fl. 1910)

Naturalist, artist and mountaineer who joined three attempts to climb Mount McKinley in 1906, 1910 and 1912. At 20,320 feet, Mount McKinley is the highest peak of the Alaska Range; both the approach and ascent are very difficult, being only three and a half degrees south of the Arctic Circle, and subject to extreme weather. Despite overcoming many setbacks, Browne's 1912 party was at last defeated by blizzards a thousand feet from the summit, but fortunately avoided the earthquake and huge avalanche that occurred a few days later and virtually altered the face of the mountain. The South Peak was climbed in 1913 by four men led by the Reverend Hudson Stuck, Episcopal Archdeacon of Yukon.

Life at base camp, Mount McKinley

While the cook was at work trails would be broken to, and water brought from, the nearest water hole, and an out-door kitchen built for cooking dog food. More boughs were brought on which to pile our freight which was covered with our sled-covers.

With the dog food cooking merrily and everything outside stowed away we would repair to the tent. A rope would be stretched along the ridgepole for our wet clothes to dry on, our beds unrolled, and we could surrender to the enjoyment of peace and warmth.

Strangely enough the fur robes in which we slept were all made of a different kind of fur. Professor Parker's was made of the skins of summer killed Lapland reindeer, La Voy's was made of Australian wombat, Aten's was composed of both summer and winter killed white sheep (*Ovis dalli*), while mine was made of timber wolf skins. For ordinary winter travel they were all equally good, but in extremely cold weather the wombat was inferior to the other skins, and during our explorations on Mount McKinley, La Voy left his wombat bag with Aten and used the sheep skins.

They were all sewed in the form of a bag. Professor Parker's was arranged with a complicated opening that buttoned over flaps; it was made (at great expense) by a New York outfitter, after the regular New York way. The other three bags were simply sacks with an open end. When you were cold you doubled the top under your head and breathed through a small hole which you made by pushing your hand out of the opening of the bag and withdrawing it. This simple arrangement is warmer, simpler, and cheaper than the New York way and is used almost universally by men who live in the north. For a hard trip the reindeer and white mountain sheep bags were superior to my wolf skins for the reason that they weighed less. My wolf skin bag complete, including a balloon-silk cover, weighed seventeen pounds, while the sheep skin bag weighed only ten pounds, and the reindeer even less. But weight for weight and warmth for warmth the white sheep bag, roughly made by the Knik Indians, was by far the best. Besides being light and warm the hair on a sheep skin does not hold moisture to any extent, and as our bags were covered with ice, from our breath freezing during the night, this fact was of great value.

Heinrich Harrer

(1912–)

Austrian mountaineer. A member of the Austro-German expedition that made the first ascent of the north face of the Eiger, Harrer continued his climbing career in the Himalayas until interned in India by the British from 1940–4. With fellow mountaineer Peter Aufschnaiter, Harrer escaped to Tibet, travelling without equipment through the Himalayas. Harrer was befriended by Tibetans and eventually became tutor to the young Dalai Lama. He spent seven years in the country, described in his famous book.

The Spider

The "Spider" on the Eiger's Face is white. Its body consists of ice and eternal snow. Its legs and its predatory arms, all hundreds of feet long, are white, too. From that perpetual, fearfully steep field of frozen snow nothing but ice emerges to fill gullies, cracks and crevices. Up and down. To left, to right. In every direction, at every angle of steepness.

And there the "Spider" waits.

Every climber who picks his way up the North Face of the Eiger has to cross it. There is no way round it. And even those who moved best and most swiftly up the Face have met their toughest ordeal on the "Spider". Someone once compared the whole Face to a gigantic spider's web catching the spider's victims and feeding them to her. This comparison is unfounded, exaggerated, and merely a cheap way of making the flesh creep. Neither the savage wall nor the lovely mountain have deserved this slur. Nor have the climbers; for climbers are not flies and insects stumbling blindly to their fate, but men of vision and courage. All the same, the "White Spider" seems to me to be a good symbol for the North Face. The climber has to face its perils on the final third of the wall, when he is tired from many hours and days of exhausting climbing and weakened by chilly bivouacs. But there is no rest to be had there, no matter how tired you are.

He who wishes to survive the spate of avalanches which sweep the "Spider" must realise that there is no escape from this dangerously steep obstacle; he must know how to blend his strength with patience and reflection. Above the "Spider" begin the overhanging, iced-up exit cracks; that is where sheer strength tells. But here the man who abandons patience and good sense for fear-induced haste will surely finish up like the fly which struggles so long in the spider's web that it is caught through sheer exhaustion.

The "White Spider" on the Eiger is the extreme test not only of a climber's technical ability, but of his character as well. Later on in life, when fate seemed to spin some spider's web or other across my path, my thoughts often went back to the "White Spider". Life itself demanded the same methods, the same qualities, when there no longer seemed to be any possible escape from its difficulties, as had won us a way out of the difficulties of the Eiger's North Face – common-sense, patience and open-eyed courage. Haste born of fear and all the wild stunts arising from it can only end in disaster.

Sir Edmund Hillary

(1919–) and Tenzing Norgay (1914–86)

Hillary and Tenzing were the first men to reach the summit of Mount Everest in 1953. Hillary was a New Zealand apiarist and mountaineer; he later became deputy leader of the British Commonwealth Antarctic Expedition under Vivian Fuchs. His son Peter joined him on expedition to the North Pole in 1985. Tenzing was the leading Nepalese sherpa and mountaineer who had been on earlier Everest expeditions in 1935, 1936 and 1938. After climbing Everest he studied mountaineering in Switzerland and became head of the Institute of Mountaineering and President of the Sherpa Association.

John Hunt

(1910–93)

English mountaineer and social reformer. Hunt was born
in India where he had a military career after being educated in England. He climbed his first Alpine peak at the
age of fifteen. Hunt led the first successful expedition to
climb Mount Everest in 1953; and other mountaineering
expeditions subsequently.

The summit (Edmund Hillary)

The ridge continued as before. Giant cornices on the right, steep rock
slopes on the left. I went on cutting steps on the narrow strip of snow.
The ridge curved away to the right and we had no idea where the top
was. As I cut around the back of one hump, another higher one would
swing into view. Time was passing and the ridge seemed never-ending.
In one place, where the angle of the ridge had eased off, I tried cram-
poning without cutting steps, hoping this would save time, but I quickly
realized that our margin of safety on these steep slopes at this altitude
was too small, so I went on step-cutting. I was beginning to tire a little
now. I had been cutting steps continuously for two hours, and Tenzing,
too, was moving very slowly. As I chipped steps around still another
corner, I wondered rather dully just how long we could keep it up. Our
original zest had now quite gone and it was turning more into a grim
struggle. I then realized that the ridge ahead, instead of still monoto-
nously rising, now dropped sharply away, and far below I could see the
North Col and the Rongbuk glacier. I look upwards to see a narrow
snow ridge running up to a snowy summit. A few more whacks of the
ice-axe in the firm snow and we stood on top . . .

I had little hope of the results being particularly successful, as I had
a lot of difficulty in holding the camera steady in my clumsy gloves,
but I felt that they would at least serve as a record. After some ten
minutes of this, I realized that I was becoming rather clumsy-fingered

and slow-moving, so I quickly replaced my oxygen set and experienced once more the stimulating effect of even a few litres of oxygen. Meanwhile, Tenzing had made a little hole in the snow and in it he placed various small articles of food – a bar of chocolate, a packet of biscuits and a handful of lollies. Small offerings, indeed, but at least a token gift to the Gods that all devout Buddhists believe have their home on this lofty summit. While we were together on the South Col two days before, Hunt had given me a small crucifix which he had asked me to take to the top. I, too, made a hole in the snow and placed the crucifix beside Tensing's gifts.

The return of Hillary and Tenzing (John Hunt)

At 2 p.m., just after the Indian Wireless News bulletin had informed the world that we had failed, five men could be seen at the top of the shallow trough about 500 yards above the camp.

Some of us started out at once, Mike Westmacott and myself ahead, while our Sherpas crowded outside their Dome tent, no less eager than the rest of us to know the result. But the approaching climbers made no sign, just plodded on dejectedly towards us; they did not even wave a greeting. My heart sank. In my weak state, this plod up the track was already an effort; now my feet felt like lead. This must be failure; we must now think of that third and last attempt.

Suddenly, the leading man in the party – it was George Lowe – raised his axe, pointing unmistakably towards the distant top of Everest; he made several vigorous thrusts. The others behind him were now making equally unequivocal signs. Far from failure, this was IT! they had made it! Feeling welled up uncontrollably as I now quickened my pace – I still could not muster the strength to break into a run, and Mike Westmacott was now well ahead. Everyone was pouring out of the tents; there were shouts of acclamation and joy. The next moment I was with them: handshakes – even, I blush to say, hugs – for the triumphant pair. A special one for Tenzing, so well merited for him personally, this victory, both for himself and for his people.

Joe Simpson

(1960–)

English mountaineer and writer, described by one reviewer as 'a specialist in the dark underside of climbing'. *Touching the Void* describes mountaineering exploits including an extremely narrow escape from death on Siula Grande in Peru in 1985, and some sticky moments in the Himalayas and the Alps.

Trouble with rockfalls

1. *The Himalayas*

I set off hurriedly. A cascade of ice dropped over steep underlying rocks in a fifty-foot step. I could see it was steep, 80° maybe, and hammered in a screw when I reached its base. I would climb it in one push, then move right.

Water was running under the ice, and in places the rock sparked as my axe hit it. I slowed down, climbing carefully, cautious of rushing into a mistake. Holding on to my left axe near the top of the cascade, I tiptoed out on my front points. Halfway into swinging my right axe, a sudden dark object rushed at me.

'Rocks!' I yelled, ducking down and away. Heavy blows thudded into my shoulder, whacking against my sack, and then it was past, and I watched Simon looking straight up at my warning. The boulder, about four-foot square, swept below me directly at him. It seemed an age before he reacted, and when he did it was with a slow-motion casualness which I found hard to believe. He leaned to his left and dropped his head as the heavy stone seemed to hit him full-on. I shut my eyes, and hunched harder as more stones hit me. When I looked again, Simon was all but hidden beneath the sack which he had swept up over his head.

'You okay?'

'Yes!' he shouted from behind his sack.

'I thought you were hit.'

'Only by small stuff. Get moving, I don't like it here.'

I climbed the last few feet of the cascade, and moved quickly right to the shelter of the rock. Simon grinned when he reached me:

'Where did that lot come from?'

'I don't know. I only saw it at the last moment. Too bloody close!'

'Let's get on. I can see the gully from here.'

Boosted with adrenalin, he climbed quickly towards the steep icy couloir visible in a corner of the main buttress. It was four-thirty. We had an hour and a half of light left.

I went on past his stance for another full rope length but the couloir seemed no nearer. The flat, white light made it hard to gauge distances. Simon set out on the last short pitch to the foot of the couloir.

'We ought to bivi here,' I said. 'It will be dark soon.'

'Yeah, but there's no chance of a snow hole, or any ledges.'

I could see he was right. Any night spent here would be uncomfortable. It was already getting hard to see.

'I'll try and get up this before dark.'

'Too late . . . it *is* dark!'

'Well, I bloody hope we can do it in one rope length then.' I didn't like the prospect of blundering around on steep ice in the dark trying to sort out belays.

I made a short traverse left to the foot of the couloir. 'Jesus! This is overhanging, and the ice is terrible!'

Simon said nothing.

2. *The Alps*

The next few seconds were unforgettable. I was inside a protective waterproof bivouac bag, half-asleep, and Ian was making final adjustments to his safety line. Suddenly and without warning, I felt myself drop swiftly. Simultaneously there was an ear-splitting roaring and grinding. With my head inside the bag and my arms flailing outside the opening at my chest I knew nothing except the sickening dread as I went plummeting down into the 2000-foot abyss below. I heard a high-pitched yelp of fear amid the heavy roaring, then felt a springy recoil. The safety rope had held. All my weight was held on my armpits, as I had accidentally caught the safety rope in the fall. I swung gently on the rope, trying to remember whether I had tied-in to the rope and gripping my arms tight just in case. The thunderous sound of tons of granite plunging down the pillar echoed and then died to silence.

I was completely disorientated. The silence seemed frighteningly ominous. Where was Ian? I thought of that fleeting yelp, and was horrified by the idea that perhaps he had not tied on after all.

'By 'eck!' I heard close by in gruff Lancastrian.

I struggled to get my head out of the tightly squeezed bag. Ian was hanging beside me on the V shaped safety rope. His head was lolling on his chest, his head-torch casting a yellow glow on to the surrounding rock. I could see blood on his neck.

I fumbled inside my bag for my head-torch, and then, carefully lifting the elastic torch strap from his blood-matted hair, I examined his injury. He had trouble talking at first, for he had hit his head hard in the fall. Fortunately the cut was a minor one, but the shock of the fall, while half-asleep in the dark, had completely confused us. It took some time to realise that the whole pedestal had detached itself from the pillar and dropped straight off the mountain face. There was a good deal of nervous swearing and hysterical giggling as, gradually, we became aware of the seriousness of our position.

At last, we fell silent. A terrible fear and insecurity had overtaken our boisterous reaction to the unimaginable event. Shining torches below, we saw the remains of our two ropes, which had been hanging beneath the ledge. They were cut to pieces, shredded by the falling rock. Turning round to inspect the safety line, we were appalled to find that the old ring peg on which we hung was moving, and that the spike of rock had been badly damaged. It looked as if one of the two attachment points would give way at any moment. We knew that if just one anchor point failed we would both be hurled into the void. We quickly searched for our equipment to see how we might improve the anchors, only to find that all of it, including our boots, had fallen with the ledge. So confident had we been in the safety of the ledge that we hadn't thought it necessary to clip our gear to the rope. We could do nothing.

To attempt to climb up or down would have been suicidal. The shadow of the huge overhang above us put paid to any idea of climbing in socks without ropes. Beneath stood a vertical wall hidden by the darkness – an obstacle we could descend only on ropes. The nearest ledges were 200 feet below, and we would certainly fall to our deaths long before we got anywhere near them.

We hung on that fragile rope for twelve interminable hours. Eventually our shouts were heard and a rescue helicopter succeeded in plucking us from the wall. The experience of that long, long night, expecting to fall at any time, one minute laughing hysterically, then silence, always with stomachs clenched, petrified, waiting for something we did not wish to think about, will never be forgotten.

Sea

Christopher Columbus

(1451–1506)

Italian navigator, and, as discoverer of the New World, one of the most famous explorers in human history. By the time he sailed on his epic voyage in 1492, Columbus had already fought in sea battles, been shipwrecked, been to Iceland and back as well as to the Cape Verde Islands and Sierra Leone. After years of effort (opposed by the ideas of men who thought the world was square), he persuaded King Ferdinand and Queen Isabella of Spain to sponsor his expedition across the Atlantic, where he expected to find India. He made four journeys. His first landfalls, which he believed to be in Asia, were at San Salvador in the Bahamas, and the Islands of Cuba and Hispaniola (now Haiti and the Dominican Republic), where he founded a European settlement. On his second voyage he reached the West Indies and on his third discovered the South American mainland. Columbus was sent home in chains for his poor administration of the 'colony' (Venezuela), and without the anticipated treasure. His final voyage, made in tired vessels and with much opposition, was to the Gulf of Mexico and Panama, where he tried but failed to find a strait – to India. This time he caught sight of Incas wearing gold, that long-sought metal but he never found the source. Columbus died within two years of returning to Spain, but his mortal remains continued to travel, being buried at Seville, transferred to Hispaniola, then to the Cathedral at Havana, and finally back to Seville.

On the shape of the earth

I have always read that the world, land and water, was spherical, and authoritative accounts and the experiments which Ptolemy and all the others have recorded concerning this matter, so describe it and hold it to be, by the eclipses of the moon and by other demonstrations made from east to west, as well as from the elevation of the pole star from north to south. Now, as I have already said, I have seen so great irregularity that, as a result, I have been led to hold this concerning the world, and I find that it is not round as they describe it, but that it is the shape of a pear which is everywhere very round except where the stalk is, for there it is very prominent, or that it is like a very round ball, and on one part of it is placed something like a woman's nipple, and that this part, where this protuberance is found, is the highest and nearest to the sky, and it is beneath the equinoctial line and in this Ocean sea at the end of the East. I call that 'the end of the East', where end all the land and islands.

Vasco da Gama

(c. 1469–1524)

Portugese navigator who discovered the sea route to the India via the Cape of Good Hope, discovered by Diaz ten years earlier. His second journey, as admiral of a fleet of twenty-one armed ships, punitively enforced the Portuguese presence in the East Indies. After doing nothing for twenty years, in 1524 da Gama was made sixth viceroy of India, but died when he reached Cochin.

Navigating to the Cape of Good Hope

During a courfe of at leaft 300 miles, we faw black gulls with white throats; their tail is like that of a fwan, and they are bigger than wood pigeons; they were catching the flying fifhes as they were flying.

On the 11th of April we were fo far, that prefisely at noon we faw the fun to the north.

At the fame time we had in the fky no mark which could help us, neither fun nor moon, but our compafs and our maps.

Then we came to another fea, where there was nothing living, neither fifh nor flefh, nor anything elfe.

On the 20th day of April the wind turned againft us, and lasted five weeks, driving us a thoufand miles out of the direct route, and we were fairly twelve days without fighting any land or fand.

On the 22nd day of May, there was winter there, and the days lafted only eight hours; and there was a great ftorm of rain, hail, fnow, thunder and lightning. The fky was open towards the Cape of Good Hope, and there was a ftorm. When we were arrived near the Cape, we directed our courfe to the north-eaft.

On the 10th day of June we could see neither the Great Bear nor the Polar Star, and we did not know the fky, which threw us in great perplexity.

Sir Francis Drake

(c. 1540–96)

English circumnavigator and admiral; Drake went to sea at the age of twelve. In 1567 he sailed with Sir John Hawkins' (**q.v.**) expedition to Guinea and Mexico where they were almost decimated by the Spanish. Ten years later he followed Magellan's (**q.v.**) route to South America on a pirate expedition sponsored by Queen Elizabeth. He plundered Valparaiso, capturing a Spanish ship laden with gold ingots from Chile, then proceeded to Lima. Returning to England, Drake landed in California and abandoning the idea of following the Arctic route, returned via Java and the Cape of Good Hope. He was the first English captain to sail around the world, returning with treasure and spices; the Queen knighted him on board the *Golden Hind* at Deptford. Drake continued his plundering career in

Spain, the Caribbean and North America. In 1588 he
defeated the Spanish Armada off Gravelines and pursued
it to Scotland. He died off Portobello in 1596.

The island of fierie-seeming-wormes

The first thing we did, we pitched our tents and intrenched ourselues
as strongly as we could vpon the shoare, lest at any time perhaps we
might haue beene disturbed by the inhabitants of the greater Iland which
lay not farre to the Westward of vs; after we had prouided thus for our
security, wee landed our goodes, and had a Smith's forge set vp, both
for the making of some necessarie shipworke, and for the repairing of
some iron-hooped caskes, without which they could not long haue
serued our vse: and for that our Smiths coales were all spent long
before this time, there was order giuen and followed for the burning of
charcoale, by which that want might be supplyed.

We trimd ourship, and performed our other businesses to our content. The place affording vs, not onely all necessaries (which we had
not of our owne before) thereunto, but also wonderfull refreshing to
our wearied bodies, by the comfortable reliefe and excellent prouision
that here we found, whereby of sickely, weake, and decayed (as many
of vs seemed to be before our comming hither), we in short space grew
all of vs to be strong, lusty, and healthfull persons. Besides this, we
had rare experience of God's wonderfull wisedome in many rare and
admirable creatures which here we saw.

The whole Iland is a through growne wood, the trees for the most
part are of large and high stature, uery straight and cleane without
bowes, saue onely in the very top. The leaues whereof are not much
vnlike our broomes in England. Among these trees, night be night, did
shew themselues an infinite swarme of fierie-seeming-wormes flying
in the aire, whose bodies (no bigger than an ordinarie flie) did make a
shew, and giue such light as if euery twigge on euery tree had beene a
lighted candle, or as if that place had beene the starry spheare. To these
wee may adde the relation of another, almost as strange a creature,
which here we saw, and that was an innumerable multitude of huge
Bats or reare mice, equalling or rather exceeding a good Henne in
bignesse. They flie with maruellous swiftnesse, but their flight is very

short; and when they light, they hang onely by the bowes with their backes downeward.

Philip Amadas

(1550–1618)

English navigator. He was one of the captains sent by Sir Walter Raleigh in 1584 to investigate the coast of North America and settle Virginia.

A sweet smell from the land of Virginia

The tenth of May we arrived at the Canaries, and the tenth of June in this present yeere, we were fallen with the Islands of the West Indies, keeping a more South-easterly course then was needefull, because wee doubted that the current of the Bay of Mexico, disbogging betweene the Cape of Florida and Havana, had bene of greater force then afterwardes we found it to bee. At which Islands we found the ayre very unwholsome, and our men grew for the most part ill disposed: so that having refreshed our selves with sweet water, & fresh victuall, we departed the twelfth day of our arrivall there. These Islands, with the rest adjoyning, are so well knowen to your selfe, and to many others, as I will not trouble you with the remembrance of them.

The second of July, we found shole water, wher we smelt so sweet, and so strong a smel, as if we had bene in the midst of some delicate garden abounding with all kinde of odoriferous flowers, by which we were assured, that the land could not be farre distant: and keeping good watch, and bearing but slacke saile, the fourth of the same moneth we arrived upon the coast, which we supposed to be a continent and firme lande, and we sayled along the same a hundred and twentie English miles before we could fine any entrance, or river issuing into the Sea. The first that appeared unto us, we entred, though not without some difficultie, & cast anker about three harquebuz-shot within the havens mouth, on the left hand of the same: and after thankes given to God for our safe arrivall thither, we manned our boats, and went to view the land next adjoyning, and "to take possession of the same, in the right of the Queenes most excellent Majestie, as rightfull Queene, and Princess of the same, and after delivered the same over to your use, according to her Majesties grant, and letters patents, under her Highnesse great Seale."

Sir Walter Raleigh

(c. 1552–1618)

English soldier, navigator, writer and courtier. A favourite of Queen Elizabeth I who endowed him with land, favours and a knighthood. Raleigh organised the expeditions to colonise Virginia, and planted his Irish estate with tobacco and potatoes they brought back. He sailed with Davis in search of the North-West Passage and in 1593 to Trinidad and Guiana (now Venezuela). He travelled 300 miles up the Orinoco River, in his search for the city of El Dorado. The victim of court intrigue at the end of Elizabeth's reign, he was condemned to death, but spared at the scaffold and put in the Tower, where he passed the time studying and writing a *History of the World*. He then returned to the Orinoco in search of gold, but the journey was beset by disaster. On his return, Raleigh was executed; before his death, he wrote an *Apology for the Voyage to Guiana*.

Dark weather. Many rainbows

Oct. 15th
Wensday morninge we saw another rainebowe and about 10 a clock it began to gather as black as pich in the south and from thence ther fell as much raine as I have seene but with little wind.

From Tuesday 12 to 12 this wensday we ran not above 14 leages, observe we could not neither munday, tweday nor wensday for the darekness of the skye which is very strange in these parts, for most of the afternoone wee stered our shipp be candellight.

From Wensday 12 to Thursday 12 we had all calmes sauing some few howers in the night and from 7 in the morning till 10 and the winde we had was so weake as we made not above 6 Lg; about 10 in the morning it began to raine and it continewed strong till 2 att after dinner, the effect of the morning rainebow. About 3 the winde the little that it was, blew att west S.W. which had not often bine seene. Captain Jennings died and many fell sick . . .

Oct 23rd

This Wensday morning we saw a thyrd rainebowe; of the two former we had the effect of foule weather, it also lightned the most part of these 2 nights which they say foreshewes raine and so we have found it hetherto. Wensdayes rainebowe gave us but one gust att night all the rest of the night being faire about 8 a clock we saw Magellans Cloude rovnd and white which riseth and setteth with the stares.

Thursday morning was faire and we oberued and found ourselves in 7 Deg: and 40 Min: from Wensday noone to Thursday noone wee made vppon a course S.W. and by S. 18 leages. We had on thursday evening a rainebow, and ther followes a foule night, and a dark Friday till noone with a winde att S.S.E. so bare as we could not lye our course, and so longe we have had those windes southerly agaynst the very order or nature in this navigation as we have cause to feare that we shall not be able to fech our port but be putt to seeward.

George Anson

(1697–1792)

British Admiral. Anson commanded ships protecting traders on the coasts of the Carolinas, West Africa and the West Indies. He commanded a squadron in the Pacific, sailed round the world and returned home wealthy. He defeated the French off Finisterre 1747, became First Lord of the Admiralty 1751–62 and was involved with reforms of naval administration and dockyards.

Scurvy

Soon after our passing Streights Le Maire, the scurvy began to make its appearance amongst us, and our long continuance at sea, the fatigue we underwent, and the various disappointments we met with, had occasioned its spreading to such a degree that at the latter end of April there were but few on board who were not in some degree afflicted with it, and in that month no less than forty-three died of it on board the *Centurion*. But though we thought that the distemper had then risen to an extraordinary height, and were willing to hope that as we advanced to the northward its malignity would abate, yet we found, on the contrary, that in the month of May we lost near double that number; and as we did not get to land till the middle of June, the mortality went on increasing, and the disease extended itself so prodigiously that, after the loss of above two hundred men, we could not at last muster more than six fore-mast men in a watch capable of duty.

This disease, so frequently attending long voyages, and so particularly destructive to us, is surely the most singular and unaccountable of any that affects the human body. Its symptoms are inconstant and innumerable, and its progress and effects extremely irregular; for scarcely any two persons have complaints exactly resembling each other, and where there hath been found some conformity in the symptoms, the order of their appearance has been totally different. However, though it frequently puts on the form of many other diseases, and is therefore not to be described by any exclusive and infallible criterions, yet there are some symptoms which are more general than the rest, and, occurring the oftenest, deserve a more particular enumeration. These common appearances are large discoloured spots dispersed over the whole surface of the body, swelled legs, putrid gums and, above all, an extraordinary lassitude of the whole body, especially after any exercise, however inconsiderable, and this lassitude at last degenerates into a proneness to swoon, and even die, on the least exertion of strength, or even on the least motion.

This disease is likewise usually attended with a strange dejection of the spirits, and with shiverings, tremblings, and a disposition to be seized with the most dreadful terrors on the slightest accident. Indeed it was most remarkable, in all our reiterated experience of this malady, that whatever discouraged our people, or at any time damped their hopes, never failed to add new vigour to the distemper; for it usually killed those who were in the last stages of it, and confined those to their hammocks who were before capable of some kind of duty; so that it seemed as if alacrity of mind, and sanguine thoughts, were no contemptible preservatives from its fatal malignity . . .

Indeed, the effects of his disease were in almost every instance wonderful; for many of our people, though confined to their hammocks, appeared to have no inconsiderable share of health, for they eat and drank heartily, were cheerful, and talked with much seeming vigour, and with a loud strong tone of voice; and yet, on their being the least moved, though it was from only one part of the ship to the other, and that too in their hammocks, they have immediately expired; and others, who have confided in their seeming strength, and have resolved to get out of their hammocks have died before they could well reach the deck; nor was it an uncommon thing for those who were able to walk the deck, and do some kind of duty, to drop down dead in an instant, on any endeavours to act with their utmost effort, many of our people having perished in this manner during the course of this voyage.

In peril on the sea

In one of these squalls, which was attended by several violent claps of thunder, a sudden flash of fire darted along our desk, which, dividing, exploded with a report like that of several pistols, and wounded many of our men and officers as it passed, marking them in different parts of the body. This flame was attended with a strong sulphureous stench, and was doubtless of the same nature with the larger and more violent blasts of lightning which then filled the air.

It were endless to recite minutely the various disasters, fatigues, and terrors which we encountered on this coast; all these went on increasing till the 22d of May, at which time the fury of all the storms which we had hitherto encountered seemed to be combined, and to have conspired our destruction. In this hurricane almost all our sails were split, and great part of our standing rigging broken; and, about eight in the evening, a mountainous over-grown sea took us upon our starboard-quarter, and gave us so prodigious a shock that several of our shrouds broke with the jerk, by which our masts were greatly endangered; our ballast and stores too were so strangely shifted that the ship heeled afterwards two streaks to port. Indeed it was a most tremendous blow and we were thrown into the utmost consternation from the apprehension of instantly foundering; and though the wind abated in a few hours, yet, as we had no more sails left in a condition to bend to our yards, the ship laboured very much in a hollow sea, rolling gunwale to, for want of sail to steady her: so that we expected our masts, which were now very slenderly supported, to come by the board every moment. However, we exerted ourselves the best we could to stirrup our shrouds, to reeve new lanyards, and to mend our sails; but while these necessary operations were carrying on, we rang great risque of being driven onshore on the island of Chiloe, which was not far distant from us; but in the midst of our peril the wind happily shifted to the southward, and we steered off the land with the main-sail only, the master and myself undertaking the management of the helm, while every one else on board was busied in securing the masts, and bending the sails as fast as they could be repaired. This was the last effort of that stormy climate; for in a day or two after we got clear of the land, and found the weather more moderate than we had yet experienced since our passing Streights Le Maire.

William Bligh

(c. 1753–1817)

Bligh was born at Plymouth; went to sea at fifteen and sailed with Captain Cook on his second voyage round the world (1772–4). As Commander of HMS *Bounty* he set off for Tahiti to collect plants of breadfruit tree for planting in West Indies in 1787. After six months at Tahiti, the crew mutinied against Bligh's alleged cruelty. Bligh was cast adrift in a 23-foot open boat with eighteen volunteers; the boat was intended for ten. After a six-week journey of incredible hardship, they landed at Timor, Java, 3618 miles across the Pacific, thanks to Bligh's skilled seamanship and good care of the men.

Salvation at Timor

Sunday the 17th. At dawn of day I found every person complaining, and some of them solicited extra allowance; which I positively refused. Our situation was miserable; always wet, and suffering extreme cold in the night, without the least shelter from the weather. Being constantly obliged to bale, and keep the boat from filling, was perhaps not be reckoned an evil, as it gave us exercise.

The little rum we had was of great service. When our nights were particularly distressing I generally served a teaspoonful or two to each person, and it was always joyful tidings when they heard of my intentions.

At noon a water-spout was very near on board of us. I issued an ounce of pork, in addition to the allowance of bread and water; but before we began to eat, every person stripped, and having wrung their clothes through the sea-water, found much warmth and refreshment. Course since yesterday noon WSW, distance one hundred miles; latitude, by account, 14° 11' S., and longitude made 21° 3' W.

The night was dark and dismal, the sea constantly breaking over us, and nothing but the wind and waves to direct our steerage. It was my intention, if possible, to make New Holland, to the southward of Endeavour Straits, being sensible that it was necessary to preserve such a situation as would make a southerly wind a fair one; that we might range along the reefs till an opening should be found into smooth water, and we the sooner be able to pick up some refreshments.

Monday the 18th. In the morning the rain abated, when we stripped and wrung our clothes through the sea-water as usual, which refreshed us greatly. Every person complained of violent pain in their bones; I was only surprised that no one was yet laid up. The customary allowance of one twenty-fifth of a pound of bread and a quarter of a pint of water was served at breakfast, dinner, and supper.

At noon I deduced my situation, by account, for we had no glimpse of the sun, to be in latitude 14° 52' S.; course since yesterday noon, WSW., one hundred and six miles; longitude made from Tofoa 22° 45' W. Saw many boobies and noddies, a sign of being in the neighbourhood of land. In the night we had very severe lightning, with heavy rain, and were obliged to keep baling without intermission.

Tuesday the 19th. Very bad weather and constant rain. At noon, latitude, by account 14° 37' S.; course since yesterday, N 81 W, distance one hundred miles; longitude made, 24° 30' W. With the allowance of bread and water, served half an ounce of pork to each person for dinner.

Wednesday the 20th. Fresh breezes ENE. with constant rain; at times a deluge. Always baling.

At dawn of day some of my people seemed half dead; our appearances were horrible, and I could look no way but I caught the eye of someone in distress. Extreme hunger was now too evident, but no one suffered from thirst, nor had we much inclination to drink, that desire perhaps being satisfied through the skin. The little sleep we got was in the midst of water, and we constantly awoke with severe cramps and pains in our bones. This morning I served about two teaspoonfuls of rum to each person, and the allowance of bread and water as usual. At noon the sun broke out and revived every one. I found we were in latitude 14° 49' S.; longitude made 25° 46' W.; course S. 88° W., distance seventy-five miles.

All the afternoon we were so covered with rain and salt water that we could scarcely see. We suffered extreme cold, and every one dreaded the approach of night. Sleep, though we longed for it, afforded no comfort: for my own part I almost lived without it. About two o'clock in the morning we were overwhelmed with a deluge of rain. It fell so heavy that we were afraid it would fill the boat, and were obliged to bale with all our might. At dawn of day I served a larger allowance of rum. Towards noon the rain abated and the sun shone, but we were miserably cold and wet, the sea breaking constantly over us; so that notwithstanding the heavy rain, we had not been able to add to our stock of fresh water. Latitude, by observation, 14° 29' S., and longitude made, by account, from Tofoa, 27° 25' W.; course, since yesterday noon, N. 78° W., ninety-nine miles. I now considered myself nearly on a meridian with the east part of New Guinea.

Friday the 22nd. Strong gales from ESE. to SSE., a high sea, and dark dismal night.

Henry Nelson Coleridge

(1798–1843)

English traveller who spent six months in the West Indies for his rheumatism. His book is an amusing account of his experiences.

Weather in the Bay of Biscay

Imaginative reader! have you ever been in a gale of wind on the edge of the Bay of Biscay? If not, and you are fond of variety, it is really worth your while to take a trip to Lisbon or Madeira for the chance of meeting with one. Calculate your season well in December or January, when the south-wester has properly set in, and you will find it one of the finest and most uncomfortable things in the world. *My* gale lasted from Sunday till Wednesday evening, which is something long perhaps for amusement, but it gave ample room for observation and philosophy. I think I still hear that ineffable hubbub of plates and glasses breaking, chairs and tables falling, women screaming, sailors piping, officers swearing, the wind whistling, and the sea roaring, which awakened me about two o'clock on Monday morning from one of those sweet dreams ... The Atlantic was gushing in through my port in a very refreshing manner, and ebbing and flowing under and around my bed with every roll of the ship. My clothes were floating on the face of the waters. I turned to sleep again, but the sea came with that after dead sledge-hammer beat, which makes a landsman's heart tremble, and the impertinent quotation of some poor scholar in the next cabin about *quatuor aut septem digitos* brushed every atom of Morphic dust from my eyes. I sat bolt upright, and for some time contemplated, by the glimmering of the sentry's lantern, the huge disarray of my pretty den; I fished for my clothes, but they were bathing; I essayed to rise, but I could find no resting-place for the sole of a rheumatic foot. However, I was somewhat consoled by a sailor who came to bale out the water at daybreak; ... "a fine breeze, Sir, only it's dead on end for us; and to be sure, I minds the Apollo and thirty-two marchmantmen were lost somewhere in these here parts.' It was kindly meant of Jack, no doubt, though he was out in his latitude by eight degrees at least.

Richard Henry Dana

(1815–52)

American lawyer and writer, born into an elite Boston family. At nineteen, Dana enlisted as a common seaman on a voyage round Cape Horn to California, where he went ashore and worked in the hide trade. His book about the voyage made a fortune for his publishers, the House of Harper. Dana also wrote a book called *The Seaman's Friend*, a popular handbook on all aspects of seamanship. As a lawyer back in Boston, he often acted as seamen's champion, his office reputedly smelled of tar. Dana kept journals of great interest throughout his life.

Heavy sea running

From the latitude of the West Indies, until we got inside the Bermudas, where we took the westerly and south-westerly winds, which blow steadily off the coast of the United States early in the autumn, we had every variety of weather, and two or three moderate gales, or, as sailors call them, double-reefed-topsail breezes, which came on in the usual manner, and of which one is a specimen of all. A fine afternoon; all hands at work, some in the rigging, and others on deck; a stiff breeze, the ship close upon the wind, and skysails brailed down. Latter part of the afternoon, breeze increases, ship lies over to it, and clouds look windy. Spray begins to fly over the forecastle, and wets the yarns the boys are knotting; ball them up and put them below. Mate knocks off work and clears up decks earlier than usual, and orders a man who has been employed aloft to send the royal halyards over to windward, as he comes down. Breast backstays hauled taut, and a tackle got upon the martingale backrope. One of the boys furls the mizzen-royal. Cook thinks there is going to be "nasty work" and has supper ready early. Mate gives orders to get supper by the watch, instead of all hands, as usual. While eating supper, hear the watch on deck taking in the royals. Coming on deck, find it is blowing harder, and an ugly head sea running. Instead of having all hands on the forecastle in the dog watch, smoking, singing, and telling yarns, one watch goes below and turns-in, saying that it's going to be an ugly night, and two hours' sleep is not to be lost. Clouds look black and wild; wind rising, and ship working hard against a heavy head sea, which breaks over the forecastle, and washes aft through the scuppers. Still, no more sail is taken in, for the captain is a driver, and, like all drivers, very partial to his topgallant-sails.

Herman Melville

(1819–91)

American writer who started life as a bank clerk but joined a whaling ship. His adventures at sea and in the South Seas, where he deserted and took refuge with 'cannibals' were used as material for his novels. Melville married and took up farming; Nathaniel Hawthorne was his friend and neighbour and encouraged him to write. He was not successful in his lifetime; and, like Hawthorne, had to take a job as a US customs official. His death was marked by only one obituary, of four lines.

Horror of whiteness

It was the whiteness of the whale that above all things appalled me. But how can I hope to explain myself here; and yet, in some dim, random way, explain myself I must, else all these chapters might be naught.

Though in many natural objects whiteness refiningly enhances ... This elusive quality it is, which causes the thought of whiteness, when divorced from more kindly associations, and coupled with any object terrible in itself, to heighten that terror to the furthest bounds. Witness the white bear of the poles, and the white shark of the tropics; what but their smooth, flaky whiteness makes them the transcendent horrors they are? That ghastly whiteness it is which imparts such an abhorrent mildness, even more loathsome than terrific, to the dump gloating of their aspect. So that not the fire-fanged tiger in his heraldic coat can so stagger courage as the white-shrouded bear or shark.

Bethink thee of the albatross, whence come those clouds of spiritual wonderment and pale dread, in which that white phantom sails in all imaginations? Not Coleridge first threw that spell; but God's great, unflattering laureate, Nature.

John MacGregor

(1825–92)

British writer who travelled widely in Europe, Russia and the Middle East. He was the great popularizer of canoeing in Britain, paddling his way all through Europe, and through the Suez Canal to the Red Sea. His 'Rob Roy' canoe was widely copied.

Night ghost at Beachy Head

Dinner done and everything set right (for this is best policy always), I slipped into my cabin and tried to sleep as the sun went down, but a little land-breeze now began, and every now and then my head was raised to see how tide or wind progressed. Then I must have fallen once into a mild nap, and perhaps a dream, for sudden and strong a rough hand seemed to shake the boat, and, on my leaping up, there glanced forth a brilliant flash of lightning that soon put everybody on the *qui vive*.

Now was heard the clink of distant cables, as I raised mine also in the dark, with only the bright shine of the lighthouse like a keen and full-opened eye gazing down from the cliff overhead.

Compass lighted, ship-lantern fixed, a reef in each sail, and, with a moment's thought of the very similar events that had passed only a few nights ago, we steered right south, away, away to the open sea.

It was black enough all around; but yet the strong wind expected after thunder had not come, and we edged away eastward, doubly watchful, however, of the dark, for the crowd of vessels here was the real danger, and not the sea.

The ghost of Rob Roy is flitting on the white sail as the lamp shines brightly. Down comes the rain, and with it flash after flash, peal upon peal of roaring thunder, and the grandeur of the scene is unspeakable. The wind changed every few minutes, and vessels and boats and steamers whirled past like visions, often much too near to be welcome.

A white dazzling gleam of forked lightning cleaves the darkness, and, behold! a huge vessel close at hand, but hitherto unseen, lofty and full-sailed, and for a moment black against the instant of light, and then utterly lost again. The splashing of rain hissed in the sea, and a voice would come out of the unseen – "Port, you lubber!" The ship or whatever it is has no lights at all, though on board it they can see mine. Ah, it's no use peering forward to discover on which side is the new danger; for when your eye has gazed for a time at the lighted compass it is powerless for a minute or two to see in the dark space forward, or, again, if you stare into the blackness to scan the faintest glimmer of a sail ahead, then for some time after you cannot see the compass when looking at it dazzled. This difficulty in sailing alone is the only one we felt to be quite insuperable.

Again a steam whistle shrieked amid the thunder, and two eyes glared out of the formless vapour and rain – the red and the green lights – the signals that showed where she was steaming. There was shouting from her deck as she kept rounding and backing, no doubt for a man overboard. As we slewed to starboard to avoid her, another black form loomed close on the right; and what with wind, rain, thunder, and ships, there was everything to confuse just when there was all need of cool decision.

It would be difficult for me to exaggerate the impressive spectacle that passed along on the dark background of this night.

Joshua Slocum

(1844–c. 1910)

Born in Nova Scotia; Slocum went to sea as cook, and became a Captain. He sailed for South America with his family in a converted barque, the *Aquidnec* in 1886. Wrecked on a sandbar off the coast of Brazil, he built a canoe from the wreckage and returned to New York in it. Slocum sailed alone around the world from Boston in the sloop, *Spray* in 1895–8. Three years later he set off again, but never returned.

Tempest off Cape Horn

It was the 3rd of March when the *Spray* sailed from Port Tamar direct for Cape Pillar, with the wind from the northeast, which I fervently hoped might hold till she cleared the land; but there was no such good luck in store. It soon began to rain and thicken in the northwest, boding no good. The *Spray* neared Cape Pillar rapidly, and, nothing loath, plunged into the Pacific Ocean at once, taking her first bath of it in the gathering storm. There was no turning back even had I wished to do so, for the land was now shut out by the darkness of the night. The wind freshened, and I took in a third reef. The sea was confused and treacherous. In such a time as this the old fisherman prayed, 'Remember, Lord, my ship is so small and thy sea is so wide!' I saw now only the gleaming crests of waves. They showed white teeth while the sloop balanced over them. 'Everything for an offing,' I cried, and to this end I carried on all the sail she would bear. She ran all night with a free sheet, but on the morning of 4 March the wind shifted to southwest, then back suddenly to northwest, and blew with terrific force. The *Spray*, stripped of her sails, then bore off under bare poles. No ship in the world could have stood up against so violent a gale. Knowing that this storm might continue for many days, and that it would be impossible to work back to the westward along the coast outside of Tierra del Fuego, there seemed nothing to do but to keep on and go east about, after all. Anyhow, for my present safety the only course lay in keeping her before the wind. And so she drove southeast, as though about to round the Horn, while the waves rose and fell and bellowed their never-ending story of the sea; but the Hand that held these held also the *Spray*. She was running now with a reefed forestaysail, the sheets flat amidship. I paid out two long ropes to steady her course and to break combing seas astern, and I lashed the helm amidship. In this trim she ran before it, shipping never a sea. Even while the storm raged at its worst, my ship was wholesome and noble. My mind as to her seaworthiness was put to ease for aye.

When all had been done that I could do for the safety of the vessel, I got to the fore-scuttle, between seas, and prepared a pot of coffee over a wood fire, and made a good Irish stew.

Joseph Conrad

(1857–1924)

Polish-born mariner and writer, born Theodor Josef Konrad Korzeniowski. He joined the French merchant navy, then became a ship's master and British subject. Conrad sailed to the Malay Archipelago, explored the Congo and visited the Ukraine, experiences that he used when he began to write novels. He left the navy and after some hard times became recognised as a writer of world status.

London Docks

This New South Dock (it was its official name), round which my earlier professional memories are centred, belongs to the group of West India Docks, together with two smaller and much older basins called Import and Export respectively, both with the greatness of their trade departed from them already. Picturesque and clean as docks go, these twin basins spread side by side the dark lustre of their glassy water, sparely peopled by a few ships laid up on buoys or tucked far away from each other at the end of sheds in the corners of empty quays, where they seemed to slumber quietly remote, untouched by the bustle of men's affairs – in retreat rather than in captivity. They were quaint and sympathetic, those two homely basins, unfurnished and silent, with no aggressive display of cranes, no apparatus of hurry and work on their narrow shoes. No railway-lines cumbered them. The knots of labourers trooping in clumsily round the corners of cargo-sheds to eat their food in peace out of red cotton handkerchiefs had the air of picnicking by the side of a lonely mountain pool. They were restful (and I should say very unprofitable), those basins, where the chief officer of one of the ships involved in the harassing, strenuous, noisy activity of the New South Dock only a few yards away could escape in the dinner-hour to stroll, unhampered by men and affairs, meditating (if he chose) on the vanity of all things human. At one time they must have been full of good old slow West Indiamen of the square-stern type, that took their captivity, one imagines, as stolidly as they had faced the buffeting of the waves with their blunt, honest bows, and disgorged sugar, rum, molasses, coffee, or logwood sedately with their own winch and tackle. But when I knew them, of exports there was never a sign that one could detect; and all the imports I have ever seen were some rare cargoes of tropical timber, enormous baulks roughed out of iron trunks grown in the woods about the Gulf of Mexico. They lay piled up in stacks of mighty boles, and it was hard to believe that all this mass of dead and stripped trees had come out of the flanks of a slender, innocent-looking little barque with, as likely as not, a homely woman's name – Ellen this or Annie that – upon her fine bows. But this is generally the case with a discharged cargo. Once spread at large over the quay, it looks the most impossible bulk to have all come there out of that ship alongside.

W.J.J. Spry

(fl. 1870s)

Spry was Sub-Lieutenant in the engine-room of the *Challenger*, a surveying ship sent round the world by the Royal Society and Hydrographic Department of the Admiralty to make scientific observations of the world's oceans for the first time. The expedition has been described as a sea-faring department of the Royal Society; it transformed our knowledge about what lay beneath the surface of the seas. The ship was surrounded by icebergs in the Arctic and narrowly avoided being crushed. Another excellent illustrated account, *The Voyage of the Challenger*, was written by Eric Linklater in 1972.

4475 fathoms

We lost the trades in lat. 17° north, and after that had a succession of easterly, north-easterly, and baffling winds, from every point of the compass except where it was wanted, thus preventing our visiting either the Carolines or Ladrones, which were passed some 100 miles to leeward. On the 23rd March, in lat. 11° 24' north, and long. 143° 16' east, bottom was touched at 4475 fathoms, the deepest successful sounding made during the whole cruise. Specimens from that depth showed a dark volcanic sand, mixed with manganese. In consequence of the enormous pressure at that depth (some five tons on one square inch) most of the thermometers were crushed. However, one stood the test, and showed a temperature of 33.9°, the surface temperature being 80°. Three other attempts were made to determine the temperature of water at these great depths, but in every instance the instruments came to the surface in a damaged condition.

James Johnston Abraham

(1876–?)

Irish-born surgeon who, threatened with tuberculosis, spent six months at sea on a cargo ship bound for Egypt and the Far East. His account of his experiences became a bestseller; after being rejected by nine publishers it went into over thirty editions. Abraham returned to Egypt in service during WWI.

Loading at Port Said

All day long we had been loading cotton for Japan. The coolies were very slow at it. It was the day of rejoicing after the fact; and extra inducements had had to be held out to them to make them work. It was also very cold and raw; and Egyptian coolies do not love the cold. Consequently it was late in the afternoon before it was all stowed.

Then we started coaling. Coaling is a nightmare. Plug your ventilators, fasten the doors of your cabin, screw up your ports hermetically, and yet the coal dust gets in.

It came alongside in lighters; and from each boat two big heavy planks were raised to the bunker doors. Up one of these planks the half-naked coolies ran, each with his basket full of coal, after dumping which he ran down the other plank to the lighter again. We, too, had a long-robed patriarch chanting verses from the Koran. It seems the men work quicker under the inspiration of the chant, and the coaling company keeps a special reciter constantly employed. But the row is something indescribable. Night fell, and still the coaling went on. The lights from the cafés on shore came in long rippling streaks across the water; and through the windows could be seen figures passing and repassing. Sometimes, the sound of music, too would come – but very rarely for the din of the coolies seemed to increase as the coal in the lighters sank lower and lower. Huge cressets burning on the lighters cast a lurid glare over the grimy, perspiring figures. It was like a scene out of the Inferno. They seemed to be working faster and faster; the voice of the chanter rose wilder and wilder; the coal in the lighters sank lower and lower. There was a sudden last shout, a sound of hurrying feet, everyone rushed to leave the ship, the planks were withdrawn, ropes cast loose, the empty lighters with their burning flares drifted into the night, and all was still.

Coaling was over. The Chief passed me, negroid with dust, where he had been measuring. I went on deck again. We looked like a Newcastle tramp. Grimy black hands had left their mark all over the spotless white paint of the deck-houses. The mate was snorting round, cursing softly to himself.

The stillness after the din was wonderful. Near the canal mouth a big German mail-boat, which had been coaling all day, had hoisted three lights on her foremast. That was the signal for the pilot to come aboard. Her three great decks were all aglow with serried rows of lights; and as she slipped silently past us, her great searchlight throwing a blinding glare in front, a hose-pipe jerking water over the stern to shake off persistent bumboat, the music of her band came clear across the water.

"What are we waiting for?" I asked.

Our signal lights had been up some time, the pilot had come aboard, the electrician had got his searchlight going. The pilot explained that there were two mailboats and a troopship just coming out of the Canal, and we could not start until they passed.

Presently the "stand-by" rang; the great searchlight in the bow burned bright; the ship seemed to wake up suddenly; and in another minute we were moving into night in the Canal.

Cecil Foster

(c. 1886–?)

Foster captained the 3000-ton cargo steamer, *Trevessa*, which left Liverpool in 1923. She later departed from Western Australia with a heavy cargo of minerals but went down half way to Mauritius. The survivors made their way to Mauritius in two open boats. Eleven men died, mostly from exposure and exhaustion. Foster gives an honest and detailed account of the ordeal.

Abandonment of the ship

JUNE 4.

NO. 1 BOAT. CAPTAIN FOSTER.

1 a.m. – I ordered all hands to the boats and wireless operator to send "SOS", giving our position and that we were abandoning the ship. All the crew were got away in the two starboard lifeboats, Nos. 1 and 3. The two port lifeboats had been damaged the day previous at 10.15 a.m. A huge sea had broken them away from gripes and flung them inboard against the rails.

2.15 a.m. – Abandoned ship; foredeck awash level with top of bulwark rail and settling fast by the head.

2.45 a.m. – Ship foundered. Boats standing by; and that was the last seen of her, standing almost on end. The lights were all burning, as dynamo had been left running. Before leaving I had stopped, gone astern, taken all way off the ship and again stopped. Perfect discipline, and all hands calm and carrying out orders promptly. Stewards passing in provisions, biscuits and milk, and rest of crew swinging out boats. Lifebelts had been issued to all hands. "SOS" answered by SS *Runic* and two steamers, names unknown. These sent "OK". We were unable to wait a reply as to whether they were coming to our assistance or as to how far they were from us. We lay to at our sea anchor all day and no vessel appeared.

3 p.m. – I had the two water-breakers and the tins (five) of biscuits and one case of milk brought aft, and hardened up the screw top of the biscuit tanks, which were nearly full. The biscuit tank and the cases of milk by the mast could not be broken into without noise. I was taking every precaution and preparing for a long voyage.

4 p.m. – Issued a small ration of biscuits – one biscuit per man.

5 p.m. – Set sail.

6 p.m. – Step of mast carried away, and No. 3 boat took us in two.

10 p.m. – The tow-line carried away, and we decided to lay to for the night. The weather being so bad, it was dangerous for the boats to get close to each other. In the meantime we were repairing the step of the mast and making the mast secure. Wedged it on either side with a case of milk, lashed it securely fore and aft and to the thwarts.

Richard Evelyn Byrd

(1888–1957)

American naval officer, aviator and polar explorer. Byrd was the first man to fly over the North Pole in 1926, forty-eight hours ahead of Amundsen. Three years later he flew over the South Pole and 1550 miles across the Antarctic continent; it took nineteen hours. In 1933–4, Byrd explored the Antarctic, from his base, 'Little America' on the Ross Ice Shelf, and spent four months in a hut 12′ × 9′, a hundred and twenty-five miles from base. Buried in ice, the only way in or out was through a trapdoor in the roof. He nearly perished in it from carbon monoxide poisoning, but was found in time. Byrd's investigations were the prelude to a massive American campaign to investigate the entire Antarctic continent from a high-tech base established in 1946. Byrd may have been the last man to be truly alone there.

Cold

1 July

It is getting cold again – 65° below zero to-day by the minimum ther-mometer. I have a feeling that it is going to be a very cold month, to make up for June. It was a great piece of luck that June was relatively so warm. [The records show that in June the cold crossed 40° below zero on thirteen days; 50° below on five days, and never once crossed 60° below.] I could not have survived otherwise. Now, when the stove is going, I keep the door cracked as wide as I can stand it; and, when it has been out long enough for the fumes to dissipate, I stuff rags (worn-out shirts and underwear, to be exact) up the engine ventilator in the tunnel and into the intake ventilator, so that the tunnel and shack won't get too cold. As a matter of fact, I do without the stove anywhere from twelve to fourteen hours a day. Believe me, it is a strain on the fortitude. Last night I froze an ear in the sleeping bag.

I'm worried about drift. Ever since I've been unable to attend to it, the drift has been deepening over the roof. This morning, when I went topside for the observations, I noticed how high the ridges were over the Escape Tunnel and the tunnels west of the shack. However, I may be able to do something about this before long. Advancing the radio schedules to the afternoon has been an immense help in bringing me back to my feet. With more time to prepare, the drain on me is not quite so heavy. To-day's schedule, though tiring, did not knock me out as the others did.

There was no news to speak of from Little America. Hutcheson said that Charlie and John Dyer were out ski-ing, and that "Doc" Poulter was with the meteor observers. Lord, how I envy them the multitudinous diversions of Little America; even, I suppose, as they must on their side envy the people home with whom they chat on the radio . . .

I sent a message approving the meteor journey, subject to its being made with full regard for its hazards.

John Steinbeck

(1902–68)

American writer. Steinbeck studied marine biology at
Stanford University as a young man. After the publication
of his epic novel, *The Grapes of Wrath*, in 1939, he took
an expedition to the Galapagos Islands, which he later
wrote about in *The Log From the Sea of Cortez*.

The collecting ship

Our collecting material at least was good. Shovels, wrecking and
abalone-bars, nets, long-handled dip-nets, wooden fish-kits, and a number of seven-cell flashlights for night collecting were taken. Containers
seemed to go endlessly into the hold of the *Western Flyer*. Wooden
fish-kits with heads; twenty hard-fir barrels with galvanized hoops in
fifteen- and thirty-gallon sizes; cases of gallon jars, quart, pint, eight-
ounce, five-ounce, and two-ounce screw-cap jars; several gross of corked
vials in four chief sizes, 100×33 mm, six-dram, four-dram, and two-dram
sizes. There were eight two-and-a-half-gallon jars with screw caps. And
with all these we ran short of containers, and before we were through
had to crowd those we had. This was unfortunate, since many delicate
animals should be preserved separately to prevent injury.

Of chemicals, we put into the boat a fifteen-gallon barrel of USP
formaldehyde and a fifteen-gallon barrel of denatured alcohol. This
was not nearly enough alcohol. The stock had to be replenished at
Guaymas, where we bought ten gallons of pure sugar alcohol. We took
two gallons of Epsom salts for anesthetization and again ran out and
had to buy more in Guaymas. Menthol, chromic acid, and novocain,
all for relaxing animals, were included in the chemical kit. Of preparing
equipment, there were glass chiton plates and string, lots of rubber
gloves, graduates, forceps, and scalpels. Our binocular microscope,
Bausch & Lomb AKW, was fitted with a twelve-volt light, but on the
rolling boat the light was so difficult to handle that we used a spot

flashlight instead. We had galvanized iron nested trays of fifteen- to twenty-gallon capacity for gross hardening and preservation. We had enamelled and glass trays for the laying out of specimens, and one small examination aquarium.

The medical kit had been given a good deal of thought. There were nembutal, butesin picrate for sunburn, a thousand two-grain quinine capsules, two-percent mercuric oxide salve for barnacle cuts, cathartics, ammonia, mercurochrome, iodine, alcaroid, and, last, some whisky for medicinal purposes. This did not survive our leave-taking, but since no one was ill on the whole trip, it may have done its job very well.

Tiny and the giant manta ray

While we were collecting on the shore, Tiny rowed abut in the little skiff in slightly deeper water. He carried a light three-pronged spear with which he picked up an occasional cushion star from the bottom. We heard him shout, and looked up to see a giant manta ray headed for him, the tips of the wings more than ten feet apart. It was rare to see them in such shallow water. As it passed directly under his boat we yelled at him to spear it, since he wanted it so badly, but he simply sat in the bottom of the boat, gazing after the retreating ray, weakly swearing at us. For a long time he sat there quietly, not quite believing what he had seen. This great fish could have flicked Tiny and boat and all into the air with one flap of its wing. Tiny wanted to sit still and think for a long time and he did. For an hour afterward he could only repeat, "Did you see that Goddamned thing!" And from that moment it became Tiny's ambition to catch and kill one of the giant rays.

Eric Newby

(1919–)

English traveller and writer, formerly an apprentice on a
four-masted barque, soldier and buyer in the fashion trade.
The Last Grain Race recounts his experiences as an apprentice on the Finnish ship, *Moshulu*, in 1939

Last man out on the weather side

'This is it,' said Kroner as I went aft, 'Upper topsails. It's going to be
really big.'

'It's the blasted "Backstern" that worries me. There's no water.'

'I'll put some on for you,' he answered. 'It'll be there when you come
back.'

'Maybe I shan't,' I said, nearer the mark than usual.

When we were all assembled the Mate slacked away the handbrake
of the upper topsail halliard winch and set it spinning. The eighty-foot
yard began to descend on its greased track on the fore part of the mizzen
mast, and as the weather sheet was progressively eased we clewed-up to
windward and manned the buntlines. With the weather clew up, the
lee was easier and the sail was furled without incident.

The fore upper topsail was the most difficult. All the buntlines
jammed and more than half the robands securing the topsail to the
jackstay had gone. The outer buntline block had broken loose and was
flailing in the air, so that when we reached the lowered yard eighty feet
above the sea, we hesitated a moment before the 'Horry ops' of the
Mates behind us drove us out on to the footropes, hesitated because
the bunt of the sail was beating back over the yard. The wind was
immense. It no longer blew in the accepted sense of the word at all;
instead it seemed to be tearing apart the very substance of the atmosphere. Nor was the sound of it any longer definable in ordinary terms.
It no longer roared, screamed, sobbed or sang according to the various
levels on which it was encountered. The power and noise of this wind

was now more vast and all-comprehending, in its way as big as the sky, bigger than the sea itself, making something that the mind balked at, so that it took refuge in blankness.

It was in this negative state of mind that could accept anything without qualm, even the possibility of death, that I fell off the yard backwards. I was the last man out on the weather side and was engaged in casting loose a gasket before we started to work on the sail, when without warning it flicked up, half the foot of a topsail, 40 feet of canvas as hard as corrugated iron, and knocked me clean off the footrope.

There was no interval for reflection, no sudden upsurge of remorse for my past sins, nor did my life pass in rapid review before my eyes. Instead there was a delightful jerk and I found myself entangled in the weather rigging some five feet below the yard, and as soon as I could I climbed back to the yard and carried on with my job. I felt no fear at all until much later on.

It needed three-quarters of an hour to make fast the weather side. Time and time again we nearly had the sail to the yard when the wind tore it from our fingers.

My companion aloft was Alvar.

'What happened?' he said when we reached the deck.

'I fell.'

'I din' see,' he said in a disappointed way. 'I don' believe.'

'I'm damned if I'm going to do it again just because you didn't see it.'

'I don' believe.'

'Orlright,' I said. 'The next time I'll tell you when I'm going to fall off.'

'Dot's bettair,' said Alvar.

Derek Lundy

(1946–)

Writer who lives in British Columbia, Canada. *The Way of a Ship* is about his ancestor Benjamin Lundy's adventures on a square-rigger at the turn of the century.

Off Cape Horn

Off the pitch of the Horn. Wind at full-gale strength, waves as high as the maintops, sometimes hail and then snow coming down thick, clouds so low they enfold the mastheads, spume and sky indistinguishable. The laden barque, down on its marks like a half-tide rock, labours to windward under three lower topsails and fore and mizzen staysails, seas sweeping the main deck like grapeshot. The hull twists, pitches and rolls; its iron plates grind and groan. The wind whistles, screams, as it encounters the vessel's four masts and their dense network of standing and running rigging. The ship is close-hauled, heading as close as possible to the direction of the wind; it must contend for every inch to the west, although in this gale, these seas, all it can manage is a stubborn retreat, a slow, grudging slide to leeward, losing as little ground as it can until things improve.

Bibliography and Index

Notes on Travel

Army and Navy Stores Limited, *General Price List, 1937 1938* (London, 1937)

Bligh, Willliam, *A Voyage to the South Seas ... for the Purposes of Conveying the Breadfruit Tree to the West Indies in His Majesty's Ship the Bounty* (Dent, 1981)

Coryate, Thomas, *Coryate's Crudities* (1611) (Glasgow, 1905)

Galton, Francis, *The Art of Travel* (1872) (David & Charles, 1971)

Harvard Travellers Club, *Handbook of Travel* (Harvard University Press, 1917)

Hatt, John, *The Tropical Traveller* (Pan Books, 1982)

Hunt, Major S. Leigh and Kenney Alexander S., *Tropical Trials: a Handbook for Women in the Tropics* (London, 1883)

Kingsley, Charles, *At Last: a Christmas in the West Indies* (London, 1889)

Kitchiner, William, *The Traveller's Oracle* (London, 1827)

Maundeville, Sir John, *The Voiage and Travailes (Which treateth of the way to Hierusalem, and of Mervayles of Inde, with Other Lands and Countryes)* (c. 1366) (London, 1839)

Pliny, *Natural History* (1634) ed. J. Newsome (Oxford, 1964)

Raleigh, Walter, *The Discovery of the Large, Rich and Beautiful Country of Guiana, 1595* (London Hakluyt Society, 1848)

Tatchell, Frank, *The Happy Traveller: a Book for Poor Men* (London, 1923)

Africa

Africanus, Leo, *The History and Description of Africa* (London Hakluyt Society, 1896)

Alvarez, Father Francisco, *Narrative of the Portuguese Embassy to Abyssinia, 1520–1527* (London Hakluyt Society, 1881)

Anon., *Travels in Africa* (Dublin, 1824)

Baker, Samuel White, *Ismailïa: a Narrative of the Expedition to Central Africa for the Suppression of the Slave Trade Organised by Ismail King of Egypt* (London, 1874)

Barley, Nigel, *The Innocent Anthropologist: Notes from a Mud Hut* (Penguin, 1986)

Barth, Heinrich, *Travels and Discoveries in North and Central Africa (Journal of an Expedition, 1849–1855)* (London, 1857)

Battel, Andrew, *Strange Adventures*, ed. E. G. Ravenstein (London, 1901)

Bruce, James, *Travels to Discover the Source of the Nile in the Years 1768–1773* (Edinburgh, 1804)

Bryce, James, *Impressions of South Africa* (London, 1897)

Cadamosto, Alvise da, *The Voyages* (1433–1480) (London, Hakluyt Society, 1937)

Caillié, René, *Le Voyage de René Caillié à Tombouctou à Travers l'Afrique* (Paris, 1932)

Cree, Thomas, *The Cree Journals. The Voyages of Edward H. Cree, Surgeon, RN, as Related in His Private Journals, 1837–1856* (Webb and Bower, 1981)

Delacroix, Eugène, *Selected Letters, 1813–1863*, selected and trans. Jean Stewart (Eyre and Spottiswoode, 1971)

Duff Gordon, Lady Lucie, *Letters from Egypt, 1863–1865* (London, 1865)

Edwards, Amelia, *A Thousand Miles Up the Nile* (London, 1877)

Haag, Michael, *Egypt* (Michael Haag, 1990; reprinted by permission of Cadegas Guides)

Ibn Battuta, *The Travels of Ibn Battuta (1304–1368)*, trans. H. A. R. Gibb (CUP/Hakluyt Society, 1958)

Kapuscinski, Ryszard, *The Shadow of the Sun: My African Life*, trans. Klara Glowczewska (Allen Lane The Penguin Press, 2001; reprinted by permission of Penguin Books Ltd; copyright © Ryszard Kapuscinski 2001)

Kingsley, Mary, *Travels in West Africa: Congo Français, Corisco and Cameroons* (London, 1897)

Lander, Richard Lemon, *Records of Captain Clapperton's Last Expedition to Africa* (London, 1830)

Lane, Edward, *An Account of the Manners and Customs of the Modern Egyptians* (London, 1837)

Livingstone, David, *Missionary Travels and Researches in South Africa* (John Murray, 1857)

Madras Officer, *The Ocean and the Desert* (London, 1846)

Marozzi, Justin, *South from Barbary* (HarperCollins, 2001; reprinted by

permission of HarperCollins Publishers Ltd; copyright © Justin
Marozzi 2001)

Martineau, Harriet, *Eastern Life, Present and Past* (London, 1875)

Murray's, *A Handbook for Travellers to Egypt* (John Murray, 1891)

Nerval, Gérard de, *Journey to the Orient* (Michael Haag, 1984)

O'Hanlon, Redmond, *Congo Journey* (Hamish Hamilton, 1996;
reprinted by permission of PFD on behalf of the author; copyright
© Redmond O'Hanlon 1996)

Park, Mungo, *Travels in the Interior of Africa* (Edinburgh, 1860)

Sarno, Louis, *Song From the Forest. My Life among the Ba-Benjellé
Pygmies* (Bantam Press, 1993; reprinted by permission of Dunaldo &
Olson, Inc; copyright © Louis Sarno 1993)

Stanley, Henry M., *Through the Dark Continent* (London, 1878)

Thomas, Elizabeth Marshall, *The Harmless People* (Secker & Warburg,
1959)

Thomson, Joseph, *To the Central African Lakes and Back. The Narrative
of the Royal Geographical Society's East Central African Expedition,
1878–80* (London, 1881)

Valle, Pietro della, *The Pilgrim*, trans. George Bull (Hutchinson, 1990)

Waugh, Evelyn, *When the Going Was Good* (Penguin, 1951)

Europe

d'Auvergne, Edmund, *The Nightside of Paris* (London, 1909)

Barton, Edward, in Hakluyt, Richard, *Voyages*, vol. 4 (Dent, 1962)

Barzini, Luigi, *Peking to Paris: Prince Borghese's Journey Across Two
Continents in a Motor-Car* (London, 1907)

Beaton, Cecil, *Diaries, The Years Between, 1963–74* (Weidenfeld and
Nicolson, 1978)

Beckford, William, *Italy, Spain and Portugal* (London, 1840)

Boswell, James, *Boswell on the Grand Tour: Italy, Corsica, and France,
1765–1766* (Willliam Heinemann, 1955)

Boulestin, X. M., *Myself, My Two Countries* (Cassell, 1936)

Burghersh, Lady, *Letters from Germany and France during the
Campaigns of 1813–1814*, ed. Lady Rose Weigall (London, 1893)

Burns, John Horne, *The Gallery* (Secker & Warburg, 1948; reprinted by
permission of Pollinger Ltd)

Byron, Lord, *Letters and Journals*, ed. Leslie Marchand (John Murray,
1976)

Byron, Robert, *The Station: Athos, Treasures and Men* (London, 1931)

Cameron, James, *Point of Departure* (Arthur Parker, 1967)

Chatwin, Bruce, *What Am I Doing Here?* (Picador, 1990)

Childers, Erskine, *The Riddle of the Sands* (Sidgwick and Jackson, 1931)

Connolly, Cyril, *The Unquiet Grave* (Hamish Hamilton, 1946)

Coryate, Thomas, *Coryate's Crudities* (Glasgow, 1905)

Covel, John, *Diaries, 1670–1679* in Bent, J. T., ed., *Early Voyages and Travels in the Levant* (London, Hakluyt Socity, 1893)

Curzon, Robert, *Visits to Monasteries in the Levant* (London, 1881)

Dallam, Thomas, *Diary, 1599–1600* in Bent, J. T., ed. *Early Voyages and Travels in the Levant* (London, Hakluyt Society, 1893)

Davies, Tony, *When the Moon Rises* (Leo Cooper, 1973)

Douglas, Norman, *Old Calabria* (Secker & Warburg, 1955; reprinted by permission of The Society of Authors as the Literary Representative of the Estate of Norman Douglas)

Duff Gordon, Lina, *Home Life in Italy: Letters from the Apennines* (London, 1908)

Durrell, Lawrence, *Spirit of Place: Letters and Essays on Travel*, ed. Alan G. Thomas (Faber and Faber, 1969, reprinted by permission of Faber & Faber)

Evelyn, John, *Diary* (London, 1850)

Fermor, Patrick Leigh, *Between the Woods and the Water. On Foot to Constantinople from the Hook of Holland: The Middle Danube to the Iron Gates* (John Murray, 1986; reprinted by permission of John Murray (Publishers) Ltd)

Flanner, Janet, *Paris Journal 1965–1971* (New York, 1971)

Ford, Richard, *The Handbook for Travellers in Spain* (John Murray, 1892)

Frazer, James, *The Golden Bough: a Study in Comparative Religion* (London, 1890)

Gibbon, Edward, *Memoirs*, ed. George Birkbeck Hill (London, 1900)

Goethe, J. W. von, *Travels in Italy* (London, 1885)

Goethe, J. W. von, *Italian Journey* (Collins, 1962)

Haydon, Benjamin Robert, *The Autobiography and Journals* (London, 1927)

Hazlitt, William, *Notes of a Journey Through France and Italy* (London, 1826)

Herodotus, *The Histories*, trans. Aubrey de Sélincourt (Penguin Books, 1972)

Hobson, Charlotte, *Black Earth City: a Year in the Heart of Russia* (Granta Books, 2001; reprinted by permission of Granta Books)

Huxley, Aldous, *Along the Road: Notes and Essays of a Tourist* (Chatto & Windus, 1925)

Irving, Washington, *Tales of the Alhambra* (London, 1850)

James, David, *A Prisoner's Progress* (Hollis and Carter, 1947)

Lear, Edward, *Edward Lear in Corsica: Journal of a Landscape Painter* (William Kimber, 1965)

Lear, Edward, *Edward Lear in Greece. Journals of a Landscape Painter in Greece and Albania* (William Kimber, 1965)

Lewis, Norman, *Naples '44* (Eland Books, 1983; reprinted by permission of Eland Publishing)

Lithgow, William, *The Totall Discourse of the Rare Adventures and Painefull Peregrinations* (Glasgow, 1906)

Madras Officer, *The Ocean and the Desert* (London, 1846)

Mansel, Philip, *Constantinople, City of the World's Desire, 1453–1924* (John Murray, 1995; reprinted by permission of John Murray (Publishers) Ltd)

Montagu, Lady Mary Wortley, *Letters and Works*, ed. Lord Wharncliffe (London, 1887)

Morris, James, *Venice* (Faber & Faber, 1960; reprinted by permission of Faber and Faber)

Moryson, Fynes, *An Itinerary* (1617) (Glasgow, 1908)

Murray's *Guide to Germany* (John Murray, 1867)

Polybius, *The Histories*, trans. Evelyn S. Shuckburgh (London, 1889)

Sévigné, Madame de, *Letters*, trans. Violet Hammersley (Secker & Warburg, 1955)

Shelley, Mary in Moore, Helen, *Mary Wollstonecraft Shelley* (Philadelphia, 1886)

Shelley, Percy Bysshe, *Select Letters*, ed. Richard Garnett (London, 1882)

Smollett, Tobias, *Travels Through France and Italy*, ed. Frank Felsenstein (OUP, 1979)

Southey, Robert, *Letters Written During a Journey in Spain etc.* (London, 1808)

Stendhal (Marie-Henri Beyle), *The Private Diaries of Stendhal*, trans. and ed. Robert Sage (Victor Gollancz, 1955)

Stevenson, Robert Louis, *An Inland Voyage* (Chatto & Windus, 1907)

Strabo, *Geography*, trans. H. C. Hamilton and W. Falconer (London, 1854)

Sumner-Boyd, Hilary and Freely, John, *Strolling Through Istanbul* (Redhouse Press, 1972)

Tatchell, Frank, *The Happy Traveller: a Book for Poor Men* (London, 1923)

Trelawney, E. J., *Recollections of the Last Days of Shelley and Byron* (London, 1858)

Wharton, Edith, *Abroad: Selected Travel Writings, 1888–1920* (Robert Hale, 1995)

Withers, Robert, *Voyage to Eastern India, 1616* in Purchas, Samuel, *Purchas His Pilgrims* (London, Hakluyt Society, 1905)

Wollstonecroft, Mary, *Collected Letters*, ed. Ralph M. Wardle (Cornell University Press, 1979)

Xenophon, *The Anabasis or Expedition of Cyrus*, trans. J. S. Watson (London, 1859)

Great Britain and Ireland

Aubrey, John, *Brief Lives* (Secker & Warburg, 1950)

Audubon, John James, *Delineations of American Scenery and Character* (London, 1926)

Ayton, Richard and William Daniell, *A Voyage Round Great Britain, 1813–14* (Tate Gallery, 1978)

Beaton, Cecil, *Diaries. The Years Between 1963–74* (Weidenfeld and Nicolson, 1978)

Belloc, Hilaire, *The Old Road* (London, 1904)

Borrow, George, *Wild Wales: Its People, Language and Scenery* (London, 1901)

Chatwin, Bruce, *What Am I Doing Here?* (Picador, 1990)

Danziger, Nick, *Danziger's Travels: Beyond Forbidden Frontiers* (HarperCollins, 1987; reprinted by permission of HarperCollins Publishers Ltd; copyright © Nick Danziger 1987)

Esquiros, Alphonse, *The English at Home*, trans. Lascelles Wraxall (London, 1861)

Evelyn, John, *Diary* (London, 1850)

Fiennes, Celia, *The Journeys (1685–1703)*, ed. Christopher Morris (The Cresset Press, 1947)

Headley, Gwyn and Meulenkamp, Wim, *Follies: a National Trust Guide* (Jonathan Cape, 1986)

Hillaby, John, *Journey through Britain* (Constable, 1968; reprinted by permission of Constable & Robinson Publishing Ltd)

Hudson, W. H., *A Shepherd's Life* (Methuen, 1919)

James, Henry, *English Hours* (London, 1905)

Jones, Barbara, *Follies and Grottoes* (Constable, 1953)

Kalm, Peter, *Account of a Visit to England on His Way to America in 1748*, trans. Joseph Lucas (London, 1892)

Lees-Milne, James, *Caves of Ice* (Faber & Faber, 1984)

Longstaff, Tom, *This My Voyage* (John Murray, 1950; reprinted by
    permission of John Murray (Publishers) Ltd)
Martineau, Harriet, *Letters from Ireland* (London, 1852)
Mundy, Peter, *Travels in Europe and Asia, 1608–1667*, ed. Sir Richard
    Carnac Temple (London, Hakluyt Society, 1919)
Murphy, Dervla, *A Place Apart* (John Murray, 1978; reprinted by
    permission of John Murray (Publishers) Ltd)
Newby, Eric, *A Traveller's Life* (Collins, 1982)
Ó'Crohan, Tomás, *The Islandman* (OUP, 1985)
O'Sullivan, Maurice, *Twenty Years A-Growing* (Chatto & Windus, 1933)
Piper, John, in Ingrams, Richard and Piper, John, *Piper's Places: John
    Piper in England and Wales* (Chatto & Windus, 1983; reprinted by
    permission of The Random House Group Ltd)
Rolt, L. T., *Narrow Boat* (Methuen, 1984)
Saussure, César de, *A Foreign View of England in the Reigns of George I
    and George II* (London, 1902)
Sitwell, Osbert, *Great Morning* (Macmillan, 1948)
Sitwell, Sacheverell, *Splendours and Miseries* (Faber & Faber, 1943)
Smollett, Tobias, *Travels Through France and Italy*, ed. Frank
    Felsenstein (OUP, 1979)
Synge, J. M., *The Aran Islands* (Dublin, 1907)
Taine, Hippolyte, *Notes on England* (London, 1872)
Theroux, Paul, *The Kingdom by the Sea* (Hamish Hamilton, 1983;
    reprinted by permission of Penguin Books Ltd; copyright © Paul
    Theroux 1983)
Victoria, Queen, *Leaves from the Journal of Our Life in the Highlands*,
    ed. Arthur Helps (London, 1868)
Wordsworth, Dorothy, *Journals, Vol. I* (Macmillan, 1941)

Near Asia

Arrian, *History of the Expedition of Alexander the Great* (London, 1813)
Baedeker's *Russia* (1914) (David & Charles, 1971)
Bartlett, W. H., *Forty Days in the Desert on the Track of the Israelites,
    or, A Journey from Cairo to Mount Sinai and Petra* (London, 1848)
Bell, Gertrude, *Letters, Vol. I*, ed. Lady Bell (Ernest Benn, 1927)
Blanch, Lesley, *The Wilder Shores of Love* (John Murray, 1954)
Blunt, Wilfrid Scawen, *My Diaries, Being a Personal Narrative of Events,
    1888–1914* (London, 1919)
Bryce, James, *Transcaucasia and Ararat* (London, 1877)

BIBLIOGRAPHY

Burckhardt, Johann Ludwig, *Travels in Arabia* (1829) (Frank Cass, 1968)
Burnaby, Frederick, *On Horseback Through Asia Minor* (London, 1877)
Carpini, Giovanni de Piano, *Journey to the Court of Kuyuk Khan, 1245–1247* in Rubruck, William of, *Journey to the Eastern Parts of the World, 1235–1255*, trans. William Woodville Rockhill (London, Hakluyt Society, 1900)
Chekhov, Anton, *Letters of Anton Tchekhov to his Family and Friends*, trans. Constance Garnett (London, 1920)
Clarke, Edward Daniel, *Travels in Various Countries of Europe, Asia and Africa* (London, 1824)
Daniel, The Abbot, in *Jerusalem Pilgrimage, 1099–1185*, eds. John Wilkinson, Joyce Hill, W. F. Ryan (London, Hakluyt Society, 1988)
Doughty, C. M., *Wanderings in Arabia Deserta* (1908) (Duckworth, 1939)
Fenton, Roger, *Letters from the Crimea*, in Gernsheim, Helmut and Alison, *Roger Fenton, Photographer of the Crimean War* (Secker & Warburg, 1954)
Glazebrook, Philip, *Journey to Khiva* (Harvill Press, 1992; reprinted by permission of The Random House Group Ltd)
Hogarth, David George, *A Wandering Scholar in the Levant* (London, 1896)
Kinglake, Alexander, *Eothen* (London, 1844)
Lawrence, T. E., *Seven Pillars of Wisdom* (London, 1935; reprinted by permission of the Trustees of the Seven Pillars of Wisdom Trust)
Maclean, Fitzroy, *Eastern Approaches* (1949) (Macmillan, 1982)
Palgrave, William Gifford, *Personal Narrative of a Year's Journey through Central and Eastern Arabia* (London, 1871)
Roberts, David, *The Holy Land* (1842–1849) (Studio Editions, 1989)
Rubruck, William of, *Journey to the Eastern Parts of the World, 1235–1255*, trans. William Woodville Rockhill (London, Hakluyt Society, 1900)
Saewulf in *Jerusalem Pilgrimage, 1099–1185*, eds. John Wilkinson, Joyce Hill, W. F. Ryan (London, Hakluyt Society, 1988)
Strabo, *Geography*, trans. H. C. Hamilton and W. Falconer (London, 1854)
Thomas, Bertram, *Arabia Felix: Across the Empty Quarter of Arabia* (Jonathan Cape, c. 1938; reprinted by permission of The Random House Group Ltd)

594

Middle Asia

Arrian, *History of the Expedition of Alexander the Great* (London, 1813)

Beaton, Cecil, *Diaries: 1939–44, The Parting Years* (Weidenfeld and Nicolson, 1965)

Bell, Charles, *The People of Tibet* (Oxford, 1928)

Bhattacharya, Jogendra Nath, *Hindu Castes and Sects* (Calcutta, 1896)

Byron, Robert, *Letters Home*, ed. Lucy Butler (John Murray, 1991; reprinted by permission of John Murray (Publishers) Ltd)

Cameron, James, *Point of Departure* (Arthur Barker, 1967)

Clavijo, Ruy Gonzalez de, *Narrative of the Embassy to the Court of Timor at Samarkand, 1403–1406*, trans. Clements R. Markham (London, Hakluyt Society, 1859)

Curzon, George Nathaniel, *Tales of Travel* (Hodder and Stoughton, 1923)

Dalrymple, William, *The Age of Kali* (HarperCollins, 1998; reprinted by permission of HarperCollins Publishers Ltd; copyright © William Dalrymple 1998)

Eden, Emily, *Up the Country* (London, 1866)

Fleming, Peter, *News From Tartary. A Journey from Peking to Kashmir* (Jonathan Cape, 1936; reprinted by permission of John Johnson Ltd; copyright © The Estate of Peter Fleming)

Forster, George, *A Journey from Bengal to England* (London, 1808)

Frater, Alexander, *Chasing the Monsoon* (Penguin Books, 1999; reprinted by permission of Penguin Books Ltd; copyright © Alexander Frater 1991)

Gama, Vasco da, *Calcoen: a Dutch Narrative of the Second Voyage of Vaso da Gama to Calicut* (Antwerp, *c.* 1504), trans. J. Ph. Berjean (London, 1874)

Hedin, Sven, *My Life as an Explorer* (Cassell, 1926)

Jordanus, Friar, *Mirabilia Descripta: the Wonders of the East* (*c.* 1330), trans. Col. Henry York, 1839 (London, Hakluyt Society, 1895)

Kipling, Rudyard, *From Sea to Sea, and Other Sketches. Letters of Travel* (London, 1910)

Lacombe, Jean de Lacombe de Quercy, in *A Compendium of the East. Being an Account of Voyages to the Grand Indies, 1668–76* (1681) (Golden Cockerel Press, 1937)

Levi, Peter, *In the Light Garden of the Angel King: Journeys in Afghanistan* (Collins, 1972)

Lutyens, Edwin, *Letters*, eds. Clayre Percy and Jane Ridley (Collins, 1985; reprinted by permission of HarperCollins Publishers Ltd)

Macaulay, Rose, *Pleasure of Ruins* (Thames & Hudson, 1953)

Magellan, Ferdinand, *The First Voyage Round the World*, trans. from the accounts of Pigafetta (London, Hakluyt Society, 1874)

Maillart, Ella, *The Cruel Way* (Heinemann, 1957; reprinted by permission of David Higham Associates)

Maitland, Julia Charlotte, *Letters from Madras During the Years 1836–1839* (London, 1843)

Maraini, Fosco, *Secret Tibet* (Harvill Press, 1952; reprinted by permission of The Random House Group Ltd)

Moorhouse, Geoffrey, *Calcutta* (Penguin, 1974; reprinted by permission of Gillon Aitken Associates Ltd; copyright © Geoffrey Moorhouse, 1973)

Mundy, Peter, *Travels in Europe and Asia, 1608–1667*, ed. Sir Richard Carnac Temple (London, Hakluyt Society, 1919)

Newby, Eric, *Slowly Down the Ganges* (Hodder and Stoughton, 1966)

Polo, Marco, *Travels* (Penguin, 1967)

Power, J. E., *Vade Mecum for Officers and Civilians Proceeding to India* (London, 1912)

Robertson, Sir George Scott, *The Kafirs of the Hindu-Kush* (London, 1896)

Roe, Thomas, *Embassy to the Court of the Great Moghul, 1615–1619*, ed. William Foster (London, Hakluyt Society, 1899)

Stewart, Stanley, *In the Empire of Genghis Khan: a Journey Among Nomads* (HarperCollins, 2000; reprinted by permission of HarperCollins Publishers Ltd; copyright © Stanley Stewart 2000)

Terry, Edward, *Voyage to Eastern India, 1616*, in Purchas, Samuel, *Purchas His Pilgrims Vol. IX* (London, Hakluyt Society, 1905)

Tully, Mark, *No Full Stops in India* (Penguin Books, 1992; reprinted by permission of Penguin Books Ltd; copyright © Mark Tully, 1992)

Varthema, Ludovico di, *The Travels* (1503–1508), trans. John Winter Jones (London, Hakluyt Society, 1863)

Younghusband, Francis, *The Heart of a Continent* (London, 1896)

Far Asia

Barzini, Luigi, *Peking to Paris: Prince Borghese's Journey Across Two Continents in 1907* (Alcove Press, 1972)

Bird, Isabella, *Unbeaten Tracks in Japan* (1880) (Virago Press, 1984)

Bird, Isabella, *The Golden Chersonese, and the Way Thither; Travels to the Far East, 1879* (London, 1883)

Bouvier, Nicolas, *The Japanese Chronicles* (San Francisco, 1992)

Dampier, William, *Buccaneer Explorer*, ed. Gerald Norris (Folio Society, 1994)

Fraser, John Foster, *Round the World on a Wheel* (London, 1899)

Gama, Vasco da, *Calcoen: a Dutch Narrative of the Second Voyage of Vaso da Gama to Calicut* (Antwerp, c. 1504), trans. J. Ph. Berjean (London, 1874)

Greene, Graham, *Ways of Escape* (Penguin Books, 1981; reprinted by permission of David Higham Associates)

Huan, Ma, *The Overall Survey of the Ocean's Shores* (1433), trans. J. V. G. Mills (CUP/Hakluyt Society, 1970)

Huc, Evariste Regis, *The Chinese Empire*, trans. W. Hazlitt (London, 1855)

Kaempfer, Englebert, *The History of Japan* (1690–1692) (Glasgow, 1906)

Kipling, Rudyard, *From Sea to Sea, and Other Sketches. Letters of Travel* (London, 1910)

Lacombe, Jean de Lacombe de Quercy, in *A Compendium of the East. Being an Account of Voyages to the Grand Indies, 1668–76* (1681) (Golden Cockerel Press, 1937)

Lewis, Norman, *A Dragon Apparent: Travels in Cambodia, Laos and Vietnam* (Eland Books, 1982; reprinted by permission of Eland Publishing Ltd)

O'Hanlon, Redmond, *Into the Heart of Borneo* (Salamander Press, 1984)

Pires, Tomé, *Suma Oriental: an Account of the East, from the Red Sea to Japan*, written in Malacca and India in 1512–1515, trans. Amando Cortesào (London, Hakluyt Society, 1944)

Prejelavsky, Nikolai, *Mongolia: the Tangut Country and Solitude of Northern Tibet*, trans. E. Delmar Morgan (London, 1876)

Redesdale, Lord, *The Attaché at Peking* (London, 1900)

Rodrigues, Joao, *Account of Sixteenth-Century Japan*, ed. Michael Cooper (London, Hakluyt Society, 2001)

Thubron, Colin, *Behind the Wall: a Journey Through China* (Penguin, 1988; published by William Heinemann and reprinted by permission of The Random House Group Ltd)

Wallace, Alfred Russel, *The Malay Archipelago* (1869) (London, 1922)

Young, Gavin, *Slow Boats Home* (Hutchinson, 1985)

North America

Audubon, John James, *Ornithological Biography, or Birds of the United States of America* (Edinburgh, 1831)

Audubon, John James, *Delineations of American Scenery and Character* (London, 1926)

Ballantyne, R. M., *Hudson's Bay, or Everyday Life in the Wilds of North America* (Edinburgh, 1843)

Bartram, John and William, *John and William Bartram's America. Selections from the Writings of the Philadelphia Naturalists*, ed. Helen Gere Cruickshank (New York, 1957)

Bartram, William (1739–1823), in Earnest, Ernest, *John and William Bartram: Botanists and Explorers* (University of Philadelphia Press, 1940)

Bird, Isabella, *A Lady's Life in the Rocky Mountains* (London, 1880)

Bossu, Jean Bernard, *Travels in the Interior of North America, 1751–1762*, trans. and ed. Seymour Feiler (University of Oklahoma Press, 1962)

Brooke, Rupert, *Letters from America* (London, 1916)

Cartier, Jacques, *Voyages* (1534–1543), trans. H. P. Biggar. Public Archives of Canada No. 11 (F. A. Acland, 1925)

Cook, Captain James, *Three Voyages Round the World*, ed. Charles R. Low (London, 1876)

Davies, W. H., *Autobiography of a Super-Tramp* (London, 1908)

Dellenbaugh, Frank S., *The Romance of the Colorado River* (Putnam, 1903)

Dickens, Charles, *American Notes* (London, *c.* 1842)

Dufferin and Ava, Marchioness of, *My Canadian Journal, 1872–8* (London, 1891)

Fearon, Henry Bradshaw, *Sketches of America* (London, 1818)

Fremont, John Charles, *Narrative of an Exploring Expedition to the Rocky Mountains in the Year 1842* (London, 1846)

Harris, Thaddeus Mason, *Journal of a Tour into the Territory Northwest of the Alleghany Mountains* (1805), see Thwaites (1904) Vol. III

Hawthorne, Nathaniel, *American Notebooks*, ed. Randall Stewart (Yale University Press, 1933)

Kemble, Fanny, *Records of Later Life, Vol. I* (London, 1882)

Llemoyne d'Iberville, Pierre, *Gulf Journals*, trans. and ed. Richebourg Gaillard McWilliams (University of Alabama Press, 1981)

Lyell, Charles, *Travels in North America, with Geological Observations on the United States, Canada and Nova Scotia* (London, 1845)

Marcy, R. B., *The Prairie and Overland Traveller* (London, 1860)

Michaux, André, *Journal 1798–1795*, see Thwaites (1904) Vol. III

Miller, Henry, *The Air-Conditioned Nightmare* (Secker & Warburg, 1947; reprinted by permission of The Random House Group Ltd)

Muir, John, *The Mountains of California* (London, 1894)

Olmsted, Frederick Law, *A Journey in the Seaboard Slave States* (New York, 1856)

Parkman, Francis, *The Oregon Trail: Sketches of Prairies and Rocky-Mountain Life* (London, 1892)

Raban, Jonathan, *Hunting Mr Heartbreak* (Harvill Press, 1990; reprinted by permission of The Random House Group Ltd)

Runciman, Steven, *A Traveller's Alphabet: Partial Memories* (Thames & Hudson, 1991)

Russell, William Howard, *My Diary North and South* (London, 1863)

Sala, George Augustus, *My Diary in America in the Midst of War* (London, 1865)

Thoreau, Henry David, *Cape Cod*, ed. Joseph Moldenhauer (Princeton University Press, 1988)

Tocqueville, Alexis de, *Journey to America* (1831–1832), trans. George Lawrens; ed. J. P. Mayer (Faber & Faber, 1959)

Trollope, Anthony, *North America* (London, 1862)

Trollope, Frances, *Domestic Manners of the Americans* (London, 1832)

Verrazzano, John de, *Certaine Voyages to Florida . . .* (1524), see Hakluyt, *Principal Navigations*, Vol. VIII (1904)

Weiser, Conrad, *Journal*, see Thwaites (1904) Vol. I

Whymper, Edward, *Travels and Adventures in the Territory of Alaska* (London, 1868)

Wolfe, Tom, *The Right Stuff* (Jonathan Cape, 1980; reprinted by permission of PFD on behalf of the author; copyright © 1980)

Central and South America and the Caribbean

Acuna, Father Cristoval de, *A New Discovery of the Great River of the Amazons* (1639) in Markham, C. R., ed. and trans., *Expeditions into the Valley of the Amazons, 1539, 1540, 1639* (London, Hakluyt Society, 1859)

Admiralty, Hydrographic Office, *The South America Pilot, Part II* (11th edition, London, 1916)

Baird, Robert, *Impressions and Experiences of the West Indies and North America in 1849* (Edinburgh, 1850)

Banks, Sir Joseph, *Journal*, ed., Joseph Hooker (London, 1896)

Bates, Henry Walter, *A Naturalist on the River Amazon* (Dent, 1969)

Beford, Sybille, *A Visit to Don Ottavio: a Traveller's Tale from Mexico* (Collins, 1960)

Bingham, Hiram, *Lost City of the Incas* (Weidenfeld and Nicolson, 1952)

Box, Ben (ed.), *Mexico and Central American Handbook* (Trade & Travel Publications, 1990)

Columbus, Christopher, *Select Letters*, trans. R. H. Major (London, 1847)

Darwin, Charles, *The Voyage of the Beagle* (Dent, 1959)

Diaz del Castillo, Bernal, *The True History of the Conquest of New Spain*, trans. A. P. Maudslay (London, Hakluyt Society, 1910)

Durrell, Lawrence, *Spirit of Place: Letters and Essays on Travel*, ed. Alan G. Thomas (Faber & Faber, 1969)

Fleming, Peter, *Brazilian Adventure* (1933) (Penguin, 1984; reprinted by permission of Kate Grimond)

Gellhorn, Martha, *The View From the Ground* (Granta Books, 1989; reprinted by permission of Alexander Matthews)

Gosling, Cecil, *Travels and Adventures in Many Lands* (Methuen, 1926)

Hawkyns, Sir John, in Hahluyt, Richard, *The Principal Navigations and Voyages, Traffiques and Discoveries of the English Nation*, Vol. X (Glasgow, Hakluyt Society, 1904)

Head, F. B., *Rough Notes Taken During Some Hard Journeys Across the Pampas and Among the Andes* (London, 1826)

Hudson, W. H., *Idle Days in Patagonia* (London, 1893)

Kingsley, Charles, *At Last: a Christmas in the West Indies* (London, 1889)

Lawrence, D. H., *Mornings in Mexico* (London, 1927)

Orellana, Francisco de, *Voyage into the River of the Amazons (AD 1540–1541)*, in Markham, C. R., ed. and trans., *Expeditions into the Valley of the Amazons, 1539, 1540, 1639* (London, Hakluyt Society, 1859)

Schaw, Janet, *Journal of a Lady of Quality, 1774–1776* (Yale University Press, 1921)

Thomson, Hugh, *The White Rock: an Exploration of the Inca Heartland* (Weidenfeld and Nicolson, 2001)

Thomson, Ian, *Bonjour Blanc: a Journey Through Haiti* (Hutchinson, 1992)

Tomlinson, H. M., *The Sea and the Jungle* (Duckworth, 1930)

Tschiffley, A. F., *Tschiffley's Ride* (William Heinemann, 1934; reprinted by permission of John Johnson Ltd, copyright © The Estate of A. F. Tschiffley)

Vespucci, Amerigo, *Letters,* trans. Clements Markham (London, Hakluyt Society, 1894)

Australasia

Banks, Sir Joseph, *Journal,* ed. Joseph Hooker (London, 1896)

Bates, Daisy, *The Passing of the Aborigines* (John Murray, 1938; reprinted by permission of John Murray (Publishers) Ltd)

Burke, Robert O'Hara, in Jackson, Andrew, *Robert O'Hara Burke and the Australian Exploring Expedition of 1860* (London, 1863)

Butler, Samuel, *A First Year in Canterbury Settlement* (London, 1914)

Carnegie, The Hon. David W., *Spinifex and Sand: a Narrative of Five Years' Pioneering and Exploring in Western Australia* (London, 1898)

Cook, Captain James, *Three Voyages Round the World,* ed. Charles R. Low (London, 1876)

Cunningham, Alan, in Lee, Ida, *Early Explorers in Australia* (London, 1925)

Earle, Augustus, *A Narrative of a Nine Months' Residence in New Zealand in 1827* (Christchurch, 1909)

Forrest, John, *Explorations in Australia* (London, 1975)

Giles, Ernest, *Australia Twice Traversed: the Romance of Exploration (1872–1876)* (London, 1889)

King, Philip P., *Narrative of a Survey of the Coasts of Australia (1818–1822)* (London, 1827)

Managku, Esther and Lawungkurr Maralngurra, in *Aboriginal Australia and the Torres Strait Islands* (Lonely Planet, 2001)

Mitchell, T. L., *Three Expeditions into the Interior of Eastern Australia* (London, 1839)

Robertson, George, *The Discovery of Tahiti, 1766–1768,* ed. Hugh Carrington (London, Hakluyt Society, 1948)

Stevenson, Robert Louis, *In the South Seas* (London, 1900)

Stuart, J. McDouall, *Journals, 1858–62* (London, 1864)

Sturt, Captain Charles, *Two Expeditions into the Interior of Southern Australia During the Years 1828, 1829, 1830 and 1831* (London, 1833)

Warburton, Colonel Peter Egerton, *Journey Across the Western Interior of Australia* (London, 1875)

The Arctic and The Antarctic

Amundsen, Roald, *The North-West Passage* (London, 1908)

Baffin, William, *The Voyages, 1612–1622*, ed., Clements R. Markham (London, Hakluyt Society, 1881)

Bellinghausen, Captain, *Voyage to the Antarctic Seas, 1819–1821*, trans. from the Russian, ed. Frank Debenham (London, Hakluyt Society, Series II, vols I & II XCI, XCII)

Cherry-Garrard, Apsley, *The Worst Journey in the World* (1922) (The Adventure Library, 1997)

Diski, Jenny, *Skating to Antarctica* (Granta Books, 1997; reprinted by permission of Granta Books)

Dufferin, Lord, *Letters from High Latitudes* (Dent, 1857)

Franklin, Sir John, *A Journey to the Shores of the Polar Sea in the Years 1819, 1820, 1821 and 1822* (London, 1824)

Frobisher, Martin, *The Three Voyages in Search of a Passage to Cathaia and India by the North-West, AD 1576–1578*, ed. Richard Collinson (London, Hakluyt Society, 1867)

Fuchs, Vivian, and Edmund Hillary, *The Crossing of Antarctica: the Commonwealth Trans-Antarctic Expedition, 1955–58* (Cassell, 1958)

Kane, Elisha Kent, *Arctic Explorations in Search of Sir John Franklin* (Nelson, 1879)

Lopez, Barry, *Arctic Dreams* (Macmillan, 1986; reprinted by permission of Macmillan, London, UK)

Mikkelsen, Ejnaar, *Lost in the Arctic: the Story of the 'Alabama' Expedition, 1909–1912* (London, 1913)

Morris, William, *Icelandic Journals* (Mare's Nest Publishing, 1996)

Nansen, Fritdjof, *Farthest North: the Norwegian Polar Expedition, 1893–1896* (London, 1897)

Nordenskiöld, N. A. E., *Voyage of the Vega in the Years 1819–1822* (London, 1885)

Scott, R. F., *Scott's Last Expedition* (London, 1913)

Veer, Gerrit de, *The Three Voyages of William Barents to the Arctic Regions, 1594, 1595, 1596* (London, Hakluyt Society, 1876)

Wheeler, Sara, *Terra Incognita: Travels in Antarctica* (Jonathan Cape, 1996; reprinted by permission of The Random House Group Ltd)

Mountains

Angeville, Henriette d', *My Ascent of Mont Blanc* (Collins, 1991)

Browne, Belmore, *The Conquest of Mount McKinley* (London, 1913)

Conway, William Martin, *Climbing and Exploration in the Karakorum-Himalayas* (London, 1894)

Cortés, Hernan, *The Fifth Letter to the Emperor Charles V, 1526*, trans. Don Pascual de Gayangos (London, Hakluyt Society, 1868)

Darwin, Charles, *The Voyage of the Beagle* (Dent, 1959)

Fitzgerald, E. A., *The Highest Andes: a Record of the First Ascent of Aconcagua and Tupungato in Argentina and the Expedition of the Surrounding Valleys* (London, 1899)

Green, William Spotswood, *The High Alps of New Zealand* (London, 1883)

Harrer, Heinrich, *The White Spider: the History of the Eiger's North Face*, trans. Hugh Merrick (Rupert Hart-Davis, 1959)

Humboldt, Alexander von, in Botting, Douglas, *Humboldt and the Cosmos* (Sphere, 1973)

Hunt, John, *The Ascent of Everest* (Hodder and Stoughton, 1953; reprinted by permission of Hodder Headline Ltd)

Longstaff, Tom, *This My Voyage* (John Murray, 1950)

Simpson, Joe, *Touching the Void* (Jonathan Cape, 1988; reprinted by permission of The Random House Group Ltd)

Sea

Abraham, James Johnston, *The Surgeon's Log* (1911) (Penguin, 1938)

Amadas, Philip, and Barlow, Arthur, *The First Voyage to Virginia* (1584), see Hakluyt, *Principal Navigations . . .* Vol. VIII (1904)

Anson, George, *A Voyage Round the World in the Years 1740–1744* (Dent, 1923)

Bligh, William, *A Voyage to the South Seas . . . for the Purposes of Conveying the Breadfruit Tree to the West Indies in His Majesty's Ship the Bounty* (Dent, 1981)

Byrd, Richard E., *Alone* (Putnam, 1938)

Coleridge, Henry Nelson, *Six Months in the West Indies* (London, 1926)

Columbus, Christopher, *Select Documents Illustrating the Four Voyages of Columbus*, Vol. II, trans. Cecil Jane (London, Hakluyt Society, 1933)

BIBLIOGRAPHY

Conrad, Joseph, *The Mirror of the Sea: Memories and Impressions* (London, 1906)

Dana, Richard Henry, *Two Years Before the Mast* (Dent, 1969)

Drake, Sir Francis, *The World Encompassed* (1572) (London, Hakluyt Society, 1854)

Foster, Cecil, *1700 Miles in Open Boats. The Loss of the Trevesa* (Martin Hopkinson, 1926)

Gama, Vasco da, *Calcoen: a Dutch Narrative of the Second Voyage of Vaso da Gama to Calicut* (Antwerp, c. 1504), trans. J. Ph. Berjean (London, 1874)

Lundy, Derek, *The Way of a Ship* (Jonathan Cape, 2002; reprinted by permission of The Random House Group Ltd)

MacGregor, John, *The Voyage Alone in the Yawl 'Rob Roy'* (London, 1868)

Melville, Herman, *Moby Dick, or The Whale* (Cresset Press, 1946)

Newby, Eric, *The Last Grain Race* (Secker & Warburg, 1956)

Raleigh, Walter, *The Discovery of the Large, Rich and Beautiful Country of Guiana, 1595* (London, Hakluyt Society, 1848)

Slocum, Joshua, *Sailing Alone Around the World* (London, 1900)

Spry, W. J. J., *The Cruise of HMS Challenger* (London, 1877)

Steinbeck, John, *The Log from the Sea of Cortez* (Heinemann, 1958; reprinted by permission of Penguin Books Ltd; copyright © John Steinbeck and Edward F. Ricketts 1941)

INDEX